POLITICS AND BELIEF IN CONTEMPORARY FRANCE

EMMANUEL MOUNIER AND CHRISTIAN DEMOCRACY, 1932–1950

by

R. WILLIAM RAUCH, Jr.

MARTINUS NIJHOFF / THE HAGUE

POLITICS AND BELIEF IN CONTEMPORARY FRANCE

POLITICS AND BELIEF
IN CONTEMPORARY FRANCE

EMMANUEL MOUNIER
AND CHRISTIAN DEMOCRACY, 1932-1950

by

R. WILLIAM RAUCH, Jr.

MARTINUS NIJHOFF / THE HAGUE / 1972

ISBN 90 247 1281 5

PRINTED IN THE NETHERLANDS

1804246

To my parents

TABLE OF CONTENTS

ACKNOWLEDGMENTS

In the research and writing of this book I have incurred more debts than I can repay or indeed formally acknowledge. To Professors Shepard Clough, Léon Roudiez, René Rémond, and Joseph N. Moody, I owe a special debt for their advice and encouragement in various stages of my work. The late Professor Yves Simon gave freely of his time and provided me with an example of the humanist scholar that I have tried imperfectly to emulate. Temple University supported my work with a research grant and a study leave. I must thank Professor Robert Schwoebel, my colleague in the History Department of Temple University, for his unfailing friendship and constant support. To my wife Patricia, a fellow historian, I am greatly indebted not only for her help but, more important, for her patience and understanding. Finally, my debt to the late Emmanuel Mounier, whom I never met, is immeasurable. As he might have said, fortunate is the man whose scholarship is more than merely an intellectual exercise!

FOOTNOTE ABBREVIATIONS

O.M., I. *Oeuvres de Mounier*. Volume I: *1931–1939*. Paris: Editions du Seuil, 1961.

O.M., II. *Oeuvres de Mounier*. Volume II: *Traité du caractère*. Paris: Editions du Seuil, 1961.

O.M., III. *Oeuvres de Mounier*. Volume III: *1944–1950*. Paris: Editions du Seuil, 1962.

O.M., IV. *Oeuvres de Mounier*. Volume IV: *Recueils posthumes. Correspondance*. Paris: Editions du Seuil, 1963.

E.M., *1905–1950*. "Emmanuel Mounier, 1905–1950," *Esprit*, Special Issue, No. 174 (December, 1950). Reprinted by Editions du Seuil, 1950.

M.S.G. Mounier et sa génération. Lettres, carnets et inédits. Paris: Editions du Seuil, 1956.

B.A.E.M. Bulletin des Amis d'E. Mounier, Nos. 1–36 (February, 1952–October, 1970).

J.O.C. Journal officiel. Débats parlementaires. Chambre des députés.

THE TRAVAIL OF CHRISTIAN DEMOCRACY,
1830–1932

> Notre vie est toute à la *Cause*
> Pour qu'elle triomphe au grand jour,
> Souffrance et mort sont peu de chose
> Pour les Chevaliers de l'Amour.
>
> Henri Colas, "Grand Semeur."

At eight o'clock on Saturday evening, October 10, 1942, during one of the blackest periods in the history of modern France, a small group of prisoners gathered in the falling dusk of the Prison Saint-Paul in Lyons in Vichy France.[1] Having removed their work clothes and prepared themselves for bed, the men pulled their bug-infested straw mattresses into a circle. Then they listened to a prisoner from cell C1 speak of his past, the meaning of the present tragedy, and his hopes for the future of his beloved Marianne. By ten o'clock, the speaker was responding to questions from his listeners and the little circle of men had been transformed into a camp of Bedouins as the men had drawn their blankets up around themselves for protection against the dampness and cold.

The prisoner who addressed this strange assemblage was Emmanuel Mounier. His talk was the culmination of a long and typically productive and energetic day. A man of incredibly wide-ranging interests, Mounier noted in his prison journal that these were his "Shakespeare weeks"; and he added with his customary sense of irony that in his cell the kings of England had done battle and Falstaff had thrown forth his magnificent jests. He had also devoted part of his day to the preparation of a critical study of the prison regime, to the writing of a scholarly book later entitled *Traité du caractère*, and to preliminary work on what he called "un grand machin sur le *Christianisme et l'époque*."[2]

Mounier's appearance and manner were not those of the intellectual that such activities may well have suggested to some of his fellow

---

[1] This account of the Prison Saint-Paul is taken from "Témoignage de Maurice Guérin," *E.M., 1905–1950*, 1035–1036; "Journaux de prison d'Emmanuel Mounier. Prison Saint-Paul, Lyon, 7 juillet 1942–octobre 1942," *E.M., 1905–1950*, 765–775; and Mounier, "Lettre à ses parents, 10 octobre 1942," *O.M.*, IV, 762.

[2] Mounier, "Lettre à Jacques Lefrancq, 28 novembre 1941," *O.M.*, IV, 721.

prisoners. He was a large, rather homely man with a fair complexion, blue eyes, and coarse features. His appearance was hardly enhanced by a childhood injury which had permanently impaired the vision in his right eye nor by the long months he had already spent in the prisons of the Vichy regime. He had first been arrested some ten months before and, after a period of provisional liberty, had been confined in the Château de Vals-les-Bains. There, the previous June, Mounier had undertaken a Ghandian hunger protest against Vichy authorities which had brought him to the verge of death and which, almost certainly, permanently impaired his health. He spoke, even in public, in a soft but rather high-pitched voice and he habitually cocked his head to one side while conversing or listening to others because of a slight deafness in one ear. Surprisingly, in view of all this, Mounier hardly looked his age. Although he was thirty-seven, he had looked like "an overgrown schoolboy" only a few years before.[3]

"If one observed him at closer range, one discovered about him an air of maturity and determination."[4] The most striking thing about the prisoner in cell C1 was his manner. It was not that of the self-assured intellectual accustomed to proposing neat but impractical solutions to painfully complicated problems. A born pedagogue – a man of dialogue, to use a more contemporary phrase – Mounier presented no ready-made or easy solutions to the problems confronting the prisoners in Saint-Paul. Instead he attempted to define the nature of these problems and often elicited from his listeners their own recognition of possible solutions. When other prisoners spoke, one of them recalls, Mounier listened "with an active and fraternal sympathy, then questioned us, making his remarks or criticisms with a charity" that this man, at least, had rarely experienced before and was seldom to encounter again.[5] A priest who often visited Mounier in his cell had difficulty in adequately describing what he encountered there. He was struck by Mounier's complete serenity and absence of discouragement in spite of the conditions in Saint-Paul. "In his cell there was a dignity, a serenity, a resolution which contrasted singularly with the atmosphere of the prison."[6]

October 10, 1942 was an important anniversary, not in Mounier's career, for he betrayed a lifelong repugnance for "building a career,"

[3] Helen Iswolsky, *Light Before Dusk. A Russian Catholic in France, 1923–1941* (New York: Longmans, Green & Co., 1942), 104.
[4] *Ibid.*
[5] "Témoignage de Maurice Guérin," 1036.
[6] "Témoignage de Mgr. Alfred Ancel, évêque auxiliaire de Lyon" *E.M., 1905-1950*, 1036.

but rather in his life. Just ten years before, he had published the first issue of *Esprit*, the monthly journal with which his life and work were inextricably bound. Two months prior to that, in August, 1932, he and a group of his friends had retired to Font-Romeu, a small resort town in the eastern Pyrenees, to lay the final groundwork for both *Esprit* and a short-lived activist movement, the *Troisième force*. The irony of the fact that the youthful founders of *Esprit* had stayed in Font-Romeu in another place named Saint-Paul, the Villa Saint-Paul, did not escape Mounier, now incarcerated in the Prison Saint-Paul in Lyons.

To the huddled figures facing him, Mounier explained the nature of the movement which had developed around *Esprit* and of the personalist and communitarian principles for which *Esprit* had been a major vehicle until its suppression by Vichy authorities the previous year. Almost certainly Mounier reviewed the founding and history of *Esprit* in terms of the present situation. Personalism, as he pointed out time and again, had no meaning outside the concrete historical circumstances in which it evolved and was intended to elucidate. Mounier's personalism was less a philosophy in the ordinary sense of the term than a frame of reference, a set of values, and a method with which a new and more human society might be constructed. In spite of the perversion of personalism by certain Vichyite thinkers and Mounier's own attempt to maintain his *présence* within the regime for well over a year, Mounier's arrest and imprisonment demonstrated that the new regime was irreconcilable with the central tenets of Mounier and *Esprit*.

On other of these evening gatherings in the Prison Saint-Paul Mounier discussed the work of Henri Bergson, Jacques Maritain, and Charles Péguy, all of whom, in one way or another, had exercised an important influence upon him. Mounier's fellow prisoners also took their turns. One of them was Mounier's cellmate, whom he referred to as "Z" in his prison journal, who was very probably Maurice Guérin, a veteran Christian democrat. After a good deal of encouragement from his fellow prisoners, Guérin recounted the legendary days of his Christian democratic youth. He spoke of Marc Sangnier and the *Sillon*, the man and movement most responsible for Christian democracy in twentieth-century France. He also discussed Abbé Jean Desgranges, one of the *abbés démocrates* whose disciple he had been, and his own long years of work in the *Confédération Française des Travailleurs Chrétiens* (C.F.T.C.) and the *Parti Démocrate Populaire*, the little Christian democratic party of the interwar years.

On Monday, October 19, these evening discussion sessions came to an end. On that day Mounier, Guérin, and thirty-odd other prisoners finally went on trial. They were charged with membership in the Resistance movement *Combat*, although the Vichy press referred to them as Communists. The trial ended a week later and the "palais d'injustice," as the prisoners called it, handed down its verdicts on October 30. Mounier was acquitted for lack of evidence and shortly thereafter he took his wife Paulette and his daughters Madeleine and Françoise to the little mountain village of Dieulefit in the Drôme. There, under the assumed name of Leclercq and in the relative safety of the Italian occupation zone, Mounier resumed his reading, writing, and Resistance activities.

Maurice Guérin and most of the other prisoners were not so fortunate. Guérin himself was convicted, fined and sentenced to a short prison term. Then he too resumed his Resistance activities as a leader of *Combat* in the Haute-Vienne, as a member of the *maquis* in the Rhône, and as the editor of a clandestine journal. Guérin and Mounier probably did not see one another again until some time after the Liberation. When Mounier returned to Paris in late September, 1944 to resume publication of *Esprit*, Guérin was already in the city. The veteran Christian democrat was busy conferring with a group of his friends preparatory to holding the constituent assembly of a new Christian democratic party, the *Mouvement Républicain Populaire* (M.R.P.). Gilbert Dru, a young student in Lyons and disciple of Mounier, however, had provided a link during 1943–1944 between Guérin and the founders of the M.R.P., on one hand, and Mounier and *Esprit* on the other. Dru journeyed between Dieulefit, where Mounier presided over several meetings of the *Esprit* group, and Lyons and Paris, where Guérin and others were laying their plans for the new Christian democratic party in a series of clandestine meetings. Young Dru had acted as the midwife for some of Mounier's ideas in the birth of Guérin's party.

Neither the intellectual *parrain* nor the young midwife were present at the founding congress of the M.R.P. in November, 1944. Dru's absence was the result of a particularly tragic event. Shortly after leaving a clandestine meeting in Guérin's home in Lyons on July 17, 1944, Dru and a young friend had been arrested by the Gestapo. Along with his friend and three other young men, Dru was taken as a hostage in reprisal for the bombing of the Café du Moulin, a restaurant on the Place Bellecour which was frequented by the Nazis. No one had been injured in the bombing, but ten days later, precisely at noon, an automobile drew up in front of the Café du Moulin. There, before the noon-hour crowd, the hostages were thrown out of the automobile and machine-gunned to death on the sidewalk. In a fitting footnote to this act of barbarism, the Germans prohibited the removal of the bodies, several of which bore signs of torture, until mid-afternoon.[7]

Ample homage was paid to the memory of the young martyr during the constituent congress of the new party. In a speech celebrating the ancestors and founders of the M.R.P., Guérin himself paid tribute to his young friend.[8] To no one's surprise only brief mention was made of Mounier and *Esprit*. Indeed, had any reference been made to Dru's debt to Mounier, a sizable portion of Guérin's audience – and perhaps an even larger proportion of the new party's inflated electoral clientele – would have been seriously alarmed. Mounier, for his part, might conceivably have denied any responsibility, even of an indirect and unintentional character, for the formation of the M.R.P. More probably he would have marked down any such reference as yet another indication of the profound and almost congenital weakness of Christian democracy and its supporters.

Emmanuel Mounier was a man of remarkable good will and unusual honesty toward even his worst enemies. But he had been and would continue to be a consistently bitter and often violent critic of both the idea of Christian democracy and the politics that he believed that this idea invariably engendered. He had noted in his journal in the Prison Saint-Paul that his cellmate "Z" was an admirable and worthy man in many respects, but, like most Christian democrats, he suffered from all the debilitating defects of the Christian democrat as a politico-religious, psychological type. Indeed almost all of the men and organizations discussed by Guérin in prison in 1942 and again before the congress of the M.R.P. in 1944 had been severely criticized by Mounier in the past.

That Emmanuel Mounier, a vigorous opponent of Christian democracy, should have provided some of the inspiration for the largest Christian democratic party in the history of France is a striking example of the complex interrelationship between the director of *Esprit* and Christian democracy and its adherents. *Esprit* was founded in 1932 upon a total and revolutionary rejection of what Mounier was to call, in a classic phrase, "the established disorder." That "the established disorder" included the ideal, the politics, and the men of Christian

---

[7] Jean-Marie Domenach, *Gilbert Dru, celui qui croyait au ciel* (Paris: Editions du livre française, 1947), 128–132; Paul Vergnet, *Les Catholiques dans la Résistance* (Paris: Editions des Saints-Pères, 1946), 199–200; Henri Amoretti, *Lyon capitale, 1940–1944* (Paris: Editions France-Empire, 1964), 305–307.

[8] Maurice Guérin, "Nous sommes en marche vers une révolution totale," *l'aube*, November 28, 1944.

democracy was implicit from the start but Mounier made this amply clear in the next several years. First in a debate in the pages of a Christian democratic newspaper and then in *Esprit*, Mounier elaborated a severe criticism of the idea of Christian democracy, of the esthetically distasteful and defective type of individual who supported it, and of the ineffectual politics that he believed Christian democracy engendered. In spite of the general coincidence between the political opinions of the *Esprit* group and those of important elements of the Christian democratic movement during the remaining years of this decade of crises, Mounier was never to alter or moderate his basic criticisms. Indeed the tenor of his criticism heightened in almost direct proportion to the size of the Christian democratic movement in the immediate postwar period.

Mounier's criticism did not, however, prevent many of the leaders of Christian democracy from admitting their own debt to Mounier and *Esprit*. Etienne Borne, an early member of the *Esprit* group, a future member of the *Académie Française*, and one of the foremost theoreticians of Christian democracy during the Fourth Republic, often referred to Mounier as one of his intellectual and spiritual masters. For a quarter of a century, Borne said, Mounier was "the prince of our youth, our equal in the fraternity of a virile friendship, but also the first among us, the man who first ventured forth and made decisions in an exemplary fashion."[9] Similarly Francisque Gay, one of the patriarchs of Christian democracy and one of its foremost polemicists during the 1920s and 1930s, paid tribute to Mounier as one of the movement's "directors of conscience."[10] And the veteran Christian democrat Paul Archambault, after being rebuffed by Mounier in his attempt to annex *Esprit* to the Christian democratic movement, indicated that he and many of his fellow Christian democrats would continue to read *Esprit* as a means of renewing their sense of indignation and revolt against a "materialistic and debased world."[11]

The validity and even the precise meaning of such encomiums are difficult to determine because the nature of Mounier's vocation and the purpose that he assigned to his journal do not lend themselves to simple definition. Jean-Marie Domenach, the present editor of *Esprit*, has

[9] Etienne Borne, "Pour un tombeau d'Emmanuel Mounier," *la Vie intellectuelle*, 27e année, June, 1956, 103.

[10] Francisque Gay, *Les démocrates d'inspiration chrétienne à l'épreuve du pouvoir* (Paris: Bloud & Gay, 1951), 19–20, 107–111.

[11] Paul Archambault, "La démocratie et la révolution. Lettre ouverte sur la démocratie," *l'aube*, March 9, 1934.

aptly stated that there are no *mouniéristes*.[12] As the tributes of Borne, Gay, and Archambault suggest, the debt of Christian democracy to Mounier and *Esprit* is not to be found in the realm of specific political programs or platforms. Mounier's influence must be examined in terms of his remarkable personal example and his effort to redefine the relationship between politics and Catholicism in the contemporary world.

The difficulty of examining the nature and extent of Mounier's influence upon Christian democracy is further compounded by the possibility that some Christian democrats may have paid tribute to Mounier in an effort to profit from his growing prestige among the younger generation of French Catholics. *Esprit*, as Michel François, Professor of History in the *Ecole nationale des Chartes*, has succinctly stated, is "the journal which has educated a Christian generation."[13] But here in a negative way an examination of Mounier's influence can be grounded in firmer evidence. There is little doubt that Mounier's example and teaching were destructive of the purposes of Christian democracy. The former were, in fact, based upon a denial of Christian democracy's *raison d'être*. The younger generation, nourished on a diet of *Esprit*, necessarily weakened the Christian democratic movement by its opposition and withdrawal. Ultimately the new generation forced the Christian democratic movement into a centrist position in the broadening spectrum of social and political Catholicism in France – and contributed in some measure to the demise of Christian democracy in 1967.

Conversely, a number of Christian democrats were equally insistent upon Mounier's debt to the tradition of Christian democracy. Unlike his Christian democratic antagonists, however, Mounier refused to recognize clearly a debt.[14] He acknowledged no historical antecedents whatsoever for the journal and movement he founded. In his *tabula rasa* project, Mounier manifested his membership in a "generation without masters." In his extreme eclecticism, Mounier owed intellectual debts to such varied men as Nietzsche, Marx, Proudhon, Sorel, Berdiaev, Maritain, and Péguy, but none of these men were Mounier's intellectual masters, not even Péguy, whose example, life, and work had such a profound and lasting effect upon him.

The contentions of the Christian democrats merit examination. As

[12] Jean-Marie Domenach, "Présence de Mounier," in *Emmanuel Mounier ou le combat du juste* (Bordeaux: Guy Ducros, 1968), 218.

[13] Michel François, "La revue qui a formé une génération chrétienne," *France-Observateur*, April 2, 1959, 12–13.

[14] For a characteristically ambivalent assessment of the debt of *Esprit* to the Christian democrats, see Mounier, "Les cinq étapes d'*Esprit*," *Dieu vivant* No. 16 (1950), reprinted in *B.A.E.M.*, No. 29 (March, 1967), 10–11.

Borne and Archambault have pointed out, for example, a rudimentary kind of personalism was implicit within the Christian democratic movement since the time of Marc Sangnier's *Sillon* at the turn of the century.[15] Similarly Marcel Prélot, a one-time leader of the small *Parti Démocrate Populaire*, has complained that the *Esprit* group was both unjust and impertinent in its refusal to support the cause of its Christian democratic predecessors.[16] In a more general and perhaps important sense, several of Mounier's friends have recognized Mounier's debt to the Christian democrats. Henri Marrou, long a member of the *Esprit* group and Professor of the History of Christianity at the Sorbonne, has argued that the labors of Mounier and the *Esprit* group would have had little chance of success without the large measure of interior liberty within the French Church which the Christian democrats, by their long and patient efforts, had helped to create. Marrou explains that the Christian democrats were among those most responsible for preventing French Catholics from passing en bloc to the conservative, monarchist, and Integralist Right which was dominated, until Mounier's day, by the *Action Française* of Charles Maurras.[17] Another of Mounier's friends, the former Marxist turned Catholic priest, Ignace Lepp, has made much the same point, although he contends that Mounier recognized his debt to the Christian democrats. Without the persistent efforts of the Christian democrats to reconcile their co-religionists with the modern world, Lepp writes, "there would have been no Catholic public to understand the appeal of Mounier."[18] And similarly Jean-Marie Domenach paid this tribute to a veteran Christian democrat at the time of the latter's death: "For more than twenty years, he was one of our beacon lights. In fact, he had advanced along the road well before us, when it was more difficult."[19]

To examine Mounier and the *Esprit* movement within this particular context is not to deny them a broader significance in the more general framework of contemporary French and European history. A recent study of contemporary French political thought does much to clarify Mounier's political ideas by examining them in the context of the gen-

---

[15] Etienne Borne, "Marc Sangnier," *l'aube*, June 4, 1950; and Paul Archambault, "Du personnalisme au marxisme: une aventure spirituelle," *Politique*, New Series, V, No. 35 (June, 1948), 482.

[16] Marcel Prélot, "Les démocrates populaires français (Chronique de vingt ans: 1919–1939)," in *Scritti di sociologia e di politica in onore di Luigi Sturzo* (Bologna: Zanichelli, 1953), III, 226.

[17] Henri Marrou, "Un homme dans l'Eglise," *E.M.*, *1905–1950*, 890–896.

[18] Ignace Lepp, *Espoirs et déboires du progressisme* (Paris: La Table Ronde, 1956), 81.

[19] Jean-Marie Domenach, "Témoignage," in *Francisque Gay. Témoignages* (Le Mans: Imprimerie commerciale, 1964), 67.

eral rethinking of French political doctrines begun in the 1930s by such contemporaries of Mounier as Simone Weil, Albert Camus, Jean-Paul Sartre, Bertrand de Jouvenal, and Raymond Aron.[20] The author of this study rightly points out, however, that Mounier was not, nor did he attempt to be, a political theorist in the classical sense. Rather, Mounier was a moralist.[21] A recent study of contemporary French social thought is more accurate. Mounier, its author states, "ranks more as a public 'educator,' or as the conscience of his generation, than as a figure in the history of philosophy."[22] Mounier was primarily concerned with the temporal implications of his religious faith and, as Henri Marrou points out, what he "discovered, felt, lived, and preached by his example is, in brief, that the spiritual is itself physical."[23] Intermittently for a hundred years prior to the founding of *Esprit*, the Christian democratic tradition had sought to reconcile Mounier's religious faith with the modern world. This tradition provides a useful context in which the significance of the life, the work, and the heritage of Mounier may be partially clarified. Such an examination serves to reveal the nature and character of Mounier's vocation and the mission he assigned to *Esprit* as well as to draw together many of the multiple elements of his *pensée engagée*. But most important, an examination of the relationship between Mounier and the Christian democrats necessarily focuses upon Mounier's foremost concern. He was first and last a profoundly committed Christian concerned with the temporal dimensions of his religious faith.

Late in his life, Mounier wrote an introduction to the philosophy of existentialism. In this study he outlined the historical development of existentialism in the form of an "Existentialist Tree." As the major roots, Mounier placed Socrates, the Stoic philosophers, St. Augustine, and St. Bernard; at the base of the trunk are Pascal and Maine de Biran; the central section of the trunk is labelled Kierkegaard; and the branches of the tree include Sartre, Heidegger, Jaspers, and, among many others, Mounier's own personalism.[24] Following Mounier's ex-

---

[20] Roy Pierce, *Contemporary French Political Thought* (London: Oxford University Press, 1966).

[21] *Ibid.*, 50.

[22] H. Stuart Hughes, *The Obstructed Path. French Social Thought in the Years of Desperation, 1930-1960* (New York: Harper and Row, Publishers, 1968), 97.

[23] Henri Marrou, "La signification religieuse de la pensée d'Emmanuel Mounier," *B.A.E.M.*, No. 28 (August, 1966), 31.

[24] Mounier, *Introduction aux existentialismes* (Paris: Editions Denöel, 1947), reprinted in *O.M.*, III, 71.

ample, an imaginary "Christian Democratic Tree" might be designed. At the base of the trunk is the first Christian democratic movement, *l'Avenir* of Lamennais; further up the trunk is the group of *l'Ere Nouvelle* of 1848; above *l'Ere Nouvelle* the tree sprouts its first and possibly largest branch, the Social Catholicism of Albert de Mun and René de La Tour du Pin (which initially receives its political nourishment from a neighboring "Monarchist Tree"); continuing up the trunk are Léon Harmel, the *Parti Démocrate Chrétien* of 1896, and the *abbés démocrates* of the turn of the century; above them is the *Sillon* of Marc Sangnier from which the trunk separates into two branches of unequal size, the small *Ligue de la Jeune-République* on the left and the larger *Parti Démocrate Populaire* on the right; and finally, to complete the tree's growth by 1932, a number of small branches including one labelled *"Esprit"* might be grafted.

The ideal of the Christian democratic predecessors of Mounier and *Esprit* was the reconciliation of a religious, moral, and spiritual tradition with a temporal, political, and social tradition. Explicit in the term "Christian democracy" are both a religious faith and a political conviction. The attempt to establish rapport between these two is the distinctive characteristic as well as the *raison d'être* of Christian democracy.[25] The precise relationship between the religious faith and the political conviction of the Christian democrat has always tended to be ambiguous. Indeed just as Mounier entitled his study of existentialism, *Introduction aux existentialismes*, rather than *Introduction au existentialisme*, there is ample reason to believe that there are "Christian democracies" rather than a "Christian democracy."

The Christian democrat has been described as one who believes that the democratic system of government and all that it implies is the most acceptable of political systems – *omnis potestas a deo per populum*. The Christian democrat also believes that the democratic system is not the product of the emancipation of human reason from religious belief but rather that democracy has religious belief as its source and that without religious belief democracy could not have reached its present development; the corollary of this is that democracy must renew and revitalize itself in Christian principles which alone can prevent its degeneration and assure its permanence. Finally, the Christian democrat believes that the greatest social problem of modern times is the condition

---

[25] The term "Christian" is used here and throughout in its specifically French usage of "Roman Catholic." This is not meant to imply either that Catholics are the only Christians in France or that non-Catholics are not democrats.

of the working class which issued from the Industrial Revolution and that it is incumbent upon him to support the progressive amelioration of this condition within the framework of democratic institutions. For the Christian democrat, therefore, "democracy is of Christian inspiration in its origins and it can be worked toward only with the continual aid of Christianity."[26]

In an effort to place the Christian democratic movement within the larger tradition of French humanism, Etienne Borne explains that the Christian democrat is inspired by the belief that *"homo politicus* can also be human," and that his essential purpose is "to humanize politics." Restating Blaise Pascal's dicta, but refusing Pascal's pessimistic resignation to the existence of monarchical absolutism, the Christian democrat believes that the purpose of politics is to conciliate justice and authority, to make what is just strong and what is strong just: justice without authority is impotent and authority without justice is tyrannical. He has triumphed over Pascal's doubt and despair concerning the possibility of uniting the two: "the synthesis of justice and authority," the Christian democrat believes," ... is not a contradictory ideal but the very end of efficacious political action."[27]

Elsewhere Borne explains that "the philosophical originality of Christian democratic thought is the search for practical and theoretical correspondances between Christianity and democracy."[28] Then, while claiming that Christian democracy is clearly aware of this problem, he succinctly summarizes the various forms that the relationship between the religious and political bases of Christian democracy have taken. Christian democracy, he states, has never really decided if democracy is a necessary corollary of Christianity, if there is only an analogous connection between the religious and political orders, or if democracy is nothing more than a legitimate temporal choice made by the Christian within the sphere of his civic liberty.[29]

Other critics of Christian democracy have been far more severe. One of them charges that while the vocation of Christian democracy was to Christianize democracy its result has been to democratize Christian-

---

[26] Jean-Baptiste Duroselle, "L'Eglise et la démocratie," *Recherches et débats du Centre catholiques des intellectuels français*, No. 14 (April, 1951), 21.

[27] Etienne Borne, "Le M.R.P. et les courants permanents de la pensée française," *M.R.P. Cahiers de formation politique*, No. 2 (n.d.), 3–4.

[28] Etienne Borne, "Ethiques politiques des Eglises. Le catholicisme," in René Rémond (ed.), *Forces religieuses et attitudes politiques dans la France contemporaine* (No. 130, "Cahiers de la Fondation nationale des sciences politiques"; Paris: Armand Colin, 1965), 14.

[29] *Ibid.*, 15–17.

ity.[30] On the other end of the political spectrum, Jean-Marie Domenach argues that Christian democracy has much in common, ironically, with its historic enemy, the religious Integralism which was allied with the *Politique d'abord* of Charles Maurras. Like its reactionary Integralist enemy, Christian democracy refuses to recognize politics as a temporal endeavor in which believers and nonbelievers are engaged on an equal footing; it refuses to recognize the existence of what Domenach calls "an autonomous political conscience"; and, finally, like its Integralist opponent, it results in, if it does not proceed from, a unitary and totalitarian view of political society which it confuses with Christendom. Christian democracy, therefore, is an essentially anti-political and clerical movement. Domenach concludes that Christian political ideology mysticizes politics and politicizes religion.[31]

As Mounier recognized, the history of Christian democracy in France offers ample evidence to support many criticisms. The relative political impotence of the movement was due in part to its tendency to mysticize politics and its religious difficulties derived from its tendency to politicize religion. To these already formidable difficulties the historical circumstances in which Christian democracy originated and developed added further problems. Although one historian of the movement finds its origins in the late Middle Ages – and like Domenach sees it as an essentially clerical and anti-political movement – Christian democracy as an organized movement does not predate the French Revolution or the Industrial Revolution which produced the social problem to which the movement addresses itself.[32] The Revolution was associated in the eyes of many French Catholics with the general attack upon religion which preceded and accompanied it. Conversely, the Catholic Church and its members appeared in the eyes of many Frenchmen as the main

---

[30] Jean Madiran, *On ne se moque pas de Dieu* (Paris: Nouvelles Editions Latines, 1957), 88–89.

[31] Jean-Marie Domenach, "Conscience politique et conscience religieuse," *Esprit*, New Series, No. 259 (March, 1958), 345–348.

[32] For this controversy over the origins and nature of Christian democracy in France, see Joseph Hours, "Les origines d'une tradition politique. La formation en France de la doctrine de la démocratie chrétienne et des pouvoirs intermédiaires," in Claude Bernardin *et al.*, *Libéralisme, traditionnalisme, décentralisation* (No. 31, "Cahiers de la Fondation nationale des sciences politiques"; Paris: Armand Colin, 1952), 79–123; Etienne Borne, "La démocratie chrétienne contre l'état?," *Terre Humaine*, No. 19–20 (July-August, 1952), 76–101; Etienne Borne and Joseph Hours, "La démocratie chrétienne et l'Etat," *Terre Humaine*, No. 22 (October, 1952), 76–85; and Jean Besson, "De l'age de la démocratie chrétienne," *Terre Humaine*, No. 27 (March, 1953), 90–98. Also of interest to students of Christian democracy is Hans Maier, *Revolution and Church. The Early History of Christian Democracy, 1789–1901*, trans. Emily M. Schossberger (Notre Dame, Indiana: University of Notre Dame Press, 1969).

bulwarks of monarchy and, after the establishment of the Third Republic, as reactionary opponents of the democratic republic.

To the alliances of Catholicism with the counter-revolutionary tradition on one hand and of hostility to Catholicism with the republican tradition on the other, the Industrial Revolution added another set of blocs. The Industrial Revolution allied the Church with the maintenance of economic power by the bourgeoisie and fixed the working class in religious nonbelief.[33] As a result of what Christian democrats often called "the great misunderstanding," as well as of the very nature of their movement, the Christian democrats ultimately attempted to bridge "the disastrous split" between Left and Right in French political and social life.

As a consequence the Christian democrats had to do battle on two fronts. On one side they were opposed by French democrats for whom Christian democracy was necessarily a form of clericalism. From the Christian democrats French democrats demanded proof of genuine democratic convictions; and that such proof was difficult to provide is indicated by the famous question: You accept the Republic, but do you accept the Revolution? On the other front the Christian democrats were opposed by a great number of French Catholics for whom democracy was anathema and Christian democracy heresy. From the Christian democrats they demanded proof of religious orthodoxy; and that this proof was difficult to provide is indicated by the constant difficulties with religious authorities encountered by the Christian democrats.

Until Mounier's day, most of the major battles of Christian democracy were fought on the front which involved other French Catholics. The movement was, in the main, both negative and clerical. Christian democracy originated and developed primarily as a negative force in French political life since it was chiefly a reaction against the alliance of religion and socio-political conservatism. As defined by the men of the M.R.P., its mission was "the break with social injustice ... and conservative political oppression by a certain number of Christians."[34] Christian democracy was clerical, first because its purpose was essentially religious rather than political – it presented a political problem

[33] Adrien Dansette, *Histoire religieuse de la France contemporaine*, Vol. I: *De La Révolution à la IIIe République* (Paris: Flammarion, 1948), 482–494, On "de-Christianization," see Joseph N. Moody, "The Dechristianization of the French Working Class," *The Review of Politics*, Vol. 20, No. 1 (January, 1958), 46–67.

[34] "Origines et mission du M.R.P.," *M.R.P. Cahiers de formation politique*, No. 6 (October, 1951), 9–10.

as a function of a religious problem[35] – and second because so many of its leaders until the twentieth century were themselves priests, or, in more recent times, the products of Catholic Action. Even when Christian democracy emerged as a significant force in French political life, its leaders were hampered by their conservative electoral clientele and they continued to place a program of civic and political education at the center of their activities.

The Christian democrats compounded their own difficulties by failing to elaborate a practicable program. In their efforts to meet the religious objections of French Catholics and the political objections of French democrats, they sought a third or middle way. The result of this quest was a strange mélange of elements more interesting, as a critic of the movement observes with obvious irony, to students of archaeology than to those of political science or history. Included in this conglomeration are such disparate factors as a fairly continual affinity for non-Marxian French socialism; an irreducible strain of moralism; a tendency towards anarchism or at least a pronounced distrust of political authority which was reinforced by the corporative theory of the Social Catholics; and a genuine attachment to democracy.[36] The moralism of the Christian democrats was one of Mounier's chief objects of criticism because, in his judgment, it not only compromised the religious faith of the Christian democrats but also rendered their politics ineffectual. While Jean-Marie Domenach recognizes that the early Christian democrats "saved ... Christian honor" by establishing "a bond between the Church and the revolt of the oppressed," he nonetheless contends that generosity and charity, while admirable virtues in themselves, are poor, and indeed dangerous, substitutes for political ability.[37] In this sense, a historian of French Catholicism is able to speak of "the political incapacity of Christians."[38] A modern Christian democrat's conclusion, with which Mounier would have been in substantial agreement, appears unchallengeable. The Christian democratic movement, Etienne Borne writes, was based upon certain vague aspirations and developed as a "generous ideal or prophetic prescience."[39]

The life, work, and difficulties of the first great forerunner of Christian democracy in France are a veritable microcosm of the history of

---

[35] Jean Lacroix, "Partis et confessions," *Esprit*, No. 80 (May, 1939), 253.
[36] René Rémond, "Les partis catholiques," in R. Carrouges *et al.*, *Le monde se fait tous les jours* (Paris: Editions du Cerf, 1953), 184.
[37] Domenach, "Conscience politique et conscience religieuse," 345–346.
[38] Rémond, "Les partis catholiques," 184.
[39] Borne, "La démocratie chrétienne contre l'Etat?," 76.

the movement's first hundred years. Abbé Hugues-Félicité Robert de Lamennais was the movement's prophet; and to it he imparted many of its essential characteristics. On October 10, 1830 a group of Catholics under the leadership of Lamennais published the first number of a short-lived journal, *l'Avenir*. With the motto "God and Liberty" on its masthead, *l'Avenir* proclaimed a program of radical reform which included universal manhood suffrage, separation of Church and State, complete religious liberty, freedom of education, the press and association, and certain communal and provincial liberties inspired by the desire for political decentralization.

In spite of this program, the members of *l'Avenir* were a politically diverse group of men.[40] They were held together less by the power of Lamennais' intellect, his philosophy or his political and social ideas than by his personality, his temperament, his great reputation as a holy man, and most especially by his ability as a writer.[41] In the course of his career Lamennais demonstrated what little importance he attached to specific political forms. He was first a traditionalist, then a proponent of an alliance between the people and the Church, and finally an advocate of a prophetic form of democratic socialism. The infallible criterion of truth in his philosophical system was the conscience of mankind rather than the changing and uncertain opinions of individual men, even of a Pope Gregory XVI. His doctrine of *sensus communis* had as its objective the moral and spiritual health of mankind and to this end Lamennais proposed first the method of authority and then the method of liberty.[42] Because of his refusal to submit to the papal condemnations of 1832 and 1834, the heritage of Lamennais was a heavy burden for his Christian democratic successors and provided their opponents additional weapons in their already well-stocked arsenals.[43] In the judgment of Emmanuel Mounier, Lamennais had succumbed to "the vaguest mystical effusions."[44]

The influence of Lamennais manifested itself again in 1848 when a

---

[40] The differences among the members of *l'Avenir* are examined in Peter N. Stearns, "The Nature of the Avenir Movement (1830–1831)," *The American Historical Review*, LXV, No. 4 (July, 1960), 837–847. See also the same author's *Priest and Revolutionary: Lamennais and the Dilemma of French Catholicism* (New York: Harper and Row, Publishers, 1967).

[41] Waldemar Gurian, "Lamennais," in M. A. Fitzsimons, Thomas T. McAvoy and Frank O'Malley (eds.), *The Image of Man. A Review of Politics Reader* (Notre Dame, Indiana: University of Notre Dame Press, 1959), 312.

[42] Marcel Prélot, *Histoire des idées politiques* (Paris: Dalloz, 1959), 474–475.

[43] See, for example Robert Havard de la Montagne, *Histoire de la démocratie chrétienne* (Paris: Amiot-Dumont, 1948), 26–27; and Jacques Marteaux, *L'Eglise de France devant la Révolution marxiste*, Vol. I: *Les catholiques dans l'inquiétude, 1936–1944* (Paris: La Table Ronde, 1958), 39-40.

[44] Mounier, "Le christianisme social," *B.A.E.M.*, No. 9–10 (December, 1956), 12.

number of veterans of *l'Avenir* joined other Catholics in publishing *l'Ere Nouvelle*. The spirit of national conciliation and fraternity which initially pervaded the revolutionaries of 1848 worked to the temporary advantage of Catholicism but the issues which ultimately divided all Frenchmen also brought to the surface profound differences among the Christian democrats, Social Catholics, and Liberal Catholics of *l'Ere Nouvelle*. Charles de Montalembert, for example, later referred to the democratic sympathies of his former friends as "the most dangerous and criminal error of our times."[45] In Mounier's estimation, "Montalembert and the Voltairean bourgeoisie effortlessly abandoned political liberty in order to safeguard their social and economic privileges."[46] The leader of the Christian democratic wing of *l'Ere Nouvelle*, on the other hand, was the recipient of one of Mounier's rare tributes to a Christian democrat. Frédéric Ozanam, Mounier stated, proposed that the central tradition of the Church be renewed: "the union of poverty and the altar."[47] Indeed, Ozanam's analogy between the new industrial working class and the barbarians – "Let us go over to the side of the barbarians," Ozanam exhorted his fellow Catholics – strikingly anticipated not only the general judgment but the precise language of Mounier a century later.[48]

Ozanam was prophetic in yet another respect. In his insistence that justice rather than charity was the only basis upon which the social problem could be resolved, he marked out one of the major differences between the Christian democratic and Social Catholic movements. With the failure of *l'Ere Nouvelle*, "social reform becomes an aristocratic 'uplift' movement rather than a democratic effort to establish a better social order. With the legitimists the undemocratic tendency reaches its extreme: Christian social reform becomes the function of the divine-right monarchy, aided by private charitable endeavors of the upper classes."[49] When Christian democracy reappeared after an eclipse of almost half a century, it carried with it traces of conservative Social Catholicism.

[45] Quoted in Jean-Baptiste Duroselle, *Les débuts du catholicisme social en France (1822-1870)* (Paris: Presses universitaires de France, 1950), 399.

[46] Mounier, *Le personnalisme* (Paris: Presses universitaires de France, 1949), reprinted in *O.M.*, III, 481.

[47] Mounier, "Court traité du catholicisme ondoyant," *Esprit*, No. 62 (November, 1937), reprinted in *O.M.*, III, 565-566.

[48] Quoted in Parker T. Moon, *The Labor Problem and the Social Catholic Movement in France* (New York: Macmillan Company, 1921), 412-413, and in Duroselle, *Les débuts du catholicisme social en France*, 296. See Mounier, "Le christianisme et les barbares," *Témoignage Chrétien*, February 1, 1957.

[49] Moon, 76.

Like the Christian democrats, the Social Catholics were convinced of the need to ameliorate the conditions of the working class and to integrate it in the society of its co-citizens.[50] Upon the modalities of this need, however, the Christian democrats and Social Catholics differed substantially. A modern historian succinctly summarizes these differences and at the same time points out one of the future difficulties of the Christian democratic movement. Jean-Baptiste Duroselle explains that Montalembert and the Social Catholics of the late nineteenth century were paternalistic; they believed that the upper classes should help and protect the proletariat without surrendering their control of the levers of authority in society. The Christian democrats, on the other hand, believed that fraternity implies not only helping the proletariat but a complete sacrifice in which the workers are given control of their own affairs. "The confusion between these two conceptions – an abyss still separates them – has always been detrimental to the representatives of Christian democracy."[51]

Although the origins of Social Catholicism in France have been traced to the 1820s, it was not until the early decades of the Third Republic that it took form as a well-organized movement.[52] Its main organ was the *Oeuvre des Cercles* under the guidance of Albert de Mun, René de La Tour du Pin, and Léon Harmel. Albert de Mun was the chief parliamentary spokesman of the movement; La Tour du Pin was its leading theoretician; and Harmel was not only the main practitioner of Social Catholicism but also the president of the short-lived *Parti Démocrate Chrétien*. The leaders of the *Oeuvre des Cercles* welcomed and rightly claimed some credit for the papal encyclical of 1891, *Rerum novarum*. This charter of Social Catholicism laid down the general principles of modern Catholic social doctrine and turned the leaders of the movement from the theoretical elaboration of their program to practical legislative and organizational activity. This activity was further encouraged the following year by the encyclical on the Ralliement, *Au milieu des sollicitudes*, which urged Catholics to accept and to work within the institutions of the Republic.[53]

[50] Duroselle, *Les débuts du catholicisme social en France*, 9–10; and Henri Rollet, *L'Action sociale des catholiques en France (1871–1901)* (Paris: Presses universitaires de France, 1950), 7.

[51] Jean-Baptiste Duroselle, "L'esprit de 1848," in Paul Archambault *et al.*, *1848. Révolution créatrice* (Paris: Bloud & Gay, 1948), 212.

[52] The standard studies of Social Catholicism are Duroselle, *Les débuts du catholicisme social en France*, and Rollet, *L'Action sociale des catholiques*.

[53] On the Ralliement, see Adrien Dansette, *Histoire religieuse de la France contemporaine*, Vol. II: *Sous la Troisième République* (Paris: Flammarion, 1951), 125–127; André Latreille *et al.*, *Histoire du catholicisme en France*, Vol. III: *La période contemporaine* (Paris: Editions

For two of the leaders of Social Catholicism the encyclical on the Ralliement posed a serious problem. Because of their monarchist political convictions, La Tour du Pin refused to rally and de Mun was at best a reluctant *rallié*. Léon Harmel, on the other hand, welcomed the policy of Pope Leo XIII without reservations. While he was president of the *Oeuvre des Cercles*, Harmel had organized *Cercles chrétiens d'études sociales*. In spite of the paternalistic connotations of "the good father," the appellation he had earned in his working community of Val-des-Bois, Harmel's new organizations were very different from the parent *Oeuvre des Cercles*. The latter was dominated by employers while the new *Cercles* were run entirely by the workers with the aid of priests who interpreted the social teaching of the Church. It was at a congress of the *Cercles* that the *Parti Démocrate Chrétien* was organized in 1896, and it was with the priests of Harmel's *Cercles*, and others like them, that the Christian democratic movement of the 1890s was to become associated.

The latter were the *abbés démocrates*, a disparate group of young priests, some of whom were obscure parish curés and others bright personalities in the world of journalism and politics.[54] In the pages of Abbé Naudet's *La Justice sociale*, Abbé Garnier's *Le Peuple français*, Abbé Trochu's *l'Ouest-Eclair*, Abbé Six's *La Démocratie chrétienne*, and numerous other little journals the cause of Christian democracy was publicized; and in the Chamber of Deputies it had worthy spokesmen in such priests as Gayraud and Lemire. The *abbés démocrates* and their followers found inspiration in the social literature of the time, particularly in such novels as *Fils de l'esprit, Les Lettres d'un curé de campagne,* and *Les Lettres d'un curé de canton* by the Christian democratic philosopher George Fonsegrive and *Lettres d'un militant* by the *abbé démocrate* Roblot.[55] That future Christian democrats frequently re-

Spes, 1962), 469–476; David Shapiro, "The Ralliement in the Politics of the 1890s," in David Shapiro (ed.), *The Right in France, 1890–1919* (London: Chatto and Windus, 1962), 13–48; and Alexander Sedgwick, *The Ralliement in French Politics, 1890–1898* (Cambridge, Mass.: Harvard University Press, 1965).

[54] On the *abbés démocrates*, see Pierre Dabry, *Les catholiques républicains; histoire et souvenirs, 1890–1903* (Paris: Chevalier et Riviere, 1905); Robert Cornilleau, *L'Abbé Naudet. Les maîtres d'une génération* (Paris: Bloud & Gay, 1934); René Rémond, *Les deux congrès ecclésiastiques de Reims et de Bourges, 1896–1900. Un témoignage sur l'Eglise de France* (Paris: Sirey, 1964); Maurice Montuclard, *Conscience religieuse et démocratie. La deuxième démocratie chrétienne en France, 1891–1902* (Paris: Editions du Seuil, 1965); and Jean-Marie Mayeur, *Un Prêtre démocrate. L'Abbé Lemire, 1853–1928* (Paris: Casterman, 1968).

[55] On Fonsegrive and Roblot, see Robert Cornilleau, *De Waldeck-Rousseau à Poincaré. Chronique d'une génération (1898–1924)* (Paris: Spes, 1926), 69–86, 207–230; Paul Archambault *et al., George Fonsegrive* (No. 11, "Cahiers de la Nouvelle Journée"; Paris: Bloud & Gay, 1928); and Pierre de Crisenoy, *Un Chevalier normand de l'Art et de la Foi. Jacques Debout*

ferred to themselves as "fils de l'esprit" and often used the slogan, "l'âme commune," contained in another of Fonsegrive's novels, testifies to both the lasting impact of this literature and the unusual character of Christian democracy itself.[56]

The political party to which many of the *abbés démocrates* belonged was organized at the third National Congress of Harmel's *Cercles* in Rheims in May, 1896. Neither the character of its program and membership nor the circumstances in which it was born boded well for its future. A careful study of an ecclesiastical congress held in August of the same year in the same city, which was attended by many of the *abbés démocrates*, reaches a conclusion that applies to the *Parti Démocrate Chrétien* in all of its essentials. The priests who gathered at Rheims were democrats for apostolic rather than political reasons. Democratic activity was viewed as a means of bringing the masses back to the Church and reviving a society based upon Christian principles. These Christian principles, however, were of conservative Social Catholic inspiration for they implied an organicist view of society which can hardly be reconciled with the individualistic basis of French political democracy.[57]

The *abbés démocrates* further manifested the uncertainty of their Christian democratic faith in the political climate engendered by the Dreyfus Affair. In 1898 the *Parti Démocrate Chrétien* entered into an electoral alliance with such groups as the *Comité Justice-Egalité* of the clerical and anti-Semitic anti-Dreyfusards, the Assumptionists of *La Croix*, the *Groupe Républicain*, and the *rallié* party of Etienne Lamy, on the basis of a vague program that called for the reform of whatever laws were contrary to the rights of Catholics.[58] Notwithstanding the sensational victory of a Christian democrat in Roubaix over the Socialist leader Jules Guesde, the elections of 1898 were disastrous for the Christian democrats.

The congresses of Harmel's *Cercles* and the *Parti Démocrate Chrétien* were, in addition, completely overshadowed by their association with the national congresses of *Démocratie chrétienne* which were held in Lyons in 1896, 1897, and 1898.[59] Present at one or another of the latter

(Paris: Bloud & Gay, 1948). Both men wrote under *noms de plume*, Fonsegrive under Yves Le Querdec and Roblot under Jacques Debout.

[56] Paul Franche, *Le Prêtre dans le roman français* (Paris: Perrin Perrin & Cie, 1902), 313.

[57] Rémond, *Les deux congrès ecclésiastiques*, 74–75. Rémond's conclusion is challenged by Montuclard, *Conscience religieuse et démocratie*, 81.

[58] Rollet, *L'Action sociale des catholiques*, 434; and Cornilleau, *De Waldeck-Rousseau à Poincaré*, 59.

[59] See Jean-Marie Mayeur, "Les congrès nationaux de la 'Démocratie chrétienne' à Lyon

were not only Harmel, Lemire, Garnier, Fonsegrive, and other Christian democrats, but such men as the editor of the notorious anti-Semitic *La France libre* and others whose positions cannot by any proper definition be called either Christian or democratic.

The failure of the *Parti Démocrate Chrétien* and the *abbés démocrates* was made complete by papal action in 1901. In that year Pope Leo XIII issued the encyclical *Graves de communi* which "de-politicized" the Christian democratic movement.[60] Henceforth the term "Christian democracy" was to mean what it had, in fact, meant to many of the *abbés démocrates* previously: "a beneficial Christian action among the people."[61] The *abbés démocrates* were placed in an equivocal and false position, for in their desire to oppose the historical solidarity of the Church and Monarchy they had supported, the encyclical implied, an equally false alliance of the Church and democracy.[62] Another result of the papal pronouncement was merely a matter of semantics. Until the terms of *Graves de communi* were altered by Pope Pius XII in 1944, the Christian democrats generally adopted the etiquette of "democrats of Christian inspiration."[63] Finally, by formally restricting the activities of the Christian democrats to social action, the encyclical contributed to a major change in the relationship of the Christian democratic and Social Catholic movements. In the words of a leader of Social Catholicism, "the meeting and quasi-fusion of the two movements, distinct and even opposed in origin, ... is one of the most important phenomena of the first half of the twentieth century."[64]

Indicative of the convergence of the Social Catholic and Christian democratic movements was the future evolution of several of the leading institutions of Social Catholicism. The *Association Catholique de la Jeunesse Française* (A.C.J.F.), the bourgeois and aristocratic youth movement founded by Albert de Mun in 1886 as an extension of the *Oeuvre des Cercles,* had among its members and leaders during the period between the two World Wars many of the future chieftains of

---

(1896–1897–1898)," *Revue d'histoire moderne et contemporaine,* IX (July-September, 1962), 171–206.

[60] Prélot, *Histoire des idées politiques,* 615.

[61] Georges Hoog, *Histoire du catholicisme social en France, 1871–1931* (Paris: Editions Domat-Montchrétien, 1946), 122; and Dansette, *Histoire religieuse,* II, 213.

[62] Dansette, *Histoire religieuse,* II, 213.

[63] See, for example, Francisque Gay, *Pour un rassemblement des forces démocratiques d'inspiration chrétienne. Mémoire confidentiel* (Paris: Bloud & Gay, 1935); and Jean Raymond-Laurent, *Le Parti Démocrate Populaire, 1924–1944* (Le Mans: Imprimerie commerciale, n.d.), 76.

[64] Joseph Folliet, "Essai sur l'évolution des idées dans le mouvement social en France," *Chronique sociale de France,* 60ᵉ année, No. 2 (April, 1952), 153.

Christian democracy. The founders of the most important Social Catholic institution, the *Semaines sociales*, were Henri Lorin and Marius Gonin, both of whom were members of the Christian democratic *Union nationale* of the *abbé démocrate* Garnier. Christian democrats regularly attended the annual *Semaines* and at one of them the decision was made to organize what was to be the *Parti Démocrate Populaire*. The Christian trade union movement, although it too had conservative Social Catholic roots, was closer to Christian democracy than to Social Catholicism during the interwar period. When the C.F.T.C. was formally organized in 1919, it adopted the formula of the *Parti Démocrate Chrétien*, "the free syndicate in the organized profession," rather than the mixed syndicate principle of conservative Social Catholicism. Gaston Tessier, the long-time secretary-general of the C.F.T.C., was in the forefront of the "democrats of Christian inspiration" and from the ranks of his organization issued many of the militants of the Christian democratic parties of the future.

In the immediate future, however, the prospects of Christian democracy were far from bright. The failure of the Ralliement to achieve its major purposes in the bitterness created by the Dreyfus Affair was followed by the anti-clerical campaigns of Waldeck-Rousseau and Emile Combes. The resultant separation of Church and State ultimately worked to the advantage of the Church, but within the Church the Christian democrats encountered serious difficulties. The attempts of the Christian democrats to reconcile the Church and modern society had their philosophical and theological counterparts in the efforts of a number of priests and laymen to "modernize" the doctrine of the Church by adopting the methods of rationalist criticism. The Modernist crisis that ensued during the first decade of the century brought with it the condemnation of Modernism by the Pope as well as a series of disciplinary measures against its leaders, Loisy, Duchesne, Brémond, Le Roy, Laberthonnière, and a number of other men.[65]

Modernism also provoked a contrary reaction of religious Integralism, several of whose leaders organized the still-mysterious organization, the *Sodolitium Pianum* or the "Sapinière."[66] These doctrinal

---

[65] On Modernism, see Jean Rivière, *Le modernisme dans l'Eglise. Etude d'histoire religieuse contemporaine* (Paris: Letouzey & Ane, 1929); Emile Poulat, *Histoire, dogme et critique dans la crise moderniste* (Paris: Casterman, 1962); Dansette, *Histoire religieuse*, II, 437–471; and Robert Rouquette, "Bilan du modernisme," *Etudes*, Vol. 289 (June, 1956), 321–343.

[66] See Louis Davallon, "'Sapinière' ou brève histoire de l'organisation intégriste," *Chronique sociale de France*, 63ᵉ année, No. 3 (May, 1955), 241–271; and Emile Poulat, *Intégrisme et catholicisme intégral. Un reseau secret anti-moderniste: La "Sapinière" (1909–1921)* (Paris: Casterman, 1969).

vigilantes arrogated to themselves the right to ride herd not only on their Modernist opponents but on anyone suspected of being a Christian democrat as well. By forming a natural alliance with the supporters of political Intransigence, the Integralists added "démo-christianisme" to their lexicon of Modernist errors, particularly in their secret delations to Rome. As a result, but not necessarily without justification in some cases, disciplinary action was taken against several of the *abbés démocrates* and in the atmosphere created by the Modernist-Integralist conflict even the *Semaines sociales* and the A.C.J.F. came under suspicion.[67] Peace reigned, but as the Christian democrats often said, it was "the peace of the cemeteries."[68]

A generation later, Emmanuel Mounier, who was himself no stranger to attacks by the Integralists and to rumors of condemnation or disciplinary action, paid tribute to the Modernists. He condemned both Modernism and Integralism as two endemic maladies of Christianity – Modernism because it temporalized Christianity and Integralism because its preference for the letter of the law killed its spirit. But he also recognized that in spite of their errors the Modernists had at least posed problems for the Church which still remained to be solved.[69] As a student in Paris, Mounier had an opportunity to appreciate at first hand the remarkable abilities of two veterans of the Modernist crisis. For a number of years he studied informally under Père Pouget, a former colleague of Loisy, and he consulted Abbé Henri Brémond, the author of the magisterial *Histoire littéraire du sentiment religieux en France*, while investigating a thesis topic. His biographer writes that Pouget's students "became and remained open and progressive minds at the same time that they were vaccinated against the virus of modernism."[70]

With the requisite reservations, the tribute Mounier paid the Modernists might also have been given the Christian democrats. For all their shortcomings, the Christian democrats persevered and gave ample evidence of their faith in the romantic ideal of Christian democracy. Not only did they survive the defeat of their Church on the terrain of republican politics and the ascendancy of the Integralists and Intransigents

[67] An excellent account of the ravages of Integralism by a prominent Social Catholic is Jean Desgranges, *Carnets intimes. Journal d'un conférencier populaire* (Paris: La Palatine, 1960), *passim*. A fascinating case study of Modernist-Integralist conflict is André Blanchet, *Histoire d'un mise à l'Index. La "Sainte Chantel" de l'abbé Brémond* (Paris: Editions Montaigne, 1967).

[68] Raymond-Laurent, *Le Parti Démocrate Populaire*, 20.

[69] Candide Moix, *La pensée d'Emmanuel Mounier* (Paris: Editions du Seuil, 1960), 281–285; and Mounier, "Responsabilités de la pensée chrétienne," *O.M.*, III, 57off.

[70] Jean Guitton, *Portrait de M. Pouget* (Paris: Editions Bernard Grasset, 1954), 26.

within the Church, but they went on to form the most fruitful Christian democratic movement in the history of France – the *Sillon* of Marc Sangnier.

In the dramatic history of the *Sillon* the previous history of Christian democracy was repeated: the predominance of enthusiasm for a cause and an ideal over any effort to define a practical political program; the confusion of Catholicism and democracy in response to the alliance of Catholicism and political reaction as it was now being manifested in *Action Française;* and the resultant intervention of religious authorities. So firmly did the *Sillon* take root, however, that not even papal action could seriously hamper the maturation of its fruits. With the *Sillon*, Christian democracy in France had at once a legend, a *mystique*, a leader, and finally a political organization.

The *Sillon* began as an informal discussion group which Marc Sangnier organized while he was a student in the Collège Stanislas in 1894. Sangnier continued this practice the following year when he entered the *Ecole Polytechnique*. After completing his military service, he concentrated his efforts on popular education among the working classes by means of *Cercles d'études sociales* and *Instituts populaires* and such journals as *Le Sillon* and *l'Eveil démocratique*. Although Sangnier jealously guarded the independence of his movement from existing Social Catholic and Christian democratic groups, their existence undoubtedly contributed substantially to the rapid success of the *Sillon*.

Precisely what the *Sillon* was is difficult to discern because it had no precise program and no formal organization. "Instead of being an association defined by statutes, the *Sillon* is 'an immaterial bond between hearts.'"[71] In a celebrated incident, a group of priests in Limoges asked Sangnier to what they were committing themselves by joining his movement. "To nothing," Marc replied. The *Sillon*, he told them, is "life" and "friendship."[72] The *Sillon* was a life to be led rather than a political movement to be joined. It was "friendship" and this friendship centered upon the person of Marc Sangnier and provided the movement with what cohesiveness it possessed. Indeed the best description of the movement is that "the *Sillon* is Marc Sangnier."[73]

Sangnier was neither a political thinker nor an effective party organizer or leader. Rather, he was a remarkable personality and an extraordinary orator. Jean Raymond-Laurent, a leader of the *Parti Démo-*

---

[71] Adrien Dansette, "Marc Sangnier et le Sillon," *La Vie intellectuelle*, (July, 1950), 17.
[72] Quoted in Desgranges, *Carnets intimes*, 19.
[73] Dansette, "Marc Sangnier et le Sillon," 10.

crate Populaire and one of the founders of the M.R.P., recalled some
forty years after the event that Sangnier "radiated dynamism." It was
a dynamism which was rooted in "divine love and human affection"
and which changed the entire existence of those with whom Sangnier
came into contact.[74] Francisque Gay, another veteran of the *Sillon*,
recalled that "for me, [Sangnier] was and would remain the most in-
genious of conquerors of souls." [75] Another description of Sangnier
refers to him as a man adept at arousing consciences.[76] And François
Mauriac, like many veterans of the *Sillon*, has testified to the lasting
effects of his membership in the *Sillon*. "All that I write today had its
beginnings fifty years ago in that little club room of the Bordeaux
Sillon, near the Madeleine," Mauriac recalled many years later.[77] He
made this admission in spite of the biting portrait of Sangnier that he
painted in one of his earliest novels.[78]

The slogans of the *Sillon* also reveal much about Sangnier and the
character of his movement. "L'Amour plus fort que la haine," "Il faut
aller au Vrai avec toute son âme," "Tout à la cause," "L'âme commune," "La trouée," and "Se laisser faire par la vie" were among the
most popular of them. It was charged that membership in the movement required "a total giving, a renunciation of one's career, perhaps of
marriage." [79] And Sangnier was accused of exercising a kind of "mystical caesarianism" over his followers.[80] Not surprisingly, the almost
religious veneration accorded its leader caused the *Sillon* to spawn a
number of schismatic men and organizations.

An almost imperceptible change in the direction of Sangnier's purposes contributed to these defections and ultimately did even greater
damage to the *Sillon*. Initially the aim of the *Sillon* was "to live Catholicism individually and collectively." Then it became a "Christian
democratic" movement within the meaning assigned the term by

---

[74] Jean Raymond-Laurent, *Figures de militants. Les origines du Mouvement républicain
populaire. Quelques souvenirs. Conférence donnée au Cours de formation civique de la Fédération M.R.P. de la Seine le 27 janvier 1947* (Paris: Editions du Mail, n.d.), 17–18.
[75] Quoted in Maurice Carité, *Francisque Gay, le militant* (Paris: Les Editions Ouvrières,
1966), 189.
[76] Simone and Hélène Galliot, *Marc Sangnier (1873–1950). Plaquête redigée à l'occasion
du dixième anniversaire de sa mort* (Le Mans: Imprimerie commerciale, 1960), 16.
[77] François Mauriac, *Mémoires intérieurs* (Paris: Flammarion, 1959), 33.
[78] See Mauriac's portrait of Jerome Servant in his *Young Man in Chains*, trans. by Gerard
Hopkins (London: Eyre & Spottiswoode, 1961), and the critical discussion of the novel in
Jean de Fabrègues, *Le Sillon de Marc Sangnier. Un tournant majeur du mouvement social
catholique* (Paris: Librairie académique Perrin, 1964), 228–233.
[79] Maurice Vaussard, *Histoire de la démocratie chrétienne* (Paris: Editions du Seuil, 1956),
74.
[80] Cornilleau, *De Waldeck-Rousseau à Poincaré*, 323.

Graves de communi. Finally, when Sangnier organized "le plus grand Sillon" in 1907, its task was to work "towards the realization of the democratic republic in our country." [81] In an atmosphere charged with politico-religious problems and strife such a change was, perhaps, unavoidable, but with it appeared a confused mingling of religious sentiments and political aspirations, for the romantic religious inspiration of the original *Sillon* remained an important component of the movement.

When Sangnier approached political questions, he did so with the moral fervor and religious zeal of a missionary. Robert Cornilleau, a future leader of Christian democracy, accurately discerned that the *Sillon* "transposed on to the terrain of republican action and civic education the élan of faith from which it had first sprung." [82] The "Cause" to which Sangnier rallied his youthful followers was "less a program than a vital élan." [83] To be a democrat meant to assume moral duties and to aid others in self-perfection, for democracy in Sangnier's generous view was less a specific social or political regime than a moral ideal. To be a democrat meant to practice the fraternity born of Christian charity.

Writing in *l'Eveil démocratique* early in 1904, Sangnier presented what was henceforth to be the classic Christian democratic, and implicitly personalist, definition of democracy. Democracy, he wrote, is "the social and political organization which aims at developing to the fullest the conscience and responsibility of each person, permitting him to take an effective part in the direction of public affairs ..." [84] Thirty years later in the heady atmosphere of the Popular Front, Sangnier spoke of the Republic in even loftier and less concrete terms: "The republic is respect for the human person; the republic is the great human fraternity which unites all men; the republic is the feeling that the goods of the earth must not be monopolized by a few but that they are, first and foremost, the common patrimony of all men." [85]

Sangnier had an almost deliberate disdain for intellectual precision and he refused to allow any systematization of his vague and generous

---

[81] Dansette, "Marc Sangnier et le Sillon," 17. See also Victor Carlhian, "Grandes étapes du Sillon," in Maurice Villain, *Portrait d'un précurseur. Victor Carlhian, 1875–1959* (Paris: Desclée de Brouwer, 1965), 133–134. Since this was written, a major study of the *Sillon* has been published: Jeanne Caron, *Le Sillon et la démocratie chrétienne, 1894–1910.* (Paris: Plon, 1967). See especially Caron, 305–408.

[82] Cornilleau, *De Waldeck-Rousseau à Poincaré*, 199.

[83] Robert Cornilleau, *Pourquoi les Démocrates-populaires ont formé un parti nouveau* (Paris: Editions "Petit démocrate," 1930), 27.

[84] Quoted in André Darricau, *Marc Sangnier* (Paris: Les Editions Ouvrières, 1953), 91.

[85] *La Jeune-République*, July 25, 1937.

ideas. The *Sillon* undoubtedly contributed to and benefited from the Catholic renaissance of the years prior to the First World War, but whether it benefited directly from the intellectual side of this renaissance is open to question. The conversions of Ernest Psichari, Charles du Bos, Paul Claudel, Charles de Foucauld, Joseph Lotte, the Maritains, and Francis Jammes belong to a separate chapter in the history of French Catholicism.[86] Certainly, his critics notwithstanding, the anti-intellectualism of Sangnier precluded any close relationship between the *Sillon* and the Modernist movement proper. "We are not modernists," a *Sillonist* accurately noted in his diary. "We do not wish to discuss dogmas or introduce a new religious life; we are content to live our faith by attempting to realize the integral Christian life." [87] That this constituted a form of "religious naturalism" akin to Modernism, as Sangnier's critics charged, is questionable.[88] What is certain is that this form of action foreshadowed, in an admittedly crude form, the idea of *témoignage* which was first clearly enunciated and practiced by Emmanuel Mounier.

All of this is not to say that Sangnier's lack of intellectual precision played no part in the difficulties encountered by the *Sillon*. His vague identification of Catholicism with a particular political system – in spite of the fact that he found the principles of this system inscribed in the Sermon on the Mount – provided effective ammunition for his opponents. In addition, Sangnier's tactics were hardly designed to allay the misgivings and fears of many members of the French hierarchy. He deliberately disregarded the terms of *Graves de communi;* he attacked the leaders of the *rallié Action Libérale Populaire;* he consistently demonstrated his antipathy towards Catholic trade unionists; he attacked the A.C.J.F. and finally even some members of the hierarchy.[89] From the point of view of the French bishops, in particular, the new potential orientation of the *Sillon* was of special concern because many of Sangnier's followers were recruited from religious organizations controlled by local bishops and priests. That many of the bishops were ardent supporters of *Action Française* only compounded Sangnier's problems.

On August 25, 1910 the long-rumored papal action against the *Sillon* was taken. In a letter entitled *Notre charge apostolique*, Pope Pius X

---

[86] See Latreille *et al., Histoire du catholicisme en France*, III, 532–543.
[87] Victor Carlhian quoted in Villain, 133.
[88] This is the criticism of Fabrègues, *Le Sillon*, 115–166 *passim*. See also Caron, 641–697.
[89] Desgranges, *Carnets intimes*, 17; Darricau, 19; Jules Zirnheld, *Cinquante années de syndicalisme chrétien* (Paris: Editions Spes, n.d.), 141–142; and Caron, 593–640.

ordered the *Sillon* disbanded and its members placed under the direction of their individual bishops in diocesan *Sillons catholiques*.[90] Although he praised Sangnier and his followers for their "generous ardour," the Pope censured them for confusing "evangelization and the advent of democracy." Catholic doctrine, the Letter stated, recognizes that justice is compatible with democratic, monarchical or aristocratic government. Some of Sangnier's enemies hoped to see in him a new Lamennais but Sangnier disappointed them by immediately submitting to the papal edict. In their future battles with the men of *Action Française*, the veterans of the *Sillon* never let their opponents forget this or that their response to the papal edict was far different from the response of Maurras and his supporters to a papal condemnation sixteen years later: *Non possumus*.

In spite of the Letter of 1910, the Christian democratic successors of the *Sillon* did not hesitate to claim Sangnier and his movement as their direct progenitors. In 1931 even Cardinal Verdier, the Archbishop of Paris, was to pay homage to the *Sillon* in a famous and often-quoted statement. "The *Sillon* is at the origin of the great contemporary social movement," he said with obvious approval.[91] Several years after Sangnier's death in 1950 a man who has been aptly called the "conscience of the M.R.P." explained the apparent contradiction between the condemnation of the *Sillon* and the approbation of its successors by the authorities of the Church:

Today it is clear that what the *Sillon* meant by democracy was not this or that institution, which is obviously relative and frail, but spiritualism applied to politics or, as is said today, a humanism of public life. That man has rights as a man and not as a result of the chances of birth, class, privilege...; that any politics which invokes *raison d'Etat* or the laws of history against the honor of only one man is a technique for degrading men and destroying social fraternity and not a true politics – these axioms, at once evident and paradoxical, profoundly revolutionary as well as conservative of authentic order, sufficiently define the purest democratic spirit...[92]

From the *Sillon* Christian democracy acquired a *mystique* rather than a doctrine or program. It also had a leader but one who by personal style and temperament, by his aversion to political programs and discipline, was unsuited for the role of a political or parliamentary chieftain.

[90] On the condemnation of the *Sillon*, see Desgranges, *Carnets intimes*, 29–135 *passim.*; Fabrègues, *Le Sillon*, 195–225; Charles Breunig, "The Condemnation of the Sillon: an Episode in the History of Christian Democracy in France," *Church History*, XXVI (September, 1957), 227–244; and Caron, 698–734.

[91] Quoted in Carité, 40–41.

[92] Etienne Borne, *De Marc Sangnier à Marc Coquelin* (Toulouse: Edouard Privat, 1953), 23–24

Sangnier's story, therefore, contains some of the elements of personal tragedy as well as some of the reasons for the failure of Christian democracy during the Third Republic. Adrien Dansette's assessment cannot be improved upon:

> The former president of the *Sillon* had a genius for popular education, but his overflowing personality, his candid and implacable logic, his instinctive horror of any organization, his aversion to concrete problems, rendered him unfit for political activity which is exercised in the contingent and the relative. Radiating in the milieu of a handful of still-faithful old disciples, he will remain unyielding and out-of-reach, and Catholics of the Left will be unable to undertake anything either with him or without him. The years will pass, his mustache will whiten, he will assume the figure of the original old man preaching in the desert, surrounded by a few young men pressing around their great misunderstood leader. Then, after the Second World War, having become a symbolic and inoffensive patriarch, his heirs of the *Mouvement républicain populaire* will raise him to a place of honor and will venerate him as a relic of heroic times.[93]

The paradox explicit in Sangnier's future role is further accentuated by the fact that the *Sillon* contributed directly and indirectly to the two Christian democratic parties of the Third Republic. The first of these parties was the *Ligue de la Jeune-République* which was founded by Sangnier in 1912. The other and numerically more important party was the *Parti Démocrate Populaire* which was organized in 1924 by a disparate group of Social Catholics, Christian democrats, and Christian trade unionists. At the time of the founding of *Esprit*, these were the chief political components of the movement of which Mounier was so very critical.

If the contributions of various organizations and intellectual currents to the elaboration of a Christian democratic doctrine and program could be precisely delineated, the most important contribution of Sangnier's *Jeune-République* would doubtless be a *mystique* of the human person. This *mystique* was that of the *Sillon* and it was an ill-defined and rudimentary form of what was to gain currency under the aegis of Mounier and *Esprit* as personalism.[94]

Like Mounier's personalism, that of the *Jeune-République* had, initially at least, a somewhat a-political cast. In fact, the *Jeune-République* was originally not a political party at all. Nonetheless, when the *Jeune-République* became a party its personalism had a much closer kinship with that of Mounier than did the implicit personalism of the *Parti Démocrate Populaire*. Almost entirely absent from the *Jeune-République* was the rather narrow sectarianism and constraining timidity of the

---

[93] Dansette, "Marc Sangnier et le Sillon," 26.
[94] Etienne Borne, "Marc Sangnier," *l'aube*, June 4, 1950.

Parti Démocrate Populaire. According to its original statutes the *Jeune-République* was "a league for economic and political action ... [which] intends to be one of the elements of that great party of the democratic republic that France needs and one of the foundation stones of the future edifice." [95] Sangnier's decision to form a league rather than a full-fledged political party was a result not only of his own aversion to ordinary political activity but of his assessment of the political climate of France in 1912. He believed that France had to be liberated from "the old parties" which no longer represented "what is best and most generous in republican aspirations." [96] There was a major crisis of faith in the republican idea and "new men" were needed to rehabilitate it.[97] What was required, Sangnier believed, was a "politics without politicians." [98]

Sangnier carried the lofty idealism of the original *Sillon* into his new organization. Just as the *Sillon* had been a "friendship," so the *Jeune-République* was "a league into which only those who are truly our friends – in perfect communion of sentiment and desire with us – will enter." [99] And just as the original objective of the *Sillon* had been to live Catholicism individually and collectively, so one of the aims of the *Jeune-République* was to end the dichotomy "between the morality of public and private life." [100] What was most lacking in French political life, Sangnier believed, was "enthusiasm, élan, confidence." [101] "We will be treated as naive men and as imbeciles," Sangnier said in an admission with which Mounier would have sympathized, but he added: "So much the better!" [102]

In later Christian democratic history the "friendship" of the *Jeune-République* was to compensate for a number of political deficiences. Until its demise many years later, the *Jeune-République* retained its almost familial atmosphere – to its members, it was always simply the

---

[95] *Ligue de la Jeune-République. Programme et statuts* (Paris: "La Démocratie," 1912), 3. See also *Compte-rendu du premier congrès national de la Ligue de la Jeune-République* (Paris: "La Démocratie," 1912), and Georges Hoog, *Vingt années d'histoire politique (1906–1925)* (Paris: "La Démocratie," 1926), 25–30.

[96] Marc Sangnier, "La politique sans les politiciens," *La Démocratie,* June 30, 1912, reprinted in Marc Sangnier, *Une politique nouvelle* (Paris: "La Démocratie," 1912), 253.

[97] Marc Sangnier, "La 'Ligue de la Jeune-République,'" *La Démocratie,* June 20, 1912, reprinted in *ibid.,* 231.

[98] Sangnier, "La politique sans les politiciens," 250–254.

[99] Marc Sangnier, "La tâche opportune," *La Démocratie,* April 21, 1912, reprinted in Sangnier, *Une politique nouvelle,* 225.

[100] Marc Sangnier, "Politique nouvelle," *La Démocratie,* June 26, 1912, reprinted in *ibid.,* 237.

[101] Sangnier, "La tâche opportune," 224.

[102] Sangnier, "Politique nouvelle," 238.

"J-R." [103] Its religious idealism, so often expressed in the demand that moral and spiritual forces be respected by the state, was similarly to leave an indelible imprint on its Christian democratic heirs. Respect for moral and spiritual forces became a kind of Christian democratic *modus operandi* during the Third Republic. Its role in Christian democratic thought was not dissimilar to that played by the defence of religious interests in the parties of the Right. As more than one critic was to point out, however, references to moral and spiritual forces became clichés and catch-alls, almost verbalisms devoid of precise or practical meaning.[104]

The *Jeune-République* assigned a utilitarian value to moral and spiritual forces which was similar to that given civic virtue by the ancient philosophers and Montesquieu. Religious belief was considered to be the source of the civic discipline needed by the individual to subordinate his personal interests to those of his fellow citizens. "To work against it is in some way to work against the country," [105] Sangnier said in an argument which was remarkably similar to that of Charles Péguy, who contended that "the de-republicanization of France is essentially the same movement as the de-christianization of France." [106]

The need for moral discipline contributed, in turn, to the emphasis the *Jeune-République* placed upon civic education. So important did the league consider this task that its secretary-general Georges Hoog stated that "the *Jeune-République* does not neglect electoral activity but it clearly subordinates it to the educational activity that it wishes to exercise on public opinion." [107] The argument Hoog used to justify the preponderant place assigned civic education merits quotation because it became stereotyped in Christian democratic circles in later years. Hoog contended that

because democracy is a social, political, and international regime which attempts to associate in the direction of public affairs, in the City, in the Factory, in Humanity itself, a continually increasing number of citizens, ... at the very base of our democratic conception an educational task is imposed. It is obvious that the participation of citizens in the direction of public affairs requires a vigorous and perservering effort by means of popular civic education. But this

---

[103] Claude Estier, *La gauche hebdomadaire, 1914–1962* (Paris: Armand Colin, 1962), 128.

[104] See, for example, Maurice Blondel, "Sens exact et fonction morale et politique des 'valeurs spirituelles,'" *Politique*, 12e année, No. 6 (July, 1937), 481.

[105] Marc Sangnier, "La tâche de demain," *La Démocratie*, April 20, 1912, reprinted in Sangnier, *Une politique nouvelle*, 215.

[106] Charles Péguy, *Temporal and Eternal*, trans. by Alexander Dru (London: The Harvill Press, 1958), 23.

[107] Georges Hoog, "Une doctrine et un programme," *La Démocratie*, No. 11 (November, 1931), 113.

education must have two aspects: a properly civic education first, . . . and another form of democratic education which is not only civic but moral. The citizen in a democracy, being himself responsible for the welfare of his country, must, at certain times at least, be capable of sacrificing his particular interest to the general interest. . . . If this moral education of the citizen is indispensable in a democracy, is this not to say that the State, far from opposing moral and religious forces, should respect them, better still support them? Democracy cannot do without religious and moral forces which can so effectively aid those who possess them in subordinating their particular interests each time it is necessary to a more general interest, to a collective interest.[108]

The central activity of the *Jeune-République* was the popular education that best suited its leader's undeniable talents. The program of the little organization was also rooted in the single idea with which Sangnier was inflamed. A young man who left the *Jeune-République* in the 1920s because of the extremely pacifist position adopted by the League after the First World War believed that Sangnier was a romantic of 1848 vintage who held that one idea alone could satisfactorily be applied to the solution of all social and political problems. This idea was the democratic idea in its classic sense. Sangnier's entire outlook, this critic continued, was colored by an individualist psychology. Sangnier and his followers continually stressed that individual reform is a prerequisite of political and social reform, that "charity must reign in our hearts before peace can reign in the world – ideas which would have been entirely correct had they been properly counterbalanced by a clear understanding of the enormous role that juridical, economic, and technical, in a word, sociological factors play in the determination of collective and individual conduct." [109]

Specific political reforms were not Sangnier's forte and the relatively short and simple program of the *Jeune-République* reflected this fact. In order to achieve "a rejuvenation of the republic itself in a democratic direction," it proposed that a greater number of people be associated in the direction of public affairs and that their association be made more effective.[110] More specifically, the *Jeune-République* advocated: the introduction of proportional representation; women's suffrage; the adoption of the English method of parliamentary dissolution and the use of the referendum; and the creation of a professional chamber which was to represent various social, economic, religious, and even

---

[108] Georges Hoog, *Histoire, doctrine, action de la "Jeune-République"* (Paris: Société coopérative d'édition et de propagande, 1925), 6.

[109] Yves Simon, *La grande crise de la République française. Observations sur la vie politique des Français de 1918 à 1938* (Montreal: Editions de l'arbre, 1941), 57–58.

[110] Hoog, *Histoire, doctrine, action de la "Jeune-République,"* 32.

intellectual interests (the *Académie Française*) and to replace the old Senate.[111]

After the First World War foreign affairs played an increasingly important part in the activities of Sangnier and the *Jeune-République*. Sangnier abandoned his moderate prewar nationalism and devoted himself almost entirely to the cause of the League of Nations, disarmament, and Franco-German rapprochement to such an extent, in fact, that a veteran Christian democrat describes the *Jeune-République* of the 1920s as "a kind of league of pacifist action." [112] To further the cause of peace Sangnier organized annual *Congrès démocratiques internationaux*, at one of which, the famous congress held at Bierville in 1926, representatives of some thirty nations were present.[113] In 1932 Sangnier resigned as president of the *Jeune-République* in order to devote himself entirely to pacifist activities through a new weekly newspaper, *l'Eveil des peuples*, and to such organizations as his *Amis de Bierville* and *Auberges de la Jeunesse*. The *Jeune-République* was henceforth free to devote itself to all of the problems of French politics as a full-fledged political party during the final decade of crises of the Third Republic.

Both the pacifism of the *Jeune-République* and the openness and progressiveness of the positions it adopted particularly in domestic politics during the 1930s make it exceedingly difficult to place the *Jeune-République* in the same "political family" with the other Christian democratic member of its "spiritual family," the *Parti Démocrate Populaire*. A number of the founders of the *Parti Démocrate Populaire* were veterans of the *Sillon* and the immediate origins of the party revealed the impatience of its founders to create the great "breach" in French politics of which the Christian democrats had always dreamed. But their desire for political success contributed to the eclecticism of the party's membership and this, in turn, was one of the major weaknesses of the party. That the *Démocrates Populaires* persevered in the face of numerous difficulties merited some small praise from even so harsh a critic as Emmanuel Mounier.

Three times during the years between the Letter on the *Sillon* and the founding of the *Parti Démocrate Populaire* in 1924 attempts were

---

[111] *Ibid.*, 37–43; Fabien France, "La reforme de l'esprit public," *Cahiers de la Démocratie*, No. 11 (April, 1934), 10–12; and Georges Hoog *et al.*, "Aspects de la crise. Problèmes d'organisation économique et sociale," *Cahiers de la Démocratie*, No. 14–15 (July-August, 1934), 8–10, 44–45.

[112] Prélot, "Les démocrates populaires française," 215. For the foreign policy of the *Jeune-République*, see Hoog, *Histoire, doctrine, action de la "Jeune-République,"* 43–78.

[113] Darricau, 35ff; and Galliot, 94–97.

made to organize a broad entente of Christian democrats. Failure in each instance did not dim the hopes of the "sons of the Spirit." In the years immediately prior to the outbreak of the First World War a number of little coteries of Christian democrats were organized or survived the condemnation of the *Sillon*. Most of these groups jealously guarded their independence not only from Sangnier's *Jeune-République* – although a few of their members belonged to the *Jeune-République* for a brief time – but also from one other. Many of these *Républicains Démocrates* had been dissident *Sillonists* and the residue of their antagonism towards Sangnier remained with them for many years and also affected their relationships with other Christian democratic groups. Only two events gave the Christian democrats any realistic basis for their irrepressible faith in the future of Christian democracy. One was the founding of a small, local weekly newspaper in December, 1912 by the members of the *Union Républicaine Démocratique de Pantin*. Robert Cornilleau's *le Petit Démocrate de Saint-Denis* carried news of interest to the inhabitants of Saint-Denis, Pantin, Aubervilliers and Noisy-le-Sec; it was eventually to become the unofficial organ of the *Parti Démocrate Populaire*.[114] In April, 1913 a member of the recently organized *Fédération des Républicains Démocrates du Finistère* was elected to the Chamber from the second district in Brest. Paul Simon, a young lawyer who had been aided in his campaign against a country squire of the extreme Right by Abbé Trochu's *l'Ouest-Eclair*, remained in the Chamber throughout the remaining years of the Third Republic as the "dean" of Christian democratic deputies.[115]

The War dispersed the already divided Christian democrats and decimated their ranks. Out of the tragedy of war, however, a new climate conducive to moderating the old and bitter differences between French Catholics and their fellow citizens developed. Even among the Christian democrats the same spirit of reconciliation took hold and it manifested itself, briefly at least, in one of the most unusual enterprises in the history of Christian democracy. On July 11, 1916 Georges Hoog published an appeal in a small journal called *Notre Etoile*. Entitled, in typical Christian democratic terms, "To men of good will," the appeal was aimed not only at Hoog's own readers but at all Catholics who wished to pursue the ideal of Christian democracy.

[114] Alfred Bour, "Dans la banilieue parisienne. Fondation du 'Petit Démocrate,'" in *Robert Cornilleau. Souvenirs et témoignages* (Rennes: Imprimerie Bretonne, 1959), 55ff; and Raymond-Laurent, *Le Parti Démocrate Populaire*, 39–40 and 58ff.

[115] Pierre Trémintin, "Dans le Finistère," in *Robert Cornilleau. Souvenirs et témoignagés*, 33ff; and Raymond-Laurent, *Le Parti Democrate Populaire*, 39.

Etienne Besson, a member of the Parisian Union, and Ernest Pezet, a young army officer who had been retired to a military censorship post because of his serious wounds, then undertook "an epistolary inquiry" to more than 500 Christian democrats, many of whom were in the trenches. Taking full advantage of his long convalescence and the free access to the battle zone that his new post offered him, Pezet travelled throughout France rallying support for a broad entente of "republican, social and democratic Catholics." Thus, while the guns on the Somme began firing and those overlooking the carnage at Verdun finally fell silent, the Christian democrats continued their work.[116]

After extensive discussions and meetings the first issue of a new journal which was to serve as the center of the proposed *ralliement* appeared. Carrying the description "Republican Weekly of Social Action" on its masthead, *l'âme française* proclaimed a vague program of "sacred union" among social and democratic Catholics.[117] The new journal rallied a large number of important Catholic leaders: Paul Archambault, a veteran of the *Sillon* and the editor of the important but much-neglected Christian democratic *Cahiers de la Nouvelle Journée;* Eugene Duthoit, the president of the *Semaines sociales;* Jean Lerolle, the president of the A.C.J.F.; Jean Raymond-Laurent; Robert Cornilleau; and, among many others, Marc Sangnier himself. Although *l'âme française* continued publication until 1924, the hopes it embodied were shattered shortly after the end of the war in particularly dramatic fashion. Late in the war Marc Sangnier had visited Rome and had been given a warm reception by Pope Benedict XV. When the war ended the eyes of many Christian democrats fastened once again upon Sangnier in spite of their past differences with him. At a meeting of the collaborators of *l'âme française* in the spring of 1919, Sangnier was offered the leadership of a new Catholic movement. To the dismay of the assembled Social Catholics and Christian democrats, he refused the offer.[118]

L'âme française clearly presaged the formation of the *Parti Démocrate Populaire*, but its failure and the events that followed must have discouraged even the most optimistic Christian democrats. In 1919 the *Jeune-République* was revived as were the various prewar federations

---

[116] On this enterprise, see Ernest Pezet, "'A l'âme française,'" in *Robert Cornilleau. Souvenirs et témoignages*, 39–54; Ernest Pezet, *Chrétiens au service de la cité, de Léon XIII au "Sillon" et au M.R.P.* (Paris: Nouvelles Editions Latines, 1965), 49–85; and Raymond-Laurent, *Le Parti Démocrate Populaire*, 35–36.

[117] Quoted in Pezet, "'A l'âme française,'" 48.

[118] Marcel Prélot, "Histoire et doctrine du Parti démocrate populaire," *Politique*, New Series, No. 19–20 (July-December, 1962), 312–313.

of *Républicains Démocrates* and *le Petit Démocrate de Saint-Denis*. In the elections of 1919 the Christian democrats and Social Catholics won in excess of forty seats in the Chamber. They failed, however, to organize a parliamentary group.[119] The Christian democrats were nothing if not persistent. In the words of one of them, the failure of 1919 "obliged the leaders to enter into conversations with one another and to ask themselves if, for want of a large union like the collaborators of *l'âme française* had prefigured, the political action of at least the Christian democrats of *Sillonist* origins might not be coordinated." [120]

These conversations bore fruit with the formation of the *Ligue nationale de la Démocratie* on August 1, 1920. Although the League had more than 4,000 members in eighteen federations and eleven deputies in the Chamber, less than two years after its organization it was disrupted by the withdrawal of its *Jeune Républicain* members.[121] The Christian democrats themselves have offered a nember of conflicting reasons for this failure. These retrospective explanations reveal the lasting antagonism of many Christian democrats toward Sangnier, the persistence of Sangnier's authoritarian tendencies, important political differences between the *Jeunes Républicains* and *Républicains Démocrates*, and the desire of the *Républicains Démocrates* to organize a fullfledged political party which conflicted with Sangnier's emphasis upon foreign policy and particularly Franco-German reconciliation.[122] Of all of the explanations for the failure of the League, the one put forward by the secretary-general of the *Jeune-République* is most convincing. "To organize a political party," Georges Hoog wrote fifteen years later, "it is not enough to share the same spiritual convictions."[123]

The truth of Hoog's simple explanation was evidenced not only the fact that Sangnier's organization broke with the *Bloc National* in 1922 but, more important, by the two Christian democratic organizations' differing policies toward Edouard Herriot's *Cartel des gauches* in 1924. The *Cartel* was supported by Sangnier and his followers because of its

---

[119] *Ibid.*, 314; Raymond-Laurent, *Le Parti Démocrate Populaire*, 37–38; and Robert Cornilleau, *Du bloc national au front populaire (1919–1924)* (Paris: Spes, n.d.), 52–53.

[120] Prélot, "Histoire et doctrine du Parti démocrate populaire," 315.

[121] *Ibid.* On the *Ligue*, see Galliot, 90–94; Darricau, 32–36; Cornilleau, *De Waldeck-Rousseau à Poincaré*, 345–347; and Raymond-Laurent, *Le Parti Démocrate Populaire*, 38.

[122] Darricau, 34–35; Prélot, "Histoire et doctrine du Parti démocrate populaire," 313–316 *passim*; and Raymond-Laurent, *Le Parti Démocrate Populaire*, 70, 80–83. For a comparison of the foreign policy programs of the two organizations, see Jean Raymond-Laurent and Marcel Prélot, *Manuel politique. Le programme du Parti démocrate populaire* (Paris: Editions Spes, 1928), 93–147, and Hoog, *Histoire, doctrine, action de la "Jeune-République,"* 43–78.

[123] *La Jeune-République*, September 12, 1937.

conciliatory foreign policy and in spite of its anticlericalism, although Sangnier himself was opposed by the Socialists in his unsuccessful bid to retain his seat in the Chamber in May, 1924. The *Cartel*, on the other hand, was vigorously opposed by the future founders of the *Parti Démocrate Populaire* although they did support Locarno. It is difficult to avoid the conclusion that the Christian democrats of this generation mistook their "friendship" and membership in the same "spiritual family" for a political program.

Having lost the support of the *Jeune-République*, the "sons of the Spirit" received the not entirely unexpected help of the leaders of the Social Catholic and Christian trade union movements with whom they had collaborated around *l'âme française*. Only two months after the *Jeune-République* withdrew from the *Ligue nationale de la Démocratie*, "a new and capital fact for our activity" appeared, a *Républicain Démocrate* wrote to one of his friends.[124] While attending the annual *Semaine sociale* at Strasbourg, Jean Raymond-Laurent was approached by Gaston Tessier. Tessier emphasized to Raymond-Laurent the growing concern not only of the members of his own C.F.T.C. but of the leaders of the A.C.J.F. and the *Semaines sociales* over the growing influence of *Action Française*. Tessier told Raymond-Laurent that an organization was needed through which Social Catholics and Christian syndicalists could channel their individual political efforts.

Two months later the enthusiastic *Républicains Démocrates* of the Paris federation organized a *Bureau d'action civique* which was to provide liaison among the "sons of the Spirit," to organize a parliamentary group in the Chamber of 1924, and hopefully to form a national political party. In 1924, although the *Républicains Démocrates*, like the *Jeunes Républicains*, suffered serious setbacks in the parliamentary elections, a *Groupe des démocrates* led by Paul Simon and Victor Balanant of the Finistère federation and numbering the requisite thirteen deputies was organized. In November of the same year the constituent congress of the *Parti Démocrate Populaire* was held.

The congress of the *Parti Démocrate Populaire* met in the Salle Saint-Georges on the street of the same name in Paris on November 15 and 16. The optimism of the party's founders was evident in a variety of ways. During the closing banquet of the congress, for example, the members of the executive commission left the Brasserie Toutvel and trooped out into the street. There, beneath a sign which read "rue de la

---

[124] Raymond-Laurent, *Figures de militants*, 40.

Victoire," they posed for a picture.[125] Robert Cornilleau, the political secretary of the party's parliamentary group, justified the new party in enthusiastic and overly optimistic terms. "The *Parti démocrate populaire*," he said, "is a truly new party because it brings to French politics an element of renovation and rejuvenation. It represents a tradition, a doctrine, [and] already existent organizations." Most parties of the Right, he continued, accentuate their patriotic or religious policies but fail to emphasize social questions. Most parties of the left, on the other hand, place proper emphasis upon the rights of workers and other aspects of the social problem but they "do not understand the necessity of respecting moral and religious forces. They approve of or aggravate sectarian politics. They erect into dogmas laws which violate the rights of conscience." He then concluded that

the originality of the *Parti démocrate populaire* rests in making a synthesis of what is just in the programs of Right and Left. It is liberal and national: it resolutely demands the right of all Frenchmen to profess, without any hindrance, the religion or opinions of their choice – and the rights of France in foreign and colonial affairs. It is social and international: it defends the interests of all those who are workers and, without ceasing to be patriotic, it is devoted to all equitable measures which will permit the organization of arbitration between nations, good feelings between peoples, in short, peace.[126]

The great "breach" in French politics which the Christian democrats had sought since the days of the *Sillon* was, in accordance with the deliberate intention of the *Démocrates Populaires*, to be the *juste milieu* of the Center. As republicans, they obviously had to break the long tradition of Catholic intransigence which Charles Maurras and *Action Française* had erected into doctrine. And as men who believed that "the first condition [for effective democratic government] is respect by the State for moral and religious forces," they similarly had to break the long tradition of republican anticlericalism which was presently embodied in Herriot's *Cartel des gauches*.[127]

The difficulties inherent in achieving these purposes were manifested in the Salle Saint-Georges. The delegates met while the threat of a new anticlerical program hung heavily in the air. The government of Edouard Herriot had come to power in May, 1924 intent not only upon withdrawing French troops from the Ruhr, but, more important, upon

---

[125] *Ibid.*, 42.

[126] *Le Parti démocrate populaire. Compte rendu de l'Assemblée générale constitutive des 15 et 16 novembre 1924 à Paris, Salle Saint-Georges* (Paris: Secrétariate général du Parti démocrate populaire, n.d.), 3.

[127] *Ibid.*, 21–24, 29–34; and "Déclaration de principes du Parti démocrate populaire," in Raymond-Laurent and Prélot, *Manuel politique*, 301.

breaking the recently restored diplomatic relations with Rome, enforcing the laws against the religious orders, and imposing the laïc laws in the recovered provinces of Alsace and Lorraine. For the first time Catholic opposition to anticlericalism was effectively mobilized; and under the auspices of the *Fédération Nationale Catholique* Catholics succeeded in defeating Herriot's anticlerical program. In doing so, French Catholics inevitably laid themselves open to the charge of clericalism and the new Christian democratic party could all too easily be accused of having religious defense as its primary *raison d'être*. The Christian democrats supported the *Fédération Nationale Catholique* and, in fact, were sympathetic to its leader, General de Castelnau, who was to be one of the *bêtes noires* of Christian democracy during the 1930s.[128]

The campaign against Herriot's program brought to the surface the latent conservative and clerical proclivities of many delegates in the congress. The latter included not only representatives of the *Républicains Démocrates*, but veterans of Jacques Piou's *Action Libérale Populaire*, delegates from the Alsatian *Union Populaire Républicaine*, and members of the A.C.J.F. and various Social Catholic groups.

The party's statement of religious policy was the subject of particularly long and heated debate. There was general agreement upon such key phrases as "religious peace is indispensable," "we demand the freedom to revise and amend those [laws] which, voted under the pressure of political passions, are contrary to the rights of citizens," and "the state must respect the sources of religious and moral life from which so many men draw the energy to devote themselves the better to the general interest." [129] On the inclusion of "laïcité de l'Etat" and several other phrases in the statement of policy, however, the delegates were deeply divided. Members of the Alsatian Union and veterans of *Action Libérale Populaire* were particularly sensitive to the religious question. Indeed the latter had refused to support the *Bloc National* in 1919 because its program contained the phrase "laïcité absolue de l'Etat." [130]

Emmanuel Desgrées du Loû, a member of the veteran Christian democratic family which published Abbé Trochu's *l'Ouest-Eclair*, and Paul Simon replied to the critics of the declaration. Desgrées du Loû attempted to mollify the Alsatians and followers of Piou by invoking

---

[128] See, for example, Ernest Pezet, "La Fédération Nationale Catholique. Une interview du Général de Castelnau," *la Vie Catholique*, February 21, 1925.

[129] *Le Parti démocrate populaire. Compte rendu*, 29–30.

[130] Jacques Piou, *Le Ralliement, son histoire* (Paris: Editions Spes, 1928) 219–220.

the names of Montalembert and Piou in a speech which clearly implied that some of the delegates wanted a confessional rather than a republican party.[131] Simon's speech, which received a resounding ovation, further clarified the declaration's distinction between *laïcité* and *laïcisme*. The former meant that the state must be impartial in dealing with various religions in a nation in which unity of belief does not exist; the latter that irreligion is a kind of religion of state. When an Alsatian persisted in arguing that his constituents might be offended by the inclusion of "laïcité de l'Etat" and misunderstand this distinction, he was told that the *Parti Démocrate Populaire* was a party of democratic education as well as an electoral organization, the obvious point being that the Alsatian should educate his supporters.[132] Having lost their major point, the Alsatians and veterans of *Action Libérale Populaire* were thanked profusely for their "valuable and conciliatory" collaboration and a later reference to a "united" but not a "unified" party brought laughter from the assemblage. Eight years later the party was not even "united," for all of the deputies from Alsace-Lorraine, with the single exception of a young man named Robert Schuman, left the *Parti Démocrate Populaire*.

There were other revealing and, in retrospect, foreboding discussions in the 1924 congress. Somewhat surprisingly, there was no serious question raised about the clearly conservative Social Catholic conception of the Republic as being "the culmination of a slow evolution which, beginning with the communes of the Middle Ages, has continued to our own day across centuries of our history." [133] There was animated debate, however, over the role of the worker in the management of his own affairs. The diluting of a statement which called for the ever-increasing participation of the workers in the management of their own professional interests in the party's final declaration of principles was a clear victory for the heirs of Albert de Mun and La Tour du Pin.[134] Like the Alsatians, eight years later some of the Social Catholic members of the *Parti Démocrate Populaire* left the party and joined a new parliamentary *Groupe Républicain et Social* which was led by Georges Pernot, a well-known collaborator of the *Semaines sociales*. Pernot's

---

[131] *Le Parti démocrate populaire. Compte rendu*, 31.

[132] *Ibid.*, 30–35. See also Paul Simon, *République et laïcité* (No. 1, "Cahiers du Parti démocrate populaire"; Paris: Editions Spes, 1925); and René Rémond, "Evolution de la notion de laïcité entre 1919 et 1939," *Cahiers d'Histoire*, IV, No. 1 (1959), 71–87.

[133] *Ibid.*, 21.

[134] *Ibid.*, 22–29.

group outnumbered the remaining *Démocrates Populaires* in the chamber.

The name of the new party provoked a major debate which pitted the *Républicains Démocrates* against a fairly united front of Social Catholics and members of the Alsatian Union. The Alsatians opposed the use of the word "démocrate" largely because it was used by a local Protestant, liberal, and bourgeois party, as did also a good number of Social Catholics because of the vestiges of their anti-republican sentiments. They supported instead the word "populaire," the former, joined by the veterans of *Action Libérale Populaire*, because of the familiar ring it would have for their constituents, and the latter because of the added emphasis this term would give to their own essentially social concerns. In support of their preference, the Social Catholics conveniently cited the papal encyclical *Graves de communi* which prohibited the political use of the term "Christian democrat." The *Républicains Démocrates*, led by Abbé Trochu and Marcel Prélot, supported the inclusion of the term "démocrate." The final solution was obviously a practical compromise. As Prélot pointed out, however, the existence of other European Christian democratic parties which used the terms "popular" and "democratic" served to place the new French party in an international political current.[135]

From a doctrinal point of view the party's name was not a compromise. This, at least, is the contention of Prélot, who writes that the members of the new party

called themselves *démocrates populaires* in spite of the slight neonasm of the term in order to underline, on one hand, their determined adherence to government "for the people" and "by the people"; in order, on the other hand, to indicate their organic and anti-individualistic conception of social life.[136]

Prélot was the foremost political theorist of the new party and his work during the late 1920s tends to contradict the contention that the *Parti Démocrate Populaire* had a ready-made doctrine at the time of the first party congress. Prélot acted as midwife not only for Sturzo's popularism – in part because he was Sturzo's French translator – but also for the theory of "Institutionalism" which was first elaborated by Maurice Hauriou, the well-known Dean of Law at Toulouse.[137] In a report to the

---

[135] On this debate, see *ibid.*, 18–20; and Prélot, "Histoire et doctrine du Parti démocrate populaire," 322–323. For Abbé Trochu's account of the founding of the party, see Paul Delourme [Abbé Trochu], *Trente-cinq années de politique religieuse ou l'histoire de "L'Ouest-Eclair"* (Paris: Editions Fustier, 1937), 257–292.

[136] Prélot, "Histoire et doctrine du Parti démocrate populaire," 323.

[137] See, for example *ibid.*, 330; Marcel Prélot, "Le théorie de l'Institution et la technique juridique," in Maurice Blondel, *Le Problème de la philosophie catholique* (No. 20, "Cahiers de

party congress of 1929 in Nancy, Prélot summarized the doctrine of the party: "Realist in its methods, institutionalist in its processes, personalist in its ends, popular democracy derives its nobility and its supreme strength from the invincible spiritualism of its inspiration."[138]

As Prélot's description indicates, the *Parti Démocrate Populaire*, like the *Jeune-République*, placed an ill-defined personalism at the heart of its doctrine. "True democracy," Jean Raymond-Laurent once said, "must favor the full development of the human personality." [139] In their search for a term and a theory to express and give substance to their personalist aims and their anti-individualism and social organicism, the theorists of the *Parti Démocrate Populaire* examined not only Hauriou's institutionalism and Sturzo's popularism, but other possibilities as well. They explored the possibility of using such phrases as "individualism with social content" and "individualism tempered by moral law." [140] Like Hauriou's institutionalism, however, these concepts proved far too complex for the average party militant to grasp. In retrospect even Prélot admits that "popular democracy was not immediately understood," and even this admission does not, perhaps, go far enough.[141]

The leaders of the new party went to great lengths to emphasize the careful attention they wished to pay not only to doctrine but to party organization and political propaganda techniques as well. They reacted in a self-conscious manner against the lofty idealism and religious sentimentality of their youth. Robert Cornilleau said that they were past the age at which "imprecise and generous tendencies" and the "ardor of a naturally enthusiastic youth" were sufficient for the task ahead.[142] The highly decentralized structure of the party, which left local federations an unusual amount of independence, was a conscious rebellion against the overly centralized and authoritarian character of the *Sillon*.[143] In addition, the executive commission of the party, which was elected by delegates of the local federations meeting three times a

la Nouvelle Journée"; Paris: Bloud & Gay, 1933), 207–216; Marcel Prélot, "Autour de la théorie de l'Institution," in Edouard Jordan, *Eugenisme et morale* (No. 19, "Cahiers de la Nouvelle Journée"; Paris: Bloud & Gay, 1932), 205–211; and Paul Archambault, "Réalisme démocratique," *Politique*, 1re année, No. 4 (April, 1927), 305–316.

[138] Marcel Prélot, "Et, de même, réformer l'Etat," *La Revue des vivants*, 6e année, No. 4 (April, 1932), 623.

[139] Jean Raymond-Laurent, *Le Parti démocrate populaire. Un effort de dix années: 1924–1934* (Paris: Editions du Parti démocrate populaire, 1935), 17.

[140] Prélot, *Histoire des idées politiques*, 619; and Paul Archambault, *Réalisme démocratique* (Paris: Editions Spes, 1930), 7–8.

[141] Prélot, *Histoire des idées politiques*, 617.

[142] Cornilleau, *Pourquoi les Démocrates-populaires ont formé un parti nouveau*, 22.

[143] Prélot, "Histoire et doctrine du Parti démocrate populaire," 320.

year in national council, spawned an extraordinary number of specialized bureaux, commissions, and organizations. Each year the party
held a national congress at which a single issue was the focus of discussion.[144] And the new party also had what should have been adequate means of publicizing its cause and activities. In addition to *le
Petit Démocrate, l'Ouest-Eclair* publicized the activities and policies of
the party in the party's main center of strength, the West; various provincial weeklies often supported the party's work; a series of *Cahiers du
Parti Démocrate Populaire* was published; the Christian democratic
monthly *Politique* often contained articles by *Démocrates Populaires;*
and Paul Archambault's *Cahiers de la Nouvelle Journée* contained contributions by party members.[145]

This flurry of journalistic activity was amazing in view of the relatively small size of the party – although, of course, journalism had
always been a particularly important Christian democratic tool. It
manifested at once the characteristic Christian democratic emphasis
upon civic education and the new party's natural desire to propagate
its ideas and program. In a communiqué given to the press after the
conclusion of the congress of 1924, the program of the party was summarized in simple and appealing language:

1. Attachment to the Republic and to political liberties (freedom of conscience,
   freedom of education and association, freedom of the press and public assembly);
2. Desire to realize democracy in social and economic organization, by a boldly
   reformist evolution and a sincere collaboration of the various elements of
   production;
3. Civic education of minds and consciences, by the appeal to moral forces and
   respect for religious convictions;
4. Foreign policy at once resolutely French and clearly favorable to methods
   of international collaboration.[146]

In more practical terms, the most distinctive feature of the party's program was the proposal that economic and social interests be given a
voice in the councils of state on every level from the region to the parliament. In its quest for a more effective democratic system, the party
proposed not only proportional representation, the use of the popular
initiative and the referendum, and women's suffrage, but such reforms
as the institution of obligatory voting, plural voting for the heads of

---

[144] *Ibid.*, 320–321; and Raymond-Laurent, *Le Parti Démocrate Populaire*, 50ff.
[145] Of the eleven members of the original editorial board ot *Politique*, at least seven were
members of the party.
[146] Raymond-Laurent, *Figures de militants*, 42–43; and "Origines et mission du M.R.P.,"
19.

families, and, in the words of Prélot, the party was "inclined" to support the establisment of a "Grand Council of the Heads of Families." [147] Like the *Jeune-République*, the party favored the replacement of the Senate by an upper chamber representing various professional, family, and other non-political interests. Unlike the former, however, the *Parti Démocrate Populaire* placed strict limitations upon governmental interference in social and economic life as its positions during the Popular Front were to demonstrate.

In foreign affairs the party supported an unusual mélange of consistent and well-reasoned support of the League of Nations, both moral and material disarmament, and measures for the protection of French security. The party's nationalism clearly separated it from the *Jeune-République*, but it was tempered by a genuine willingness to undertake projects of international cooperation, particularly with the Christian and Popular democratic parties of Belgium, Austria, Poland, Italy, and Czechoslovakia.

Moral and civic education were basic components of the program of the *Parti Démocrate Populaire* and the argument used to justify the unusual attention given this activity was precisely the same as the *Jeune-République* used.[148] Even during the crises of the 1930s the leaders of both Christian democratic parties insisted that one of their central purposes was to change "habits" as well as laws; that at the center of the crisis was a moral crisis and that a change in the hearts of men, a "moral revolution," was a prerequisite of institutional or organic reform.[149] This assessment was not an unusual one; it was shared by Mounier and the *Esprit* group as well as by many other *Jeunes équipes* of the time. Unlike *Esprit* and the other *Jeunes équipes*, the Christian democrats were political parties, however, and they could be criticized for thinking that moral reform constituted a viable political program or, in the case of the *Parti Démocrate Populaire*, using moral reform as an excuse for political inaction.

The *Parti Démocrate Populaire* was more open to such criticism than was the *Jeune-République*. Until after the resignation of Sangnier in 1932, the *Jeune-République* was nothing more than a league for civic

---

[147] Prélot, "Et, de même, réformer l'Etat," 614–615. For the program of the party, see Raymond-Laurent and Prélot, *Manuel politique*; and Jean Raymond-Laurent, *Face à la crise* (Paris: Spes, 1935).

[148] See, for example, Raymond-Laurent, *Face à la crise*, 131–161; and France, "La réforme de l'esprit publique," 62.

[149] See, for example, Raymond-Laurent, *Pour sortir de la crise. Le Plan Démocrate Populaire* (Paris: Editions du Parti Démocrate Populaire, [1936]).

education; and when it did become a full-fledged political party its program was immeasurably more adventurous than that of the *Parti Démocrate Populaire*. In some respects it even went beyond that of the Popular Front. The *Parti Démocrate Populaire*, on the other hand, increasingly emphasized its program of moral and civic education and its character as a "school of thought" rather than an "electoral committee." [150] As early as 1929 the editor of *le Petit Démocrate* made the surprising statement that "the conquest of mandates, the possession of power certainly have considerable importance, especially in a country as unified and centralized as France ... But politics is not everything. It is not even of the first order." [151] That such a statement could be made by a leader of a political party is partially explicable because of the possibility that Cornilleau was referring to politics in the grossest sense of the simple acquisition of power and the probability that he was reacting in typical Christian democratic fashion to the complete separation of morality and politics explicit in the *Politique d'abord* of the recently condemned *Action Française*. Nonetheless the statement reveals a good deal about both the character of one form of Christian democracy and the shortcomings of the *Parti Démocrate Populaire*.

Somewhat ironically, Robert Cornilleau also made what was one of the most imaginative and prophetic policy proposals in the entire history of his party. In an article entitled "Pourquoi pas?" in *le Petit Démocrate* of January 23, 1927, he suggested, albeit tentatively and with careful qualifications, that the *Parti Démocrate Populaire* collaborate with the Socialist Party.[152] In succeeding articles Cornilleau defended and further amplified his suggestion, although he now referred to it as a "hypothesis." The prophetic character of Cornilleau's proposal as well as the courage he displayed in making it are amply clear. In the early years of the Fourth Republic the Christian democratic M.R.P. collaborated not only with the Socialists but with the Communists as well. More immediately, Cornilleau's "Pourquoi pas?" became something of a *cause célèbre*. Cornilleau was the object of angry attacks and even denunciations to ecclesiastical authorities. He and his fellow *Démocrates Populaires* were quickly saddled with such epithets

---

[150] Raymond-Laurent, *Le Parti démocrate populaire. Un effort de dix années*, 25.

[151] Robert Cornilleau, *Lettres à un jeune sur la Démocratie populaire* (Paris: Editions du "Petit démocrate," 1929), 23.

[152] Reprinted in Robert Cornilleau, *Pourquoi pas? Une politique réaliste* (Paris: Librairie Valois, 1929), 5–15. The account of the controversy surrounding Cornilleau's proposal is taken from this work.

as "Red Christians" and "so-called Christian democrats." [153] Even Cornilleau's own friends severely criticized him. Responding to an attack by his old friend Abbé Trochu of *l'Ouest-Eclair*, Cornilleau complained: "This is a veritable political indictment, a disavowal and condemnation of all of my work." [154]

Cornilleau's suggestion was made at a particularly important moment in the political history of his party. At one point during the long series of governmental crises of 1926, Edouard Herriot attempted to form a government of left-wing Radical Socialists and Moderates. Among those to whom the original *bête noire* of the *Parti Démocrate Populaire* offered a ministerial post was Auguste Champetier de Ribes, who was a member of the Finance Commission and who was to become president of the *Parti Démocrate Populaire* in 1929. Champetier de Ribes refused the post in a government which intended to impose a capital levy which the conservative propensities of the *Démocrates Populaires* led them to oppose.[155] It is too much to contend that the future of the party was foreclosed by this reaction against the Left, but the fact remains that a pattern was soon established. Very simply, this pattern was a refusal to enter into any majority of the Left – as was suggested in early 1927 by Cornilleau and again in the fall of 1929 when Paul-Boncour offered a post to Champetier de Ribes – and support of the short-lived conservative governments of Tardieu, Laval, and Daladier in the 1930s. Only in the desparate days following the *Anschluss* did the party depart from this pattern; in March, 1938, Paul Simon, the president of the party's parliamentary group, proposed the formation of a government "from Louis Marin [of the moderate *Fédération Républicaine*] to Léon Blum." In keeping with the *raison d'être* of Christian democracy, the *Parti Démocrate Populaire* pursued a policy of republican concentration as a means of breaking the "two blocs" which had long dominated French political life. The leaders of the party however, were not noted for their political audacity and they were generally unwilling to risk what little political success they enjoyed in any new or original departure. Mention must be made, on the other hand, of the proposals for political reform made by Marcel Prélot at the national congress of Nancy in 1929. Prélot's proposals compare

---

[153] Jean Le Trécorrois, *Les déviations du Parti démocrate populaire* (Paris: Editions Fernand Roches, 1932), vi, 83–88, and *passim*; and Auguste Cavalier, *Les Rouges "Chrétiens"?* (Paris: Editions Bossard, 1929).

[154] Quoted in Delourme, 277.

[155] Vaussard, 97–98; and Prélot, "Histoire et doctrine du Parti démocrate populaire," 332.

favorably with other programs of basic institutional reform put forward during the interwar years.[156]

The *Parti Démocrate Populaire* was at once something more than a political party or electoral formation in the eyes of its members and something less than a political party in the general context of French political life. Leaders of the party were particularly fond of pointing out that the *Parti Démocrate Populaire* was only the formal political manifestation of a much broader social and doctrinal movement. Raymond-Laurent and Prélot, for example, took pride in citing André Siegfried's contention that the *Démocrates Populaires* were the heirs of a long Catholic tradition dating from the early nineteenth century and in the inclusion of "the social Christian family" in Albert Thibaudet's classic *Les Idées politiques de la France*.[157] There is some justification for Raymond-Laurent's contention that although his party contributed only a beginning in the general reclassification of French political parties, it accomplished a good deal more in the realm of attitudes and ideas by demonstrating that religious belief was no longer an adequate criterion for classifying political parties.[158]

On the other hand, the leaders of the *Parti Démocrate Populaire* may well have attempted to rationalize their electoral and parliamentary shortcomings by emphasizing the non-political aspects of their strenuous efforts. By 1932 the *Parti Démocrate Populaire* had reached the zenith of its success. On the parliamentary level its original group of thirteen members was increased by one in February, 1927 and reached its maximum of eighteen members after the elections of 1928 when, among others, Robert Schuman joined the party's parliamentary group. Its secretary-general claims that the parliamentary group could normally count on some thirty votes after 1928.[159] The elections of 1932, however, were disastrous, for not only were five deputies not returned to the chamber but the party lost the support of a number of Social Catholics who formed their own *Groupe Républicain et Social* in the chamber. In 1937 the parliamentary group was further reduced to eleven members.

Throughout its sixteen-year history the *Parti Démocrate Populaire* had an average of twelve or thirteen deputies and normally received

---

[156] Prélot, "Et, de même, réformer l'Etat," 610–623; and "Documents sur la réforme de l'Etat," *Politique*, New Series, I, No. 3–4 (June, 1945), 322–368.
[157] Prélot, "Les démocrates populaires français," 218; and Raymond-Laurent, *Le Parti démocrate populaire. Un effort de dix années*, 25.
[158] Raymond-Laurent, *Le Parti Démocrate Populaire*, 75.
[159] *Ibid.*, 66.

about three per cent of the total ballots cast in any national election.[160] It was a regional party for not only did it fail to present candidates in as many as half of the districts in any national election, but its electoral strength was concentrated in the departments of the West, the North, and the Northeast. There is, in fact, a direct correlation between the party's geographical centers of strength and those areas of France which have been designated, in the classic studies of Fernand Boulard, as "pays pratiquants" as distinct from "pays indifférents" and "pays détachés." [161] Some of the reasons for the party's lack of success put forward by veterans of the party itself range from the existence of an electoral system which prevented the dissolution of the traditional politics of the "two blocs" and the absence of a great political chieftain comparable to the Radicals' Herriot or the Socialists' Blum, to the basic conservatism of the party's electoral clientele and the excessive prudence of the party's leadership. Doubtless all of these factors contributed in some measure to the relative political failure of the party.[162] Certainly the leaders of the party were largely technicians and none had the prestige that Georges Bidault brought to the M.R.P. in 1944 as a result of his leadership during the Resistance. There were within the party, however, a surprisingly large number of local and municipal office-holders. That the almost elemental conservatism of the party's supporters, especially in the West of France, hamstrung many of the efforts of the party's more progressive leaders is undoubted. The great Christian democratic daily l'Ouest-Eclair became increasingly conservative in the course of the 1930s, excluded the progressive Abbé Trochu, and opposed a Christian democrat in the elections of 1936.[163]

The failure of the Parti Démocrate Populaire is somewhat less comprehensible when it is viewed in the context of a series of events which were either almost contemporaneous with or followed shortly upon the formation of the party. These events, which have been described as the "second Ralliement," should in normal circumstances have offset some

[160] Alain Bomier-Landowski, "Les Groupes Parlementaires de l'Assemblée Nationale et de la Chambre des Députés de 1871 à 1940," in François Goguel and Georges Dupleix (eds.), Sociologie Electorale (No. 26, "Cahiers de la Fondation Nationale des sciences politiques"; Paris: Armand Colin, 1951), 82–89.

[161] See A. Coutrot and F. Dreyfus, Les Forces religieuses dans la société française (Paris: Armand Colin, 1965), 316. The great majority of the party's deputies came from the Finistère, Vendée, Haute-Rhin, Bas-Rhin, Moselle, Basses-Pyrénées, and Ille-et-Vilaine. Only one was elected in a "pays détaché" (Paris) and one in a department which is part "détaché" and part "indifférent" (Loiret).

[162] Prélot, "Les démocrates populaires français," 221–225; and Raymond-Laurent Le Parti Démocrate Populaire, 96–97.

[163] On the exclusion of Abbé Trochu, see Delourme, 351–439 passim.

of the party's serious deficiencies. This Ralliement was prepared by the reestablishment of diplomatic relations between France and the Vatican; the papal encyclical *Maximam Gravissimamque* which permitted the organization of Diocesan Associations in accordance with the Law of 1905; the conciliatory character of many new members of the French hierarchy; and the failure of the anticlerical policies of the *Cartel des gauches*. Only the serious problem of the Catholic schools, which has been called "the most tangible expression of a philosophical conflict between the Catholic Church and the lay Republic," remained to plague relations between the Church and the State.[164]

Within the French Church itself the central events of the second Ralliement took place. The condemnation of *Action Française* was the most crucial event. The condemnation was especially advantageous to the Christian democratic movement, for just as the Letter on the *Sillon* had prevented Marc Sangnier from identifying the Chruch with republican doctrines and parties, the condemnation of *Action Française* had the practical effect of opposing the Church to the contrary alliances. In what followers of Maurras called "the revenge of the *Sillon*," [165] the condemnation of 1926 finally disengaged French Catholics and the French Church from monarchist parties and doctrines. Although the devotées of *Action Française* were not all Catholics and the organization itself was to have a long posthumous heritage, "a page was turned [and] a new story began" in the history of French Catholicism.[166] "It finally became clear to the Church that a republican regime did not necessarily mean Jacobinical anticlericalism and that a republic could provide as good an environment as a monarchy for the Church's mission." [167]

Two other events were somewhat overshadowed by the *affaire* of *Action Française*, highlighted by the famous *non possumus* of Charles Maurras. One concerned the C.F.T.C. In this case a small *affaire* resulted in the Christian syndicalist movement receiving official Vatican approval.[168] Having acquired recognition within the Church, the C.F.T.C.

---

[164] Coutrot and Dreyfus, 53. On the new Ralliement, see Latreille *et al.*, *Histoire du catholicisme*, III, 578ff; and Harry W. Paul, *The Second Ralliement: The Rapprochement Between Church and State in France in the Twentieth Century* (Washington, D.C.: The Catholic University of America Press, 1967).

[165] Havard de la Montagne, 128.

[166] Latreille *et al.*, *Histoire du catholicisme*, III, 588. See also Raoul Girardet, "L'Héritage de l'Action française," *Révue française de science politique*, VII, No. 4 (October-December, 1957), 765–792.

[167] Paul, 185.

[168] The entire *affaire*, complete with reprints of the most important documents, is sum-

lent increasing, though unofficial, support to the Christian democratic movement. The other event concerned the venerable A.C.J.F. The A.C.J.F. was reorganized into a number of specialized movements in such a way that it could be accurately described as "the *Sillon* reabsorbed." [169] Some indication of the new orientation which resulted from this reorganization is to be found in the fact that on the executive committees of the A.C.J.F. during these years were no less than five men who were to become ministers during the Fourth Republic as members of the M.R.P.[170] During the same period, the young Emmanuel Mounier belonged to the A.C.J.F. in Grenoble and contributed to its journal.

The effects of the second Ralliement penetrated almost every facet in the life of French Catholicism. In 1927 a young Jesuit priest, Pierre Lhande, published *Le Christ dans la banlieue* and thereby gave dramatic voice to the new concern of the Church for the "de-Christianized" proletariat, a concern which was to culminate in the priest-worker experiment after the Second World War. In the same year the young philosopher Jacques Maritain broke with *Action Française* and published his influential *Primauté du spirituel*. Few men were to play as important a role in the intellectual life of French Catholicism and in the advent of a new pluralism among French Catholics, less because of his key role in the revival of Thomistic philosophy than because of the social and political implications of such books as his *Humanisme intégrale* of 1936.[171] Among the members of the new generation who attended the almost legendary meetings of intellectuals, writers, and artists at Maritain's home in Meudon, outside of Paris, was the founder of *Esprit*.

At the same time a variety of Catholic newspapers and journals at once reflected and contributed to this transformation. As one of the foremost students of Catholicism in contemporary France has aptly pointed out, "since French Catholicism entered into the age of the press with Lamennais, periodicals have always been the most visible expression of its internal divergencies and their principal mode of organization ..." [172] Late in 1924 a partner in the publishing house of Bloud et

---

marized in René Rémond, *Les catholiques, le communisme et les crises, 1929–1939* (Paris: Armand Colin, 1960), 21–29.

[169] Marrou, "Un homme dans l'Eglise," 894.

[170] On the reorganization of the A.C.J.F., see Adrien Dansette, *Destin du catholicisme français, 1926–1956* (Paris: Flammarion, 1957), 81–118.

[171] See Henry Bars, *Maritain en notre temps* (Paris: Bernard Grasset, 1959), 113–140; and Hughes, *The Obstructed Path*, 72–81.

[172] Rémond, *Les catholiques, le communisme et les crises*, 14.

Gay founded a new weekly, *La Vie Catholique*. Francisque Gay's journal had the support of Pope Pius XI and it became one of the bulwarks of the "democrats of Christian inspiration" during the 1930s.[173] Early in 1932 Gay and Gaston Tessier founded the first Christian democratic daily newspaper in Paris since the demise of Marc Sangnier's *La Démocratie* in 1914. Around the newspaper, which was optimistically called *l'aube*, a veritable army of Christian democrats gathered in what was to be the most fruitful expression of Christian democracy since the *Sillon*.[174] In 1927 even *La Croix*, the famous organ of the Assumptionists, underwent a major editorial change. In that year the Vatican appointed Père Léon Merklen director of *La Croix* and he ended the political intransigence of the old anti-Dreyfusard paper.[175]

The following year, again at the request of the Holy See, the French Dominicans founded a monthly journal called *la Vie intellectuelle*. Under the leadership of Père Bernadot, the Dominicans of Juvisy published a number of remarkable journals.[176] Perhaps the most notable was the weekly *Sept*. The history of *Sept* is, in itself, an important chapter in the history of the changing political orientation of French Catholicism.[177] The Dominicans who published *Sept* and the other journals were to be in the forefront of many of the most important changes within French Catholicism in the next two decades. One of their closest friends and admirers was Emmanuel Mounier.

The existent Christian democratic organizations did not benefit from this outburst of Catholic intellectual and journalistic activity. Indeed the new journals contributed further to the fragmentation of the already divided forces of Christian democracy. Each of the new journals had its group of "friends" who were loyal to their particular circle of friends. Although the *Amis de l'aube* and the *Amis de Sept* were progressive in their social and political views, such fraternal organizations as the *Parti Démocrate Populaire* and the *Jeune-République* were extremely independent of them. In addition, the Christian democratic parties were weakened by the organization of numerous *Jeunes équipes*. In this

---

[173] Françoise Mayeur, *l'aube. Etude d'un journal d'opinion, 1932–1940* (No. 144, "Cahiers de la Fondation nationale des sciences politiques"; Paris: Armand Colin, 1966), 12–18.

[174] *Ibid.*, 5–32; and Carité, 75–109.

[175] René Rémond, "L'Evolution du journal 'La Croix' et son role auprès de l'opinion catholique (1919–1939)," *Bulletin de la Société d'histoire moderne*, No. 7 (1958), 3–10.

[176] See "Le dossier de la quinzaine. Un artisan de la presse catholique moderne. Le Père Bernadot (1883–1939)," *Informations catholiques internationales*, No. 147 (July 1, 1961), 15–25; and "Le Père Maydieu," *La Vie intellectuelle*, Special Number (August-September, 1956).

[177] See Aline Coutrot, *Un courant de la pensée catholique. L'hebdomadaire "Sept" (mars 1934–aout 1937)* (Paris: Editions du Cerf, 1961).

respect, if in relatively few others, they had much in common with other French political parties.

The *Jeunes équipes* were groups of young men just reaching maturity who were profoundly disillusioned with French political life. They attacked the old parties and the old men for failing to recognize what they, in their youthful vision, considered to be a revolutionary crisis not only in France but in the entire Western World. In response to the *Jeunes équipes*, the *Jeune-République* organized its *Equipes de Jeunes de la Jeune-République* and initiated what it called a "Jeune politique." Similarly, in 1931 the *Parti Démocrate Populaire* welcomed into its ranks a group of young men from the A.C.J.F., which included Georges Bidault, and organized its *Jeunesses Démocrates Populaires* in November, 1932. Ultimately, however, the Christian democrats were unable to obtain the support of the new generation. Of all the *Jeunes équipes*, only one survived; this was the *Esprit* group founded in 1932 by Emmanuel Mounier. Mounier was to be the foremost critic of Christian democracy from a vantage point which was without precedent in the history of Christian democracy in France.

CHAPTER II

THE ESTABLISHED DISORDER:
EMMANUEL MOUNIER AND THE FOUNDING OF
ESPRIT

> Une vie n'est pas brisée qui a porté un grand témoignage. Nous savons la fragilité de nos forces et du succès, mais nous savons aussi la grandeur de notre témoignage. C'est pourquoi nous poussons sans trouble notre tâche dans la certitude de notre jeunesse.
>
> Mounier, "Certitude de notre jeunesse," May, 1933.

Perched on the right side of the road leading from Perpignan into the Cerdagne and thence through the old Spanish enclave of Llivia to Andorra is the small resort town of Font-Romeu. The main buildings in the little town are hotels and villas which are usually filled with vacationing Frenchmen during the August holiday. On August 16, 1932 a group of fifteen or twenty young men arrived at the Villa Saint-Paul which had been placed at their disposal by Madame Madeleine Daniélou, the wife of Charles Daniélou, a former Minister of Public Health, and herself the directress of the Collège Sainte-Marie in Neuilly. Among the young arrivals were Madame Daniélou's son, Jean, a seminarian; her son-in-law, Georges Izard, a promising lawyer who had been her husband's private secretary; André Déléage, a student of Marc Bloch and librarian at the University of Toulouse; Louis Galey, who had been a classmate of Déléage in Bourges and was now a student at the Beaux-Arts in Paris; and Emmanuel Mounier, a philosopher who had taught in Madame Daniélou's school and in the Lycée de Saint-Omer. During the following week the young men enjoyed the sun and quiet air of the surrounding Pyrenees, but their purpose in Font-Romeu was neither quiet nor peaceful. They were revolutionaries of a peculiar variety. "The basis of our accord," they explained several months later, "is the common impossibility of living." [1]

What the young men experienced in Font-Romeu left its mark on most of them for the rest of their lives. Jean Daniélou has had an illustrious career as a highly influential and original philosopher and theologian since his ordination as a Jesuit priest in 1938. In 1969 he was made a prince of the Church. Daniélou has remained extremely sympathetic to, though not entirely uncritical of, the work of his friends at

---

[1] "Chronique du mouvement," *Esprit*, No. 1 (October, 1932), 129.

Font-Romeu.[2] Almost twenty-five years later Georges Izard said that he was not aware that he had deviated from the path he had set out upon at Font-Romeu.[3] After a comparatively brief political career, Izard became one of the most prominent lawyers in France as counsel in the celebrated cases involving Kravchenko, Mendès-France, Robert Barat, the Neo-Destour, the Bey of Tunis, and Mitterand. Galey, after an even briefer political career, devoted himself entirely to his work as an architect and scenarist, but he, like Izard, acknowledged a lasting debt to the experience that had begun at Font-Romeu.[4] The cases of some of the other young men remain problematical. Galey's classmate, André Déléage, for example, began a brilliant but tragically short-lived career as a medievalist at the Universities of Strasbourg and Nancy. After writing his magisterial *La Vie rurale en Bourgogne jusqu'au début de XIe siècle*, Déléage met his death during the von Rundstedt offensive in 1945.[5]

In spite of the undeniable brilliance of many of its members, the little group in Font-Romeu was dominated by Emmanuel Mounier. What bound the young men together was Mounier's intention "to remake the Renaissance" and his revolutionary opposition to what he was later to call "the established disorder." [6] At Font-Romeu the little band of moral rebels laid the groundwork for *Esprit*, the journal, and the movement which were to carry forward the unusual task described by Mounier.

The founders of *Esprit* were youthful visionaries and in retrospect several of them have admitted the naïveté of some of their early hopes.[7] With a large number of other *Jeunes équipes*, they moved in a broad current of revolutionary, moral, and largely negative opposition to the men, institutions, and ideologies of the Third Republic, and, indeed,

---

[2] See Jean Daniélou, *Dialogue avec les Marxistes, les Existentialistes, les Protestants, les Juifs, l'Hindouisme* (Paris: Le Pottulan, 1948), 21–32, and Jean Daniélou, "La vie intellectuelle en France," *Témoignage Chrétien*, September, 1945.

[3] Georges Izard in "Qu'as-tu fait de ta jeunesse? Une grande enquête de Gilbert Ganne sur les mouvements intellectuels d'avant-guerre. Cette semaine: *Esprit*," *Arts*, No. 561 (March 28–April 3, 1956).

[4] Louis-Emile Galey in *ibid*.

[5] See "Souvenirs de André Déléage," *Esprit*, New Series, No. 340 (July-August, 1965), 189–208; and Mounier, "André Déléage," *Esprit*, No. 107 (February, 1945), 476–477.

[6] Mounier, "Refaire la Renaissance," *Esprit*, No. 1 (October, 1932), 1–51. This article is a revised version of the report given at Font-Romeu, "Les directions spirituelles du mouvement '*Esprit*'" B.A.E.M., No. 13–14 (March, 1959), 1–48. The article in *Esprit*, like many of Mounier's most important writings, was later included in a book, *Révolution personnaliste et communautaire* (Paris: Fernand Aubier, 1936), 14–63. This book, in turn, is included in *O.M.*, I, 129–416. Henceforth, in similar cases, references will be made to the *Oeuvres* and will include the original date of publication in *Esprit*.

[7] See, for example, Galey in "Qu'as-tu fait de ta jeunesse?"

of contemporary Western civilization as a whole. "It is difficult to imagine the revolt which then aroused young intellectuals if one did not live through it," a student of the *Jeunes équipes* writes. "Maurrasiens, Marxists, Christians rebelled – a few years later a youth's journal was called *L'Insurgé* – against a world of deception which horrified them." [8] "It was," a member of the *Jeunes équipes* recalls, "literally the end of *a* world, perhaps of *the* world. ... It seemed urgent to take part. Commitment had to be complete and exclusive." [9]

The formation of the various *Jeunes équipes* followed an almost identical pattern. A group of young intellectuals, united only by friendship and certain common and vaguely-felt aspirations, gathered in a study circle. They then began the publication of a journal and through it the intellectual life of the group developed and took form. None of them found a school of thought they could accept or a political party to whose discipline they could submit. The war and the crises which followed it had erected insurmountable barriers between the old ideological and political cadres and these young intellectuals who despised the "mentality of the war veteran" and the France of Poincaré. Characteristically, one of them stated: "We are more than a new party: we are a new generation." [10]

The *Jeunes équipes* were deliberately less representative of positive and constructive political points of view than of "a spirit and a method." [11] In December, 1932 *La Nouvelle Revue Française* published a special "Cahier de revendications" to which thirteen leaders of the *Jeunes équipes* contributed.[12] After an examination of their grievances, Paul Archambault accurately discerned that the *Jeunes équipes* had nothing in common but a refusal to accept the established order.[13] Another contemporary accused them of "revolutionary conformism"

[8] Pierre Andreu in "Qu'as-tu fait de ta jeunesse?" A valuable study of the *Jeunes équipes* of 1930–1934 is the doctoral thesis of Jean-Louis Loubet del Bayle, *L'esprit de 1930. Tentative de renouvellement de la pensée politique française*, which examines *Esprit, l'Ordre Nouveau*, and the "Jeune Droite." Since this was written, it has been published as *Les non-conformistes des années 30. Un tentative de renouvellement de la pensée politique française* (Paris: Editions du Seuil, 1969).

[9] Philippe Muller, "Emmanuel Mounier. Il faut nous donner tout entiers," *Coopération*, No. 51 (December 18, 1965). Italics added.

[10] Quoted in Pierre Démagny, "Les Jeunes équipes," *Politique*, 2e année, No. 5 (May, 1929), 462–463. Démagny is concerned, of course, with the *Jeunes équipes* of the late 1920s, but his description fits those of the early 1930s equally well.

[11] *Ibid.*, 464.

[12] "Cahier de revendications," *La Nouvelle Revue Française*, XXXIX, No. 231 (December, 1932), 801–845. Mounier's contribution was "Ce ne sont pas ceux qui disent: esprit, esprit," 824–826, reprinted in *O.M.*, I, 845–847.

[13] Paul Archambault, "Cahier de revendications," *Politique*, 7e année, No. 1 (January, 1933), 95–96.

and Henri Daniel-Rops commented in a book aptly entitled *Les années tournantes* that "the expression, spiritual revolution, is one of those that finds the best reception among young men today."[14] Robert Garric, the veteran leader of the Catholic youth movement the *Equipes sociales*, pointed out the importance which the *Jeunes équipes* attached to the words "refusal" and "revolution." "These great words are dishonored by becoming the daily coin of our passions and our dreams," Garric charged, "and real revolutionaries must be disquieted by this degradation of the vigor of a myth and a word." [15] There was a kind of revolutionary romanticism among the *Jeunes équipes*.[16]

Like many youthful revolutionaries, the *Jeunes équipes* were far more certain of what they opposed than of what they proposed to do. They were anti-rationalist and anti-materialist in philosophy, anti-bourgeois in spite of their own social origins, and both anti-Communist and anti-capitalist.[17] In addition, although the spirit of the *Jeunes équipes* penetrated the Radical and Socialist parties, the new generation was harshly critical of the traditional game of politics, of parliamentarianism, of political parties, and even of politics itself as a means of resolving the revolutionary crisis.[18] Denis de Rougemont, a leader of the team of *l'Ordre Nouveau*, began a study of the problems confronting his generation with the simple declarative statement: "I have a kind of natural aversion for politics." [19]

The essential a-politicism of many of the *Jeunes équipes* enabled the spirit of the new generation to penetrate almost every sector of the spectrum of traditional French social and political milieux.[20] None of the traditional economic and political categories had any specific ap-

---

[14] Pierre Démagny, "Mouvement de jeunes et jeunes équipes," *Politique*, 7ᵉ année, No. 4 (April, 1933), 457; and Daniel Rops, *Les années tournantes* (Paris: Editions du Siècle, 1932), III.

[15] Robert Garric, "Pourquoi nous acceptons," *La Revue des Jeunes* (February, 15, 1933), 159.

[16] Raoul Girardet, "La droite nationaliste," in Jean Touchard, Raoul Girardet, and René Rémond, *Le Mouvement des idées politiques dans la France contemporaine* (Paris: Amicale des élèves de l'Institut d'études politiques de Paris, 1958–1959), II, 95.

[17] Jean Touchard, "L'esprit des années 1930: une tentative de renouvellement de la pensée française," in *Tendances politiques dans la vie française depuis 1789* (Paris: Hachette, 1960), 103.

[18] See Alexander Werth, "Le mouvement 'Jeune turc,' une phénomene radical de l'entre-deux guerres," *Cahiers de la République*, No. 2 (1956), 100–105; and Marcel Prélot, *L'Evolution politique du socialisme français, 1789–1934* (Paris: Spes, n.d.), 267–296.

[19] Denis de Rougemont, *Politique de la Personne. Problèmes, doctrines et tactiques de la Révolution personnaliste* (Paris: Editions "Je Sers," 1934), 7. For a valuable recollection of the founding of *l'Ordre Nouveau*, see Denis de Rougemont, *Journal d'une époque, 1926–1946* (Paris: Gallimard, 1968), 89–110 *passim*.

[20] Touchard, "L'esprit des années 1930," 87–118.

plicability to the *Jeunes équipes*. The method they intended to use in their quest for new syntheses and a general and profound renovation of French life was intellectual action pure and simple. They wished to assume their character as intellectuals because they felt "that political men are engulfed in shabby battles [and] that writers too often delight themselves in subtle refinements." [21] They believed it was their duty to think and to act; to consider the problems of the human condition; and also to participate and to bear witness. Their very vocation as intellectuals, they believed, predisposed them to understand popular aspirations better than others, and contact with the people, they thought, would give vigor to their intellectual action. For them, "intelligence is neither a mirror nor a tool: intelligence is a sword. A kind of ideocratic fever is thus diffused among the intellectuals." [22]

The spirit of the *Jeunes équipes* is perhaps best described by the words and phrases to which these young men were addicted: "refusal," "revolution," "spirit," "neither right nor left," "disquiet," and "beyond" with reference to Marxism, nationalism, socialism, and democracy. Also revealing are the titles they gave to their manifestoes: Daniel-Rops' *Le Monde sans âme*, Thierry Maulnier's *La crise est dans l'homme*, Robert Aron and Arnaud Dandieu's *Décadence de la nation française*, and, not least, Mounier's "Refaire la Renaissance." The extent of the revolt of the *Jeunes équipes* is clear: the economic and political crises were, in their judgment, but manifestations of a profound moral and spiritual crisis.

Although the *Jeunes équipes* admired, and in their extreme eclecticism drew upon, the work of Georges Bernanos, Georges Sorel, Friedrich Nietzsche, and André Malraux, on the loftiest pedestals in their pantheon were two men who, like Bernanos and Nietzsche, were essentially moral or spiritual rebels against their times: Pierre-Joseph Proudhon and Charles Péguy.[23] The vogue of the poet-patriot Charles Péguy was especially strong among the *Jeunes équipes* as it was to be again during the great moral crisis brought about by the defeat of 1940. "This was the generation of péguysme." [24]

Mounier once told a new collaborator of *Esprit* that "here we are Proudhonians" [25] and the influence of Proudhon is evident in his early

---

[21] *Ibid.*, 98.
[22] *Ibid.*
[23] *Ibid.*, 109.
[24] Stanley Hoffmann, "Paradoxes of the French Political Community," in Stanley Hoffmann *et al.*, *In Search of France* (Cambridge, Mass.: Harvard University Press, 1963), 33.
[25] M. M. [Marcel Moré], "Luminaire," *Dieu vivant*, No. 16 (1950), 7.

writings,[26] but Mounier was correct in his contention that Péguy "was the uncontested master of a generation without masters." [27] Admiration for Péguy was a kind of badge of membership in many of the *Jeunes équipes* no matter what their members' past or future political propensities. To Mounier, Péguy was the eternal rebel, at once a socialist, a humanist, and a Christian. He was a true revolutionary because he "placed upon the portal of the great revolution which is advancing in the world this banner: 'The revolution will be moral or there will be no revolution.'" [28] Daniel-Rops of *l'Ordre Nouveau* found meaning for the much-used "spiritual revolution" of the *Jeunes équipes* only by giving the term a *péguyste* content.[29] And to Jean-Pierre Maxence, a leader of the *Jeune Droite*, Péguy was simply "alive." "Péguy," he wrote, "remained among us. He commanded our acts, our thoughts ..." [30] Péguy, who had been an angry opponent of *Action Française*, was even adopted by Henri Massis, a disciple of Maurras. In his view, Péguy "accomplished for the soul what a Maurras has accomplished for the intellect. Both had an identical objective: the *salvation* of France." [31]

The bond represented by Péguy was one of moral and spiritual protest and it proved too fragile to survive the crises of the 1930s. The pressure of events – the riots of February, 1934, the problem of the Fascist leagues, the Ethiopian War, the "New Crusade" of Franco, the Popular Front – all of these forced the *Jeunes équipes* to make a number of difficult political choices. Like most French intellectuals, who since the time of the Dreyfus affair had oscillated between a-politicism and political commitment, many of the *Jeunes équipes* were polarized by these events.[32] As early as the February riots of 1934, for example, Henri Massis accused Mounier of constructing a "synthetic Péguy." "The *Agrégé* [Mounier]," he charged, "has made a cadaver of him." And, he added, "the writers of *Esprit* ... invoke Péguy only in order to betray him ceaselessly." [33] Three members of the *Jeune Droite*, Robert Francis, Thierry Maulnier and Jean-Pierre Maxence, dedicated their manifesto, *Demain la France*, "to the dead of February 6 [1934]. First

[26] See especially Mounier, "Anarchie et personnalisme" (April, 1937), *O.M.*, I, 653–725.

[27] Mounier, "Et maintenant," *Esprit*, No. 66 (March, 1938), 806.

[28] Mounier, "Péguy ressuscité," *B.A.E.M.*, No. 12 (June, 1958), 6–7.

[29] Daniel-Rops, *Les années tournantes*, 120.

[30] Jean-Pierre Maxence, *Histoire de dix ans, 1927–1937* (Paris: Gallimard, 1938), 145 and 152.

[31] Henri Massis, *Maurras et notre temps. Entretiens et souvenirs* (Paris: Plon, 1961), 426.

[32] René Rémond, "Les Intellectuels et la Politique," *Revue française de science politique*, IX, No. 4 (December, 1959), 867–876 *passim*.

[33] Henri Massis, *Débats* (Paris: Plon, 1934), I, 117–127.

witnesses of the coming revolution, killed by the bullets of an inhuman, anti-social, anti-national regime." [34] And two members of *l'Ordre Nouveau* argued that "when order is no longer order, it is necessary that there be a revolution: and the revolution that we envisage is the revolution of order." [35] The years 1934 and 1935 witnessed a series of "battles of manifestoes" which revealed the tremendous divergencies among the *Jeunes équipes* and effectively broke the common spirit of the early 1930s.[36] It was not until the time of the Liberation – following another revival of interest in Péguy – that common commitment by the intellectuals once again became the order of the day.[37]

Of all of the reviews of the *Jeunes équipes* of the 1930s only one survived: "that which was the first to choose when it judged it necessary to do so: *Esprit*." [38] Like the other *Jeunes équipes*, the men of *Esprit* had as their common bond the unshakable conviction that France and the Western world were undergoing a revolutionary crisis. In spite of the high caliber of its contributors and collaborators, it was Mounier's thought and character which imprinted themselves so completely upon the journal that a history of *Esprit* has necessarily to be identified with Mounier's personal history.[39] "*Esprit*," Mounier noted, "was myself and my personal history." [40]

Mounier's decision to found a journal and lead a movement is inexplicable solely in terms of his family background and early training. He was born in Grenoble on April 1, 1905, the son of a pharmacist "in a sector of the most humble, provincial petite-bourgeoisie." [41] He often referred in his personal writings to his beloved Grenoblois countryside and his happy childhood there.[42] He was a somewhat shy and retiring boy and two childhood afflictions, one which slightly affected his hearing and the other which reduced the sight in his right eye to less than one tenth of its normal vision, perhaps contributed to his penchant for

---

[34] Robert Francis, Thierry Maulnier, and Jean-Pierre Maxence, *Demain la France* (Paris: Bernard Grasset, 1934), 7.

[35] Robert Aron and Arnaud Dandieu, *La Révolution nécessaire* (Paris: Bernard Grasset, 1933), xiv.

[36] Touchard, "L'esprit des années 1930," 108.

[37] Rémond, "Les Intellectuels et la Politique," 877.

[38] Touchard, "L'esprit des années 1930," 110.

[39] *Ibid.*, 93; and Albert Béguin, "Une vie (textes de liaison)," *E.M.*, *1905–1950*, 995.

[40] Mounier, "Entretiens VIII, 13 mai 1934," *O.M.*, IV, 548.

[41] Henri Marrou, "L'action politique d'Emmanuel Mounier," *Cahiers de la République*, No. 2 (1956), 91.

[42] See, for example, Mounier, "Lettre à Xavier de Vireu, 1er mars 1950," *O.M.*, IV, 41;3 and Mounier, "Lettre à Paulette Leclercq, 30 avril 1933," *O.M.*, IV, 414.

solitude and meditation.[43] A somewhat apathetic student, Mounier nonetheless excelled in literature and philosophy and had a serious interest in music. While he dreamed of a brilliant literary career, his parents, in part perhaps to compensate for his meditative nature, encouraged him to pursue a career in medicine.

Mounier dutifully embarked upon a program of pre-medical studies. By March of his first year he had become so intensely unhappy that he stopped eating, and, in fact, despaired to the point of contemplating suicide.[44] While attending a religious retreat he made a decision – of such magnitude that a man who knew him well calls it a "conversion"[45] – to give up his medical studies and prepare himself for a career in teaching. In this decision Mounier was encouraged by Jacques Chevalier, a professor of philosophy in the University of Grenoble.

Both Mounier and his father had attended lectures by Chevalier on Malebranche and César Franck, and one day they approached the philosopher after class. Chevalier recorded his first impression of his future student: "Emmanuel is a large, fair boy, with blue eyes, and a pale complexion. He looks at me intensely, without staring (because of a slight defect of vision). He seems very intimidated by my presence." And Chevalier added that young Mounier was extraordinarily quiet and spoke hardly at all.[46] For three fruitful years, from 1924 to 1927, Mounier studied philosophy under Chevalier.

Although Mounier was among the youngest of Chevalier's students, he quickly demonstrated an aptitude for his new work. So highly did Chevalier think of him that Mounier lectured on Plato to his class during the absence of the professor. It was Mounier who transcribed Chevalier's course of lectures on Bergson for the *Revue des Cours et Conférences* in the winter of 1925–1926 and who later helped Chevalier correct the proofs of his book on Bergson. Not surprisingly, Mounier was one of the leaders of a *Groupe d'études* composed of Chevalier's students, who discussed Spinoza, Maine de Biran, Maritain, and other philosophers and philosophical topics. Maine de Biran provided especially fruitful study for the young student; in reviewing a thesis on the philosopher, Mounier praised the revival of interest in a man who, like Pascal, had once been scoffed at as a proponent of "mysticism" and "superstition." [47] Many years later Mounier paid tribute to Maine de

[43] Béguin, "Une vie," 936–937.

[44] Mounier, "Lettre à Jacques Lefrancq, 25 aout 1933," *O.M.*, IV, 417.

[45] Jean Lacroix, "Les trois conversions d'Emmanuel Mounier," *Témoignage Chrétien*, March 30, 1950, reprinted in *B.A.E.M.*, No. 16–17 (April, 1961), 11–12.

[46] "Journal de Jacques Chevalier. Samedi 15 mars 1924," in *E.M.*, *1905–1950*, 941.

[47] Mounier, "A propos d'une thèse sur Maine de Biran: la leçon d'une vie," *la Vie Catholique*, No. 153 (September 3, 1927).

Biran as "the modern precursor of French personalism." [48] In his final
year at Grenoble Mounier studied Descartes: his *mémoire* for the
Diplôme d'Etudes Supérieures was "Le conflict de l'Anthropocentrisme
dans la philosophie de Descartes." [49]

What Mounier received from Chevalier is not easy to assess. Mounier
undoubtedly admired his master at Grenoble. In a letter to Francisque
Gay, Mounier asked if Chevalier's course on Bergson did not merit some
mention in the columns of Gay's newspaper.[50] Mounier painted a
charming word portrait of his mentor and Chevalier's teaching methods
for Gay's journal in 1926, and several years later he wrote a laudatory
review of one of Chevalier's books for the same paper.[51] Within a year
after Mounier left Grenoble, however, Chevalier was already privately
expressing his reservations concerning the young man's new interests
and new friends.[52] Increasingly, the paths of the two men diverged.
Chevalier did not approve of *Esprit*, of the influence of "the other
Jacques" (Maritain), or of the political options of Mounier and *Esprit*,
especially at the time of the Popular Front and the Spanish Civil War.
"I don't know who has turned your head," Chevalier wrote his former
student.[53] Ultimately Mounier was to be imprisoned by the very regime
which Chevalier supported and served briefly as a minister. Nonetheless, Mounier defended his old master when the latter was tried in 1946
for his supposed collaborationist activities. In a letter to Chevalier in
1946, Mounier broke the lengthy silence between himself and Chevalier
with a heartfelt statement: "behind all that has separated us I find a
bond once tightened in loyalty. I have never forgotten it."[54]

In the words of the philosopher Jean Conilh, Mounier received from
Chevalier a predilection for "philosophy conceived of not as an abstract intellectual exercise – the idealism which then reigned in the
Sorbonne was the *bête noire* of Chevalier, as it was for the masters of the
neighboring universities, Aix-en-Provence and Montpellier – but as a
patient and methodical approach to the real, invoked and dominated

[48] Mounier, *Le personnalisme*, O.M., III, 436.

[49] The conclusion of Mounier's *mémoire* has been published in *Les Etudes philosophiques*,
No. 3 (Paris: Presses universitaires de France, 1966), 319–324.

[50] Mounier, "Lettre à Francisque Gay, 8 février 1926," O.M., IV, 420.

[51] Mounier, "Un penseur français: Jacques Chevalier," *la Vie Catholique*, No. 79 (April 3,
1926); and Jacques Mersennes [E. Mounier], "Méditations dans La Forêt," *la Vie Catholique*,
No. 301 (July 5, 1930).

[52] "Réflexions et souvenirs de J. Chevalier. Juillet 1950 (A la suite du journal du 28 octobre
1928)," in *E.M., 1905–1950*, 944–945.

[53] Quoted in Béguin, "Une vie," 982.

[54] Mounier, "Lettre à Jacques Chevalier, 13 mars 1946," O.M., IV, 804.

by the spiritual exigency." [55] Time and again, Mounier himself was to recognize that he had escaped *sorbonnardisme* and was immune to the "poison of the Sorbonne." [56] Less than a year after arriving at the Sorbonne itself, he wrote his sister Madeleine, to whom he was unusually close: "Oh, the narrow minds, the men seated in their chairs on the rostrum, in their armchairs, the self-satisfied men, the intellectuals, the *academicians!*" [57]

Following his arrival at the Sorbonne, Mounier continued his study of "philosophy as an apostolate" and he retained what a friend called a "confused and bastard conception of teaching." [58] There was relatively little to distinguish Mounier from a number of his contemporaries who were preparing themselves for what undoubtedly would be successful careers in lycées or provincial universities and eventually, perhaps, in the Sorbonne itself. Mounier excelled in his studies; in July, 1928 he passed his *agrégation*, second only to Raymond Aron, and for the next three years he was a *boursier de doctorat*. He also began teaching in the Collège Sainte-Marie in Neuilly and in 1931–1932 in the Lycée de Saint-Omer.

The young *agrégé* encountered real difficulties in his quest for a thesis topic. He first considered working on the sixteenth-century Spanish mystic, John of the Angels, and in pursuit of this project he made a brief trip to Spain in the spring of 1930. Then he considered a thesis on sin but this topic too was abandoned. Finally, he determined to write on human personality – an interest which bore bruit more than a decade later when he began work on his *Traité du caractère* – and a complementary thesis on John of the Angels.[59] With the prospective and humor that years alone can provide, Mounier later told a friend that "John of the Angels is at least a lovely title for a thesis." [60] Mounier's difficulty in selecting a topic for his major research was less a matter of personal indecisiveness than a manifestation of his increasing effort to harmonize his formal and public life with his innermost convictions and aspirations. "A thesis, in my eyes, is far more a human work than an intellectual work," he said.[61]

[55] Jean Conilh, *Emmanuel Mounier. Sa vie, son oeuvre avec un exposé de sa philosophie* (Paris: Presses universitaires de France, 1966), 4.

[56] See, for example, Mounier, "Lettre à Jacques Lefrancq, 25 août 1933," *O.M.*, IV, 418.

[57] Mounier, "Lettre à Madeleine Mounier, 12 janvier 1928," *O.M.*, IV, 430.

[58] Lacroix, "Les trois conversions," 12.

[59] Mounier, "Rapport sur les projets de thèse adressé à M. le directeur de la Fondation Thiers, 22 mars 1930," *O.M.*, IV, 463–467.

[60] Mounier, "Lettre à une amie, 1er avril 1941," *E.M.*, *1905–1950*, 965.

[61] Quoted in *O.M.*, IV, 438.

During these "years of metamorphosis," Mounier's intellectual horizons were broadening but his interests were also gradually shifting from purely literary and philosophical questions to the social and political dimensions of his original interests. The most decisive event in Mounier's life during his early years in Paris was not directly related to his studies although it was to have a profound effect upon both his academic work and his future life. This was the death of his most intimate friend, Georges Barthélemy, on January 6, 1928. For a solitary young man not given to easy friendships or camaraderie, the loss of a confidant was a severe blow. Several days after Barthélemy's death, Mounier wrote Jean Guitton that Barthélemy was "the only real friend that circumstances and my own excessive reserve have permitted me to know intimately." [62] And seven months later, he confessed to Guitton that:

I have had many "friends" in the eyes of everyone [but] I have had only one true friend in my own eyes, the one I lost in January, although our friendship, slow and hesitant because it was so profound, consisted much more of unfulfilled promises than of actual exchanges.... I have the distinct impression – one of those certainties that are beyond human expression – that my friend bequeathed me an ensemble of spiritual heritages. Perhaps someday I will tell you its painful history. Be that as it may, I feel that I do not have the right to ordain my life as if his had not been destroyed.[63]

Mounier then added that he had been on the verge of succumbing to the "mentality of the university machinery" but that Barthélemy's death had saved him from this danger. "Perhaps," he told Guitton, "I am also not much of a philosopher: does the philosopher consider a friendship more precious than a thesis?" [64]

Barthélemy's death acted as a partial catalyst on Mounier's slowly increasing awareness that his vocation was not that of an academic philosopher and teacher. In the year or two after his young friend's death, Mounier underwent what was in his own words "an intellectual and religious reconversion." [65] During the Christmas vacation of 1928–1929 Mounier made the discovery which not only enabled him to recover from the loss of his friend but altered the course of his life. Referring to his loss, Mounier said: "Péguy saved me from it." [66] And concerning his final decision to give up his studies, he later said: "It

---

[62] Mounier, "Lettre à Jean Guitton, Paris, mardi 9 janvier 1928," *E.M.*, *1905–1950*, 951.
[63] Mounier, "Lettre à Jean Guitton. Le Pinet d'Uriage, le 10 août 1928," in *Revue Montalembert* (Special Issue: "Jean Guitton"), No. 4–5 (1963), 163.
[64] *Ibid.*, 163–164.
[65] Mounier, "Lettre à Madeleine Mounier, mars 1935," *O.M.*, IV, 427.
[66] Mounier, "Lettre à Jéromine Martinaggi 18 mai 1930," *O.M.*, IV, 468.

[the study of Péguy] crystallized the entire extra-university part of my life and, moreover, gave a death blow to the University." [67]

For the rest of his life Mounier, like Péguy, betrayed a great distaste for the men of the University. "Alas, university training," he once said, "which has its strengths, is at the same time a terrible disease from which it takes a long time to recover." [68] A longtime friend testifies that "until his death, he kept, like a deep scar, the retrospective horror of what he had been on the way to becoming: a professor, an academician exercising influence over youths, certainly, but at the same time building a 'career.'" [69] Another friend, Albert Béguin, states that Mounier's abrupt change in 1931–1932 from philosophy as an apostolate to commitment in temporal affairs is inexplicable without Péguy. "Péguy," Béguin contends, "would authorize Mounier inwardly to become what he was to be." [70]

Mounier first interrupted his studies to collaborate with Péguy's son, Marcel, and Georges Izard on a book about Péguy. Then, as Jacques Maritain recalls, Mounier and Izard, joined by André Déléage, decided that their book on Péguy should not remain "a manifesto without a future." The three men wished to form a group, a center from which "the *péguyste* work" could be continued in the context of the crisis of the early 1930s. This task was first and foremost the dissociation of "the Christian order from the powers of money and the 'established disorder,' and its first requirement was a pitiless examination of conscience by Christians themselves." [71] Few statements are more revealing of what Mounier was to become – and what *Esprit* was to be – than Mounier's response to Izard's suggestion that a new review be founded:

Good! We are right and penniless. But it is only enterprises founded on poverty that succeed. I will give up the University and install myself in Paris. I have only to explain this to my family, but I am certain they will understand. I will take the editorship – assuming that there will be something to edit. At any rate, this cannot be worse than [Péguy's] *Cahiers de la Quinzaine*.[72]

Some indication of the impact of Péguy upon Mounier is apparent in Mounier's correspondence and activities in the course of these years.

[67] Mounier, "Lettre à Jéromine Martinaggi, 1er avril 1941," *O.M.*, IV, 452.
[68] Mounier, "Les cinq étapes d'*Esprit*," 43.
[69] Lacroix, "Les trois conversions," 13.
[70] Béguin, "Une vie," 964. See also Georges Izard, "La fondation d'*Esprit*," *Express*, March 29, 1960, reprinted in *B.A.E.M.*, No. 16–17 (April, 1961), 6–7.
[71] "Notes de Jacques Maritain," in *E.M.*, *1905–1950*, 974. See also "Naissance et début de la revue 'Esprit' évoqués à travers les rapports de Maritain et de Mounier. (Lettres, notes, articles) 1931–1933," *B.A.E.M.*, No. 34–35 (November, 1969), 3–65 *passim*.
[72] Quoted in *The Tablet* (London) (April, 1950), 255.

Mounier's discovery of Péguy in 1928–1929 was, in fact, a rediscovery. While a student in Grenoble, he had read the Tharauds' *Péguy* and had referred to the poet-patriot as a "source of consolation and hope." [73] But increasingly, beginning in the spring of 1928 after the death of Barthélemy, Mounier's letters, particularly to his sister and his former teacher in Grenoble, were filled with references to Péguy. To Madeleine Mounier, he referred to a "delightful lecture on Péguy" he had attended in Gentilly.[74]

Mounier's knowledge of the life and work of Péguy owed much to his association with two organizations during his first years in Paris. One was the *Davidées*, an organization of Catholic laywomen who taught in public schools, led by a remarkable woman named Marie Silve. From 1928 to 1931 Mounier took an active part in the meetings of Mlle. Silve's group. In August, 1928 at a meeting of the *Davidées* at Notre-Dame du Laus, Mounier spoke for four hours on Péguy. In the various periodicals of Mlle. Silve's groups Mounier clearly, but perhaps unconsciously, revealed his evolving interests. In March, 1929 he published an article on "L'idée d'irrationnel"; in December, 1930 he wrote an article entitled "L'événement et nous"; and in July, 1931 he entitled an article of obvious *péguyste* inspiration, "Temporel et spirituel." [75]

The other organization was the "Paulins" or *Compagnie de Saint-Paul*, a religious group founded by Mounier's friend, Jean Daniélou, who directed the *Maison de la Jeunesse* where Mounier lived in Paris. The members of the "Paulins" organized a *Cercle d'études péguystes* which included not only Mounier but Daniélou and Izard as well.[76] Daniélou recalls that Mounier did not know Péguy's work very well and that he persuaded Mounier to read the works of the man whose influence upon Mounier, in Daniélou's judgment, was decisive.[77]

The actual project of a book on Péguy was decided upon in the monthly meetings of artists and intellectuals held in Jacques Maritain's home in Meudon. Mounier began to attend these meetings in 1928 and Péguy was discussed there time and again. Maritain encouraged Mounier in his project and arranged for the publication of the book in the "Roseau d'or" collection of Librairie Plon. Like Mounier's association with the *Davidées*, his attendance at the meetings at Meudon also indicated his gradually changing interests. He first discussed his various

[73] Mounier, "Lettre à Madeleine Mounier, mai 1925," *O.M.*, IV, 419.
[74] Mounier, "Lettre à Madeleine Mounier, avril 1928," *O.M.*, IV, 432.
[75] Béguin, "Une vie," 966.
[76] *Ibid.*, 963.
[77] Jean Daniélou, "La mort d'Emmanuel Mounier," *Etudes*, CCXV (May, 1950), 250.

research projects with Maritain and other members of the Meudon group. Then the major topic of conversation was the book on Péguy. And finally, it was *Esprit* itself that was the focus of attention.[78]

During the same period Mounier wrote Henri Bergson about his Péguy and received "a pleasing letter from Bergson" in return.[79] He visited Péguy's mother in Orléans in January, 1930 and, the following June, he attended the dedication ceremonies of a bust of Péguy in Orléans, in company with all of the Péguys, many of the veterans of the *Cahiers* – Daniel Halévy, Henri Massis, and others.[80] As Mounier began to devote his time and energy entirely to the journal which was to continue the work of Péguy, he said: "It is Péguy who cleaves the air before us." [81] And in an interview published a number of years later, he succinctly summarized his debt to Péguy in recalling that he, Izard, and their friends suffered

in our youth from the knowledge that certain disorders used spiritual values and made certain realities that were most dear to us appear hypocritical. This suffering in our twentieth year crystallized on one man: Péguy. I wrote my first book on his thought ten years ago, and at the time when vocations are formed I lived long months in intimate contact with his work.

Oh, I did not try to annex him. I pretended even less to continue his work. He is much greater than we. Furthermore, one really continues only what one tries to recreate. To be truthful, when I decided to found *Esprit*, I did not for a moment think of a pastiche or a resurrection of the *Cahiers*. I was still, with reference to that recent influence, in that retreat and abstinence which follow any strong influence, especially after the publication of a book. It is only since then, as our work advances, that I see my debt to him grow day by day.[82]

Most of Mounier's contemporaries were insistent upon his intellectual and spiritual debt to Péguy. On the occasion of a ceremony in the rue de la Sorbonne in 1939 commemorating the founding of the *Cahiers de la Quinzaine*, Georges Hourdin, a leading Christian democratic publicist, said without qualification that Mounier and *Esprit* had received the heritage of Péguy and the *Cahiers* and were continuing their work.[83] Not without careful qualifications, but with similar emphasis, Paul Archambault put forward the same contention in a study of Péguy which was one of the first in the renaissance of Péguy's fame and in-

[78] Béguin, "Une vie," 967.

[79] Mounier, "Lettre à Madeleine Mounier, 6 mai 1929," *O.M.*, IV, 445.

[80] Mounier, "Entretiens II, 23 janvier 1930," *O.M.*, IV, 456–459; Mounier, "Entretiens III, 23 juin 1930," *O.M.*, IV, 469; and Mounier, "Avec Mme Charles Péguy, 23 juin 1930," *L'Amitié Charles Péguy*, No. 85 (June, 1961), 24–25.

[81] Quoted in Béguin, "Une vie," 977.

[82] Mounier, "Action temporelle des catholiques," in Dominique Auvergne (ed.), *Régards catholiques sur le monde* (Paris: Desclée de Brouwer, 1938), 68, reprinted in *B.A.E.M.*, No. 18 (December, 1961), 13.

[83] Georges Hourdin, "Péguy," *l'aube*, January 22–23, 1939.

fluence during the War and the Reisstance.[84] And it was the kinship with Péguy that came to the mind of Pierre-Henri Simon when Mounier was buried in the little cemetery in Châteny-Malabry, outside of Paris, in March, 1950.[85]

That the life and work of Péguy exercised a profound influence on Mounier is beyond dispute, but the precise character of that influence is difficult to delineate clearly and concretely. In one respect at least, it will always elude the grasp of even the most diligent and sympathetic observer; so profound was it that to trace it requires one to plumb the most secret and innermost depths of the character of a remarkable man. This problem is further compounded by the fact that Mounier's vocation, which he discovered through Péguy, was an extraordinary one. In the introduction to the collaborative work on Péguy, Mounier himself wrote that "Péguy is not dead; his work is unfinished." [86] Jean Conilh says, "Mounier was not a disciple [and] *Esprit* was not the continuation of the *Cahiers*. It was an authentic creation ... We do not know the secret path nor the profound motivations of that creation." [87]

To penetrate beyond the articles and the books, even beyond the remarkable letters and diary entries that Mounier left behind, is therefore, in the final analysis, an impossible task. Mounier's friend, the priest-worker Abbé André Depierre, aptly states that "Mounier is not first read, he is not first studied, he is encountered!" [88] Although Depierre does not use the word "encounter" in the literal, physical sense, the recollections of two of Mounier's students, one in the Collège Sainte-Marie in Neuilly and the other in the Lycée de Saint-Omer, cast some light upon Mounier during the two years immediately prior to the founding of *Esprit*.

When he began teaching in Neuilly, he appeared to be somewhat restrained and impersonal in revealing his own philosophical convictions to his students. He was generous, perhaps to a fault, especially to those students in whom he detected any possibility of a genuine interest in philosophy. More important, this former student says, when Mounier confronted human facts, then he became "a man of action."

---

[84] Paul Archambault, *Charles Péguy. Imagines d'un vie heroïque* (No. 2, "La Nouvelle Jounée"; Paris: Bloud & Gay, 1939), 149–152.

[85] Pierre-Henri Simon, "Péguy pamphletaire," *l'aube*, May 8, 1950.

[86] Mounier, "Avant-propos," in Marcel Péguy, Georges Izard, and Emmanuel Mounier, *La pensée de Charles Péguy* (Paris: Plon, 1931), reprinted in *O.M.*, I, 14.

[87] Conilh, 6–7.

[88] André Depierre, "Mounier ou évangile du salut et monde moderne," *B.A.E.M.*, No. 28 (August, 1966), 11.

It was then that he became more open and vitally concerned with providing his students with the intellectual means for pursuing their work. Most significantly, he never attempted to impose any sort of dogmatism upon his class.[89]

At Saint-Omer in 1931–1932 Mounier's manner more accurately reflected the character of the man and his vocation. His students had been forewarned that they were being given an opportunity to work under a very prominent young man. But then Mounier entered the classroom, "very large, very thin, [and] dressed in a blue suit" which he seemed always to wear. In fact, this student recalls meeting him by chance in a store in 1946 and he seemed to be wearing the same suit. Although the class was somewhat chilled by his presence initially – perhaps because of their forewarning – almost immediately the new teacher demonstrated that he was unlike any teacher his students had encountered before. Other professors demanded complete silence while they lectured but Mounier welcomed interruptions, questions, and even objections to what he was talking about. "He had a horror of professors who present their courses *ex cathedra.*" He intended his words to be the beginning of decisions on the part of his students. He spoke of the necessity of commitment; "the principles of moral action reveal themselves to our intelligence only if we practice them, and only this practice awakens us to them," he told the class. He lectured on Pascal, often repeating the aphorism, "one possesses only what one gives." To one of his students he gave a brief memorandum which contained his views on his three favorite thinkers: Plato, Bergson, and Péguy.[90]

These recollections are admittedly only suggestive of the manner of man Mounier was on the eve of the founding of *Esprit*. But they suggest certain similarities between Mounier and Péguy. Indeed, there are a number of similarities – as well as a number of differences, primarily of time, space and temperament – between the two men.[91] The most apparent but certainly not the only parallels are the themes that are common to the lives and work of the two men. The most important of the latter were implicit in Mounier's contribution to the collaborative *La pensée de Charles Péguy* entitled "La vision des hommes et du

[89] "Note de Mme Paul Vignaux," in *E.M., 1905–1950*, 955.
[90] "Témoignage de Mme Duhameaux," and Mounier, "Carnet. Noël 1931," in *E.M., 1905–1950*, 955–957.
[91] See Albert Béguin, "Vies parallèles de Péguy et Mounier," *L'Amitié Charles Péguy*, No. 12 (May, 1950), 1–3; Béguin, "Une vie," 963–964; Lucien Guissard, *Emmanuel Mounier* (Paris: Editions universitaires, 1962), 27–36; and Moix, 15ff.

monde." [92] There, in an attempt to synthesize the thought of Péguy, Mounier examined four inter-related topics.

In the first chapter, he analyzed Péguy's "denunciation of ready-made thought." Like Mounier, Péguy was Bergsonian in his opposition to the idealism of the University, to the "intellectual party," the Kantians, and to any ready-made, rigid, and closed intellectual system. Péguy's definition of a "great philosophy" was, in fact, one way of defining Mounier's personalism. "A great philosophy," Péguy said, "is not that which passes final judgments, which takes a seat in final truth. It is that which introduces uneasiness, which opens the door to commotion." [93] There exists no "scholastic" personalism and no one distributes diplomas of *mouniérisme*, Jean-Marie Domenach aptly states. [94] This radical opposition to "intellectualism," to any sort of secluded intellectualizing, to any effort to abstract thought from concrete reality, did not, however, lead either Péguy or Mounier to self-righteous moralizing. Both men's writings are distinguished by their moral tone and fervor which never descend to the level of cheap and easy moralizing. [95]

The second chapter of Mounier's study of Péguy is devoted to "The servitude of the Spirit: the world of habit." Here Mounier analyzed the intellectual and spiritual dangers of habit, and the virtues of "youth", not in the sense of age but in the sense of remaining flexible and open to men, events, and ideas. Péguy himself once said that "what is most contrary to salvation is not sin but habit." [96] And in his study of Péguy Mounier wrote: "Ready-made thought is not an accident on the surface of our intelligence. It represents a form of habit, and habit is, an 'immense and universal parasitism,' a torpor which insinuates itself into all of the activities of our soul and of the world." [97] Just as Péguy believed that "it is a good principle that each *Cahier* should displease a third of the subscribers, [98] so Mounier often repeated: "Don't satisfy the public too much. Take care not to flatter our readers!" [99] Few

---

[92] Mounier, "La vision des hommes et du monde," *O.M.*, I, 19–125.

[93] Charles Péguy, *Basic Verities*, trans. by Anne and Julian Green (Chicago: Henry Regnery Company, 1965), 47.

[94] Domenach, "Présence de Mounier," 217.

[95] For a highly critical assessment of Péguy, see Hans A. Schmitt, *Charles Péguy. The Decline of an Idealist* (Baton Rouge, La.: Louisiana State University Press, 1967). A more sympathetic treatment is Marjorie Villiers, *Charles Péguy. A Study in Integrity* (London: Collins, 1965.

[96] Péguy, *Basic Verities*, 112.

[97] Mounier, "La vision des hommes et du monde," 59.

[98] Quoted in Villiers, 122.

[99] Quoted in Jean-Marie Domenach, "Emmanuel Mounier," *Psyché*, 5ᵉ année, No. 4 (June, 1950), 499.

words are more descriptive of Mounier's life and work than "disquiet" and "confrontation"; and one of his most important and characteristic works is entitled *L'Affrontement chrétien.*

Closer still to the profound kinship of Péguy and Mounier and intimately connected with their sense of perpetual disquiet is the third theme Mounier examined in his study of Péguy: "To the heart of destitution."

Both men had a deep, almost unfathomable, sense of poverty, as distinct from destitution. The former they practiced in all of its dimensions as the greatest of virtues and the latter they condemned with a rare vigor and consistency. Both Péguy and Mounier were acutely suspicious, if not actually fearful, of material success. Although Péguy had no reason to voice such a fear concerning his *Cahiers,* the fame of *Esprit* after the Second World War led Mounier to fear lest his journal become "*la Revue des Deux-Mondes* of personalism." [100] Both men, on the other hand, condemned destitution and this was one of the most important elements of their anti-capitalism, their non-doctrinaire socialism, and, most important, their criticism of Christendom in the name of Christianity. Here the differences between the two men are striking but not sufficiently important to conceal a basic community of spirit. Péguy's evolution had led him from socialism to Christianity while Mounier's commitment to Christianity was to lead him to a form of humanist socialism. But as socialists neither man ever submitted to the doctrine or discipline of a party. Mounier's socialism was very much akin to Péguy's "religion of temporal salvation," [101] since its moral content was far more striking and original than its technical aspects. Just as Péguy opposed the *politiques* of both the Dreyfusards and the anti-Dreyfusards, Mounier found no political party to which he could give his unqualified support. Both attacked the political parties of their times, although Péguy did this with a vehemence, a violence, and a vituperation that were characteristic of his temperament and polemical style but hardly of Mounier's. This is not to say that there are not some striking similarities between the literary styles of the two men. "What first strikes the reader is the tone of Mounier. This incisive, almost brutal style is at once seductive and irritating," wrote one of his admirers.[102] A student of Mounier's personalist esthetics described

[100] Mounier, "Situation du personnalisme," *Esprit,* No. 118 (January, 1946), 4.
[101] Péguy, *Basic Verities,* 76.
[102] H. B. Vergot, "Présence de Mounier," *L'Agora* (Angers), April-June, 1960, reprinted in *B.A.E.M.,* No. 16–17 (April, 1961), 9.

Mounier's style as "ample, poetic and precise." [103] A friendly critic probably came closest to the mark when he stated that "certainly Mounier was not a great classic like Péguy. He wrote badly; he had neither the leisure nor the concern to make his language a work of beauty." [104]

Time and circumstance as well as style and temperament also serve to explain Péguy's emphasis upon the ancient traditions of France and his idealization of the ageless French peasant in contrast to Mounier's resolute confrontation of the future, his optimistic assessment of modern technology, his love of the proletariat, and finally his attempted dialogue with the Communists. There are other differences of emphasis and style between the two men but their kindred criticism of what may best be termed the sociological extension of Christianity in the name of the poor, the downtrodden, and the dispossessed – in the name of Christianity itself – more than compensates for such differences. "Mounier," in the view of one of his contemporaries, "was the living protest against *bien-pensantisme*," [105] and precisely the same thing can be said of Péguy.

Significantly, Mounier entitled his examinaton of destitution "The decadence of the world and the incarnation of the Spirit," and he devoted the final chapter of his study of Péguy to "Salvation through hope." His foremost concern was that of Péguy: to incarnate the spiritual in the temporal without compromising religion (clericalism) or mysticizing the temporal (*angélisme*). Because both men were so profoundly convinced of the truth of the doctrine of the Incarnation, the pessimism evident in the foregoing did not dominate their thought and action. Indeed, both men believed that the history of man, in this sense, was the history of God also; the spiritual was also temporal. And in their lives and work, the perspective gained by this vision of man and history was clearly evident. The emphasis was always upon the future possibilities of man rather than upon his fallen nature: this was the essence of Mounier's "tragic optimism." On the basis of his own optimism, Péguy could say that "it has happened very frequently in history that very small companies of small good people have succeeded in achieving what has been refused to great companies of men of good

---

[103] J. Charpentreau and L. Rocher, *L'Esthétique personnaliste d'Emmanuel Mounier* (Paris: Les Editions Ouvrières, 1966), 137.

[104] Robert Rouquette, "Positions et oppositions d'Emmanuel Mounier," *Etudes*, CCXVI (February, 1951), 146.

[105] François Perroux in "Qu'as-tu fait de ta jeunesse?"

will." [106] And Mounier could respond to the early criticism of the revolutionary position of *Esprit* with this testament of faith: "A life is not broken when it carries a great witness. We know how fragile are our forces and success, but we also know the grandeur of our witness. This is why we carry forward our work without uneasiness in the certainty of our youth." [107] The spiritualism of Péguy and Mounier precluded any tendency to evade the confrontation of temporal events. Nor did it carry with it any tendency to proselytize. Rather, the operative words were *témoignage* and *engagement*. "Unfortunately, it is not enough to be a Catholic," Péguy once said. "One must still work in the temporal if one wishes to tear the future from temporal tyrannies." [108]

The most practical example of the relationship between the spiritual and the temporal in the thought of Péguy was his classic distinction between the *mystique* and the *politique*, a distinction which has been called one of the most significant in modern French political thought.[109] It was this distinction that provided one of the original bases of Mounier's *Esprit* movement. Nowhere in his writings, however, did Péguy define, *ex professo*, the terms *mystique* and *politique* nor did he explain the full meaning of his often-quoted epigram, "everything begins as a *mystique* and ends as a *politique*." [110] But he clarified their meaning in the context in which he used them in one of his most famous *Cahiers*, *Notre Jeunesse*. There Péguy applied them to the republican regime and the Catholic Church in France.

Péguy described the republican *mystique* as the ideal or the faith of the whole of France: the pagan France of the Renaissance and the humanists, the Christian France of St. Louis and Joan of Arc, the France of tradition and the France of revolution, the France of the Monarchists and the Republicans.[111] He exclaimed: "Don't talk so airily about the Republic; it was not always a pack of politicians, behind it there is a mystique, it has its mystique, behind it lies a glorious past, an honorable past, and what is perhaps more important still, nearer the essence, there is a whole race behind it, heroism and perhaps sanctity." [112] The republican *mystique*, Péguy wrote, had degenerated

---

[106] Péguy, *Basic Verities*, 76.
[107] Mounier, "Certitude de notre jeunesse" (May, 1933), *O.M.*, IV, 16.
[108] Péguy, *Basic Verities*, 106.
[109] David Thomson, *Democracy in France. The Third and Fourth Republics* (London: Oxford University Press, 1958), 133.
[110] Mounier, "La vision des hommes et du monde," 71.
[111] Charles Péguy, *Temporal and Eternal*, trans. Alexander Dru (London: The Harvill Press, 1958), 33.
[112] *Ibid.*, 24.

into a *politique:* republicans had sacrificed their belief in the Republic to their desire for power; republicans no longer believed in the Republic but were concerned only with politics in the grossest sense, that is, with the political struggle to make their policies prevail.[113] Similarly, Péguy condemned French Catholics without condemning their religion. Catholicism too had degenerated into a *politique:* Christianity was no longer the religion of the poor, of the depths, but the religion of the bourgeois, of the rich, "a wretched sort of distinguished religion." The Church therefore was nothing and meant nothing.[114]

The process by which the republican and Christian *mystiques* had degenerated into their corresponding *politiques* was one and the same, Péguy said. The Dreyfus affair was the last operation of the republican *mystique;* after it had come the modern world. The inhabitants of this world believed in nothing, devoted themselves to nothing, and sacrificed themselves to nothing. "More precisely," Péguy continued, "this is the world of those without a mystique . . . The de-republicanization of France is essentially the same movement as the de-christianization of France. Both together are one and the same movement which makes people no longer believe in the Republic and no longer believe in God, no longer want to lead a republican life and no longer want to lead a Christian life . . . One and the same sterility withers the city and Christendom." [115]

"Mysticism may be the laughing stock of politics," Péguy maintained, "but all the same it is the mystic who nourishes politics." The mystics "make things and men, peoples and races" while the politically-minded are parasites who demolish and bring ruin.[116] In religion, Péguy argued, the Church had been freed of its political burdens by the Separation of 1905, but it had not cast off its social burdens. The Church had to accept the cost of "a *temporal* revolution for *eternal* salvation. . . . The economic, social and industrial price must be paid, the temporal price. Nothing can evade it, not even the eternal, not even the spiritual, not even the inward life." [117]

At the founding congress of the *Esprit* movement in Font-Romeu in August, 1932, Mounier presented a report in which he outlined the *mystique* of *Esprit* and condemned the *politiques* of both the Republic

---

[113] *Ibid.*, 40.
[114] *Ibid.*, 82.
[115] *Ibid.*, 22–23.
[116] *Ibid.*, 48–49.
[117] *Ibid.*, 67.

and the Church.[118] Mounier's report was a personal statement of principle and it was the culmination of a series of personal convictions which had crystallized over a period of several years. The first conviction was that with *La Nouvelle Revue Française* half-dead a cycle of French creativity had come to a close. Second, Mounier was suffering more and more from seeing "our Christianity joined with what I was to call a little later 'the established disorder,'" and he wished to rupture this connection. Finally, he perceived that beneath the growing economic crisis there was a total crisis of civilization.[119]

Mounier began his report with the *péguyste* statement that what bound the *Esprit* group together was not a matter of "politics and cartels, but of justice and truth." [120] What united the *Esprit* group, Mounier continued, adopting the phrase of Jacques Maritain, was its members' recognition of the "primacy of the spiritual."[121] The latter was "a principle, an indignation, a cry of alarm." The *Esprit* group was to bear witness for goods other than its property. Mounier then criticized the old bourgeois habit of confusing order with complacency. Echoing Péguy, he suggested that complacency was always a form of disorder. As an example of the extent and depth of this disorder, Mounier then discussed the habitual French temptation to pose all problems in purely political terms. Implicitly, he contended that the degeneration of the Christian and republican *mystiques* into their respective *politiques* was apparent in the association of certain values with the political Right and Left. To the Right belonged honor, moderation, and prudence; to the Left belonged audacity and generosity. Charity was at the Right with the Academy, religion, the Minister of War, the soul, Latin, the liberal economy, the notaries, and the great families, he said with obvious irony. Justice was at the Left, and with it was associated an equally disparate mélange: Picasso, the civil service, social hygiene, feminism, liberty, peace, and experimental psychology. The bloc of values usually assigned to the Right masked beneath a materialistic ethos such basic values as personal dignity, love of country and the past, and the religious sentiment itself. Conversely, attached to the Left by a complex of historical and psychological reasons was a betrayal of the "sons of the spirit," a tendency to confuse the spiritual with

---

[118] Mounier, "Les directions spirituelles du mouvement 'Esprit,'" 1–48.

[119] Mounier, "Lettre à Jéromine Martinaggi, 1er avril 1941," *O.M.*, IV, 476–477.

[120] Mounier, "Les directions spirituelles du mouvement 'Esprit.'" Unless otherwise indicaꝟd, the following is taken from this report.

[121] Jacques Maritain, *Primauté du spirituel* (Paris: Plon, 1927).

the reactionary. Thus, Mounier concluded, "the spirit is domiciled at the Right and resides at the Left."

The immediate task of the founders of *Esprit* was "to detach spiritual values from the temporary unreality called 'the Right'" in order to free the Christian *mystique* from its *politique*. This task transcended politics not only because the Christian *mystique* should not be associated with a Leftist *politique* but because the ultimate purpose of *Esprit* was not "the well-being, the comfort, the prosperity of the city, but the spiritual flowering of man." In addition, Mounier told his friends in Font-Romeu, there were other more fundamental tasks. One was to become aware of a disorder which, for lack of a better term, could be called "the bourgeois age." The bourgeois age was characterized by egoism, cupidity, and complacency which had made the spiritual a refuge rather than a vital life force. At this point in his talk, Mounier broached a problem that was one of his major concerns as well as the basis of one of his criticisms of the Christian democrats. The misuse and abuse of the spiritual, he said, normally took one of three forms: for some men the spiritual was the servant of the temporal; for others the spiritual was a technique for evading the temporal; and for still others the spiritual was a refuge, an artifical life of exile from the world.

Returning then to his statement of the purposes of *Esprit*, Mounier explained that the nature of the disorder he had outlined necessitated a general revision of values and that this revision of values was a genuinely revolutionary task. Only after a revision of values had been accomplished could *Esprit* turn to political action. And even this political action would be of a special nature. It would be based upon two principles. "The first is that we will act by what we are as much as and more than by what we will do and say." The second was that "our action is not directed essentially towards success but towards bearing witness. Such is our very special optimism." The remainder of Mounier's report in Font-Romeu was an analysis of the various dimensions of the human person and critiques of materialism, idealism, and individualism.

In the most general historical sense, there is little reason to doubt that Mounier by his consistent a-political *engagement* in the affairs of his time, by his confrontation of the most difficult problems of his time, and by his own remarkable witness experienced a large measure of success in his purpose of dissociating Christianity from traditional Rightist politics. This is not to say that the Catholic Right in France succumbed to his merciless criticisms, but rather that he was a Catholic of the avant-garde who was the exemplar of a new Catholic Left which by its very existence demonstrated the emergence of a genuine pluralism among French Catholics. Nor is it to say that Mounier entirely avoided the danger of associating Christian values with a Leftist *politique*. One of his critics, the writer Pierre de Boisdeffre, is correct when he says that the history of *Esprit* was very much a part of Leftist thought in France for twenty years.[122] Mounier, in his perpetual ambivalence, admitted at Font-Romeu that the "royal way" of truth was on the Left and later confessed not only that the *Esprit* group used the language of the Left but that it possessed a definite Leftist bent which he attributed to a kind of "collective bourgeois bad conscience." [123]

There was a definite change in the major object of Mounier's efforts over the years. Shortly before his death he himself admitted that in the early years of *Esprit* he had attempted to instill a revolutionary temper in the "spiritualists," while in later years he tried to guide the revolutionaries in the direction of the "spiritual." [124] Among the "spiritualists," Mounier's message was quickly rebuffed by such men as François Mauriac and Robert Garric, or its full implications misunderstood as Mounier's encounter with the Christian democrats of *l'aube* in 1934 was to make clear.[125] Mounier himself described his "Refaire la Renaissance" as "unjust, brutal, artless," and as a rebellion against any "references" and "deferences." [126] His use of the word "revolution" was shocking and imprecise enough to put fear into the hearts of many of his otherwise sympathetic readers.[127] But it was his intention to overcome complacency and tranquility and his language served this purpose admirably. Moreover, although the material or economic revolution was most urgent, the material and spiritual revolutions were, in Mounier's *péguyste* terms, inextricably connected. To ask Christians to be themselves, Mounier told the "spiritualists," was to ask for a revolution. Later, when Mounier turned his efforts toward the revolutionaries of the Left, he was confronted by a new *mystique;* and it was his attempt to revise what he called "scholastic Marxism" into an

---

[122] Pierre de Boisdeffre, *Des vivants et des morts. Témoignages, 1948–1953* (Paris: Editions Universitaires, 1954), 12.

[123] Mounier, "Extraits du rapport privé sur 'Esprit' à l'usage de Mgr. Courbe et de l'archevêque de Paris, juin 1936," *O.M.*, IV, 592; and *Journal intérieur des groupes Esprit*, October, 1937, quoted in Moix, 254.

[124] Mounier, "Les cinq étapes d'*Esprit*," 50.

[125] See François Mauriac, "Les jeunes bourgeois révolutionnaires," *L'Echo de Paris*, March 25, 1933; and Garric, "Pourquoi nous acceptons," 159–173.

[126] Mounier, "La vision des hommes et du monde," 77.

[127] Moix, 81–92.

"open Marxism" that provided the greatest drama as well as the greatest misunderstanding of his position in the last years of his life.

The general revision of values which Mounier proposed as a corollary of "the profound awareness of disorder" was an undertaking which, because of its very nature, he pursued for the rest of his life. The spiritual revolution was an endless process. Nonetheless, Mounier himself was cognizant of important changes which took place in the general orientation of *Esprit*. In the early years the journal tended to be doctrinaire; special issues were devoted to important problems: capitalism, labor, property, money, anarchism, corporatism, and others.[128] Beginning in 1934 the pages of *Esprit* were filled with reflective analyses of contemporary political events; *Esprit* entered upon what Mounier was to call its "period of *engagement*." [129] This *engagement*, however, was not ordinary political activity although it did at times reflect an internal ambience or tension between the form of action outlined at Font-Romeu and more ordinary political *engagement* aimed at concrete temporal success. It has been suggested that in spite of Mounier's amazing consistency in his pursuit of the intentions of Font-Romeu, after the Second World War the journal based its criticism of "the established disorder" on political bases whereas before the War the journal had done the reverse: it had proceeded from a general criticism of civilization to a consideration of concrete political problems.[130]

Paralleling these changes of emphasis, in what Mounier had called at Font-Romeu a continual adaptation to "the new revelation," to historical change, was the increasing attention which he gave to communitarian rapports among persons. As Jean Lacroix says, Mounier went from the "person" to "personalism." [131] Not until late 1934 and early 1935 was "personalism" joined by "communitarianism" in the pages of *Esprit*. Then Mounier called for the construction of a "personalist and communitarian democracy." Still later, when humanist socialism came into vogue, socialism replaced "communitarianism" as one of Mounier's central themes.

If these changes were in an important sense a measure of the constancy of Mounier's original intentions, they also reflected the character of the final task which Mounier proposed for the new journal and

---

[128] Mounier, "Les cinq étapes d'*Esprit*," 41.
[129] *Ibid.*, 43.
[130] Jean Touchard, "La gauche non communiste," in Touchard, Girardet and Rémond, *Le Mouvement des idées politiques*, III, 317. For a good, schematicized introduction to Mounier's critique of civilization and culture, see Ganne, 13–28.
[131] Jean Lacroix, "Mounier éducateur," *E.M.*, *1905–1950*, 841.

its movement at Font-Romeu. They would "bear witness." The idea of "bearing witness" was so fraught with difficulties and so open to misunderstanding that Mounier was consistently attacked for practicing an ineffectual form of action. From Garric's question, "if the revolution does not occur. ... what will you do with your life?," to an attack by Marc Beigbeder, a former member of the *Esprit* movement who charged Mounier, *Esprit*, and the entire postwar Christian Left with complete political impotence, Mounier was often misunderstood in this respect.[132]

Making reference to Mounier, Jean-Paul Sartre and Merleau-Ponty an American observer judiciously commented that these men "may be sowing seeds for the future, [but] they are not taking an effective political stand at this hour." [133] Other critics were less judicious. Raymond de Becker, whose movement *Communauté* was associated for a brief time in 1934 with *Esprit*, launched a bitter personal attack against Mounier in 1942. Mounier, he said sarcastically, "directed the review and preached the good word." For him, Mounier was the type of intellectual who was inaccessible to reality and for whom everything was resolved in abstractions. "Ugly and badly dressed, he was, in reality, only a kind of disinherited. He could put people on the wrong track for a certain period of time by means of the esoteric character of his speculations but inevitably the emptiness of these speculations become apparent before long." [134] In a crude caricature, another critic said that "Emmanuel Moonlight" writes in his column "Imaginary Actualities": "It is evident that in the sharpening consciousness of our refusal of events, which tempers the anxiety of a true realism, joined to an adherence to principles, with all of the reserves of a true idealism, that our way is discovered." [135]

Mounier himself was troubled by the antimony of purity and efficacy, by his ambivalent "temptation to political action" and his attempt to revise values on the level of theoretical criticism. For him this was "a permanent inner drama." [136] One of his major essays in the early years of *Esprit* was an examination of precisely this dilemma: "is not any action condemned to inefficacy to the extent that it will be

[132] Garric, "Pourquoi nous acceptons," 164; and Marc Beigbeder, *Lettre à "Esprit" sur l'esprit de corps et la contrainte par corps* (Paris: Gallimard, 1951) and *Les vendeurs du temple* (Paris: Editions de minuit, 1951).

[133] Kenneth Douglas, "The French Intellectuals: Situation and Outlook," in E. M. Earle (ed.), *Modern France. Problems of the Third and Fourth Republics* (Princeton, N. J.: Princeton University Press, 1951), 68.

[134] Raymond de Becker, *Livre des vivants et des morts* (Brussels: Editions de la Toison d'Or, 1942), 166.

[135] Quoted in Marrou, "L'action politique d'Emmanuel Mounier," 92–93.

[136] Moix, 22.

pure, impure to the extent that it will be efficacious?" [137] The form of action Mounier undertook was determined in some measure by his own temperament and by his own abilities. In this regard, the brief story of the association between the journal and Mounier, on one hand, and the *Troisième force* of Georges Izard, André Déléage and Louis Galey, on the other, is instructive.

As early as October, 1931 Georges Izard was of the opinion that the new journal should be the intellectual expression of a movement which was in time to become a political party.[138] Indeed Izard's movement predated the journal and there is some reason to believe that the loyalty of many of its members always centered upon the *Troisième force* rather than upon *Esprit* itself. Jean Maze has recalled that Izard, Déléage, Galey, Edmond Humeau and other members of the *Troisième force* "would always remember with rare feeling this intense movement of their youth. ... Those who had the opportunity to live that exemplary adventure were never to forget it. The *Troisième force* experience will remain, among all those of the inter-war period, one of the purest, but also spiritually one of the richest." [139]

The real history of the *Troisième force* and *Esprit*, however, is largely the story of the friendship of Mounier and Georges Izard. In the spring of 1932 Mounier attempted to define the relationship between the journal and the movement in a lenghty letter to Izard.[140] He as director of the journal and Izard as the chieftain of the movement would complement one another because of their different temperaments. He then discussed the two postulates underlying the future action of the journal and movement in terms which clearly revealed his own acute awareness of how poorly equipped he was for political leadership and of his own distaste for ordinary political activity. He told Izard that no one could be indifferent to the political action which would result from the movement. "We are not whimsical intellectuals." "But action has its requirements," Mounier added, "short-cuts, exaggerations, silences and disciplines, originating publicity, inflation of leaders, artificial agitation, pre-emptory proclamations of ill-conceived ideas, a whole ensemble of *necessary* impurities to which those who affirm spiritual bases cannot submit." Mounier made a clear distinction between the journal and its

---

[137] Mounier, "Pour une technique des moyens spirituels" (November, 1934 and February, 1935), *O.M.*, I, 314.

[138] "Notes de Georges Izard," in *E.M.*, *1905–1950*, 978.

[139] Jean Maze, quoted in Pierre Andreu, "'Esprit' (1932–1940)," *Itinéraires*, No. 33 (May, 1959), 42.

[140] Mounier, "Lettre à Georges Izard, 23 mars 1932," *O.M.*, IV, 491–493.

team which he would direct and the movement which Izard would lead and represent on the executive committee of the journal. *Esprit* would concern itself with doctrinal problems and the movement with public lectures and debates, and eventually with candidates and an extra-parliamentary party. Significantly, Mounier added that he himself had no confidence in parliamentary methods and envisaged direct action among the masses on the part of the movement.

Almost immediately Mounier began to have serious misgivings about the orientation of the *Troisième force*. He first worried about the total ignorance of the review exhibited by some members of the movement and the tendency of the movement to lose itself in matters of political tactics.[141] Then he grew fearful of the Leftist political tendency of both the journal and the movement as a result of the expulsion of the Rightist team of *l'Ordre Nouveau* from the movement.[142] By late May, 1933 the *Troisième force* had been asked to join Bergery's *Front commun contre le fascisme* and Mounier was convinced that a break between the journal and the movement was inevitable.[143]

In July, 1933 the split between the journal and the movement was formally announced in a joint statement by Mounier and Izard.[144] After the separation Mounier saw his worst fears confirmed. The youths of the *Troisième force*, which Izard estimated at 8,000 to 9,000, adopted some of the tactics of the *Jeunesses Patriotes* and *Camelots du Roi* and actually battled members of the latter on the boulevard Saint-Michel.[145] On the evening of February 6, 1934 Déléage led a group of some forty militants of the *Troisième force* to the Place de la Concorde.[146] In November, 1934 the *Troisième force* joined Gaston Bergery's *Front commun* in a premature effort to form an anti-Fascist front. Izard himself joined Bergery's *Parti Frontiste*, was elected to the Chamber in 1936, and was the political editor of his party's journal, *La Flèche*. In 1937 he left Bergery and joined the Socialist Party. The evolution of other members of the *Troisième force* was not dissimilar. Galey, however, organized a short-lived movement as a refuge for those veterans of the *Troisième force* who were unable to support Bergery. But, although he had opposed the fusion of the *Troisième force* with Bergery's *Front commun*, Galey eventually became secretary-general of

[141] Mounier, "Lettre à Georges Izard, 11 avril 1933," *O.M.*, IV, 526–527.
[142] Mounier, "Entretiens VII, 7 mai 1933," *O.M.*, IV, 529.
[143] Mounier, "Entretiens VIII, 23 mai 1933, *O.M.*, IV, 531–532.
[144] Mounier and Izard, "Avertissement," *Esprit*, No. 10 (July, 1933), 454–456.
[145] Izard in "Qu'as-tu fait de ta jeunesse"; and Léon Derne in "Souvenirs d'André Déléage," 199.
[146] Armand Vincent in "Souvenirs d'André Déléage," 201.

La Flèche. And Bergery himself, after a checkered political career, became first one of Pétain's *missi dominici* and then a Vichy ambassador.

In Mounier's estimation, membership in the *Esprit* group had been only a foyer to ordinary political action for many of the men of the *Troisième force.*[147] Late in 1934 he complained in his diary that their "political enthusiasm was primary. ..."[148] Within Mounier's frame of reference, the evolution of the movement constituted a vivid illustration of the degeneration of a *mystique* into a *politique.* His reactions to the activities of the *Troisième force* were governed far less by considerations of a purely political nature than by his own distaste and ineptitude for political action and his belief in the degenerative effects of political action *per se.* "Action," he wrote to his future wife Paulette Leclercq with reference to the *Troisième force,* "is a terrible devourer of men."[149] He wrote to Georges Izard: "I believe that ... you have been victims of the old conception of parties and their game. The masses do not make history, but the values which act upon them flowing from minorities resolute in their faith."[150] When Izard's movement joined the *Front commun,* Mounier told a friend: "The further I go ... the more I sense my incompetence in matters of political tactics and the necessity for work which is completely foreign to them."[151] A few months before he had noted in his diary:

Left to myself, I would spend my life making *Esprit* a pure witness; I would give my life in order that this testimony never cease. But to organize a stratagem, attacks, in a word, a revolution, I care nothing for that. That does not interest me in itself (I do not say that the fate of the men affected by the revolution does not interest me, ... but so many revolutionaries ... think more about acting for the revolution than about what will result from it). I do not think of success. I would die without regrets having never realized what we want.
   I exaggerate, most certainly, I exaggerate, for I like men and life; I want them to have bread and liberty.... I wish only to emphasize one of my essential characteristics. I am like a calm and steady force, radiating, not made for conquest but seduction, not for attack but for being present.[152]

From this recognition of his vocation and this renewed confidence in the efficacy of his *témoignage,* Mounier seldom deviated.

Mounier's function and that of his journal, as he reiterated in his "Programme pour 1933," was not merely to add words to words, "but

[147] Mounier, "Entretiens VIII, 15 février 1935," *O.M.,* IV, 566.
[148] Mounier, "Carnets, 22 novembre 1934," *E.M., 1905–1950,* 989–990.
[149] Mounier, "Lettre à Paulette Leclercq, 1er avril 1933," *O.M.,* IV, 524.
[150] Mounier, "Lettre à Georges Izard, 16 octobre 1934," *O.M.,* IV, 558.
[151] Mounier, "Lettre à Georges Izard, 6 novembre 1934," *O.M.,* IV, 559.
[152] Mounier, "Entretiens VIII, 5 juin 1934," *O.M.,* IV, 551.

to instill in others, in the heart of a despiritualized humanity, a foyer of protest and witness." [153] His function was to prepare men for the political action that he himself could not undertake. He possessed what one of his lifelong associates aptly called "an almost constitutional repugnance for the idea of political strategy." [154] He was a prophet who understood many of the necessities of politics but whose personal function was "to recall to those who are engaged more directly in action the requirements of the absolute and the constant necessity for self-criticism." [155] Julien Benda denounced the "betrayal of the intellectuals," and Mounier denounced the "betrayal of the men of action." [156] He condemned politicians for sacrificing principle but he also condemned the idealists and spiritualists, much to their dismay, for refusing to take into account the requirements of history and concrete reality.[157]

It would be exceedingly tempting to treat Mounier as "a gentle dreamer, as a chimerical intellectual, or to make irony of the formula, 'Spiritual revolution,' to which he remained attached for so long." [158] But in spite of his tendency to underrate the importance of politics and his own lifelong aversion to political activity, Mounier fought against any sort of purely negative a-politicism or anti-politicism. If he himself sought efficacy on the level of theories and the criticism of ideas, he did not clearly prohibit his readers from deciding upon a more concrete political commitment for themselves. Because he considered the pros and cons of every problem, however, he sometimes gave the impression of "spiritual timidity." [159] On occasion Mounier led his readers to the very brink of a definite political commitment and then criticized them for this commitment or, by his rigorous examination of the complexities of a particular problem, foreclosed any sort of effective political activity. However, as Pierre-Henri Simon, a longtime member of *Esprit*, said, Mounier was rigorous and honest to an extent that has rarely been equalled "in this century of propagandists and falsifications." Had he undertaken a different form of *engagement*, he might well have had more spectacular results, Simon believed, but he would have "touched and impregnated consciences less." [160] Mounier was primarily a teacher, and his teaching was in that border area where

---

[153] Mounier, "Programme pour 1933," *Esprit*, No. 3 (December, 1932), 363.
[154] Pierre-Aimé Touchard, "Dernier dialogue," *E.M., 1905–1950*, 785.
[155] Henry Duméry, "Hommage à Mounier," *B.A.E.M.*, No. 27 (January, 1966), 19.
[156] Moix, 329.
[157] Mounier, *Manifeste au service du personnalisme* (1936), *O.M.*, I, 484.
[158] Marrou, "L'action politique d'Emmanuel Mounier," 99.
[159] Pierre-Henri Simon, "Vocation de Mounier," *Nouvelles littéraires*, July 12, 1951.
[160] *Ibid.*

truth or principle converge with action and concrete, historical events. "It is clear," Mounier wrote, "that we are operating on a mixed level. A philosophy which is totally oriented towards politics must be judged politically, by its political success of failure. We cannot over-emphasize the fact that Personalism is not fundamentally centered in political action, but that it is a total effort to comprehend and outgrow the whole crisis of twentieth-century man." This effort, he said, might be undertaken politically in various ways and it might result in various tactical errors. But it could no more refuse political *engagement* than it could withdraw from anything that concerned man. But "if it excludes certain choices which are imcompatible with its master intentions, it does not lay down infallibly the direction of political choice." [161] Mounier's personalism, therefore, was neither a systematic philosophy (Mounier was no systematizer) nor a program of political action (Mounier was certainly no politician), but rather the basis from which the principles of political choice could be drawn.[162]

It should not be concluded from the foregoing that the *Esprit* movement was completely void of political content. In a country where even the cults of Charles de Foucauld and Joan of Arc have certain political connotations, such a feat would be difficult, if not impossible. By Mounier's own admission the *Esprit* team was forced to place itself on the Left. The politics of Mounier and *Esprit*, however, consisted primarily of the recognition of the existence of certain problems, an analysis of these problems, and an assignment of priorities to their solution. The *raison d'être* of *Esprit* and of Mounier's personalism was grounded in general analyses of concrete political events.

Mounier recalled in later years that there were two explanations for the economic crisis which began in 1929: "The Marxists said: classic economic crisis, crisis of structure. Adjust the economy and the sickness will be cured. The moralists contended on the contrary: crisis of man, crisis of morality, crisis of values. Change man and the society will recover." Neither of these explanations was entirely satisfactory to Mounier. He revised Péguy's aphorism, "The revolution will be moral or there will be no revolution," to read: "The moral Revolution will be economic or there will be no Revolution. The economic Revolution will

---

[161] Mounier, *Qu'est-ce que le personnalisme?*, (1947), *O.M.*, III, 204, trans. Cynthia Rowland in Mounier, *Be Not Afraid. A Denunciation of Despair*. (New York: Sheed and Ward, n.d.), 144.

[162] Lacroix, "Mounier éducateur," 839–851; and Jean-Marie Domenach, "Les principes du choix politique," *E.M., 1905–1950*, 820–838.

be 'moral' or it will be nothing." [163] Corresponding to this attempt to synthesize two divergent points of view, the *Esprit* movement represented the convergence of two types of men. According to Mounier, those of Christian or spiritualist background discovered in the crisis the profound socio-economic roots of all human problems; and others, especially of Socialist origins, discovered the human dimensions of the crisis and the necessity of posing the revolutionary problem in terms much larger than the purely economic.[164] "It was ... between these two crises of conscience that the encounter from which *Esprit* sprang was made. The encounter was made, therefore, along the lines of a kind of humanist socialism." [165]

In joining *Esprit*, the Christian members made a judgment concerning the comportment of their co-religionists in the face of the crisis. They were convinced that Catholics were making no contributions to the purely technical solutions required by the situation. This neglect had left the way open for the intellectually bankrupt Socialists and the proponents of totalitarianism of the Right and Left to attempt to impose their solutions.[166] Mounier believed that the great majority of French Catholics were guilty of one or the other of two serious errors. They either failed to recognize the existence of a revolutionary crisis and continued to support a corrupt system, thereby compromising the Christian *mystique* in "the established disorder"; or they made this *mystique* a harmless and ineffectual refuge, an inhuman spiritualism or *angélisme*, thereby denying its relevance to temporal affairs.[167] "There is, first, in personalism," Mounier later explained, "a reaction, let us say, against spiritualism, that is, against misunderstanding, in the name of noble sentiments, of the realities taking form at our feet." [168] The Christian members of *Esprit* wanted to dissociate the Christian *mystique* from "the established disorder" and to bring about what they called, in a celebrated issue of the journal, the "rupture entre l'ordre chrétien et le désordre établi." [169] They were also determined to project Christianity "from that kind of ghetto into which those who are organ-

[163] Mounier, *Qu'est-ce que le personnalisme?*, O.M., III, 183.
[164] Mounier, "Les cinq étapes d'*Esprit*," 38–39. See also "Enquête sur la revue *Esprit*," in *Les Revues européenes*, November, 1946, reprinted in *B.A.E.M.*, No. 15 (March, 1960), 3.
[165] *Ibid.*
[166] Mounier, "Extraits du rapport privé sur 'Esprit,'" 586.
[167] *Ibid.*
[168] "Dialogue entre Pierre Emmanuel et Emmanuel Mounier, sur le livre de celui-ci: le Personnalisme. Radiodiffusion française, Paris, 23 décembre 1949," *B.A.E.M.*, No. 15 (March, 1960), 12.
[169] This is the title of the special issue of *Esprit*, No. 6 (March, 1933).

izing new forms of civilization are attempting to drive it, in order to re-incarnate it in all of the problems of our times . . ." [170]

The other members of *Esprit* justified their acceptance of a spiritual-ist *mystique* on the basis of what they considered to be the insufficien-cies of the Socialist "catechism" and the purely economic explanation of the crisis.[171] The ferment and crises within French Socialism during the early 1930s, the organization of a Protestant Christian Socialist movement under the aegis of André Philip and others, and even the publication in France of the early letters of Karl Marx which, some believed, showed Marx to have been less a materialist than many of his French disciples – all of these events contributed to the adherence of a number of young Socialists and Communists to *Esprit*.[172] Mounier later recalled that these members of *Esprit* attempted to renovate an out-of-date socialism by returning to the "profound socialist tradition" of Proudhon, Jaurès and the other "prophets" of French Socialism.[173] The result of the collaboration of Christians and Socialists in *Esprit* was not, however, the construction of a "Christian Socialism." Mounier objected vehemently to the formula, "Socialist because Christian," which gained currency during the mid-1930s and culminated in the organization of a group of *communistes spiritualistes*.[174] "If we fought against the idea of 'monarchist because Christian' or 'conservative because Christian,'" he said, "it was not to arrive at the idea of 'social-ist because Christian.'" [175]

One of the initial bonds of the *Esprit* team was the reciprocal curiosi-ty of Catholics and non-Catholics.[176] More important still, this pluralist collaboration was a step in the integration of French Catholics into the society of their fellow citizens. It was also a necessity if French Catho-lics were to rid themselves of their "ghetto complex." [177] It meant, in addition, that *Esprit* itself was not a Catholic journal. This in itself was a novelty in 1932. It ran counter to the historical disposition of many French Catholics and was one of the reasons that Mounier and his jour-nal encountered difficulties with ecclesiastical authorities. In 1936 Mounier responded to his critics by preparing a lengthy report in which

---

[170] Mounier, "Extraits du rapport privé sur 'Esprit,'" 585–586.

[171] *Ibid.*; and Mounier, "Les cinq étapes d'*Esprit*," 40.

[172] Touchard, "L'esprit des années 1930," 97–108 *passim*.

[173] Mounier, "Les cinq étapes d'*Esprit*," 41. See also Mounier, "Personnalisme et socialis-me," *Cité-Soir*, August 14, 1945.

[174] Mounier, "Vision socialiste et vision chrétienne" (September, 1933), *O.M.*, I, 849–855; and Mounier, "Chrétiens et révolutionnaires," *Esprit*, No. 33 (June, 1935), 423–424.

[175] "Enquête sur la revue *Esprit*," 3.

[176] Mounier, "Les cinq étapes d'*Esprit*," 41.

[177] Mounier, "Extraits du rapport privé sur 'Esprit,'" 586.

he explained that the Catholic members of the group were not collaborating with non-Catholics in religious matters. Rather, he said, they were working fraternally with non-Catholics in the area of "free questions." [178] All Catholics should work "as Christians" without losing contact with the religious faith that should guide their every action, but the solutions they proposed to various temporal problems could not be presented "as Christian solutions." [179] Mounier followed the lead of Jacques Maritain in making this important distinction. [180]

One of the most important lessons that Mounier gave his co-religionists was that they should bear witness to their religious faith in the multiple organizations of a pluralist society rather than in the traditional Catholic organizations of religious defense or conquest. The depth and steadfastness of Mounier's own religious convictions colored his life and work to an extent that is impossible to exaggerate. "Intransigence," one of his friendly critics wrote, "was the style of his thought as of his life. There was nothing of the Modernist in him. He was of the Church without question; and if he suffered so badly because the Church is identified with Christendom, ... it was because of the absolute character of his faith." [181] To a subscriber who complained about the Catholicism of *Esprit*, Mounier responded that he was a Catholic, but a Catholic who was far more aware of the paganization of the great mass of Catholics than a non-Catholic. "My best friends are nonbelievers," he said, making reference to such members of the *Esprit* team as Pierre-Aimé Touchard, Georges Duveau, P.-L. Landsberg, François Goguel, and many others. "It is not only my desire but the *very axis of my vocation* ... to make the ones [Christians] and the others [non-Christians] work together: to communicate to non-Christians some less grimacing image of Christian practice" and to make Christians aware of the distasteful "sociological projection" of their faith.[182]

What bound the *Esprit* group together, consequently, was not an attempt to construct a "Catholic order" or a new "Christendom", but rather an unsystematic philosophical frame of reference called perso-

---

[178] *Ibid.*; Mounier, "Action temporelle des catholiques," 78–91 *passim.*; and Mounier, "Chrétiens et incroyants," (February, 1936), *O.M.*, I, 859–869.

[179] Mounier, "Extraits du rapport privé sur 'Esprit,'" 587–589; and Mounier, "Lettre à un abonne inconnu; extraits adressés par un tiers, 19 septembre 1934," *O.M.*, IV, 556–557.

[180] Mounier, "Pluralisme chrétien," *Esprit*, No. 32 (May, 1935), 284–285.

[181] Borne, "Pour un tombeau d'Emmanuel Mounier," 106.

[182] Mounier, "Lettre à un abonne inconnu," *O.M.*, IV,556.

nalism.[183] The personalism of Mounier has been described in a variety of ways: as a "pedagogy: a philosophy of service and not of domination"; as a "philosophy of ambivalence"; and as "an open adventure" which has no meaning outside the historical situations it is meant to elucidate.[184]

That Mounier's personalism can be described in various ways is due in large part to the fact that it was not a philosophy in the ordinary sense of the word. Mounier often used the language of the discipline in which he was trained – especially in his definition of the nature of the human person – but, in part because of his rebellion against academic philosophy, he was not a great or original philosopher, a fact that even his longtime friend Jean Lacroix acknowledges.[185] Even the term "personalism" did not originate with Mounier.[186] Moreover, such philosophers as Maurice Nédoncelle, Paul Ricoeur, and Paul-Louis Landsberg provided more profound analyses of the purely philosophical roots and aspects of personalism than did Mounier.[187] Landsberg, a student of Max Scheler in Germany, began an extremely fruitful collaboration with *Esprit* in late 1934; and, in Mounier's own estimation, his contributions to *Esprit* on the nature of action and *engagement* "marked crucial dates in our history." [188] Ricoeur testifies that "in the internal history and in the thought of the *Esprit* movement," Landsberg's importance was almost comparable to that of Mounier himself; and Jean-Marie Domenach states succinctly that Landsberg helped to save *Esprit* from purely speculative, detached, and impotent attitudes in the face of concrete historical situations.[189] What Mounier did was to give personalism a new vocabulary, new themes, and new perspectives.[190] An English personalist contends that even though the philo-

[183] Mounier, "Etienne Gilson: Pour un ordre cathoilque," *Esprit*, No. 30 (March, 1935), 959–964; and Rouquette, "Positions et oppositions d'Emmanuel Mounier," 147–148.

[184] Domenach, "Présence de Mounier," 222; Jean Lacroix, "Un témoin et un guide," in *Emmanuel Mounier ou le combat du juste*, 46–47; and Etienne Borne, "Une philosophie ouverte: le Personnalisme," *l'aube*, March 25–26, 1950.

[185] Jean Lacroix, "Le dixième anniversaire de la mort de fondatuer d'*Esprit*," *Le Monde*, March 23, 1960, reprinted in *B.A.E.M.*, No. 16–17 (April, 1961), 13.

[186] Mounier, "Quelques réflexions sur le personnalisme," *Synthèses* (Brussels), No. 4 (1947), 25.

[187] See, for example, Maurice Nédoncelle, *La réciprocité des consciences* (Paris: Aubier, 1942); Paul Ricoeur, *Histoire et vérité* (Paris: Editions du Seuil, 1955); and Paul-Louis Landsberg, *Problèmes du personnalisme* (Paris: Editions du Seuil, 1952).

[188] Mounier, "Paul-Louis Landsberg," *Esprit*, No. 118 (January, 1946), 155–156.

[189] Paul Ricoeur, "P.-L. Landsberg," *Esprit*, No. 180–181 (July-Aug., 1951) 263, and Jean-Marie Domenach, "L'Evénement politique," *B.A.E.M.*, No. 30 (September, 1967), 9–10.

[190] Joseph Folliet, "Emmanuel Mounier," *Chronique sociale de France*, 64ᵉ année, No. 4 (July, 1956), 357–358.

sophical roots of personalism are to be found in the work of Scheler, Berdiaev, Kierkegaard, Jaspers, and Gabriel Marcel, "It is Emmanuel Mounier ... who is the founder and inspirer of Personalism regarded as a movement," and Jean Lacroix says simply that *"Esprit* has popularized the themes [of personalism] especially on the social, economic, and political planes." [191]

Mounier defined the human person, albeit in terms that had a "very philosophical allure," [192] in the following manner: the human person is an absolute which has three dimensions: vocation, incarnation, and communication or communion. [193] In his final definition of personalism, Mounier said that since the central affirmation of personalism is the existence of free and creative persons, personalism carries with it a principle of unpredictability which precludes any kind of definitive systematization. [194] "What makes Personalism very difficult for some to understand is that they are trying to find a system, whereas Personalism is perspective, method, exigency." It is perspective because it opposes a spiritual realism to abstract idealism and materialism, in a continuous effort to remake the unity broken by these two perspectives. It is method because it rejects both the deductive method of the dogmatists and the crude empiricism of the realists, and because it refuses the proposition that the constants of the human condition can be defined in some sort of definitive schematic. It is exigency, finally, because it demands commitment "which is at once total and conditional." [195] Mounier then declared:

We are not putting forward some myth of the concept of man, or some dream about humanity. We are setting out on a project, a human project in the truest sense of the word, taken to its fullest possible extent, the gathering together of the fundamental data of civilisation, the perpetual search for the synthesis which no age will fully realize. Man's permanence is in adventure. The nature of man is artifice. To undertake this adventure, to direct this artifice so that man, in each of his always unexpected appearances, shall be more truly man, such seems to be the task to which both tradition and revolution incite us in perpetual dialogue. [196]

---

[191] J. B. Coates, *The Crisis of the Human Person. Some Personalist Interpretations* (London and New York: Longmans, Green and Co., 1949), 15; and Jean Lacroix, "Les orientations de la philosophie française," *Le Monde*, October 6, 1945.

[192] Hervé Chaigne, "Le personnalisme de Mounier," in *Emmanuel Mounier ou le combat du juste,* 148.

[193] See *ibid.,* 137–175, for a good brief introduction.

[194] Mounier, *Le personnalisme, O.M.,* III, 429–430.

[195] Mounier, *Qu'est-ce que le personnalisme?, O.M.,* III, 242–243.

[196] *Ibid.,* 243.

The personalism of Mounier, consequently, can be defined only in a particular historical context. Mounier himself defined and redefined his personalism many times in the course of his lifetime.[197] And a number of men, whose temporal commitments bore little or no resemblance to those of Mounier and *Esprit*, called themselves "personalists." The men of *l'Ordre Nouveau*, for example, were "personalists" but in Mounier's judgment their concept of the human person was a confused Neitzschian and aristocratic one.[198] During the War and Occupation a number of men who called themselves "personalists" were among the active doctrinal proponents of Pétain's National Revolution. And after the Liberation, Mounier felt it necessary to examine the possible ambiguities of personalism and to condemn various perversions and distortions of it.[199] Mounier also defined and redefined personalism within various philosophical contexts: in its relationship with anarchism, Marxism, and existentialism.[200] In his final statement Mounier said that "one might thus distinguish an existentialist tangent of personalism comprising Berdiaev, Landsberg, Ricoeur, Nédoncelle, a Marxian tangent often concurrent with this one, and another tangent, more classical, in the French philosophic tradition (Lachièse-Rey, Nabert, La Senne, Madinier, J. Lacroix)." [201] The essence of Mounier's personalism is best described by Jean-Marie Domenach as "a manner of living, of comporting oneself, of communicating, which has very numerous applications in various situations and métiers." [202]

Mounier's intention was practical and concrete. It was to distinguish between the human person and the individual of both the individualists and the collectivists. It was to combat the individualists' attempt to isolate the individual and center him upon himself and the collectivists' attempt to use the individual and to treat him as an interchangeable object. The way in which Mounier often introduced his readers or listeners to his personalism reflected these specific historical concerns. For example, several months before his death in an interview with his friend the poet Pierre Emmanuel, he said:

---

[197] In addition to the works already cited, see Mounier, "Personnalisme catholique," *Esprit*, Nos. 89, 90, and 91 (February, March, and April, 1940), 220–246, 395–409, and 57–72, reprinted as "Personnalisme et christianisme," *O.M.*, I, 729–779, and published anonymously as "Catholic Personalism Faces Our Times," in Joseph T. Delos *et al.*, *Race: Nation: Person* (New York: Barnes & Noble, Inc., 1944), 323–380.

[198] Mounier, "'Esprit' et les mouvements de jeunesse," 842.

[199] Mounier, *Qu'est-ce que le personnalisme?*, *O.M.*, III, 229–241 *passim*.

[200] See Moix, 175–202, 211–227.

[201] Mounier, *Le personnalisme*, *O.M.*, III, 438.

[202] Domenach, "Presence de Mounier," 219.

E[mmanuel]. M[ounier]. – You know, Pierre Emmanuel, that the word personalism and the idea that it expresses were born spontaneously. I dread ideologies. A doctrine that can be placed in the service of man, in a given epoch, ought to be progressively disengaged from a kind of familiarity with the epoch.

P[ierre]. E[mmanuel]. – In other words, the ideas were born of living experience?

E.M. – Yes, but not haphazardly: dominated by a directive intuition. We found, if I may say so, the requirements of an ardent and demanding fidelity to the idea of the human person as a result of the questions posed by the fascisms, communism, existentialism, and also by our most mundane difficulties.[203]

Mounier's reference to "the fascisms, communism, existentialism," in his response to Pierre Emmanuel was somewhat misleading. His criticism of Fascism and Marxism was always secondary to his unequivocal and life-long opposition to what he considered to be the historical causes of the two. "Our entire doctrinal effort," he said in 1936, "has been to free the sense of the person from individualist errors and the sense of communion from collectivist errors." [204] But both forms of collectivism, he believed, were primarily responses to the failures of capitalism and liberal democracy: Fascism was the final and totalitarian phase, a kind of defensive reaction, of a bankrupt democratic system; and "Marxism," Mounier said at the time of the founding of *Esprit*, "is the rebellious son of capitalism." [205]

Consequently, Mounier sought the roots of the contemporary crisis in the distant past and initially defined personalism in this particular context. Drawing upon the work of Nicolas Berdiaev, the Russian Orthodox Catholic philosopher who was an early supporter and collaborator of *Esprit*, Mounier's "Refaire la Renaissance" meant to assist "in the downfall of an era of civilization born towards the end of the Middle Ages, ... capitalist in its structures, liberal in its ideology, bourgeois in its ethics." [206]

At the risk of doing injury to the complexity and the richness of Mounier's thought, two themes may be said to run continuously through his work. They are a radical anti-capitalism linked with support for the construction of an "economy decentralized to the person"

---

[203] "Dialogue entre Pierre Emmanuel et Emmanuel Mounier," 10–11.
[204] Mounier, "Extraits du rapport privé sur 'Esprit,'" 589.
[205] Mounier, "Des pseudo-valeurs fascistes" (January, 1934), *O.M.*, I, 224–225; and Mounier, "Extraits du prospectus annonçant la publication d'Esprit," *O.M.*, IV, 490.
[206] Mounier, *Manifeste au service du personnalisme*, *O.M.*, I, 486. See Nicolas Berdyaev, *Un nouveau Moyen Age* (Paris: Plon, 1927); Béguin, "Une vie," 966; and Nicolas Berdyaev, *Dream and Reality. An Essay in Autobiography*, trans. Katherine Lampert (New York: Macmillan Co., 1951), 275ff. In addition to the materials published in *O.M.*, IV, see also "Correspondance entre Mounier et Berdiaeff," *B.A.E.M.*, No. 33 (February, 1969), 5–17.

which Mounier identified after the Second World War with a renovated form of socialism; and in the words of François Goguel, "the consciousness of what is formal, incomplete, and therefore vain in the institutions of a liberal democracy installed by and for the bourgeoisie, and the appeal for its overthrow by the revolutionary creation of a more authentic democracy organized on all levels of collective life and not only on that of the traditional state." [207] Although Mounier treated neither of these themes systematically in his own writings – and both of them are intimately, indeed, inextricably connected with his primary intention of dissociating Christianity from "the established disorder" – they can be treated separately for purposes of brief summary.

Mounier's anti-capitalism was basic to all of his temporal commitments between 1932 and 1950. From the prospectus announcing the publication of *Esprit* in February, 1932 to his last article in the journal, Mounier's anti-capitalism was clear.[208] The prospectus announcing *Esprit* stated that "capitalism reduces a growing multitude, through destitution or through comfort, to a state of servitude that is irreconcilable with the dignity of man. ..." [209] What distinguished Mounier's anti-capitalism and constituted its originality was that it was less technical than moral; it was rooted less in Marxism than in the sense of spiritual destitution of Charles Péguy.[210]

In Mounier's exaggerated assessment, almost all of the evils of modern society – crises, wars, destitution, corruption, hatred, tyranny, and injustice – resulted from capitalism in one way or another.[211] Most important, however, the profit motive of capitalism perverted all human values. The primacy of profit created the "bourgeois spirit" which in turn infected the other classes in the social organism. The bourgeois individual was possessed by his goods and devoted his life to his own personal well-being, to his material comfort, and to nothing else. He and his fellows, Mounier said in terms reminiscent of Péguy, "understand nothing, believe in nothing, above all, would die for nothing, neither for God, the revolution, France, nor their neighbor."[212] Worse still, the bourgeois spirit deformed, disfigured, and made a caricature of Christianity. Bourgeois Christianity, the distasteful, "sociological extension" of Christianity against which Mounier fought with-

---

[207] François Goguel, "Positions politiques," *E.M., 1905–1950*, 798.
[208] Mounier, "Extraits du prospectus annonçant la publication d'*Esprit*," 490; and Mounier, "Fidélité" (February, 1950), *O.M.*, IV, 17–21.
[209] Mounier, "Extraits du prospectus annonçant la publication d'*Esprit*," 490.
[210] Jean-Marie Domenach, "Les principes du choix politique," *E.M., 1905–1950*, 821–822.
[211] Mounier, "Pour une technique des moyens spirituelles," 346.
[212] "Anticapitalisme" (June, 1934), *O.M.*, I, 272.

out respite, substituted security, economy, and social immobility for faith, hope, and charity. It was therefore a facade used to mask the most sordid kind of self-interest beneath its false idealism.[213] The world, Mounier wrote his sister not long after his arrival in Paris, had lost "the meaning of the verb *to give* (even intelligence has become a private possession) and this is the cause of a great many human ruins." [214]

The injustices for which Mounier held capitalism and the bourgeois spirit responsible were, in his view, legalized within an immense apparatus of oppression – individualist liberal democracy. Mounier agreed with Marx that many of the rights granted the citizen in the liberal democratic state were abrogated by the conditions of his economic and social status.[215] And he agreed with Proudhon that individualist, liberal democracy was only a form of tyranny, the tyranny of numbers, and little more than a form of absolutism, the absolutism of the majority.[216] In terms remarkably similar to those used by Marc Sangnier, Mounier argued that "the essence of an ideal democracy ... is to ask for each citizen a maximum of participation and responsibility ... in public affairs. Liberal democracy has made that participation illusory and that responsibility worthless." [217] "Democracy," he charged in another statement worthy of the founder of the *Sillon*, "has developed a tyranny of the public man over the private man. ...."[218]

Mounier's criticism of liberal, parliamentary democracy was launched almost entirely from the position of his radical and total anti-capitalism. The bourgeoisie had transformed democracy into a statism controlled by large capital and industry.[219] The political system was monopolized by the bourgeoisie who, through their political parties, attempted to impose their views and values upon the rest of society. This tendency towards totalitarianism was analogous, in Mounier's judgment, to the transformation of communism into Stalinist dictatorship and "Hitler's submission to the banks and to the Reichswehr." [220] A

[213] Mounier, *Manifeste au service du personnalisme, O.M.*, I, 492–498; and Mounier, "Confession pour nous autres chrétiens" (March, 1933), *O.M.*, I, 373–392 *passim*.

[214] Mounier, "Lettre à Madeleine Mounier, 28 janvier 1928," *O.M.*, IV, 431.

[215] Mounier, *Manifeste au service du personnalisme, O.M.*, I, 515.

[216] Mounier, "Anarchie et personnalisme," 688–689.

[217] Mounier, "Les nouvelles conditions de la vie publique en France," *Esprit*, No. 94 (November, 1940), 62–63.

[218] Mounier, *Révolution personnaliste et communautaire, O.M.*, I, 410.

[219] Mounier, "Lettre ouverte sur la démocratie," *l'aube*, February 27, 1934, reprinted in *O.M.*, I, 296.

[220] Mounier, "Pour une technique des moyens spirituels," 347.

student of French political thought aptly pointed out that "this assi-milation of French democracy to totalitarianism under the control of occult capitalist powers was common fare for French social critics during the early nineteen thirties, when Mounier expressed these views." [221] The same critic also noted that there was a shift in Mounier's critical position in the late 1930s after the failure of the Popular Front. In a profound analysis of what he called "la mythique de gauche," Mounier addressed himself to the liberal theory of Alain. Although he believed Alain to be correct in his suspicion of power-holders, he doubt-ed that "the doctrine of the distrustful peasant" was a viable attitude for citizens to take toward their government and toward one another.[222] Always far more concerned with human attitudes than with political structures, Mounier said that what France needed was "a certain un-animity on fundamentals, limited to objective relationships, of course, but unquestioned and living. ..." [223]

In place of "the established disorder" of capitalism, liberal demo-cracy, and the bourgeois spirit Mounier had no utopian plan to propose. His refusal to enclose himself in any sort of utopian constructions and the consequent freedom that this allowed him in taking account of un-foreseen historical contingencies were decisive factors in the survival and expanding influence of *Esprit*. The very nature of his personalism included a far-reaching and profound criticism of the civilization, the culture, and the institutions of the society in which he lived, but it pre-cluded the elaboration of a rigid schematic of economic, social, and political institutions which would constitute an ideal society. "The history of man." Mounier said, "is not a geometry in black and white, but a perpetual vicissitude of light and shadow. The shadow extends to the end of history." [224]

What Mounier did set down were the guidelines or conditions for a personalist and communitarian (or socialist) economy and political regime. But these guidelines were general and they were always sub-ordinated to the work which was his true métier: the criticism of cul-ture, human attitudes and the falsification of values. In this task, on occasion he contradicted himself and violated some of the basic canons of his own critical methods. Although he himself often warned his

---

[221] Pierce, 59.

[222] Mounier, "Bilan spirituel: court traité de la mythique de gauche" (March, 1938), *O.M.*, IV, 40–75, cited in *ibid.*, 59.

[223] Quoted in Pierce, 60.

[224] Mounier, "Réunion et désunion pour la vérité" (April, 1933), reprinted as "Révolution et révolution," *O.M.*, I, 848.

readers of the danger of adopting the opposite of what one opposes or condemns, his own broad description of the prerequisites of a personalist or socialist economy was almost a perfect antithesis of the capitalist system he condemned.[225] "A non-capitalist society," he wrote in 1934, "whatever its mechanisms, must start from principles diametrically opposed to those of the present economic system." [226]

Mounier argued that a personalist economy would substitute the primacy of the needs of the human person for the tyranny of undisciplined economic liberty, profit, capital, and production.[227] Moreover, a personalist economy would be based upon the "primacy of the person expanding within organic communities." The new regime would put an end to capitalist anarchy and tyranny by creating natural communities in which the private and public lives of the individual could flourish; and the decentralization explicit in the formation of these communities would protect the individual against both the return of capitalist anarchy and the oppression of an overly centralized economic apparatus. Before the reign of money could be extricated from the social and economic machinery, however, cupidity, violence, pettiness, and mediocrity had to be irradicated from the hearts of men and this, in turn, posed an educational problem.[228] In all of his work Mounier's emphasis remained remarkably consistent: the economy must be subordinated to essentially human needs and this could be accomplished only by a spiritual revolution or a revision of values and this, in turn, was an educational task. If Mounier used different terms to express essentially the same aims this was but one measure of his consistency of purpose and his constant effort to adapt himself to changing historical circumstances. In 1936, for example, he defined an economy of personalist inspiration as a "pluralist economy" and after the Second World War he often substituted the word "socialism" for his earlier "communitarianism." [229]

Mounier's attempts at political innovation are at once inseparable from and subordinate to his concern for economic and social change. Like his socialism, his political proposals were extremely flexible. His *Manifeste au service du personnalisme* contained his fullest examination of a personalist and communitarian democracy but even here his

---

[225] See, for example, Mounier, "Feu la chrétiente" (1949), *O.M.*, IV, 705.
[226] "Anticapitalisme," 274.
[227] *Ibid.*, 274–275.
[228] *Ibid.*, 276.
[229] Mounier, *Manifeste au service du personnalisme*, *O.M.*, I, 605; and Mounier, "L'inquiétude de la liberté dans la France contemporaine," *Suisse contemporaine* (Lausanne), October, 1946, reprinted in *B.A.E.M.*, No. 19 (October, 1962), 10.

aversion to specific political forms, institutions, and techniques was clear. Indeed, Mounier devoted far more attention to the principles of personalist education, to outlining "a pluralist statute for education," to the problems of personal life, culture, and a personalist economy than to specifically political questions. In terms clearly reminiscent of the classic *Sillonist* definition of democracy, Mounier declared that a personalist democracy "is only the search for the political means to assure all persons ... the right to free development and maximum responsibility." [230] Later he defined true democracy as "any regime which places concern for the human person at the base of all public institutions." [231] In what was perhaps his most concrete proposal, Mounier was insistent that a "fundamental statute for the human person" be inserted into the fabric of the state. In his final definition of personalism, Mounier said that "the crucial problem for personalism is that of the legitimacy of power wielded by man over man, which seems incompatible with the interpersonal relationship ..." [232]

For both Mounier and the Christian democrats, democracy was an instrument for fulfilling human potentialities rather than a rigid political form; and for both of them, democracy was always in the making and never fully achieved, for the human person always sought but never achieved perfection. This did not preclude membership in the *Esprit* movement of a number of men who were concerned with matters of political techniques and forms but such men never played a particularly significant role in its affairs.

Not long after the separation of *Esprit* and the *Troisième force*, a new period in the history of *Esprit* began to unfold. In a retrospective assessment of the deficiencies of *Esprit* during its early "doctrinaire" period, Mounier pointed out that his journal, like *l'Humanité* at the time of its founding by Jean Jaurès, was too much a journal of *agrégés*.[233] Mounier discerned "a deficiency on a particularly important plane, that of politics itself, and that deficiency persisted for a long time in *Esprit*." [234] Indeed Mounier admitted that his journal never had a team which would distinguish itself for its political creativity.[235] Rather, the pressure of external events, as well as a new awareness of the danger of "purism," provided the impetus for *Esprit* to enter upon a period of

[230] Mounier, *Manifeste au service du personnalisme*, O.M., I, 623.
[231] Mounier, "Pour une démocratie personnaliste," *le Voltigeur*, No. 3 (November 2, 1938), reprinted in *B.A.E.M.*, No. 23–24 (December, 1964), 9–13.
[232] Mounier, *Le personnalisme*, O.M., III, 518–521.
[233] Mounier, "Les cinq étapes d'*Esprit*," 15.
[234] *Ibid.*, 16.
[235] *Ibid.*, 15–16.

engagement in which Mounier and the *Esprit* team quickly distinguished themselves for their reflective analyses of the great events of their time.

The new period in the history of *Esprit* was preceded by a grave crisis in the always marginal finances of the journal itself – a crisis so serious that Mounier broached with Madame Daniélou the possibility of resuming his teaching in Neuilly. This crisis, in turn, was made more acute by a reorganization of the publishing house of Desclée de Brouwer which forced Mounier to vacate his little office at 76, rue des Saints-Pères. Through his friend Georges Zérapha, Mounier found new quarters at 137, faubourg Saint-Denis, and through the continued efforts of Gilbert de Véricourt, one of *Esprit*'s staunchest supporters in Lille, the precarious financial condition of the journal was alleviated sufficiently for publication to continue. Mounier himself lived a precarious material existence, especially after his marriage in July, 1935 to Paulette Leclercq. Prior to his marriage Mounier had taught in the French lycée of his fiancée's native Brussels. After his marriage Mounier, his wife and their first daughter Françoise lived with the family of Jacques Lefrancq in the Lefrancqs' *maison Gilsoul* in Brussels. Mounier kept his teaching position and his wife worked in a Brussels museum until the birth of Françoise. Mounier had to commute between Brussels and Paris until the family moved to Paris in June, 1939. Even as late as 1938, when the finances of the journal had improved considerably, Mounier received only 2,500 francs a month from the journal, as compared, for example, with the 6,000 francs Henri Massis received from the *Revue Universelle*.[236] In the spring of 1938 Mounier, Lefrancq, and several other members of the *Esprit* group began to lay plans for a small *Esprit* community – a phalanstery, according to their critics – which was to be both a center for the *Amis d'Esprit*, and a *Centre psycho-pédagogique*. Not until after the War, however, did the *Esprit* community in Châtenay-Malabry finally materialize.

The reorganization of the *Esprit* group which followed the financial crisis was primarily a reorganization of the *Amis d'Esprit* founded in July, 1933.[237] By the latter part of the summer of 1934 there were various specialized *Esprit* groups: a philosophy group which studied such problems a; "the technique of spiritual means," the metaphysics of the person and the community, and Marxism; a social group which examined the nature of the Corporation, the State, and Federalism; and a group of artists who, at the *Esprit* congress of September, 1937, de-

---

[236] Mounier, "Lettre à Emile-Albert Niklaus, 6 septembre 1938," *O.M.*, IV, 617–618.
[237] See "Constitution des amis d'*Esprit*," *Esprit*, No. 10 (July, 1933), 457–462.

cided to establish a new poetry journal called *Droit de Survivre*. On July 6, 1934 Mounier noted in his diary: "A beautiful end of the year, with its miracles for *Esprit* and departures of capital importance. ... I truly feel that *Esprit* is on the way of turning smoothly towards its true destinies." [238]

Included in these various *Esprit* groups and among the journal's collaborators or participants in one or more of the congresses of the movement during the remaining years of the 1930s were men and women who comprised a veritable intellectual *Who's Who in France*: Etienne Borne, Pierre-Henri Simon, Jean Lacroix, Marcel Moré, André Philip, Joseph Folliet, François Goguel, Pierre-Aimé Touchard, Adrian Miatlev, Henri Marrou, Jacques Madaule, Rabi, Victor Serge, Henri Guillemin, Edmond Humeau, Georges Duveau, and innumerable others. [239] One of the contributors to *Esprit*, Hélène Iswolsky, the daughter of the last Tsarist ambassador to France, has charmingly described the *Esprit* congresses, usually held in the summertime on the campus of a boys' school in Jouy-en-Josas, near Versailles:

I shall always remember these inspiring meetings, where young people assembled from all parts of France and from abroad – students, young teachers and priests, philosophers in the bud – and there were also some more mature men present – doctors, economists, writers – for Mounier's movement attracted people of all ages and professions....

The congresses usually lasted three or four days. We sprawled on the lawn in the warm July sunlight, and Mounier would sit in the middle of our circle in an old sweater and flannel pants, which made him look more than ever like a schoolboy. He would conduct the discussion which went on heatedly for the greater part of the day....

In spite of this atmosphere of familiarity and youthful nonchalance, the members of *Esprit* and their leader, Mounier, were very intent on their job. We observed a carefully worked-out schedule; a series of philosophical, social, and economic problems was examined in turn, and often led to animated debates. Mounier directed them with great skill and prevented them from ending in general confusion....

In spite of all their differences, these young men had much in common, and especially their deep devotion to ideals, their feeling for justice and humanity, and – I should say – their purity. So much has been written after the defeat, about the "demoralization of French youth" and of Frenchmen in general, that I am glad of this opportunity to recall those young people I met at the congresses of *Esprit*. [240]

As Hélène Iswolsky's account indicates, *Esprit* was an international review and movement almost from its inception. It was not, however,

---

[238] Mounier, "Carnets, vendredi 6 juillet 1934," *E.M.*, *1905–1950*, 992.
[239] Béguin, "Une vie," 992.
[240] Iswolsky, *Light Before Dusk*, 107–110.

until after 1945 that the fame and influence of Mounier and his journal became an international phenomenon of intellectual significance. In France itself during the 1930s the circulation of the journal was exceedingly small but, as one historian wrote, *Esprit* "quickly conquered in public opinion a place comparable to that which the *Cahiers de la Quinzaine* had occupied twenty-five years before." [241]

Among the readers of the early issues of the journal were a number of the intellectual leaders of Christian democracy. Indeed the advent of *Esprit's* period of *engagement* coincided with an encounter between Mounier and one of the latter. In the pages of the new Christian democratic daily *l'aube*, Paul Archambault asked Mounier to rally to the support of Christian democracy. Mounier's encounter with Archambault and the Christian democrats enabled him to bring to bear upon one particular problem his anti-capitalism, his opposition to French democracy, and, most important, his condemnation of the tight historical bonds between his fellow Christians and "the established disorder."

241 A. Latreille *et al.*, *Histoire du catholicisme*, III, 604.

CHAPTER III

THE PARAPLEGICS OF VIRTUE:
MOUNIER AS A CRITIC OF CHRISTIAN DEMOCRACY,
1932–1934

Mardi soir, conférence aux Sillonistes.
Pauvres pâles généreux débris épuisés de douceur...

Mounier, "Entretiens VIII, 8 juin 1934."

Shortly after Emmanuel Mounier's death, a controversy took place in the pages of *Témoignage Chrétien*, the progressive Catholic weekly founded during the Resistance. It was triggered by Henri Marrou who had paid heartfelt tribute to Mounier as a *témoin*.[1] Mounier's influence, Marrou contended, was so profound that its true nature and extent could be discerned only with the aid of historical perspective. In the first decade of the century, Marrou explained, French Catholicism consisted largely of "little chapels" in which a Léon Bloy or a Charles Péguy prophesized in solitude, a few discouraged or suspect "liberal milieux," and, most important, "the ghetto of the bien-pensants." Contaminated by money, the bourgeois spirit, and the neo-paganism of *Action Française*, French Catholics looked upon Taine, Barrès, Maurras, and even Drumont as great thinkers. They were excluded from contemporary life, from political life, and from the main movements of art and science. All of this had to be recalled, Marrou stated, in order to appreciate fully the great historic revival which put an end to the tendency of French Catholicism to immigrate to its own interior and which destroyed the walls of the ghetto: "in this movement, Emmanuel Mounier was one of the most powerful influences and *Esprit* a center of ralliement."

There were immediate and angry reactions to Marrou's attempt at historical retrospection. J.-E. Bonnoront, a Social Catholic in Lyons, complained that Marrou had neglected not only the Social Catholic movement but the *Sillon* itself. The rebirth of which Marrou spoke, Bonnoront continued, was not the work of *Esprit* but rather of the *Sillon* before World War I. At that time, he added sarcastically, Mou-

---

[1] Henri Marrou, "Un témoin," *Témoignage Chrétien*, March 31, 1950

nier was about ten years old. "In contrast to the popular movement of the *Sillon, Esprit* has been purely intellectual and, consequently, has had only a very slight influence. It has included intelligent men but rarely men of practical action, and it has exercised no influence on the political life of France." The doctrine of the *Sillon*, on the other hand, produced not only the *Jeune-République*, but the M.R.P. as well. A similar complaint came from François Desgrées du Loû, the scion of the veteran Christian democratic family in Britanny which had founded *l'Ouest-Eclair* in 1898. The Social Catholics who organized the *Semaines sociales* and joined the *Sillon* did not fit Marrou's description, the director of the rechristened *l'Ouest-France* complained.[2]

The participants in this debate presented some of the elements of the misunderstanding and differences which had separated Mounier and the Christian democrats. These misunderstandings and differences are difficult to comprehend in all their multiple facets because, on Mounier's part in particular, they were rooted in factors which were not only historical and political but psychological and religious as well. In recounting the history of *Esprit* in December, 1944, Mounier touched briefly upon most of these factors. Making reference to such anterior movements as the *Sillon* and certain Christian democratic groups, he explained that although he could not deny their contributions nor that, in the main, *Esprit* had been their heir, their existence, nonetheless, was neither solely advantageous nor solely disadvantageous to *Esprit*: "they simply existed." [3] Following this ambivalent tribute to the Christian democratic predecessors of *Esprit*, Mounier devoted himself to delineating the differences between the Christian democrats and the *Esprit* movement. Whereas the former had developed within a confessional context or with a view to political activity, *Esprit* was less confessional and concerned itself with "a crisis of civilization and culture." "If you wish to use a gross word, our movement had a slightly more intellectual 'allure.' " [4] Then in a more clear but still left-handed tribute to Christian democracy, Mounier explained that the efforts of the Christian democrats had often resulted in confusion. "I do not reproach them for this. We had the advantage of coming afterwards and consequently we were able to avoid their errors and to profit from them." [5] The errors of the Christian democrats, Mounier stated fairly explicitly, consisted primarily of a confusion between the political and

[2] Réponses à Marrou," *Témoignage Chrétien*, April 14, 1950.
[3] Mounier, "Les cinq étapes d'*Esprit*," 10–11.
[4] *Ibid.*, 11.
[5] *Ibid.*

the spiritual. Mounier suggested that they failed to discern the profound bond between the political and the spiritual as well as the relative autonomy of temporal problems and spiritual problems. Moreover, they succumbed to clericalism not only in its most crude and obvious forms but in its more diffuse and serious forms. The latter resulted in a failure to confront real problems and a proclivity for rapid assimilations of a purely sentimental nature.[6] Later in the same lecture, Mounier made passing reference to one of the essential and perhaps most original facets of his criticism of the Christian democrats; Christian education, he said, cultivated on the part of its recipients inner debates and scruples at the expense of decisiveness in action.[7]

In 1932 and 1933, however, Mounier made few specific references to Christian democracy and its adherents although even the most superficial reader of *Esprit* could hardly have failed to perceive that Mounier's revolt against "the established disorder" and his condemnation of the "ghetto of the bien-pensants" had some applicability to the Christian democrats. In the third issue of the journal Mounier defended the members of the *Troisième force* against the charge that they were a "group of neo-Christians" by stating rather cryptically that the Catholic members of *Esprit* had learned the lesson of both the *Sillon* and *Action Française*.[8] In his contribution to the special issue of *Esprit* devoted to "Rupture entre l'ordre chrétien et le désordre établi," Mounier condemned the historic habit of Catholics of joining together in temporal affairs solely on the basis of common religious interests. And, in a bit of sarcasm to which the Christian democrats were to become accustomed, he referred to their program as a "recipe" which included equal portions of "doctrinal advances" and "advanced doctrines," "a little courage," and "many precautions" to dilute the total mixture.[9] In the same issue, Mounier inventoried the forces available to "us other Christians," and explicitly excluded the Christian democrats:

All of the tendencies of resistance to social conformism were paralyzed after the war by the double cadre that the heritage of the past offered: that of the *Action Française* in which liberal and parliamentary democracy was fought against courageously, but to the advantage of a traditionalist conformism which was compromised in a pagan conception of the city; that of the *Sillon* whose survivors, dispersed in the *Jeune-République* or the *Parti démocrate populaire*

---

[6] *Ibid.*
[7] *Ibid.*, 17.
[8] Mounier, "Les Jeunes radicaux et nous," *Esprit*, No. 3 (December, 1932), 493–494.
[9] Mounier, "Confessions pour nous autres chrétiens" (March, 1933), *O.M.*, I, 379–380.

compromised their generous efforts in vague political compromises and a permeated ideology.[10]

The most fruitful work was being carried on in other areas, Mounier believed: by Charles Blondel and Jacques Maritain, by Robert Garric's *Equipes sociales*, by the *Jeunesse Ouvrière Chrétienne* (J.O.C.), and the Christian syndicalist movement.[11]

It was clear that the Christian democrats were accomplices in Mounier's "established disorder." What was less clear in the early days of *Esprit* was that Mounier was to reserve a special place for the Christian democrats near the head of his rather lengthy list of *bêtes noires*. Indeed the very special character of his opposition to Christian democracy and its adherents was largely concealed at first. Even in his personal journals Mounier's references to the *Jeune-République* and the *Parti Démocrate Populaire* contained only suggestive glimmerings of his future criticisms. An entry for May 7, 1926, describing the character of the circle of studies under Professor Chevalier, stated: "It matters little whether one comes from *Action Française*, provided that force is not erected into a system, or from *Jeune République*, provided that liberalism is not made into a dogma." [12] And in November, 1932 while meditating on the future of the journal, Mounier noted in his journal: "Finally, to establish *our tone*. Without the unctuous tone, a caricature of charity à la popular democracy." [13]

Other intimations of Mounier's attitude toward the Christian democrats might conceivably have been drawn from the character of the milieux in which Mounier had lived both in Grenoble and in Paris in the decade or so prior to the founding of *Esprit*. These milieux were not those of "ghetto Catholicism," of the political Intransigents and religious Integralists, but rather those which were generally sympathetic in breaking down the walls of the ghetto and to the reconciliation of French Catholicism and the modern world.

The religious milieu of Grenoble underwent a rather marked change during Mounier's youth and young manhood. Although references to "the piety of Grenoble" remained fairly commonplace, the religious outlook of most Catholics evolved from "a rather limited piety to

---

[10] Mounier, "Ceux qui ont commence: catholiques," *Esprit*, No. 6 (March, 1933), 1025–1026.

[11] *Ibid.*, 1029.

[12] Mounier, "Entretiens II, 7 mai 1926," *O.M.*, IV, 421.

[13] Mounier, "Entretiens VI, 10 novembre 1932," *O.M.*, IV, 511.

larger preoccupations with evangelization and social action." [14] The
Sillon, for example, held its regional congress in Grenoble in 1907 and
the meeting was greeted with great enthusiasm, especially by students.
In the summer of 1907, however, the local bishop, Msgr. Henry, prohibited the dissemination of *Sillonist* literature in the Catholic schools
and forbade members of the clergy to belong to the *Sillon*. In 1910 the
bishop expressed his joy over the disappearance of a movement which
pursued "suspect paths." [15] Msgr. Henry's successor, Msgr. Maurin,
was a "vigilant guardian of doctrine," but he, in turn, was succeeded
in 1917 by Msgr. Caillot, a strong and progressive ecclesiastic. Although
he once a year affirmed the importance of the private schools and was
not unsympathetic to *Action Française*, Msgr. Caillot abstained from
intervening openly in political affairs and vigorously enforced the ban
on membership in *Action Française* in 1927.[16] More important still,
the bishop actively supported the work of the diocesan *Union* of the
Association Catholique de la Jeunesse Française (A.C.J.F.) and ultimately promoted Abbé Emile Guerry, one of its organizers, to the vicar-
generalship of the diocese. In the motto of the A.C.J.F., "Piety, study,
action," emphasis was always placed upon "study." [17]

Mounier belonged to a study circle in Abbé Guerry's working-class
parish of Saint-Laurent. Guerry was to be one of the founders of the
J.O.C. in France; later be became Archbishop-Coadjutor of Cambrai
and Secretary of the Assembly of Cardinals and Archbishops of France.
One of Mounier's friends believes that Guerry had a decisive influence
upon Mounier's religious development.[18] Mounier and Guerry remained
lifelong friends and both were staunch supporters of a group of men who
undertook an action of *présence* among the working masses at the end
of the Second World War – the controversial priest-workers. In
January, 1941 Mounier noted in his diary that Guerry was one of those
rare men who completely understood "the advent of a new phase in the
action of Catholics in profane, temporal affairs ..." [19] Mounier's
youthful experience in Guerry's parish, as well as his membership in the
Conférence de Saint-Vincent-de-Paul, the Social Catholic organization
founded by Frédéric Ozanam, initiated him into the world of poverty

---

[14] Pierre Barral, *Le Départment de l'Isère sous la Troisième République, 1870–1940. Histoire
sociale et politique* (No. 115, "Cahiers de la Fondition nationale des sciences politiques"; Paris:
Armand Colin, 1962), 273.
[15] *Ibid.*, 420.
[16] *Ibid.*, 244, 404.
[17] *Ibid.*, 264ff.
[18] "Témoignage de L. Maggiani," in *E.M.*, *1905–1950*, 948.
[19] Mounier, "Entretiens XI, 14 janvier 1941," *O.M.*, IV, 689.

and working-class misery for which he was to demonstrate such consistent and profound concern.

The study circle of Saint-Laurent took part in organizing the diocesan *Union* of the A.C.J.F. in Grenoble, and for a time Mounier was an editor of the local bulletin of the A.C.J.F., *La Jeune Dauphiné*.[20] The A.C.J.F. of this period had already come a long way from its conservative Social Catholic origins. Under the leadership of Charles Flory, the A.C.J.F. joined the *Semaines sociales* and the C.F.T.C. in separating itself from the Maurrasien Right and perhaps as a consequence from the great mass of French Catholics. Henri Marrou described the A.C.J.F. as "the last bastion of resistance by 'Catholicism of the Left' and the base for offensive action against *Action Française.*" In the judgment of Marrou, however, Mounier escaped "that frenzy of quasi-propaganda activity which characterized the period of 'Catholic Action' and its 'specialized movements.'" [21]

A former leader of the A.C.J.F., the historian and political scientist René Rémond, presented a different assessment. While the practical relationship between the A.C.J.F. and *Esprit* was to be largely one of mutual neglect, the tendencies of the specialized branches of the A.C.J.F. and those of *Esprit* went in very similar directions. The members of the J.O.C., *Jeunesse Etudiante Chrétienne* (J.E.C.), *Jeunesse Agricole Chrétienne* (J.A.C.), and other groups engaged themselves in the affairs of their respective socio-professional milieux and there they pursued their religious objectives by means of *présence* and *témoignage* rather than by attempts at outright religious conquest and active proselytizing. Rémond believed that such methods were entirely in keeping with the spirit of the *Esprit* movement.[22] Mounier, on the other hand, believed that the J.O.C. and other Catholic Action organizations were not sufficiently "open": they tended to become stultified by working within specifically Catholic milieux or towards narrowly confessional ends.[23] More serious still, the character of their spiritual training ill-prepared the members of the specialized movements for effective political action, as Mounier contended in an argument that was fundamental to his criticism of the M.R.P.[24]

[20] Barral, 264.
[21] Marrou, "Un homme dans l'Eglise," 894.
[22] René Rémond, "Droite et gauche dans le catholicisme français," *Revue française de science politique*, VIII, No. 3 (September, 1958), 542–543.
[23] Mounier, "Entretiens XI, 14 janvier 1941," *O.M.*, IV, 689.
[24] Mounier, "La jeunesse comme mythe et la jeunesse comme réalité – bilan 1940–1944," *Esprit*, No. 105 (December, 1944), 146–147.

In Grenoble, finally, Mounier probably had little direct contact with *Action Française* and its fervent adherents. Not until January, 1909 was an *Action Française* group organized in Grenoble, and even after the War when it was reorganized Maurras had few disciples in the city. Against what has been described as "the influential nucleus" of *Action Française* in the University, however, a *Ligue d'action universitaire républicaine et socialiste* was organized in 1926.[25] As Marrou noted, Mounier himself was "always profoundly foreign and hostile to the tendencies of *Action Française*" not only because of his social background but even more because of his education. Jacques Chevalier warned his students against "'pride, the eternal heresy, that of *Action Française*,'" and he viewed Maurras' organization as the embodiment of "the greatest heresy of modern times since the Reformation." [26] Mounier appears to have largely escaped what has been called "the tyranny with which the furious clan of *Action Française* then burdened French Catholicism" and "the atmosphere of police-like terror that reigned in the Church because of the Integralism incarnated in the men of *Action Française*." [27] In later years the youths of *Action Française* often tried to break up meetings of the *Amis d'Esprit* in provincial towns, but neither this nor the venomous attacks upon *Esprit* from the pens of the supporters of Maurras prevented Mounier from occasionally equating the errors of the Christian democrats with those of *Action Française*. This was in part a measure of Mounier's antipathy towards Christian democracy but it was also perhaps a result of the fact that Mounier had not lived as a youth or young adult in a milieu dominated by the *Polititique d'abord* of *Action Française*. Even during the late 1920s and 1930 the Rightist leagues had little success in Genoble.[28]

There is also perhaps some significance in the fact that the political climate of Grenoble was largely Radical in *laïcist* circles and only moderately conservative in Catholic circles. The influence of Jacques Piou's *rallié Action Libérale Populaire* was profound and lasting in Grenoble. It was not unusual for almost all of the parliamentary liberals in the city to attend the speeches of Paul Jouvin, the local leader of *Action Libérale Populaire*. After the First World War most of the veterans of Piou's party joined the conservative *Fédération Républicaine*. In 1925 local members of Catholic Action formed a federation of

[25] Barral, 308, 404. See also Eugen Weber, *Action Française. Royalism and Reaction in Twentieth-Century France* (Stanford, Calif.: Stanford University Press, 1962), 174–177.
[26] Marrou, "Un homme dans l'Eglise," 894.
[27] Marrou, "La signification religieuse de la pensée d'Emmanuel Mounier," 26.
[28] Barral, 404–405.

the *Parti Démocrate Populaire* which at one time had in excess of 2,000 members in the Isère. Among the latter was one of the best-known professors in the University, Jean-Jacques Chevalier. The little *Jeune-République*, on the other hand, had only three fairly prominent militants in Grenoble.[29]

Among Mounier's associations during the years preceding the founding of *Esprit*, several merit particular attention. One was the *Davidées*.[30] Between 1929 and 1932 Mounier contributed regularly to the various journals of the *Davidées* and attended several of its weekend meetings in the South of France. Mounier's full debt to his association with the *Davidées* is difficult to measure, but the intensity of feeling with which he recorded his meetings with Mlle. Silve and her organization in his diary and letters leaves little doubt as to the importance that he himself attached to it. He referred to a meeting of the *Davidées* as "days of purity and light" which were the most beautiful hours of his life. "No false mysticism, no earthly pride, no duplicity." [31] To his sister Madeleine, Mounier referred to "that incomparable Mlle. Silve" and said that among the *Davidées* he could breathe freely without any of the constraints or barriers of party-taking and with the profound assurance that there would be no attempt "to justify the unjustifiable, to make half-truths pass for articles of faith." She could never know, he told Madeleine, the joy with which he encountered such a group.[32]

Among the thirty some articles which Mounier contributed to the little journals of the *Davidées*, a number give substance to Mlle. Silve's later contention that "they can almost be considered to be the outline of his entire [future] work." [33] In "L'étranger," "L'événement et nous," and "De l'action intellectuelle ou de l'influence," Mounier revealed several of his most constant characteristics and concerns: his remarkable openness to men and events; his continuous battle against the debilitating effects of habit; his opposition to the distorted religiosity of "ghetto Catholicism"; and his belief in the efficacy of intellectual action.[34] On the occasion of an attack upon the *Davidées* by Marceau

---

[29] *Ibid.*, 335, 375.

[30] On the *Davidées*, see Jean Guitton, *les davidées. Mouvement d'apostolat laïc, 1916–1966* (Paris: Casterman, 1967).

[31] Mounier, "Entretiens II, 29–31 août 1929, Journées intellectuelles à Notre Dame du Laus," *O.M.*, IV, 449.

[32] Mounier, "Lettre à Madeleine Mounier, 18 avril 1929," *O.M.*, IV, 444.

[33] Quoted in P.M. [Paulette Mounier], "Liminaire," *B.A.E.M.*, No. 3 (April, 1953), 2.

[34] Mounier, "L'étranger" and "L'événement et nous," *Aux Davidées*, May, 1930, and December, 1930, reprinted in *B.A.E.M.*, No. 3 (April, 1953), 3–16; and Mounier, "De l'action intellectuelle ou de l'influence," *Revue de Culture Générale*, October-December, 1931, and January-May, 1932, reprinted in *B.A.E.M.*, No. 4 (January, 1954), 2–16.

Pivert of the *Ligue de l'enseignement,* Mounier defended Mlle. Silve's movement against the charge that their Catholicism and their obligations to the state were irreconcilable: that as lay teachers they were committed not to interfere in the religious training of their students, but that as Catholics they were incapable of doing so. In answering this charge, Mounier wrote a brief history of the *Davidées* and described its objectives in a manner which revealed nearly as much about himself and his debt to the *Davidées* as it did about Mlle. Silve and her movement.[35]

The *Davidées* began spontaneously and informally on the eve of the First World War. It consisted of a small group of young Catholic women who taught in the public schools of the small villages of the Basses-Alpes. Under the leadership of Marie Silve, who taught in Saint-Pons, the young women adopted the name *Davidées* from Davidée Birot, the heroine of René Bazin's novel of the same name. In this fictional character they found "the example of a delicate conscience and a devoted soul, sustained by the same love of her [teaching] profession and the same desire for loyalty." The motives of the young women were spiritual, professional, and cultural: spiritually, they sought to renew and deepen their religious lives which had been either disrupted by their years in the *Ecole Normale* or made more difficult by the circumstances of their profession; professionally, they were committed to teaching in public schools and improving their pedagogical methods; and culturally, they were committed to their own intellectual development which they believed was inseparable from their spiritual growth. Mounier pointed out that deepening and sustaining the spiritual lives of its members was therefore both the point of departure and the final purpose of the *Davidées.*

The unity that Mounier discerned in these multiple purposes presaged much of his own later work. Even his description of the communal spirit, the mutual affection, the fraternal confidence, and the common approach to important questions without jeopardizing the individuality of its members which were characteristic of the *Davidées* brings to mind many of the elements which were to be the basis of the *Esprit* movement. "The group labors particularly for the conquest of itself, for it professes that the work of conversion is more exacting for the Christian than for any one else," Mounier said. "Their adversaries ... who expect to find sectarians, are very surprised to encounter only

---

[35] François Chauvières [Emmanuel Mounier], "Une amitié spirituelle: les Davidées," *la Vie spirituelle,* Vol. 27 (April, 1931), 66–91, reprinted in Guitton, *les davidées,* 82–108.

open ... persons ... 'Large in spirit, a *Davidée* is accustomed to en-
countering views which differ from her own and does not set herself
up as a judge.'" In his conclusion, Mounier suggested that the future
perhaps belonged to Christians like the *Davidées* – an elite which sought
the truth not in habit or in sentimentality but rather in the study
necessary to increase its own competence.

It is only a slight exaggeration to say that the young *agrégé* who attended the meetings of the *Davidées* was very much the same man who
guided the *Esprit* movement for almost two decades. Mlle. Silve has
recalled that

> what struck me about him were the two great virtues which characterized him,
> it seems to me, throughout his short life. First, a great love of truth; on this
> subject he expressed himself with unforgettable intensity. Then, an immense
> generosity which was already oriented in the direction of the people, towards
> those who suffer from the social conditions in which they work.[36]

In view of all this, it is perhaps unfair to append the fact that even the
Davidées did not escape Mounier's penchant for criticism. The journal
of the movement, he complained, suffered somewhat from "a spirit of
the catacombs." [37]

Other young *agrégés* and teachers attended the meetings of the
Davidées. Among them were Etienne Borne, Jean Lacroix, André Latreille, Jacques Madaule, Joseph Hours, and Jean Guitton. Guitton was
a friend both of Mounier and a priest who was largely responsible for
Mounier's solid religious training. The priest was an aged Lazarist
named Père Pouget, who was also a good friend of Jacques Chevalier;
indeed, Chevalier always sent his best students to Pouget upon their
arrival in Paris. During his lifetime, Pouget, like Teilhard de Chardin,
exercised a profound influence within the confines of a relatively small
and select group of Catholic intellectuals. And like Teilhard de Chardin also, Pouget was a man of encyclopedic knowledge and interests
whose fame was to be almost entirely posthumous.[38] His interests
ranged from theology and philosophy through Greek, Hebrew, and
Latin to mathematics, physics, and geology. At a time when Mounier's
own interests were somewhat diffuse, he undoubtedly found the company of the Lazarist both congenial and rewarding.

From late 1927 until Pouget's death in early 1933 Mounier studied

---

[36] "Notes de Mlle Marie Silve," *E.M.*, *1905–1950*, 961–962.
[37] Mounier, "Entretiens II, 5 mars 1930," *O.M.*, IV, 462.
[38] The posthumous fame of Pouget is due largely to Jean Guitton's books: *Portrait de M.
Pouget* (Paris: Nouvelle Revue Française, 1941); *Dialogues avec Monsieur Pouget* (Paris:
Grasset, 1954); and *Monsieur Pouget* (Paris: Gallimard, 1954).

with the old priest in his little room on the rue du Bac in Paris regularly two afternoons a week. He filled little notebooks with material on the Bible, the history of religions, the two Saint Theresas, St. John of the Cross, the themes of action and meditation, and other subjects of a similar nature.[39] Jean Daniélou recalled that Mounier also studied the papers of Pouget which "were really courses in theology." [40] Unlike his association with the *Davidées*, Mounier's debt to Pouget, apart from his solid grounding and marked interest in theology, remains elusive. One fact, however, seems certain. Pouget, who was a one-time colleague of Loisy the Modernist leader, was an opponent of the Integralists and he would not have guided his pupil in the direction of the restricted and narrow views of his old antagonists. Jean Guitton contended that Mounier strengthened his own extremely efficacious conception of Christianity in the cell of Pouget and there also found a "sublime example of evangelical poverty and of sovereign and humble independence." [41] In a letter to Jacques Chevalier Mounier wrote of Pouget simply that "when I am in his presence it seems to me that I am confronting the truth." [42]

Mounier's other friendships in Paris were with circles that were noted for their interest in the many problems relating to the adaptation of Catholicism to the modern world. Jean Daniélou was to be one of the leaders of the progressive Jesuit community of Fourvières. Henri Brémond, under whom Mounier investigated one of his thesis topics, was no friend of the Integralists. Dominican Père Henri de Lubac, who after a period of difficulties with his religious superiors emerged as a *peritus* at the Second Vatican Council, was also a long-time friend of Mounier, as were other Dominicans of Juvisy. Through their Editions du Cerf, the latter published *la Vie spirituelle* and *la Vie intellectuelle*, and Mounier contributed articles to both of these monthly journals. Later when the Dominican Père Bernadot founded *Sept*, Mounier and other members of the *Esprit* group contributed to the journal. Mounier, as has been noted, also contributed to Francisque Gay's *La Vie Catholique* and he was conversant with the *Cahiers de la Nouvelle Journée*, the Christian democratic series of books edited by Paul Archambault. None of the foregoing – priests, laymen, and journals – belonged to the "ghetto of the bien-pensants."

[39] Editor's note, Mounier, "Lettre à Jacques Chevalier, novembre 1927," O.M., IV, 428–429; and Béguin, "Une vie," 958–959.
[40] "Témoignage du R. P. Jean Daniélou," E.M., 1905–1950, 959.
[41] "Notes de Jean Guitton," E.M., 1905–1950, 959.
[42] Mounier, "Lettre à Jacques Chevalier, novembre 1927," O.M., IV, 428–429.

This was particularly true of the monthly meetings of intellectuals and artists organized by Jacques and Raïssa Maritain in their home in Meudon. These Sunday meetings were an outgrowth of the *cercles d'études thomistes* which Maritain had initiated in late 1919.[43] The first members of the group were personal friends of the Maritains and some of Maritain's students from the *Institut Catholique* who gathered in the house on the rue du Parc for informal discussions of Thomist philosophy and its relevance to contemporary life. The meetings gradually expanded to include men and women of all ages, students and professors, laymen and clerics, philosophers, doctors, poets, musicians, Catholics, Protestants, Jews, members of the Orthodox faith, and agnostics. Although Thomism remained the central interest of Maritain himself, over the years the Meudon gatherings discussed an incredibly wide range of subjects. "An incessant stream of visitors arrived [at Meudon] by the little electric train from Paris," one of the visitors recalled. "In the Meudon villa, I saw most of the men who contributed at that time to the French Catholic revival, as well as many distinguished writers and artists, who though not participating in this movement, were personal friends of Maritain." [44] Nicolas Berdiaev, who often visited the Maritains and hosted similar gatherings in his own home in Clarmat, characterized the members of this circle as "the flower of contemporary French Catholicism." [45] Among the visitors to Meudon were Catholics and non-Catholics: Abbé Louis Journet, Henri Ghéon, Jean Cocteau, Maxime Jacob, Etienne Gilson, Yves Simon, Charles du Bos, Gabriel Marcel, Ramon Fernandez, Daniel Halévy, Merleau-Ponty, Stanislas Fumet, Louis Massignon, Igor Stravinsky, Marc Chagall, Nicholas Nabokoff, and many others.

On Sunday, April 17, 1932 a "less well attended meeting" was held at Meudon, "especially for *Esprit*." [46] Among the visitors who were to collaborate with *Esprit* were Berdiaev, Izard, Déléage, Etienne Borne, Claude Bourdet, and Hélène Iswolsky. Berdiaev recalled, however, that "I was present at the meeting at which *Esprit* was founded. This took place in the home of I. [Izard], a left-wing Roman Catholic, subsequently a Deputy and a member of the Socialist Party .... I was greatly moved when at the foundation meeting it was unanimously adopted that the fundamental purpose and concern of *Esprit* should be the vindication

[43] Jacques Maritain, *Carnet de notes* (Paris: Desclée de Brouwer, 1965), 183.
[44] Iswolsky, *Light Before Dusk*, 85, 70–87.
[45] Berdyaev, *Dream and Reality*, 264.
[46] Maritain, *Carnet de notes*, 227.

of man." [47] Meudon provided Mounier with an opportunity to meet such men as Maritain, Marcel, and Berdiaev, who gave the fledgling *Esprit* movement invaluable, and perhaps indispensable, support. Of equal importance, at Meudon and Clarmat Mounier met a great number of noted intellectuals and artists with whom the adherents of "ghetto Catholicism" had little or no contact and with whom even the "democrats of Christian inspiration" had little or no contact because of their tendency to limit their friendship and associations to other "sons of the Spirit." Perhaps the Meudon meetings also impressed upon Mounier the possibility of duplicating in the *Esprit* movement the atmosphere of friendship and sympathetic understanding among an extremely diverse group of men and women which characterized the Meudon meetings. Mounier's first examination of the problem of cooperation between "Christians and nonbelievers" in *Esprit* drew directly upon Maritain's work.[48]

If in some respects Mounier's debt to Maritain and the Meudon meetings is fairly clear, the relationship between the two men was not without its complexities. Philosophically, Mounier had little sympathy for Maritain's Thomism. He was far more sympathetic to the work of two other visitors to Meudon, Gabriel Marcel and Nicolas Berdiaev. On the "existentialist tree" in his *Introduction aux existentialismes*, Mounier labeled a neighboring branch of his own personalism branch G. Marcel, and another branch of the tree is labelled Berdiaev.[49] A long-time friend of Mounier wrote that

From the point of view of political temperament, and even of temperament alone, Marcel is the complete opposite of Emmanuel Mounier, who was the herald of the emancipation of the poor and the uncontested leader of a numerous team of young intellectuals, who were all far from sharing his Christian beliefs. It was, however, as a disciple of Gabriel Marcel that Mounier realized more and more the irreducible character of the human act and understood the dignity of the person, which one is not entitled to sacrifice to any temporal end. He also derived from Marcel the profound unease which never allowed him to rest on the ready-made, in the certainty of a tranquil possession of his sociological position as well as his Christian faith. During the twenty years of my acquaintance with Mounier, I never saw him engage in the "dialectic of having." Being, existential being, was his main preoccupation.[50]

And, of Mounier's debt to Berdiaev, the same man wrote that Mounier

---

[47] Berdyaev, *Dream and Reality*, 274.

[48] Mounier, "Chrétiens et incroyants" (February, 1936), *O.M.*, I, 859–869; and Mounier, "Pluralisme chrétien," *Esprit*, No. 32 (May, 1935), 284–285.

[49] Mounier, *Introduction aux existentialismes*, *O.M.*, III, 71.

[50] Ignace Lepp, *A Christian Philosophy of Existence*, trans. Lilian Soiron (Springfield, Ill.: Templegate, 1954), 115.

had a profound admiration for the Russian exile. "The two men had the same keen sense of the involvement of the spiritual in the temporal history of humanity, and the same horror of a disembodied intellectualism which took no account of the economic and political realities of the human condition, or compromised itself with outworn forms of civilization." [51]

In a tribute to Péguy and Maritain in 1939, Mounier himself stated that the "renewal of Christian realism" was due to these two men. Mounier explained that Péguy and Maritain were the masters of Christian personalist youths, the former because he "oriented us, body and soul, in the direction of the Incarnation," and the latter because he turned these youths away from the sin of *angélisme*.[52] Maritain, on the other hand, was critical of Mounier's Font-Romeu manifesto, of what he considered to be Mounier's exaggerated emphasis upon "the necessary revolution," of Mounier's supposed neglect of doctrinal work in *Esprit*, and of Mounier's tendency to give greater credit to modern thought than to such traditional philosophies as Maritain's own Thomism.[53] Later in the 1930s Maritain found himself allied with Mounier and *Esprit* on the question of the Spanish Civil War, and in 1942 he wrote that "despite certain inevitable errors, the work of *Esprit* was extremely fruitful particularly as regards the chief aim indicated above: to destroy the prejudices and misunderstandings which caused Christianity to be confused with the forces of wealth and social reaction." Along with several other journals of the Catholic avant-garde, Maritain said, *Esprit* "planted in French soil the seeds of reconciliation between the ancient opposing traditions – the France of religious faithfulness and spirituality, and the France of human emancipation." [54]

To describe the milieux in which the attitudes and ideas of the young Mounier matured is not merely to belabor the obvious. Nor is it necessarily to assign politico-social labels to Mlle. Silve, Père Pouget or others, although there are certain general correlations between doctrinal tendencies and political options within French Catholicism.[55]

---

[51] *Ibid.*, 115–116.

[52] Mounier, "Hérésiophages," *Esprit*, No. 81 (June, 1939), 439.

[53] Béguin, "Une vie," 982; Mounier, "Entretiens VI, 23 septembre 1932," *O.M.*, IV, 503–504; Mounier, "Entretiens VI, 9 novembre 1932," *O.M.*, IV, 511. See also the correspondence between Mounier and Maritain published in *B.A.E.M.*, No. 34–35 (November, 1969), 3–65 *passim*.

[54] Jacques Maritain, "Religion and Politics in France," *Foreign Affairs*, Vol. 20, No. 2 (January, 1942), 273.

[55] For a brilliant examination of this question, see René Rémond, "Droite et gauche dans le catholicisme française," *Revue française de science politique*, VIII, No. 3 (September, 1958), 529–544, and No. 4 (December, 1958), 803–820.

Rather, in a country where intellectial circles and friendships play such an important role, such factors can be ignored only a great risk. Moreover, the foregoing suggests that Mounier's rebellion against "the established disorder" had some special reference to the Catholic avant-garde which his writings in *Esprit* in 1932 and 1933 did not clearly reveal. This possible ambiguity in Mounier's position was irrevocably removed as a result of a debate in the pages of *l'aube* in the first months of 1934.

Mounier's antagonist in this debate was Paul Archambault who, of all of the "democrats of Christian inspiration." probably paid closest attention to Mounier and the young *Esprit* movement in 1932 and 1933. To his encounter with the young director of *Esprit* Archambault brought impeccable credentials as both a veteran Christian democrat and as a philosopher. Archambault had been a member of the *Sillon*, the entente of Christian democrats and Social Catholics formed around *l'âme française* in 1919, and the *Parti Démocrate Populaire*. He was also a collaborator of *Politique*, Francisque Gay's *La Vie Catholique, le Petit Démocrate*, Sangnier's *l'Eveil des peuples*, and *l'aube*, as well as the founder and director of the *Cahiers de la Nouvelle Journée*. Archambault was a philosopher of note. A disciple of Maurice Blondel, the philosopher of "L'Action," Archambault was for thirty years professor of moral and social philosophy in the Collège Sainte-Croix in Neuilly as well as a laureate of the *Académie des Sciences Morales et Politiques*. He has been variously praised as having accomplished a symbolic liaison between Sangnier and Péguy, as a "philosopher of disquiet," and as a personalist philosopher before personalism itself was an acceptable term within Christian democratic and Social Catholic circles.[56]

The latter explains, at least in part, the sympathy with which Archambault greeted the publication of *Esprit* as well as the slight resentment he was to betray in later years when personalism was regarded by many as being something of a private preserve of the *Esprit* movement. In 1913 Archambault published an *Essai sur l'Individualisme* in which he examined the work of such early "personalists" as Renouvier and Laberthonnière. Archambault pointed out that Christian democrats were confronted with the task of elaborating a philosophy which manifested their opposition to any doctrine of individualism. For such a

---

[56] See Etienne Borne, "Actualité du Blondelisme. A la mémoire de Paul Archambault," *Terre humaine*, No. 2 (February, 1951), 90–96; Jacques Nanteuil, "Paul Archambault, philosophe de l'inquiétude," *La Démocratie*, No. 5–6 (February-March, 1932), 372–377; "Paul Archambault, témoin d'une génération (1883–1950)," *Etudes*, CCLXVIII, No. 6 (February, 1951), 254–255; and Pierre Dournes, "Paul Archambault," *L'Amitié Charles Péguy*, No. 19 (January, 1951), 5–7.

Christian democratic philosophy, Archambault proposed, but did not use, the terms "personalism" or "spiritualism." [57] He did not use the term "personalism," he later explained, because the times were not propitious: among Social Catholics "personalism" had a certain Kantian ring and among his fellow *Sillonists* even the term "human person" had *laïcist* and rationalist connotations. Otherwise, he said, the book would have been entitled *Essai sur le Personnalisme*.[58]

In the late 1920s and early 1930s, however, Archambault proposed that the *Parti Démocrate Populaire* adopt the term "personalism" and he paid particular tribute to Maurice Hauriou's theory of Institutionalism for its "personalist perspective" as well as to Marcel Prélot and Robert Cornilleau for "rediscovering" the personalist inspiration of Christian democracy.[59] Whether or not this was merely a verbal coincidence with Mounier's personalism is difficult to determine – certainly Mounier believed it to be nothing more than this – but there are a number of general similarities between Archambault's own philosophical position and some of the social and political inferences he drew from it, on one hand, and Mounier's *pensée engagée*, on the other.

Like Mounier, Archambault rejected Julien Benda's proposed solution to the problem of "intellectuals and citizens." [60] Archambault's view was that a philosophy which neglected the practical world of the man of action was a betrayal of the function of the intellectual. Thought must necessarily submit to the requirements of the practical and the real. Moreover, not unlike Mounier's *pensée engagée*, Archambault's philosophy was rooted in the conviction that thought finds its ultimate fulfillment in action. For Archambault, as for the *Jeunes équipes*, "intelligence is a sword." Archambault's solution to the problem posed by Benda, therefore, was not "intellectuals *or* citizens" but rather "intellectuals *and* citizens." Like Mounier also, Archambault believed that "disquiet" is a permanent element of the human condition. Just as Mounier condemned the inherent dangers of habit, Archambault welcomed "disquiet" as a necessary and natural condition of thought and action. At the very heart of Archambault's "philosophy of

[57] Paul Archambault, *Essai sur l'Individualisme* (Paris: Bloud, 1913), 2–4.
[58] Archambault, "Du personnalisme au marxisme: une aventure spirituelle," 482.
[59] See, for example, Paul Archambault, "Introduction" in Maurice Hauriou, *Aux sources du droit* (No. 23; "Cahiers de la Nouvelle Journée"; Paris: Bloud & Gay, 1933), 7; and Archambault, "Réalisme démocratique," 305.
[60] Paul Archambault, "Clercs et citoyens," *Politique*, 2ᵉ année, No. 2 (February, 1928), 97–109.

disquiet" was an attempt to embrace and to synthesize all of the complexities, diversities, and contradictions of human nature.[61]

Archambault's philosophy precluded the possibility of constructing a utopian City. The "better City" in the title of one of Archambault's most important books, *Pierres d'attente pour une Cité meilleure*, was not an ideal or perfect City but rather a never-ending effort to make "habitable the temporal abode in which we must live, in which our children are being prepared to live in their turn, and to this end to draw up an inventory of our difficulties and resources, to recall the permanent exigencies of human destiny, of the human vocation, to mark out the paths now available for our labors ..." [62] If there was much in *Pierres d'attente* with which Mounier and a devotée of *Esprit* would have vigorously disagreed, there was ample evidence that Archambault was a close student of *Esprit* and the other *Jeunes équipes*, and that he was not unsympathetic to many of their aims and aspirations.

As early as November, 1932 after the publication of the first two issues of *Esprit*, Archambault commented on the new journal. *Esprit*, he said in language hardly pleasing to Mounier, was not only a review but a tradition to be maintained and an effort to be continued. "We feel at home with the founders of *Esprit*." Archambault nonetheless found *Esprit* dissatisfying in many respects. "The faculty of repudiation of these young men is excessive," he complained. What they were against was amply clear: materialism, egoism and hypocrisy, capitalist exploitation and Communist tyranny, nationalism, militarism, and a certain kind of pacifism, the bourgeois and the barbarians.

> They tell us endlessly of the action to be begun, of the betrayals to be denounced, of the false values to be revised, of the revolutions to be undertaken. They proclaim themselves united above all by a "common impossibility of living." They thus participate, in the highest degree it would seem, in that catastrophic and apocalyptic mentality which is one of the signs of our time. But for what and for whom are they...? What precise formula of thought and action do they propose to use?
>
> Of course I think that I can see what troubles them. All political groups are repugnant to them and any technical correction to their views seems to them to be compromise. Comprising men of different religious and metaphysical beliefs, they do not wish to identify themselves with any specific philosophy.

Archambault then asked if this position was a tenable one in view of the fact that the members of *Esprit* contended that their group was not only a "meeting place" but a center of life and action. Could the spiri-

---

[61] Paul Archambault, *Plaidoyer l'Inquiétude* (Paris: Bloud & Gay, 1932).

[62] Paul Archambault, *Pierres d'attente pour une Cité meilleure* (No. 29; "Cahiers de la Nouvelle Journée"; Paris: Bloud & Gay, 1935), 7.

tual be put forward as a principle of action without considering its temporal applications, Archambault asked. "It is well to talk about assuring the worker the integral benefits of his work, etc., but is this a futuristic myth or a positive position? At the time when I must choose between a Popular Democrat and a Socialist, I will want *Esprit* to tell me for whom I ought to vote." In addition, the incessant use of the word "revolution" in the pages of *Esprit* troubled Archambault. "Do you really believe," he asked Mounier, "that you can construct the society of tomorrow without making any impression upon the society of today? With what will I work if you crush between your hands those instruments of civilization and culture to which the past has devoted so much sincere effort, whatever you may think of them?" [63]

Later Archambault's criticism became even more biting. In an examination of *Esprit* and other journals of the *Jeunes équipes*, Archambault was struck by the various uses to which the term "personalism" was put by the new generation.[64] He praised Mounier's personalism as an "open" humanism but confessed his irritation at Mounier's tendency to "gush forth" with sentiments and ideas which lacked doctrinal coherence. Mounier's facility of enthusiasm and indignation were not, in Archambault's judgment, matched by his power of analysis, organization and concrete realization. Although Archambault sympathized with what he called Mounier's "social romanticism," he added that Mounier could continue to reject the discipline necessary to make his position effective only at great risk.[65]

Thus began a debate between Mounier and one of the foremost Christian democratic philosophers of the interwar decades. Archambault had already revealed the main elements of the Christian democratic response to Mounier and *Esprit*. Nothing was more characteristic of that response than Archambault's statement that "we feel at home with the founders of *Esprit*," and his complaint that *Esprit* failed to provide him with guidance when he entered the voting booth. Archambault's response reflected the basic and necessary reformism of the Christian democrats which Mounier's revolutionary opposition to "the established disorder" precluded him from accepting. But Archambault invited Mounier to join forces with the "democrats of Christian inspiration." "Why," Archambault asked, "considering all that you attribute

[63] P.A. [Paul Archambault], "Esprit," *Politique*, 6ᵉ année, No. 11 (November, 1932), 1034–1036.
[64] Paul Archambault, "Destin d'un mot," *Politique*, 8ᵉ année, No. 2 (February, 1934), 154–156.
[65] *Ibid.*, 158–159.

to it or bring to it, why do you keep yourself so much outside of the great democratic tradition – I mean the democratic tradition of spiritualist and personalist inspiration which alone counts in our eyes?" "Your place," Archambault added, "is not among those who strive to discredit the democratic idea. It is in the avant-garde of those who fight for it." [66]

The avant-garde to which Archambault referred was the entente of "sons of the Spirit" which had gathered around the new Parisian daily *l'aube*. *L'aube* was almost entirely the result of the labors of the veteran Christian democratic publicist Francisque Gay. Gay was a veteran of the *Sillon* and a partner in the publishing house of Bloud et Gay. Except for a brief period immediately after the First World War when he was secretary-general of the Seine federation of the *Jeune-République*, Gay belonged to no political party, Christian democratic or otherwise. In 1924 he began publication of the weekly *La Vie Catholoque* which "affirmed the primacy of the name Catholic over all intellectual or political differences." [67] The new venture was initially a great success. It obtained the support of Catholics ranging from Sangnier and Archambault to such supporters of *Action Française* as Henri Massis and Maurice Denis as well as of influential members of the hierarchy both in France and Rome. The unity of *La Vie Catholique* was shattered, however, by the crisis of the condemnation of *Action Française* during which Gay quickly established himself as one of the foremost defenders of the papal action.[68] Indeed, Gay's battles against the men of *Action Française* were characterized by a violence which alienated even some of his own friends and made him a "marked" man for the rest of his life.[69] With the unity of *La Vie Catholique*'s clientele broken, the possibility of publishing a Parisian daily which would be completely separated from the Maurrasian Right was explored and after a lengthy search for collaborators and sufficient finances, *l'aube* appeared on January 20, 1932. Completely independent of religious authorities, of various groupings of the Christian democratic family, and of external financial pressures, *l'aube* nonetheless suffered from what Gay himself called its "original sin." "Neither Emmanuel Mounier nor Jacques Maritain, especially, would excuse it from being in some way the off-

[66] Paul Archambault, "La démocratie et la révolution. Lettre ouverte à M. Emmanuel Mounier," *l'aube*, January 21–22, 1934.

[67] Mayeur, *l'aube*, 12.

[68] See Francisque Gay, *Non, l'"Action française" n'a bien servi ni l'Eglise, ni la France* (Paris: Bloud & Gay, 1927), and *Comment j'ai défendu le Pape* (Paris: Bloud & Gay, 1927).

[69] Mayeur, *l'aube*, 13.

spring of *La Vie Catholique* and the heir of quarrels with *L'Action française.*[70]

Unlike *La Vie Catholique*, *l'aube* was a political journal. The masthead of the paper proclaimed: "*L'Aube*, organ of a spiritual family: unity of orientation but diversity of tendencies." Both of its editors, Gay and Gaston Tessier, disclaimed the possibility, or even the desirability, of any strict correlation between religious convictions and the political positions of the paper. *L'aube* was not an organ of the "Catholics of the Left," but the manifesto of the paper made it clear that "Catholics are not necessarily reactionaries and nationalists. ... It is toward men of the Left, toward men of the Left alone, that we must obstinately turn ourselves in order to demand and claim our place in the avant-garde of the partisans of social progress and international accord."[71] The original collaborators in this avant-garde included Marius Gonin of the *Chronique sociale;* André Cochinal, Georges Bidault, Robert Cornilleau, and Raymond-Laurent of the *Parti Démocrate Populaire;* Georges Hoog and Louis Dannenmüller of the *Jeune-République;* Adéodat Boissard of the *Semaines sociales;* Joseph Zamanski of the *Confédération française des professions;* Paul Archambault and Jean Lacroix of the *Cahiers de la Nouvelle Journée;* and innumerable other Catholics. Speaking for this somewhat disparate group, Archambault issued his invitation to Mounier.

Archambault argued that those facets of democracy condemned by Mounier were merely historical accidents with which the system had become contaminated. Capitalism, individualism, statism, and parliamentarianism did not constitute the essence of the democratic system. Democracy, Archambault stated, repeating the classic definition of his *Sillonist* youth, was any regime in which the human person could fulfill himself by the continuous expansion of his participation in the affairs of his community. "Person" and "community," he added, were words close to the heart of the editor of *Esprit.* To call for the revolutionary overthrow of the democratic republic because of its temporary shortcomings was both illusory and unjust. It was illusory because, even granting the availability of the forces necessary to undertake a revolution at the present time, such a revolution would have to be undertaken against the best French democrats, including those of Christian inspiration. It was unjust because it would involve the repudiation of the democratic *mystique* for which "the solution is not to

[70] *Ibid.,* 18.
[71] *l'aube,* November 9, 1932.

overthrow the democratic republic but to reform it and renew it. ..."

The editor of the *Cahiers de la Nouvelle Journée* concluded his open letter with a short lecture which Mounier, in his youthful rebellion against his elders, was to find particularly distasteful. The *Esprit* group, Archambault predicted, would descend from the "sky of abstract principles to the ground of our daily battles" just as Jacques Maritain had done by elaborating a Christian democratic program. "Your place," Archambault told Mounier, "is not among those who strive to discredit the democratic idea. It is in the avant-garde of those who fight for it – wherever they fight, so that they may profit from your youthful vigor and enthusiasm."

Archambault's reference to Maritain's "Christian democratic program" was immediately denied by the Thomist philosopher.[72] Mounier's response, on the other hand, was delayed more than a month by what he told Archambault were "the unexpected events through which we are living." [73] Mounier's reference was to the violence of February, 1934 which ushered in the final crisis years of the Third Republic and to which Mounier reacted by writing his first commentary on a specific contemporary event: "Leçons de l'émeute ou la révolution contre les mythes." [74]

Even today the true nature of the riot of February 6, 1934 is the subject of historical debate. The events themselves, however, are well known. On the evening of February 6 a large mob of some 40,000 Parisians, including members of various veterans organizations and such anti-republican and para-military leagues as *Action Française's Camelots du Roi*, Pierre Taittinger's *Jeunesses Patriotes*, and Colonel de La Rocque's *Croix de Feu*, attempted to storm the Chamber of Deputies. The ostensible reason for the demonstration was to protest the government's failure to prosecute those responsible for the Stavisky scandal – a bond scandal in which a number of politicians and bureaucrats were implicated – as well as the dismissal of Jean Chiappe, the Rightist Prefect of Police in Paris. The demonstration was staged to coincide with the presentation of a new cabinet (the sixth in eighteen months) headed by the Radical-Socialist Edouard Daladier. By the early hours of the morning of February 7 fifteen people had been killed and over

---

[72] "Au sujet de 'la démocratie et la révolution.' Une lettre de M. Jacques Maritain," *l'aube*, January 25, 1934.

[73] Mounier, "La démocratie et la révolution. Lettre ouverte à Paul Archambault, 20 février 1934," *l'aube*, February 27, 1934, reprinted in *O.M.*, I, 292–297.

[74] Mounier, "Leçons de l'émeute ou la révolution contre les mythes" (March, 1934), *O.M.*, I, 361–369.

1,000 injured, many of them seriously. The following day, with the threat of further violence in the air, the Daladier government resigned and a new "government of national union" headed by Gaston Doumergue was organized, only the extreme Right, the Socialists and Communists being excluded. Tension was further heightened when the Communists called for a demonstration on February 9 to bring about the dissolution of both the Chamber and the Rightist leagues and when the *Confédération Générale du Travail* called for a general strike on February 12. The anti-fascist demonstration of February 9 resulted in the death of six men and the general strike of February 12 brought all but essential services to a stop for twenty-four hours. Most significantly, the Left organized itself to "bar the route of fascism" and in the following two years the Popular Front was built. The Popular Front, the alliance of Radical Socialists, Socialists, and Communists, "would never have been possible without a common and deeply rooted conviction that the Sixth was a carefully planned assault on the Republic, a recurrence of the desperate attacks of the 1880s and 1890s by reactionaries who were now dressed up as 'fascists.'" [75]

In January, 1934 Mounier had warned of the dangers of the infiltration of Fascist "pseudo-values" into France.[76] His immediate response to the events of February, 1934, however, did not mark a departure from his "neither-nor" position. Certainly he refused to accept either the Left's belief that February 6th was a "fascist plot" or the Right's contention that Daladier intended to set up some sort of Jacobin dictatorship of the Left in alliance with the Communists. Later Mounier contended that in March, 1934 he had denounced the "pre-fascism" of February 6th as well as the way in which the Communists had exploited the situation, but that at the same time he had "very clearly recognized what was promising in the reaction of February 12." [77] A careful reading of Mounier's "Leçons de l'émeute ou la révolution contre les mythes" confirms the judgment of Jean-Marie Domenach, who can hardly be suspected of being unsympathetic to Mounier. Domenach points out that Mounier's response to February, 1934 "seems to me still to bear the mark of that purism that he was soon to reject so vigorously." [78]

[75] Philip C. F. Bankwitz, "Paris on the Sixth of February, 1934: Riot, Insurrection, or Revolution?," in Brison D. Gooch (ed.), *Interpreting European History*, Vol. II: *From Metternich to the Present* (Homewood, Ill.: The Dorsey Press, 1967), 338.
[76] Mounier, "Des pseudo-valeurs spirituelles fascistes" (January, 1934), *O.M.*, I, 223–228.
[77] Mounier, "Les cinq étapes d'*Esprit*," 18.
[78] Domenach, "L'Evénement politique," 11.

The events of February, Mounier wrote, served to bring "the established disorder" into the realm of public recognition. The visible disorder, he explained, was far less important than "the massive proliferation of falsehood and the spiritual dangers with which this burdens the revolutionaries themselves." "Against the revolution of parades," he proclaimed, "we wish to undertake the painstaking revolution of the poor." The first task was "a revolution against myths" – against the myth of the honor of the party, the myth of the young leader, the myth of the fascist bands, the myth of the people of Paris, the myth of the veterans organizations. Because these myths had been propagated on all sides, *Esprit* could not join forces with any of the political revolutionaries. On the side of the Communists, "where the presence of misery and revolutionary vigor attracts us," *Esprit* would be forced to accept the materialism and atheism which it rejected more than the political positions of the party. On the side of the Fascists, "where nothing attracts us," *Esprit* would have to accept "hypocritical capitalism," "warlike politics," and "the mediocre dictatorship of mediocre aristocracies of interests." The unavoidable conclusion, Mounier contended, was that the spiritual revolution could not be undertaken in the present political circumstances without betraying that revolution. The action proposed by Mounier was: first, a revolution against myths; second, an inexorable battle against the world of money; third, long-range preparation of the spiritual revolution; and finally, abstention from all political parties but vigilant participation in new movements which were sufficiently rooted in the general positions of *Esprit*.[79] As Domenach points out, Mounier's "revolution against myths" failed to take into account the urgency of a *rassemblement* against the growth of Fascism and was therefore "a little remote from reality," and a "utopian view." [80]

As his response to Archambault revealed, the Christian democratic entente of *l'aube* was clearly not among Mounier's "new movements." Mounier opened his letter with a general criticism of the Christian democrats of *l'aube*. They were divided, he charged, between their "democratic fidelities," their "spiritual aspirations," and their "more or less revolutionary generosities." [81] Whether or not Mounier was aware of the extent to which the Christian democrats of *l'aube* had been divided amongst themselves over the events of February is uncertain,

---

[79] Mounier, "Leçons de l'émeute ou la révolution contre les mythes," 361–368.
[80] Domenach, "L'Evénement politique," 11.
[81] Mounier, "Lettre ouverte sur la démocratie," 292.

but their differences provided some validity to his initial criticism. A number of the leaders of the *Parti Démocrate Populaire* were sympathetic to the demonstrators of February 6 and all of the party's deputies voted against Daladier. In fact, Georges Lebecq, a *Démocrate Populaire* and member of the Municipal Council of Paris, led what one of his fellow party members delicately described as "the pacifist procession of the U.N.C. [*Union National des Combattants*]" into the Place de la Concorde on February 6. The two deputies of the *Jeune-République*, on the other hand, voted for Daladier and their party was an avid proponent of "barring the route to Fascism." [82]

Mounier then indicated that much of what separated the young rebels of *Esprit* from their elders of *l'aube* was a matter of age. The men of *l'aube*, Mounier told Archambault, had formed their political views, indeed, their entire outlook, during the years between 1890 and 1914.[83] "The entire drama between you and us consists of the fact that the world has changed, that positions have been upset, and that ... you propose to us *the same* alternatives, that is, alternatives based upon the past, upon academic assumptions, in response to the problems of a new world." Mounier charged that the Christian democrats were republicans of pre-1914 vintage: of 1789 in their ideology, of 1875 in their generous optimism, of 1905 in their errors of style. "The liberal and parliamentary republic as you knew it, and because you knew it when it was adolescent and endangered, is almost a kind of natural sacrament for you." Mounier admitted that the men of *Esprit* would appear ungrateful to Archambault and his fellow Christian democrats. "As you wish, for gratitude is a virtue of historians. Youth, life, creation are ungrateful. ... The person who preoccupies himself with references at age twenty or thirty begins to dig his own grave." Certainly, Mounier said, the Christian democrats had selflessly, and often unknowingly, provided living riches for Mounier and his generation. But what the men of this generation would do with this heritage would astonish the Christian democrats, "as the son astonishes his father."

Mounier, therefore, granted that Archambault and the men of *l'aube* had aided the forces of the future but nowhere did he clearly specify what this heritage was. Rather, he insisted that the men of *Esprit* were not concerned with the outdated problems to which he believed the Christian democrats still addressed themselves. That the Christian democrats might have contributed to making these problems ana-

[82] Mayeur, *l'aube*, 71–73; and Raymond-Laurent, *Le Parti Démocrate Populaire*, 137–142.
[83] Mounier, "Lettre ouverte sur la démocratie," 292ff.

chronistic was a possibility that Mounier did not consider. He stated: "Civilizations give way, others surge forward. Barbarians will appear. We were not born in one of those periods in which man glides along on an assuring tradition ... This is not the time to look back."

Having cut himself off from his Christian democratic forerunners, Mounier turned his radical iconoclasm to the contemporary political regime. To a careful reader of *Esprit* little of what Mounier now said was particularly new. Mounier drew a distinction between totalitarian regimes and true democracy, placing not only Fascism and Stalinist Communism but also "statist and capitalist 'democracies'" in the former category. True democracy, he said, was "the regime which reposes on the responsibility and functional organization of all persons who make up the social community." Granted this definition of democracy, "we are on the side of democracy," Mounier told Archambault. But, as Archambault must have expected, Mounier told him that *"this democracy has never been realized."* Democracy in France *"is a future to realize and not an acquisition to defend."*

Mounier then somewhat half-heartedly admitted that Archambault's letter provided evidence that the Christian democrats shared some of his criticisms of the existing democratic regime. These common criticisms, however, concealed serious differences between the Christian democrats and the men of *Esprit*. The latter reproached the Christian democrats for their refusal to repudiate completely the impurities of the system and for their failure to seek out "the audacious tradition" which would place them in the avant-garde rather than in the position of political paralysis which had too often made them "the final and scandalous rearguard of reaction." More specifically, Mounier charged that the Christian democrats failed to condemn the basic evil of capitalism. "Here again," Mounier told Archambault, "I read in your Letter some harsh words against the corruption that submerges us. Here again, I fear that you see the evil as merely an external thing, as dirty grease on a sound piece of machinery." The Christian democrats failed to recognize that the machinery itself was defective. They had too much affection for "precious old things." A radical change was necessary, Mounier concluded, and "a radical change is always called a revolution." Given recent events, Mounier continued, the question was no longer whether or not a revolution would occur but rather whether the revolution would save human values or strangle them. "This is why youths ... turn to you who defend the past and say: *The great democratic tradition, yes. But not the small. And for the great, great paths.*"

The day after the publication of Mounier's letter, Archambault's response appeared in *l'aube*.[84] With obvious sarcasm Archambault protested Mounier's "simplistic" description of his formative years. "My style, alas, was in fact formed in 1905," Archambault admitted. But "I was too little in 1789, and not much larger in 1875." After registering several other protests, Archambault attempted to mark out the common ground between *Esprit* and Christian democracy. The Christian democrats also believed that democracy was "a future to realize," Archambault told Mounier. Moreover, much that *Esprit* repudiated had already been repudiated by the Christian democrats. And all that Mounier and his friends supported, with the notable exception of the idea of a revolution, the Christian democrats had long supported. For each of Mounier's positive proposals and for almost all of his negative ones, Archambault said, "I could amuse myself, if the times were amusing," by reproducing similar suggestions from the publications of the A.C.J.F. or the *Sillon* and from the *Chronique sociale, Politique,* or *la Vie intellectuelle.* Among the "revolutionary measures" supported by Mounier there were few that the Christian democrats could not accept; and among the "reformist" or "renovating" measures supported by the Christian democrats there were few that Mounier could not incorporate into his program. "You, like Maritain, carry our infants in your arms," Archambault told Mounier.

On the basis of these assumptions, Archambault asked Mounier what separated *Esprit* and the Christian democrats. In his judgment, neither age nor differing mentalities was a sufficient explanation. Rather, the middle ground between totalitarianisms of the Left and the Right was broad enough to encompass both the patient and reformist Christian democrats and the impatient and enthusiastic *Esprit* team. The Christian democrats, Archambault admitted, "are perhaps too attached to their methods and habits" and the men of *Esprit* "too defiant of any method and any habit." But "these two forces go together ... like fuel oil and a spark," Archambault submitted.

In his final response to Archambault, Mounier shifted the bases of the debate by addressing himself primarily to an explanation of the nature and function of the *Esprit* movement.[85] *Esprit*, he said, was not a political movement nor was its function to make a revolution. Rather the

---

[84] Paul Archambault, "La démocratie et la révolution. Réponse à Emmanuel Mounier," *l'aube*, February 28, 1934.

[85] Emmanuel Mounier and Paul Archambault, "La démocratie et la révolution. Un dernier mot avec Emmanuel Mounier," *l'aube*, March 9, 1934.

purpose of the journal was to provide a *mystique* and doctrine for the revolution which was certain to take place. "We do not address ourselves to the masses, or to the proletariat, or to the middle classes, or to democrats, but to each man considered in terms of his personal endeavors in his day-to-day life and within the concrete collectivities which sustain him." *Esprit* would welcome anyone who would join with its members in preparing the spiritual revolution.

"Perhaps I have had harsh words for certain movements to which you give your friendship," Mounier told Archambault. "If you frequented us, you would know that we are more severe toward our own errors than toward those of others," Mounier wrote, in an effort to emphasize the perpetual self-criticism practiced by the members of *Esprit* – and perhaps also to blunt the edge of his criticism of the Christian democrats. Mounier then reiterated his central point. "When you pose the question of collaboration between groups on the level of political activity," he told Archambault, "you should address your appeal to political movements." This exchange of letters, he concluded optimistically, would perhaps contribute to clarifying purposes, orienting good intentions, and arousing audacity.

Archambault's final response to Mounier revealed that Mounier's optimism was unwarranted. Archambault summarized his understanding of the position of Mounier and *Esprit*, First, he expressed his mistaken belief that Mounier was concerned solely with the spiritual and that, although Mounier believed a temporal revolution was inevitable, he would limit himself to examining spiritual matters in the future. Second, Archambault stated that *Esprit* would not attempt to sustain a new political movement but rather would pursue its spiritual work among already existent groups. And finally, Archambault interpreted Mounier's criticism of the Christian democrats as constituting something short of a series of anathemas. "Thus clarified [*sic*], the situation appears clearer and more encouraging. As we have in good number gotten into the habit of doing, we will continue to go to the pages of *Esprit* to renew our faculties of indignation and revolt. . . . On the other hand, we can hope to see systematic discredit no longer hurled at the patient, more prosaic, but also necessary work of political reform, economic organization, and social liberation which we wish to pursue."

Archambault returned to his original criticism of Mounier a year later in a book published in his *Cahiers de la Nouvelle Journée* in which he elaborated the principles and program of Christian democracy. He repeated his charge that *Esprit* had adopted an unrealistic *tabula rasa* position and again urged Mounier to forget his dangerous revolutionary position and support the Christian democrats in using existing "foundation stones" in constructing a "better City." [86] In addition, however, Archambault contended even more explicitly than he had in early 1934 that "the principle which illuminates the less transparent pages of *Esprit*" was one which any veteran of the *Sillon* could recognize. He had often thought, Archambault wrote, that had it not been used by the *Sillon* for such a long time, the best slogan for *Esprit* would be: "And we, we believed in love." [87] Of all the leaders of the *Jeunes équipes* who denounced the "permeated ideologies" of the Christian democrats, Archambault said, the one to whom they felt closest was Emmanuel Mounier.[88] In later years Archambault persisted in his contention that *Esprit* owed an important debt to its Christian democratic predecessors. Although he was cognizant of both the problems and varieties of personalism, Archambault contended once again that the personalism of *Esprit* had been implicit in Christian democratic circles long before it became popular as a result of Mounier's work.[89] "Emmanuel Mounier," he said in his last commentary on Mounier, "invented neither the word not the thing," making reference to the personalism of the original *Sillon*. But with characteristic fairness Archambault added: "It is with E. Mounier ... that personalism has taken the form of a defined doctrine explicit at once in its doctrinal premises and its practical conclusions." [90]

The response of another Christian democrat of Archambault's generation to Mounier and *Esprit* was very similar. A year after the debate in *l'aube*, Francisque Gay wrote a lengthy and revealing *Mémoire confidentiel* in which he examined the past errors and the future possibilities of the "democratic forces of Christian inspiration." Gay expressed his belief that in spite of their disclaimers the young men of *Esprit* were within "our tradition." But while the *Jeunes équipes* were developing new *mystiques*, Gay complained, the *mystique* of Christian democracy was being dissipated. "We don't even understand what these young men, who treat us with even greater disdain than the *Sillonist* of thirty years ago treated the 'old beards' of reaction or radicalism, want." Try to make a *Jeune Républicain* or a *Démocrate Populaire* read an issue of

---

[86] Archambault, *Pierres d'attente pour une Cité meilleure*, 16, 31–44.
[87] *Ibid.*, 11–12.
[88] *Ibid.*, 37.
[89] Paul Archambault, "Problèmes et doctrines du personnalisme," *Politique*, 13e année, No. 40 (April, 1939), 374–376.
[90] Archambault, "Du personnalisme au marxisme: une aventure spirituelle," 481–483.

Esprit, Gay said, and what a shock he would get. "Yet, in spite of certain excesses ... how can one deny that many of these young men are clearly within our tradition. They want none of our tutelage," Gay complained in conclusion.[91]

Two years later, after political events had forced *l'aube, Esprit*, and several other journals into a camp which their opponents on the Right consistently labeled "Red-Christian," Gay published another *Mémoire confidentiel*. Making reference to the Archambault-Mounier controversy of 1934, Gay expressed his conviction that in the interval Mounier had recognized the shortcomings of some of his earlier positions. "We are totally in accord with E. Mounier when he concludes: 'The great democratic tradition, yes. But not the small. And for the great, great roads.' Since that letter was written," Gay stated, "more than once we have met E. Mounier on the great roads that, before him and in the footsteps of our elders, we have already trod." [92] Like Archambault, the editor of *l'aube* paid tribute to the generosity and enthusiasm of the *Esprit* group and to the character and talent of Mounier personally, but he questioned their audacity – "an audacity that disturbs even the *audacious*," he said with obvious irony. Unlike a number of Christian democrats who were sympathetic to *Esprit*, Gay refused to accept any comparison between *Esprit* and the *Sillon*. He believed that the purely intellectual preoccupations of *Esprit* would prevent it from exercising the "incomparable" influence of the *Sillon*. Gay persisted in including *Esprit* among the intellectual resources of the Christian democratic movement and he echoed Archambault's sentiments:

It is sad to see *[Esprit]* ... reject both those who have never tried to comprehend the changes being prepared and those who have been unable to make themselves understood, those who are intent upon precipitating the ruin of a democratic regime to which they attribute all of the evils of the present hour and those who, applying themselves to the construction of the new order, do not consent to the impetuous overthrow of the edifice in which public liberties still find refuge.

Of Mounier himself, Gay said: "One cannot always agree with him, as he knows, but it is difficult to refuse him our high regard, sympathy, and confidence." [93]

Shortly after Mounier's death Gay paid tribute to Mounier for "the gift of dialogue" and for his elaboration of a *pensée engagée* which was

---

[91] Francisque Gay, *Pour un rassemblement des forces démocratiques d'inspiration chrétienne. Mémoire confidentiel* (Paris: Bloud & Gay, 1935), 50.

[92] Francisque Gay, *Pour en finir avec la legende: "Rouges-Chrétiens." Mémoire confidentiel* (Paris: Editions de 'l'aube,' 1937), 154.

[93] *Ibid.*, 273–274.

an instrument for the construction of "a communitarian and personalist France." [94] This homage was something more than a demonstration of charity and good will towards a deceased opponent. A year later without any mention of his earlier effort to enlist Mounier and the *Esprit* group as a kind of intellectual cadre of Christian democracy, the surviving elder statesman of Christian democracy in France gave Mounier the ultimate accolade. Himself a harsh and disillusioned critic of the M.R.P., Gay adopted a substantial portion of Mounier's own criticism of Christian democracy.[95]

Marcel Prélot, the veteran political theoretician of the *Parti Démocrate Populaire* was a self-styled personalist. At the *Semaine sociale* of Rheims in 1933 he declared that democracy was the supreme refuge of personalism.[96] And four years later at the *Semaine sociale* of Clermont-Ferrand, which was devoted to "the human person in peril," he suggested some sort of corporative system as the best means of effecting the personalist *rassemblement* necessary to save French democracy.[97] It was primarily in retrospect that Prélot expressed himself somewhat cryptically concerning the relationship between *Esprit* and Christian democracy. He was unable to hide his pique over the fortunes which awaited the terms "popular democracy" and "personalism." "Many, unfortunately, were able to comprehend this terminology only when it had been adulterated in other hands." [98] The other hands to which Prélot referred were undoubtedly those of the Communist satellites of post-World War II Europe and the personalists of *Esprit*. "Even before Emmanuel Mounier had given the word [personalism] its great audience," Prélot complained, "Paul Archambault had suggested it. ..." [99] And of Mounier's refusal to associate himself with the Christian democrats, Prélot commented brusquely: "The *Esprit* group, so anxious to distinguish itself – even impertinently and unjustly – from its predecessors, could not join in defending 'the Cause.'" [100]

The voice of Marc Sangnier was not silent on the *Jeune équipe* of *Esprit*. Like Archambault and Gay, Sangnier felt "at home" with

---

[94] Francisque Gay, "Sur Marc Sangnier," *l'aube*, May 30, 1950.

[95] Gay, *Les démocrates d'inspiration chrétienne à l'épreuve du pouvoir*, 19–20, 107–111.

[96] Marcel Prélot, "Les catholiques sociaux devant la crise et la reforme de l'Etat," *Politique*, 7e année, No. 9 (September, 1933), 7–8.

[97] Marcel Prélot, "Personne et société politique," *Semaines sociales de France. Clermont-Ferrand XXIXe Session 1937. La personne humaine en péril. Compte rendu in extenso des Cours et Conférences* (Lyons: Chronique sociale de France, 1938), 433–451.

[98] Marcel Prélot, "Les démocrates d'inspiration chrétienne entre les deux guerres (1919–1939)," *la Vie intellectuelle*, December, 1950, 558.

[99] Prélot, "Histoire et doctrine du Parti démocrate populaire," 330.

[100] Prélot, "Les démocrates populaires français," 226.

Mounier. On March 22, 1934 Mounier presented a lecture on "The Spiritual Revolution" to Sangnier's pacifist *Foyer de la Paix* in the *Maison de la démocratie* on the boulevard Raspail. Mounier's talk touched upon all of the essential elements of his revolt against "the established disorder," but the great chieftain of Christian democracy commented that Mounier was a defender of "the Cause" and that his ideas were essentially those of the original *Sillon* expressed in a rejuvenated form.[101]

The members of the younger generation of Christian democrats, as well as the elders of the *Jeune-République*, responded to Mounier and *Esprit* in a somewhat different fashion. Although they were critical of the radical revolutionism of *Esprit*, they made little or no effort to annex *Esprit*. The responses of these younger men suggest that the misunderstandings and differences between Mounier and the Christian democrats were not due solely, or even in any significant measure, to a gap between generations. Among the younger members of the *Parti Démocrate Populaire* Pierre Démagny was a particularly close observer of the *Jeunes équipes*.[102] He was aware of the general outlook and aspirations of the *Jeunes équipes* and was especially concerned with their belief that the dissociation of Christianity from the established order was a prerequisite of a better City. Démagny recalled the tradition of *l'Avenir* and the efforts of many French Catholics to dissociate the Church from monarchical ideas and integral nationalism. *Esprit*, which he described aptly as "a kind of intellectual meeting place," was one of those groups which was attempting to disengage the Church not only from all political activity but especially from the capitalist system. Démagny accurately perceived that the most clearly definable positions taken by *Esprit* were essentially negative. "It is a position of rupture, of refusal to submit to the present order, a complete dissociation of religious and moral values from the organization of the City." Démagny charged that most of the collaborators of the journal "appear to be animated by a catastrophic mysticism." He then raised the most common Christian democratic questions concerning *Esprit*. "First, can one accept an indictment of the capitalist world which does not take into account the undeniable gains made in the lot of the workers in the past thirty years?" In addition, "when does a situation require a revo-

---

[101] Mounier, "La révolution spirituelle. Conférence faite au Foyer de la Paix, le 22 mars 1934," *l'Eveil des peuples*, April 1, 1934, and April 8, 1934. Sangnier's comments are in the issue of April 1, 1934.

[102] Démagny, "Les Jeunes équipes," 457–466.

lution?" With obvious irony but little accuracy, Démagny stated that neo-Thomism, which had once been in the service of "order," was now being used to justify a revolution. Démagny also contended that the revolution proposed by *Esprit* would be a bourgeois revolution for the benefit of the proletariat. "All of this is perhaps good literature," Démagny remarked with obvious sarcasm, "but we are anxious to learn more about all of this." Démagny concluded his assessment with a rhetorical but prophetic question: "After having denounced the abuse of confidence perpetrated by the bourgeoisie in confusing its own values with religious values, will not the men of *Esprit* end up by associating the religious sentiment with a revolutionary conformism?" [103]

Two other younger Christian democrats were far more sympathetic to *Esprit*, probably in large part because their assessment of Mounier and his team had the advantage of greater historical perspective than did Démagny's. Writing in *l'aube* in November, 1938, Jean Thévenot placed *Esprit* among those movements of French youth which were seeking a third way. In a book published several years earlier by the presses of the *Jeune-République* and dedicated to the president of the *Jeunes de l'aube*, Thévenot had already, implicitly at least, accepted part of Mounier's criticism of the republic.[104] Now, making specific reference to the *Esprit* movement, he stated that *Esprit* was seeking a solution to the urgent problems confronting France which was neither Fascist, Communist, nor what had been "abusively called the old morass democracy." [105] "*Esprit*," Thévenot concluded, "is certainly one of the best – if it is not the best – [movement] that we have in France today." [106] Another young Christian democrat was equally generous and appreciative of the work of Mounier and *Esprit*. Writing in *Politique* in July, 1939, Max André criticized the early negativism of *Esprit* but praised its later and more constructive work.[107] "*Esprit* remains essentially a movement of ideas, a spiritual animator, the guardian of a certain doctrine which must be preserved from many impurities. Without ignoring the temporal, *Esprit* intends to avoid being adulterated by it," André said. André concluded by pointing out that the influence of *Esprit* was profound, particularly on French youths.

[103] Pierre Démagny, "Mouvements de jeunes et jeunes revues," *Politique*, 7e année, No. 4 (April, 1933), 357–365.
[104] Jean Thévenot, *Destin de la République* (Paris: "La Démocratie," n.d. [1935?]), 10–14.
[105] Jean Thévenot, "Panorama de la Jeunesse française: VI: A la recherche d'une troisième voie," *l'aube*, November 10, 1938.
[106] *Ibid.*
[107] Max André, "Chronique du reveil français," *Politique*, 13e année, No. 7 (July, 1939), 636.

No sampling of the reaction of the Christian democrats to Mounier's rebellion against "the established disorder" is complete without mention of two men who were both Christian democrats and collaborators of *Esprit* during the 1930s. One of them was Joseph Folliet, a contemporary of Mounier who was later to be one of the foremost leaders of Social Catholicism as the editor of the prestigious *Chronique sociale de France*. Folliet recalled that he was privy to the decision of Mounier and Izard to found *Esprit* and that he immediately expressed serious reservations concerning the project.[108] The first issue of *Esprit* confirmed Folliet's initial misgivings "because of an imprecision and confusions which seemed dangerous to me." Shortly thereafter, after a long discussion with Mounier while Folliet was conducting a survey of the tendencies of the new generation for *l'aube*, these misgivings vanished. "Although I sometimes collaborated in *Esprit*, I was never of *Esprit*," Folliet wrote. The journal was too intellectual, too Parisian for Folliet. Concerning the relationship between Mounier and the Christian democrats, Folliet believed that Mounier's chief errors were errors of omission – most notably Mounier's failure to recognize clearly the heritage of personalism upon which he drew. Folliet also contended that Mounier was very much a man of his generation, the immediate postwar generation of 1918 which was "influenced, consciously or not, by the thought of Charles Maurras. That he was concerned about seeing himself assimilated by the Christian democrats, I undertsand only too well," Folliet said. But Folliet added that by both temperament and deliberate intention Mounier brushed aside far too casually a past to which he owed a genuine debt. Mounier, ironically, lacked a "sense of historical continuity."

Etienne Borne, on the other hand, regarded himself as a kind of intermediary between *Esprit* and the Christian democratic movement. Borne asserted that he "was faithful to *Esprit* until the war." [109] His fidelity to *Esprit* was based upon his conviction that the work of Mounier's group did not conflict with that of the Christian democrats and for this reason he also collaborated in *l'aube*. Borne's conviction proved to be unfounded and "after the war, when it was necessary to make a choice, I made my decision." Borne chose the M.R.P. and in the pages of *l'aube* he challenged some of Mounier's political options. In his own judgment, nonetheless, Borne remained faithful to his earlier com-

---

108 The following is taken from Fr. Genièvre [J. Folliet], "Emmanuel Mounier," *Témoignage Chrétien*, March 31, 1950; and Joseph Folliet, "Emmanuel Mounier," *Chronique sociale de France*, 64ᵉ année, No. 4 (July, 1956), 355–361.
109 Borne in "Une grande enquête de Gilbert Ganne."

mitment. "I am today a personalist," he claimed, and there is a good deal of validity in Borne's contention. He can accurately be described as a "director of conscience" of Christian democracy and he fulfilled this unusual function by accepting some of Mounier's criticisms of Christian democracy.[110] Like so many other Christian democrats, Borne was also insistent upon Mounier's debt to his Christian democratic forerunners. On the occasion of the death of Marc Sangnier, Borne wrote that

> By democracy, Marc and his followers meant something other than a political regime or form of government, objects of partisan preference, but a *mystique* of the human person, of his liberty, of his dignity, that the Christian because he believes in the soul and its sacred destiny cannot forget in his political and social engagements.... The democracy of the *Sillon* was already, in a form that was insufficiently elaborated and lacked rigorous philosophical justifications, the personalism of Emmanuel Mounier.[111]

Borne accused Mounier of refusing to admit his debt to the tradition of Christian democracy. And of Mounier's lifelong battle against the Christian democrats, Borne lamented: "So many windows fully and justifiably opened to the unknown and to danger and [yet] this door closed to [Mounier's] closest friends. ... At the risk of admitting the limits of my understanding, I confess that in this battle there was something I cannot comprehend. ...." [112] In spite of this, and undoubtedly in part because of his high personal regard for Mounier, Borne could find no greater tribute to pay the *Esprit* movement than to say it was for him and his contemporaries "our *Sillon*, that is, the first hope and the first élan." [113]

The reaction of members of the *Jeune-République* to the *Esprit* movement is of special significance for a number of reasons. Not the least of these reasons is the irony implicit in the relations between the *Esprit* group and the *Jeune-République* during the 1930s as well as after the Second World War. The *Jeune-République* pursued policies that were far more in accord with the political options of *Esprit* than those of any other political component of the Catholic avant-garde; and yet as the direct heir of Sangnier's *Sillon* the *Jeune-République* was the object, implicity at least, of some of Mounier's most severe strictures. In addition, unlike so many other Christian democrats, the men of the *Jeune-*

---

[110] See, for example, Etienne Borne, *1944–1954. Le sens de notre engagement. Texte du rapport présenté par Etienne Borne au 10ᵉ Congrès National du M.R.P. Lille 27, 28, 29, 30 mai 1954 (Forces Nouvelles*, Special Issue, June, 1954), 24ff.

[111] Etienne Borne, "Sur un episode de la vie de Marc," *l'aube*, June 4, 1950.

[112] Borne, "Pour un tombeau d'Emmanuel Mounier," 111–112.

[113] Etienne Borne, "La parti intellectuel contre la Troisième force," *l'aube*, January 11–12, 1948.

République attempted neither to obtain the support of *Esprit* nor to convince Mounier of his debt to his Christian democratic forerunners.

Paul Chanson, one of the little party's leading publicists, very early criticized Mounier's revolutionary opposition to parliamentary democracy. "Open to criticism though it is ... the parliamentary regime constitutes the irreplaceable safeguard of the imprescribable rights of the human person. You wish to undertake a *coup d'état*, if need be with the Communists, and you soothe yourselves with the hope of directing the triumphant revolution towards 'personalism.'" [114] What should be done, Chanson said, was to insert positive, day-to-day reforms within existing institutions. The secretary-general of the *Jeune-République* responded to Mounier in a similar vein. Georges Hoog cited Archambault's open letter to Mounier as having cleared the confusion between the principles of democracy and certain contemporary institutions. Hoog took particular umbrage at Mounier's contention that *Action Française* had "fought courageously against liberal and parliamentary democracy." A veteran of long years of abuse at the hands of Maurras and his followers, Hoog replied angrily:

First, it was against all democracy that *Action Française* fought. Furthermore, if a certain "liberal and parliamentary democracy," which is presently vegatating before our eyes, is a "permeated ideology," it is not true that democracy, as Paul Archambault now defines it, as we define it and have always defined it, is a dead organism.... Nonetheless, true democracy remains to be built. A constructive and total effort is required. The methods? Radical reform of institutions; profound reform of the hearts of men.[115]

The *Jeune-République* acted upon its recognition of the "new spirit" of *Esprit* and the other *Jeunes équipes* in a far more vigorous and concrete manner than did any other Christian democratic group. In mid-1932 the party proposed the idea of a "Jeune Politique," the purpose of which was "to urge men of youthful spirit, in all clearly democratic parties, to a concerted effort of political rejuvenation by means of a reform of institutions and public morality." [116] Making specific reference to "the revolt of the youth," Hoog explained that the very essence of a "Jeune Politique" was the total renovation of all institutions based upon "respect for the eminent dignity of the human person." [117] In the flurry of activity which accompanied the initiation of the project, a banquet was held in July, 1932; and both Georges Izard and Emmanuel

---

[114] Paul Chanson, "Révolution violente?," *La Jeune-République*, June 2, 1933.

[115] Georges Hoog, "La démocratie en péril," *La Jeune-République*, January 28, 1934.

[116] Georges Hoog, "La Jeune-République, les réformes de structure et la défense de la paix," *Cahiers de la Démocratie*, No. 51 (August, 1938), 5–18.

[117] Georges Hoog, "La révolte des jeunes," *La Jeune-République*, July 28, 1933.

Mounier were present.[118] The actual program of the "Jeune Politique" was outlined in a manifesto which called for reforms which went well beyond those of the future Popular Front. Published on February 4, 1934, "Pour une Jeune Politique" proclaimed that "money is king"; that Fascists were using scandals to conceal their opposition to the republican regime; that parliamentarianism was in a state of decay; and that between Fascism and a decrepit parliamentarianism, only a radical transformation of society could save human liberty.[119] The *Jeune-République* also formed its *Equipes de Jeunes de la Jeune-République* and one of its leaders wrote in the pages of *Esprit* itself that he found in the spiritual idealism of his party the source of his "revolutionary indignation against the present world in which money reigns supreme." [120] In an appeal published in *l'aube* by the youths of the *Jeune-République*, any supporter of *Esprit* would have found the kind of language with which he was familiar. "The Republic is dying, you say? And we answer you: it was never alive," the appeal stated. "Never has anyone attempted to suppress the powers of finance. Never has anyone given the workers the place that they merit in the direction of our economy. The result: shameless oppression by capitalism." [121] Such appeals were more than brave but empty verbalisms. Less than four months later the *Jeune-République* became the only Catholic organization to join the Popular Front and thence to support in the Chamber in the form of specific legislative measures the reforms it had so often advocated in its declarations.

But the *Jeune-République* was no more exempt from Emmanuel Mounier's merciless criticism than were the moderate and conservative members of the Christian democratic movement. Mounier carefully maintained his independence even from such activities as the "Jeune Politique" of the *Jeune-République*, although this movement might conceivably be considered to have fit one of the requirements Mounier had laid down in his article on the events of February, 1934: "vigilant participation in new movements which are sufficiently rooted in the general positions of *Esprit*." In 1935 Mounier paid only a typically cryptic tribute to the "living youthfulness" of the *Jeune-République*.[122]

---

[118] "La Jeune Politique devant la crise mondiale," *La Jeune-République*, July 15, 1932.

[119] Reprinted in Georges Hoog, "La Jeune-République et Rassemblement Populaire," *Cahiers de la Démocratie*, No. 41–42 (October-November, 1936), 37–38.

[120] Philippe Wolff, "La Jeune-République et le communisme," *Esprit*, No. 25 (October, 1934), 164–165.

[121] "Appel des Equipes de la Jeune-République," *l'aube*, March 22, 1935.

[122] Mounier, "'Esprit' et les mouvements de jeunesse," *O.M.*, I, 845.

Several reasons for Mounier's opposition to Christian democracy are too obvious to belabor. Mounier was no party man and any attempt to enlist him in a political movement was foredoomed to failure. He was relatively indifferent to political techniques and, like all French democrats, the Christian democrats were in his judgment too attached to the techniques of French democracy. "Defense of democracy" was a damning criticism in Mounier's lexicon. Mounier once wrote Francisque Gay, "a criticism coming from *Esprit* always seems to you to be a family wound." But he added: "the faults common to democrats are also common to the Christian democratic parties."[123] So serious did Mounier consider these faults that he occasionally equated them with the shortcomings of *Action Française*, a judgment that a man like Gay, who according to his own calculations had been involved in some seventeen legal actions with Maurras, must have found well-nigh incomprehensible.[124]

Mounier's criticisms of the political defects of the Christian democrats are scattered unsystematically throughout his prolific writings. He once sarcastically referred to the "little group of Christian democrats who form a kind of peaceful and friendly Andorra" in French politics. This description appeared in a lengthy analysis of the sociological, psychological, and historical ambiguities of what he called "la mythique de gauche." [125] Adopting *Action Française*'s use of the term "Catholics of the Left," Mounier divided the Christian democrats into two families, one that can be roughly, and admittedly with some injustice, identified with the *Jeune-République* and the other, with similar qualifications, with the *Parti-Démocrate Populaire*. Mounier believed that the first family was habitually afraid of not being sufficiently open on its Left and of not being protected on its Right. Infected, like all "Catholics of the Left," by the virus of *sinistrisme*, it manifested the extent of its infection by tending to politicize the spiritual at the Left rather than by attempting to spiritualize the Left. Mounier reserved his harshest criticism for the other family of "Catholics of the Left," the *Parti Démocrate Populaire*. It too suffered from *sinistrisme*: it feared that it was not sufficiently open on the Right and not properly protected on its Left. What it feared most was any transgression towards the Left. For its own tranquility, it was fortunate that there were other "Catholics of the Left" who protected its Left flank and minimized its mistakes.

[123] Mounier, "Lettre à Francisque Gay, 9 février 1940," *O.M.*, IV, 655–656.

[124] "Dépositions de M. Francisque Gay," *Le procès de Charles Maurras. Compte rendu sténographique* (Paris: Editions Albin Michel, 1946), 175.

[125] Mounier, "Court traité de la mythique de gauche," 46–47.

At the same time, Mounier referred to the *Jeune-République* as being "paralyzed by a sickly refusal to think and under the influence of a parliamentarianism, not to mention a frantic search for electoral success, which has made it fail completely in the good mission that it might have accomplished." [126] Mounier admitted the existence of a current of personalism within the *Jeune-République*, but he was quick to add that the personalism of the *Jeune-République* was far too complacent and reformist. The *Parti Démocrate Populaire*, Mounier said in the same report, was being "progressively weighted down by its conservatism in spite of intermittent shifts." Elsewhere Mounier described the history of the *Parti Démocrate Populaire* as the story of its *embourgeoisement* and of the long and massive resistance of the Catholic world and part of the clergy to any understanding of the social problem.[127] It was a party of "pious and overly cautious petit bourgeois" which was guided by a few bourgeois paternalists and responded in Catholic milieux to the same needs that Radical Socialism satisfied in laïc areas.

Mounier's political criticisms of the Christian democrats increased in a kind of geometrical progression with the importance of the role played by Christian democrats in French political life. During the Resistance, as the Christian democrats began the work which was to culminate in the organization of the M.R.P., Mounier wrote his wife that the Christian democrats of the Third Republic understood nothing at all: "Their narrow outlook, their absence of intellectual and civic vitality, their way of always offering what is not asked of them, their verbalism and that sterile bad humor in which so many of them enclose themselves today place them outside the field of living forces." [128] They thought of themselves, Mounier continued, as members of the avant-garde but they had not changed since around 1910. A little more than a month later, Mounier protested vehemently against the accusation that he was a Christian democrat. In a letter to the Secretary-General of the Police in June, 1942 he said:

As to the political Christian democrats who, before the war (if I recall distant memories clearly), formed the *Parti Démocrate Populaire*, I believe that the poverty of their political sense, their social timidity, and sometimes the very questionable illumination of their Christianity distinguished them neither for historical intelligence nor for the revolutionary action required by the times.

---

[126] Mounier, "'Esprit' et l'action politique," *Esprit*, No. 73 (October, 1938), 48, 59.
[127] Mounier, "Paul Delourme: Trente-cinq années de politique religieuse ou l'histoire de l'Ouest-Eclair," *Esprit*, No. 52 (January, 1937), 687–688.
[128] Mounier, "Lettre à Paulette Mounier, 4 mai 1942," *O.M.*, IV, 739.

If I must be devoured, is it not permissible to choose the sauce with which I am to be eaten? [129]

Shortly after the Liberation Mounier recognized that "the M.R.P. has its roots in the old *Parti Démocrate Populaire*" and that "everyone considers it to be the political heir of the prewar Christian democratic movement." The latter, Mounier added somewhat ambiguously, was not a great political heritage but it was a great spiritual heritage.[130] Far more characteristic of the intensity of Mounier's views concerning the largest Christian democratic party in the history of France was his description of its program as "that tasteless pap of deceptions, poor abstractions, devious calculations and moral élans that our M.R.P. [serves us] as the platter of Christian civilization." [131]

Many of Mounier's criticisms of Christian democracy were not dissimilar to those that he leveled at other political parties.[132] Even the charge that the Christian democrats failed to recognize the revolutionary requirements of their times was not an unusual one. Francisque Gay, for example, complained that the leaders of the "democrats of Christian inspiration" played the game of politics as if nothing had changed since before the First World War. They were plagued by old habits and "singular timidities" which resulted in lamentable mediocrity.[133] Georges Hoog complained in 1938 that the history of Catholics in France was the story of eternal *ralliés*, of men who were always one generation in arrears.[134] In retrospect, two leaders of the *Parti Démocrate Populaire* echoed some of Mounier's criticisms. Marcel Prélot said of his former colleagues:

Courageous – their wounds and medals from the First War and their Resistance records during the Second generally prove this – they were, nonetheless, timid to an extent that is stupifying in retrospect. Most of them had all of the private virtues; ... but almost none of them was aware of the requirements for success in public life.[135]

Raymond-Laurent probably recognized the same problem when he attempted to justify the politics of his old party on the grounds that its "politics of *présence*" required compromises and slow and steady efforts

---

[129] Mounier, "Lettre à Monsieur le Secretaire général à la Police, 19 juin 1942," *O.M.*, IV, 748–749.

[130] Mounier, "Politique confessionnelle," *Cité soir*, Novembre 3, 1945, reprinted in *B.A.-E.M.*, No. 29 (March, 1957), 37.

[131] Mounier, "Lettre à Xavier de Virieu, 1er mars 1950," *O.M.*, IV, 828.

[132] See, for example, Mounier, "Court traité de la mythique de gauche," 40–75.

[133] Gay, *Pour un rassemblement des forces démocratiques d'inspriation chrétienne*, 49–50.

[134] Georges Hoog, "La République et le spirituelisme," *La Jeune-République*, September 25, 1938.

[135] Prélot, "Histoire et doctrine du Parti démocrate populaire," 337.

within existing institutions. The party, he argued, could not afford a "politics of opposition" with its attendant luxuries of intransigence and disregard for public opinion and concrete circumstances. While the *Jeune-République* bore witness in the milieux of the Left, the *Parti Démocrate Populaire* sought to penetrate Catholic milieux in order to free them from their conservative and reactionary propensities.[136]

The Christian democratic parties were different from other parties in Mounier's judgment, however, and it was this difference which aroused his bitter ire. A veteran of *Esprit* testified that Mounier was normally courteous and charitable with his adversaires but that he rarely mentioned the Christian democrats in any but the most cutting and sarcastic terms.[137] Scattered throughout his writings are criticisms of the Christian democrats which clearly suggest that the primary source of Mounier's bitter antipathy toward them was far more than merely political in character. Mounier told the congress of the *Esprit* movement at Jouy-en-Josas in 1938 that the most effective service *Esprit* could perform for the Christian democrat would be to splash "a dash of vinegar into his holy water." [138] A year later on the occasion of the lifting of the Vatican's ban on *Action Française,* he accused the Christian democrats of having grafted on to the condemnation of Maurras "a kind of political confessionalism and moralism which turned anti-Maurrasianism into monomania and constantly mingled political criticism with a kind of sacred vehemence and moral discourse which are so deadly for the lucid analysis of problems." [139] In a letter to Francisque Gay, Mounier charged that the Christian democrats "too often compromise the subordination of politics to morality in a kind of moralism which we feel the need of disengaging today, a spirituality on one side, a politics on the other, the one and the other more distinct. ..." [140]

Mounier's major criticism of the Christian democrats was that they had compromised their faith in "the established disorder." The Christian democrats were included in Mounier's classic "Feu la chrétienté" which, as Etienne Borne aptly pointed out, might more properly have been entitled "Feu sur la chrétienté." [141] The Christian democrats were survivors of a moribund Christendom. They were on the wrong side of

---

[136] Raymond-Laurent, *Le Parti Démocrate Populaire,* 44–45.
[137] Marrou, "Un homme dans l'Eglise," 895.
[138] Mounier, "'Esprit' et l'action politique," 50.
[139] Mounier, "La soumission de l'Action Française," *Esprit,* No. 83 (August, 1939), 695–696.
[140] Mounier, "Lettre à Francisque Gay, 9 février 1940," *O.M.,* IV, 656.
[141] Etienne Borne, "Emmanuel Mounier, juge de la démocratie chrétienne," *Terre humaine,* No. 2 (February, 1951), 67.

history. They contributed to "l'agonie du christianisme." The idea they supported, their background and training, their indiscriminate mingling of religion and politics, even their temperament – all of these factors, and more, made the Christian democrats unsuited for the great task of constructing a new and more human civilization.

Like the Christian democrats, Mounier believed that the Christian should bring to temporal affairs the unique resources of his religious faith and spiritual life. In the process, however, the Christian encountered a number of serious dangers: remaining complacent or indifferent in the face of the injustices of "the established disorder"; failing to confront temporal problems by making the Christian faith a refuge or a kind of disembodied idealism rather than a vital source of life and action; temporalizing or politicizing Christianity; and succumbing to the temptation of moralism. At one time or another, Mounier accused the Christian democrats of each of these errors, but in his only full-scale analysis of "Christian politics" he placed special emphasis upon one of them. Several months after the debate in *l'aube*, he asked if there were such a thing as a Christian politics and in his response said that moralism was "one of the permanent malformations of the Christian world." [142]

The main thrust of Mounier's criticism of "Christian politics" rested on his contention that the moral and religious education of Christians very often had a debilitating effect upon their temporal activity. Because they were brought up to believe in certain absolutes – eternity, justice, and truth – Christians were ill-prepared for the anguish and uncertainty inherent in seeking solutions to the unfamiliar and perplexing problems of the temporal order. To their confrontation of temporal problems, they often brought their habitual sense of the absolute. They submitted to what Mounier called "a certain clericalism of the intelligence" in their proclivity for arrogating to themselves sovereign judgments on all political problems in the name of vague and generous principles or ideals. Too often Catholics used encyclicals and even the Bible as shields against the contradictions and ambiguities of temporal action. How many times, Mounier complained, did Catholics present such principles as the common good, justice, charity, and morality as a magnificent and ready-made synthesis which precluded any further effort.

Mounier believed that Christians must place themselves, like others, in "the humble school of experience. ... For it has not been said to

[142] Mounier, "Ya-t-il une politique chrétienne?" (June, 1934), *O.M.*, I, 394–406.

them that they will be the only ones who need not sweat for their spiritual bread." They must rid themselves of their pious verbiage, their easy assurances, and their ready-made systems and admit the existence of extremely complex, if not nearly insoluble, problems. When Christians, with their "social homilies", gave the impression of not having confronted reality, it was not, however, because their principles were deficient. It was rather because these principles had been deformed into an "insipid piety" and a "proliferation of verbalism and moral discourse." Mounier contended that "moral discourses are responsible for average positions and mediocrities in action. For the morality of moralism is a bastard and degenerate offspring of spiritual life." Then, with some exaggeration, Mounier stated that he had not denied the services rendered by the Christian democrats. Rather, he had invited them to reflect on their errors. Instead of making ineffectual appeals to good will, he urged them to regain contact with reality. The Christian democrats were not to suppose that "the inner life dispenses competence" in temporal affairs.

Mounier concluded his analysis of "Christian politics" with a consideration of the question of confessional parties. In them, he explained, the danger of submitting to political moralism was especially acute. If Christians agreed upon certain principles which precluded the pursuit of certain ends and the use of certain methods in politics, this did not mean that they were necessarily in agreement upon the "ensemble of historical and practically-determined judgments which is the only basis of effective political action." To unite more than a very small fraction of Catholics in a political party on the basis of their common religion would be "to condemn oneself to [political] impotence through eclecticism" and to create that "'sociological extension' of religion which is its constant internal menace." Mounier concluded that "to unite for political action such disparate adherents, even after agreement on principles has been reached (for example, on an encyclical), can be done only on the level of a vague moralism which, as we said above, is as foreign to the affairs of the world as it is to the powers of the spirit."

Mounier believed that the Christian democrats were not only guilty of being democrats but, more important, that they were both politically ineffectual and spiritually dangerous. Much of his criticism of "Christian politics" in general and of Christian democracy in particular was not particularly original. Even the moralism he attributed to the Christian democrats was not an unusual accusation for, as he himself recognized, the religious moralism of the Christian democrats had been attacked by the men of *Action Française* and the politics of religious moralists had long been the object of Marxist criticism.[143] What distinguished Mounier's criticism of the Christian democrats was the vantage point from which he launched his merciless attacks; the consistency with which he returned to his criticism in the most disparate contexts in almost all of his major writings; the explanation he offered for the Christian's proclivity for political moralizing; and the extent to which moralism, in his judgment, vitiated the political efficacy of Christian democracy and debilitated the necessary vigor of Christian spirituality. In the end, as Etienne Borne discerned, a kind of archetype – a sociologically and psychologically determined character – of the Christian democrat emerged from Mounier's many-faceted critique.[144]

The vehemence of Mounier's attacks upon the Christian democrats cannot be comprehended outside the general context of his condemnation of "the late Christendom" of which the Christian democrats were inhabitants. Nowhere was this vehemence more evident than in *L'Affrontement chrétien*, written in Dieulefit during the winter of 1943–1944.[145] Admittedly *L'Affrontement chrétien* voiced Mounier's almost apocalyptic response to the fall of France and his recent experiences in the prisons of the Vichy regime. "Did a French Catholic at any time during the last hundred years," Mounier asked, "readily imagine that it might be more normal for him to be found in prison than on a safe public platform?" Nonetheless, what Mounier wrote in 1943–1944 was entirely consistent with the corpus of his work.

L'Affrontement chrétien began with a series of half-rhetorical questions which established the tone of Mounier's angry attack on Christendom:

Is it true that Christianity is a poison to young muscles, an enemy of manly strength and natural grace, a soft sickness of the Orient fallen upon Greek man because a little fanatic of Tarsus in an evil day survived a tempest?

Exhaustion of the instincts, abdication of the will or inconsistency of spirit, that indefinable something which surrendered at the first warcry, could all this be but a remote effect of the disease of Christianity?

Is Christianity a pseudonym for the coalition of the feeble and the timorous? Does it hang about the street-corners of decadence? And insofar as it conceals

---

[143] Mounier, "Morale et révolution," *Cité soir*, October 22, 1945, reprinted in *B.A.E.M.*, No. 29 (March, 1967), *33*.

[144] Borne, "Emmanuel Mounier, juge de la démocratie chrétienne," 66–67.

[145] Mounier, "L'Affrontement chrétien," *O.M.*, III, 9–66, trans. Katherine Watson as *The Spoil of the Violent* (London: The Harvill Press, 1955).

a power of rebellion, is it only the insurrection of the servile against the exalted, of mediocrity against nobility, of torpor against life, of stupidity against culture, of the hard against the elite? [146]

Although Mounier's answer to these questions was a vigorous no, he expressed his conviction that if one day Christians were to be confronted with the option of surrendering their physical comforts or abjuring their faith there is little doubt that this religion of habit "would crumble away in enormous sections." He added: "On that day it will be possible to question whether there is a single Christian left in the civilized world. It will be necessary to search in byways and thickets for that heroic Christianity which will remake, with the boldness of life, a new vision of the eternal tradition." In almost white anger, Mounier complained that "if the Christian is congenitally a sick man, quick, then, let him be *made* to die. Mankind is weary of wasting its best strength in fighting against a perpetually moribund invalid. So speaks the young neo-pagan." And Mounier obviously agreed with his Nietzschean "young neo-pagan."

L'Affrontement chrétien contains a lengthy but unsystematic catalogue of the deficiencies of the inhabitants of contemporary Christendom. Christianity is rapidly becoming a religion of women, old men and petty tradesmen. The Christian is a fundamentally feminine character who relaxes in the "comfortable certainty" he believes his faith provides him. "The hard element of our populations, the working-class element," is almost entirely absent from Christianity. Repeating an old criticism, Mounier contended that the reason for the decadence of contemporary Christendom "lies for the most part in the progressive monopolizing of western Christianity by the bourgeois class." Faith, hope, and charity have given way to the conservative, defensive, sulky propensities of the bourgeoisie. Bourgeois Christianity is like the bourgeois house, "a shuttered house," and like the bourgeois heart, "a heart circumspect and cautious." What is necessary is "a Christianity of the open air," "a virile Christianity," "a plebian Christianity." Admittedly, Mounier continued, the average Christian has good intentions but such intentions invariably "carry him headlong and unerringly into every lost cause." He is paralyzed by his own moral scruples and racked by secret demons. He is a *"paraplegic of virtue."* The outside world is always a fearful challenge to him and he retreats into "idealistic effusions," "too-gentle and ingenuous manners," and "habits of inflated or piously unctuous speech." He and his

[146] The following is taken from Mounier, *The Spoil of the Violent*, 1–85 *passim*.

fellow Christians "congregate in little coteries, speaking the language of the parish, their feebleness keeping them from the broad highways and the dangers to be met there."

With similar lack of system, Mounier explained the development of the weak, "devirilized" and "devitalized" Christian largely in terms of his family and educational upbringing. A Christian family upbringing and a confessional education seriously hamper the Christian in his ability to confront the affairs of the temporal world. The Christian mother, in particular, "makes the son." She is overly protective and furnishes him with pious literature and sentimental illusions. By her very tenderness she hinders his progress towards maturity. Confessional education continues this prolongation of Christian adolescence. It produces a "nice little, rather bewildered, rather dreamy . . . young man." Its authoritarian character, the kind of moral intimidation inculcated by the catechisms of the pious press, does nothing to develop initiative, judgment or leadership. "The man who, throughout his upbringing, was first and foremost protected, continues to protect himself for the rest of his life." He and his fellow Christians "are all to prone to confound evangelical brotherhood with a taste for little coteries, and to carry, even into political associations, under the pretext of giving them a family atmosphere, a domestic sentimentality which is as embarassing spiritually as it is aesthetically."

Within this general context, Mounier's criticism of the Christian democrats takes on added meaning. He also discerned an historical reason for the psychological malformation of the Christian democrat. The fear of Modernism and the endemic strife between Modernists and Integralists since the first decade of the century had forced many Christians to give themselves over to "religious sentimentality." "The propagation of an insipid spirituality by means of a widely read, pious literature, the reduction of the Christian tradition to a family tradition, which was so widespread in some milieux, the fear of ideas exhibited by so many pious men and their indifference to theological training . . . , all of this impoverishment of Christian vigor is the offspring of an era which believed it possible to defend Charity, or the effusions that it mistook for Charity, by depriving it of [intellectual] light." [147] His own generation, Mounier was quick to point out, had escaped the contaminations which afflicted the Christian democrats. It had been trained to be

---

[147] Mounier, "Responsabilités de la pensée chrétienne," *O.M.*, III, 571–572.

intellectually hard and precise and found soft ideas, compliance, and intellectual pusillanimity distasteful.[148]

In one of his most concise criticisms, Mounier said in a lecture only a year before his death that since the beginning of the century "the Christian political conscience" had been either purely and simply conservative or affected by romanticism, indiscriminately intermingling politics, religion, and impulses of the heart. The latter, he told his audience, was one of the weaknesses of the *Sillon* and of the Christian democratic movement generally. Following the condemnation of *Action Française*, Catholic youths reacted excessively against the separation of morality and politics. They fell back towards a "purely spiritual" education, and without economic or political education "when they found themselves confronted with economic or political problems [they] were tempted to resolve them in the climate in which they had been trained, by a short-circuiting from spiritual considerations to practical problems through the confused intermediary of good will and moral approximations." [149]

From the foregoing, it is possible to extract a portrait of a man like Marc Sangnier. After an encounter with some of Sangnier's disciples in 1934, Mounier noted in his diary that these men were "Poor, pale, generous debris enfeebled by softness." [150] Eight years later he painted this remarkable picture of a veteran of the *Sillon*: "Yesterday at dawn a quaint pensioner joined us: mustached [like Sangnier], ... his eyes brimming over with kindness and vague idealism. ... I quickly diagnosed [his illness]: a *Sillonist*. I wasn't wrong. The father of six brats, four pipes in his pockets. ... Why must these men, as good as gold, all appear to be a little foolish? They have such fervor that one feels a little ashamed of criticizing them." [151]

This facet of Mounier's criticism of the Christian democrats is nowhere more incisively summarized – albeit with much of the same sarcasm of which he accused Mounier – than by Etienne Borne. Borne responded to the posthumous publication of some of Mounier's letters and diaries which contained the foregoing descriptions of the *Sillonists* by writing that "Emmanuel Mounier never liked the Christian democrat as a sociologically and psychologically determined species." Mounier believed that there were well-defined varieties of the *homo genre*,

[148] Mounier, "Aux avant-gardes de la pensée chrétienne" (September, 1947), *O.M.*, III, 678–679.
[149] Mounier, "Feu la chrétienté," *O.M.*, III, 705–706.
[150] Mounier, "Entretiens VIII, 8 juin 1934," *O.M.*, IV, 552.
[151] Mounier, "Journaux de prison. Prison de Clermont, jeudi 5 février 1942," *E.M.*, *1905–1950*, 728.

Borne said. "The Christian democrat is a mixture of *homo politicus* and *homo religiosus* whose first error is in being hopelessly 'unesthetic.'" Mounier's Christian democrat is an overly good man who suffers from prolonged adolescence and the overly careful protection of confessional education or he is a sentimental old man who pours out his heart in verbal rhetoric. Mounier's Christian democrat lacks "a certain kind of virile and aggressive maturity." As a species he is soft. "A sweet animal without temperament who practices confusions, such is the Christian democrat in the merciless analysis of Emmanuel Mounier." [152]

The validity of Mounier's criticism is not readily verifiable. It is, perhaps, only a most unusual coincidence that an *abbé démocrate*, who sat in the Chamber of Deputies during the 1930s as a supporter of the *Parti Démocrate Populaire* and who was himself a veteran of the *Sillon*, referred to Sangnier in precisely the terms used by Mounier to describe the old veteran of the *Sillon* whom he encountered in 1942. Abbé Jean Desgranges had noted in his diary a few years earlier: "It is a little sad to see [Sangnier] ... always occupied with grandiose dreams, *a little foolish.*" [153] Similarly the slogans and mottoes to which the Christian democrats – including those of the Fourth Republic – were addicted were suggestive of the existence of a peculiar Christian democratic temperament. Archambault's reaction to *Esprit* and Mounier was characteristic: he felt "at home" with them. Christian democracy was always "the Cause." Christian democratic organizations were something more than ordinary political groups: they were "foyers of life, of friendship, of civic education." Christian democratic parties were consistently bound together by "friendship." Even the M.R.P. was "the party of friendship." The chants and slogans of the original *Sillon* echoed through the meeting halls of the *Jeune-République*, the *Parti Démocrate Populaire*, and even the M.R.P.: "Our life is all for the Cause," "And we, we believed in Love," and "Love is stronger than Hate." All of this provides some substance to Mounier's charge of excessive good will, perpetual moral discourse, domestic sentimentality, and piously unctuous speech. The Christian democrat habitually referred to his colleagues as a "son of the Spirit" or even as a "good apostle." He relied heavily upon "moral forces" and "spiritual forces" to achieve his objectives. His activities as a Christian democrat were inseparable from "a way of life." He repeated time and again that he

---

[152] Borne, "Emmanuel Mounier, juge de la démocratie chrétienne," 66–67.
[153] Jean Desgranges, *Journal d'un prêtre député, 1936–1940* (Paris: La Palatine, 1960), 148. Italics added.

and his fellow Christian democrats were all members of the same "spiritual family."

Some support is lent Mounier's critique also by the criticisms of several Christian democrats. In a retrospective assessment of the deficiencies of the *Parti Démocrate Populaire*, Marcel Prélot pointed out that "each time that the general policy of the party was challenged in a vote or by a speech, [the party's leaders] were racked by scruples and serious misgivings. Certainly, these scruples were always honorable and these misgivings often justified. But even if their arguments were acceptable, ultimately an almost complete paralysis of action resulted." [154] In the course of a lengthy criticism of the *Parti Démocrate Populaire*, Georges Hoog said that if democracy in France was not sufficiently spiritualist it was because, for fifty years, too many "sons of the Spirit" had been forthright and generous in thought but far too timid, hesitant, and reticent in action. "The essential thing in politics is not merely to ask for reforms [but] to vote for them." After citing numerous examples of the great disparity between the doctrine of the *Parti Démocrate Populaire* and its political actions, Hoog commented that some parties assessed a reform proposal not in terms of what it was intended to achieve but rather in terms of the motives they suspected were behind it.[155]

In his auto-critique of the "democratic forces of Christian inspiration" in 1935, Francisque Gay also touched upon several facets of the *mouniériste* criticism. He charged that the Christian democrats had been intimidated both by the haunting fears left by the Letter on the *Sillon* and by the possibility of being accused of clericalism. As a result, the Christian democrats took "infantile precautions." They were guilty of "little cowardices" and even of a lack of confidence in their own programs. Too many militants of Christian democracy, Gay contended, had a tendency "to 'clericalize'" all of their political activity. Too many Christian democrats, he clearly implied, looked for "light and strength . . . in the Gospel and in the directives of the Church" not only for their private lives but for their politics as well.[156] Finally, a young Christian democrat named Marc Scherer addressed himself to explaining the relative inefficacy of the efforts of the Christian democrats in 1939. The moralism and sentimentalism of the Christian democrats, Scherer wrote, explained many of their failures. Scherer argued that the moral-

---

[154] Prélot, "Histoire et doctrine du Parti démocrate populaire," 322.

[155] Hoog, "La République et le spirituelisme."

[156] Gay, *Pour un rassemblement des forces démocratiques d'inspiration chrétienne*, 30–46 *passim*.

ism, sentimentalism, and good will of the Christian democrats provided them with an excuse for changing nothing in the "established order" by allowing them "to believe that they have done their duty by denouncing injustice and by proclaiming the 'requirements of the Christian conscience.'"[157]

Even more suggestive of the existence of a Christian democratic temperament were two novels written by Robert Cornilliau. Explicit even in the titles of his novels was Cornilleau's recognition of the existence of a Christian democratic social and psychological type: *Le Champ de ronces. Roman de moeurs politiques* and *Le Navire sans capitaine. Etude psychologique et sociale*.[158] Both novels belong to the tradition of Christian democratic social literature of such men as George Fonsegrive and Cornilleau's friend Abbé Roblot.

Written under the pseudonym of Jacques Hardanges, *Le Champ de ronces* had as its chief protagonist a young hero of the First World War named Jacques de Villeneuve. The heir of two conflicting traditions – his paternal grandfather was a Catholic, a royalist, and an army officer, while his maternal grandfather was a country doctor, a good republican, a free-thinker, and communard – the very mixture of blood flowing in his veins made Cornilleau's hero a symbol of the Christian democratic attempt to bridge the historic chasm between Right and Left in French life. And the originality of this attempt was suggested by the young protagonist's name. Jacques de Villeneuve was an extremely mild-mannered, almost timid young man who was undecided about his future career. He took refuge in reading history and there his awareness of social injustice and suffering was sharpened to such an extent that he dreamt in traditional Social Catholic terms of a great reconciliation between the governing classes and the popular classes. But Cornilleau's hero was also a democrat of the *Sillonist* variety. He confided to an old priest: "You talk to the people. You continue, to a certain extent, the vocation of Christ. What I like about democracy is its completely Christian obligation of descending to the most humble, even the most worthless."

With the encouragement and support of a wartime friend named Folletière, Jacques then decided to enter politics as a candidate in

---

[157] Marc Scherer, "Regard sur vingt années d'action sociale," in E. Borne, J. Lacroix, and M. Scherer, *Options sur demain* (No. 6; "La Nouvelle Journée"; Paris: Bloud & Gay, 1939), 109–110.

[158] Jacques Hardanges [Robert Cornilleau], *Le Champ de ronces. Roman de moeurs politiques* (Paris: Librairie Valois, 1928); and Robert Cornilleau, *Le Navire sans capitaine. Etude psychologique et sociale* (Paris: Bloud & Gay, 1931). The synopses that follow are taken largely from Jacques Nanteuil, "L'écrivain," in *Robert Cornilleau. Souvenirs et témoignages*, 95–101.

Rheims. In a novel heavily laden with obvious symbolism, the political campaign that followed provided the central theme and justified the title: "Politics is a field of brambles and its combatants are naked. Upon it even those who are least hurt leave shreds of their flesh." In the course of the campaign, Jacques was aided by Folletière who was the antithesis of the Christian democrat both socially (as an "authentic plebian") and temperamentally (as a man of action). But even Folletière could not compensate for the political defects of his friend or the tactics of their opponents. Opposing Jacques de Villeneuve was a Radical who was supported by the Socialist workers and the anticlerical bourgeoisie. With typical impetuosity and optimism, Jacques determined to break the false dichotomy of Right and Left by organizing a new political party. His opponents on both the Right and the Left resorted to calumny and violence. The young Christian democrat was defeated. Apparently the slogan of the *Sillon* had been proven false for, as Jacques Nanteuil, a literary critic and veteran of the *Sillon*, aptly pointed out, this time hate had been stronger than love. Love had its recompense, however, because Cornilleau's hero married the only daughter of an old conservative Catholic who had instigated some of the calumnies against him. Cornilleau concluded on a hopeful note, therefore. He seemed to contend that it was better to have fought well and lost than to have used unethical methods and possibly have won. That the undoubtedly fine personal virtues of a Jacques de Villeneuve were no substitute for the acumen necessary for political success was a conclusion that Cornilleau significantly failed to draw.

In writing *Le Navire sans capitaine* three years later, Cornilleau abandoned his pseudonym and dedicated his book to Jean Raymond-Laurent, the secretary-general of the *Parti Démocrate Populaire*. The chief character, but hardly the hero, of this sequel to *Le Champ de ronces* was Folletière who had recently won a resounding victory in Rheims and become the leader of a small group of deputies in the Chamber. Folletière's *Démocrates Sociaux* sat in the center of the Chamber, opposed both self-seeking conservatism and violent revolution, and had hopes of using their strategic position and their firm convictions and enthusiasm to compensate for their numerical weakness. More important, they had to change the political habits of their fellow deputies and create a breach through which their own influence could be exercised. Unhappily, Folletière was quickly seduced by the old political habits of the Chamber (and more literally by the charms of a young woman who was the instrument of corrupt politicians). Part of the meaning of Cornilleau's title thus becomes clear. The small crew of *Démocrates Sociaux* was left without a captain. Jacques de Villeneuve then reappeared. He told himself: "Today I am seeking the captain of the ship. ... I am obeying, unconsciously, that penchant which leads so many Frenchman to seek a man, a chief, a savior. ... No, Catholicism has no need of a man, of a political captain, to surmont the situations of the future: there is the Church of God." Jacques had obviously lost none of his idealism in spite of his disastrous political campaign. He was clearly the perfect Christian democrat – motivated by a vague idealism, relying upon his religion to provide the answers to political problems, a man of unusual character who possessed all of the Christian virtues. For a brief moment, however, even the perfect Christian democrat was on the verge of despair. When Folletière withdrew from politics, Jacques complained to his wife that "humanity is ugly and wicked." His wife responded: "Not you. ... You are not like the others." Fortunately, even some of the opponents of the *Démocrates Sociaux* in the Chamber discerned this difference. One of the former sounded the concluding note of the novel with these words: "They have the faith; that is the essential thing. ... Their ship is still small, but what astonishes and concerns me is that without a captain it still maneuvers among the reefs as if a light which is invisible to us guides it through the fog."

Whether or not Emmanuel Mounier had occasion to read the novels of Robert Cornilleau is uncertain. If he did, he undoubtedly found in Jacques de Villeneuve the confused religious-political temperament that was so distasteful to him "The Church of God," he might have said, provides the Christian with immeasurable resources; and certainly he must practice the Christian virtues. But the Church cannot provide the leadership needed by Cornilleau's *Démocrates Sociaux*. The "light" of religious faith does not provide a guide through the "fog" of difficult political choices. Jacques de Villeneuve, Mounier might well have said, should not have regarded himself as being different from "the others." The whole point of Mounier's criticism of the Christian democrats was that in politics the Christian must regard himself as being like "the others," for religion does not dispense political competence. Mounier might very well have agreed with Cornilleau that "politics is a field of brambles and its combatants are naked," but to be properly clothed, Jacques de Villeneuve should have appealed not to his Church, not to good will or generous sentiments, but rather to the hard and virile school of experience and historical judgment.

Mounier himself entered this school during particularly difficult circumstances. Just as the final and fateful crises of the Third Republic began, Mounier abandoned what he himself recognized as the "dangerous purism" which had characterized the early and doctrinaire years of the *Esprit* movement. Nineteen thirty-four marked a turning point in the history of *Esprit*. Mounier said in retrospect that "in the concrete historical circumstances in which we are always immersed, whether we wish it or not, we have a certain number of obligations, obligations of decision and of commitment, and to pose problems without reference to historical situations is basically to evade the human condition." [159] The efficacy of personalism as a guide for political choice was thus to be tested. Many of the most serious crises of the 1930s – the Ethiopian crisis, the Spanish Civil War, and the Popular Front, for example – involved religious as well as political issues and consequently Mounier's conception of the role of the Christian in politics underwent a severe and practical test. In the course of this test, Mounier was to be acutely aware that "historical things are always mixed," for more than once he found himself allied with the *"paraplegics of virtue."* Indeed, he was already cognizant of the necessity for prudence in affairs that concerned the Church. In September, 1933 he had written Georges Izard that "a condemnation of us [will involve] the entire movement of the Catholic 'Left,' even the least advanced [who have been] paralyzed for a generation." [160]

---

[159] Mounier, "Les cinq étapes d'*Esprit*," 17.
[160] Mounier, "Lettre à Georges Izard, 6 septembre 1933," *O.M.*, IV, 538.

CHAPTER IV

THE BROKEN IDOL:
MOUNIER, THE CHRISTIAN DEMOCRATS, AND THE
CRISIS YEARS OF THE THIRD REPUBLIC, 1934–1939

> L'idole est brisée, l'idole pour gens tranquilles. Le petit saint.
>
> Mounier, "Entretiens VIII, 17 mai 1935."

Early in the summer of 1936 Pierre-Henri Simon, a veteran of the
Esprit movement, received an urgent summons from Msgr. Chollet, the
aged Archbishop of Cambrai.[1] Simon, a professor of French literature
at the University of Lille as well as a teacher at the Collège of Roubaix,
was received by a visibly upset prelate. Simon himself may well have
expected an unpleasant meeting, for although he had long maintained
fairly cordial relations with Msgr. Chollet, the Archbishop was a strict
Thomist, Maurrasian in his sympathies, and was reputed to have referred to the Cardinal's hat given his much younger and progressive
suffragan, Bishop Liénart of Lille, as a "cocked hat." When Simon
was received by Msgr. Chollet, his host was holding a copy of Simon's
recently published book, *Les Catholiques, la politique et l'argent*. The
book bore ample evidence of having been carefully read; its pages were
filled with marginal notations and underlined passages. "You have
written," Simon recollects the good prelate as saying, "an absurd work
which offends good sense and tact, which is going to divide Catholics a
little more and weaken the position of the Church in our unhappy country." For the next half hour the Archbishop attempted to substantiate
his criticism of Simon's book and then, finally closing the volume, he
told Simon: "This said, having read you line by line, I must say that
there is not a word contrary to either dogma or morality in the book
and that you limit yourself in it to the order of natural opinion and
disputed questions in which a Christian remains free to write nonsense."
Msgr. Chollet concluded the interview by pointing out that no ecclesiastical authority could take action of a doctrinal or disciplinary

---

[1] The following is taken from Pierre-Henri Simon, *Ce que je crois* (Paris: Bernard Grasset,
1966), 40–44; Pierre-Henri Simon, *Les Catholiques, la politique et l'argent* (Paris: Editions
Montaigne, 1936); Etienne Borne, "Un débat grave," *Esprit*, No. 45 (June, 1936), 450–452;
Béguin, "Une vie," 1000–1001; Coutrot, 107–113; and Rémond, *Les catholiques, le communisme et les crises*, 150–155.

character against a Catholic layman for exercising his liberty in such matters, whether that Catholic was an intellectual, an academician, or even an army general.

Msgr. Chollet's mention of an army general was a reference to General de Castelnau, the famous "Capuchin in army boots" of the First World War, the leader of the *Fédération Nationale Catholique* (F.N.C.), and a regular contributor to the Rightist *l'Echo de Paris*. In the pages of this paper Castelnau had vehemently attacked Simon's book. The book was clearly polemical in tone and was designed, in Simon's own words, "to demonstrate how the habitually reactionary and conservative attitude of Catholic milieux is tied to a capitalist morality and to monied interests." Within the context of the elections of the Popular Front, the occupation of the factories, and the angry humiliation of the bourgeoisie, "a number of pages in particular [including an appendix specifically attacking Castelnau], in which I affirmed that the electoral duty of a Christian, conscious of the fundamental exigencies of his morality, would be to prefer a candidate of the Left, even a *laïcisante* candidate, who proposes a program of social justice, to a clerical of the Right who defends the abusive privileges of property, appeared singularly scandalous." Castelnau's response was characteristic of the president of the anachronistic F.N.C. and other Catholics who were still obsessed with possible Masonic and *laïcist* influences infiltrating the Church.[2] The general charged that Simon was a "masked enemy of the Church introduced into a Catholic University." Castelnau's diatribe constituted a veritable anthology of the themes familiar to the Catholic Right – religious defense, nationalism, social paternalism. A little civil war ensued. Simon was hissed by students in the corridors of his university; the entire city of Lille was divided, most of it hostile to Simon; many parents threatened to withdraw their children from the school; and certain members of the administration demanded that Simon vacate his chair. Only the support of Cardinal Liénart and the judicious position taken by Msgr. Chollet prevented Simon from losing his position.

At almost precisely the same time, Emmanuel Mounier was fighting for the life of his journal. Indeed, this was not a new experience, for as early as May, 1933 Mounier and *Esprit* had been accused of Modernism and, because Catholics collaborated with non-Catholics in *Esprit*, of

---

[2] See, for example, Mounier, "Croquemitaines," *Esprit*, No. 22 (July, 1934), 623–624; and A. G. Michel, *La France sous l'étreinte maçonnique* (Paris: Fédération Nationale Catholique, n.d. [1934]).

renewing the error of the *Sillon*. The cause of *Esprit* had been taken up in a meeting of the Council of Vigilance of the Paris Archdiocese and only the support of ecclesiastical friends and an understanding Archbishop had saved Mounier and *Esprit* from being subjected to some sort of disciplinary measure.[3] Now, almost precisely three years later, the cause of *Esprit* was again in question. For some eighteen months, Castelnau and what Mounier referred to as *"Action Française* and its satellite milieux" had been waging "a systematic and very well organized attack" both in public print and by traditional Integralist delations to religious authorities "against all those whom they place under the label of Catholicism of the Left." [4] The forces of the Catholic Right and Integralism indiscriminately placed *Esprit, l'aube,* the Dominican-sponsored *Sept,* and the strange "Christian Marxist" journal *Terre Nouvelle* in the same camp. All were "Red Christians." At the end of May, 1936 Mounier received a letter from a friend who relayed "news from a very reliable source in Rome" that the condemnation of *Esprit* was imminent. Mounier spent two days in a state of extreme agitation until he received encouraging news from another friend who reported that matters were not quite as serious as had previously been thought. Mounier turned to his friend Msgr. Courbe for advice and was told to prepare a report on *Esprit* for Cardinal Verdier, the Archbishop of Paris, and to request a meeting with the Archbishop. He prepared a lengthy report and gave it to the Cardinal's secretary who, in turn, took it with him to Rome where the Cardinal was attending a Consistory. In late June Mounier was informed by an ecclesiastical friend that *Esprit* had not been mentioned once in all of his conversations with high personages in Rome. Finally, Mounier was received by the Archbishop of Paris, who expressed confidence in "our spirit and the necessity for our activity." [5] Not until more than a decade later were there to be rumors of disciplinary action being taken against *Esprit* and once again the rumors proved to be unfounded.

In this way Mounier, Simon, and *Esprit* encountered one of the most difficult problems confronting the Catholic in French politics – a problem with which the Christian democrats were only too familiar. And

---

[3] Marrou, "Un homme dans l'Eglise," 892; Béguin, "Une vie," 982; and Mounier, "Entretiens VII, 16 mai 1933," "Entretiens VII, 19 mai 1933," "Entretiens VII, 21 mai 1933," "Entretiens VII, 22 mai 1933," "Entretiens VII, 26 mai 1933," "Entretiens VII, 27 mai 1933," and "Entretiens VII, 14 juin 1933," *B.A.E.M.*, No. 34–35 (November, 1969), 41–58 *passim*.

[4] Mounier, "Entretiens IX, 30 mai 1936," *O.M.*, IV, 582.

[5] *Ibid.*; Mounier, "Extraits du rapport privé sur 'Esprit,'" and "Entretiens IX, 26 juin 1936," *O.M.*, IV, 582–595; and Béguin, "Une vie," 1000–1001.

Mounier also found himself and *Esprit* forced into an ironical alliance with the Christian democrats of *l'aube* and their friends of *Sept* by their common opposition to Castelnau and the Catholic Right. Indeed, between 1934–1935 and the War, as Mounier demonstrated the necessity of committing himself to increasingly definite political positions, he found himself in the company not only of the men of *l'aube* and *Sept* (and its successor *Temps présent*) but of the Christian democrats of the *Jeune-République* and, to a lesser extent, of the *Parti Démocrate Populaire*. Mounier, however, did not abandon or even moderate his opposition to Christian democracy and its adherents. Similarly, the Christian democrats did not alter their reservations concerning *Esprit*. When Pierre-Henri Simon published his "landmark in the political evolution of the Catholic world," as Mounier called Simon's controversial book,[6] *l'aube* published a cautious review, and even this was excessive in the opinion of Francisque Gay. Gay, who had been absent at the time, told his editorial assistant upon his return that "it would have been better not to have published it." [7]

In entering the realm of political controversy, Mounier was not only continuing his war of words on the confusion of Catholicism and "the established disorder," but he was also demonstrating that personalism was a guide to political choice, that he himself, as an observer noted, "was not a man of the study; he was not a colorless theoretician, but rather an energetic spirit, a militant Christian to whom knowledge meant a call to duty." [8] The position adopted by Mounier and *Esprit* were fairly typical of those of many members of the French political Left. In foreign affairs, Mounier's position evolved from pacifism in 1934–1935 to outright opposition to the Munich Agreement by way of condemnation of Mussolini's aggression against Abyssinia, opposition to Hitler's remilitarization of the Rhineland, and sympathy for the cause of the Spanish Republic against Franco and the Nationalists. In domestic affairs, Mounier's "purism," his "neither-nor" response to the riots of February, 1934, changed to support of the Popular Front. Certainly Mounier's political options were not always realistic or free of error, as even his friends admit.[9] Nor were they entirely free of the ambivalence which was characteristic of much of Mounier's work. In

---

[6] Mounier, "P.-H. Simon: Les Catholiques, la politique et l'argent," *Esprit* No. 44 (May, 1936), 225–228.

[7] Quoted in Carité, 131.

[8] Arnold Bauer, "Emmanuel Mounier," *The Personalist*, XXXI, No. 3 (July, 1950), 311.

[9] See, for example, Domenach, "L'Evénement politique," 10; and Goguel, "Positions politiques," 812.

retrospect, Mounier himself said that "from the moment we rejected the comfort of Olympian attitudes," the *Esprit* team was compelled to make decisions which were incompatible with theoretical purity. Such decisions never had the heroic character Mounier wished them to have. The tension between the early purism of *Esprit* and its immersion in temporal affairs persisted for a long time, Mounier confessed. "We could always find sufficiently good grounds in the enemy's camp, sufficient baseness and ignominy in that of our allies, to risk altering our decision. ... Our struggles towards decision were many and the outcome never certain." [10] Mounier's political options were notable for their honesty, for the consistency with which they reflected his personalist perspectives, and perhaps most important for the manner in which they revealed the remarkable moral resources Mounier brought to every task to which he addressed himself.

Mounier's first total immersion in the murky waters of political controversy occurred early in 1935 during the heated debate over the extension of the French military conscription law from one to two years. In January of that year General de Castelnau argued in *l'Echo de Paris* that not only did German military preparations necessitate this action but the Christmas message of Pope Pius XI, *Dissipa gentes quae bella volunt*, made it incumbent upon Catholics to support the passage of the law.[11] On March 1 in its review of the press, the Catholic weekly *Sept* cited the English weekly *Catholic Herald* which had criticized Castelnau and added its own commentary to the effect that recourse to armaments was an "intolerable scandal" in the eyes of a sincere Christian. A little more than a week later, General de Castelnau responded to his critics. The General said the latter were "foreign agents" and "defeatists." At this juncture, the response to Castelnau came not from *Sept* but from the editor of *Esprit*.

The General's endorsement of the two-years law coincided with the return of the Saar Basin to Germany and was followed shortly by Hitler's repudiation of the military clauses of the Versailles Treaty; and even short of such provocations, the law could be justified on the basis of the rapidly decreasing number of Frenchmen of military conscription age. Mounier's attack upon General de Castelnau, however, did not reflect concern with any of these developments. Rather, he took the General to task for buttressing his demand for armaments with

---

[10] Mounier, "What is Personalism?," in *Be Not Afraid*, 126.
[11] The controversy is recounted in Rémond, *Les catholiques, le communisme et les crises*, 79ff.; and in Coutrot, 267ff.

papal statements and for accusing his opponents of being unpatriotic and, implicitly, less Catholic than the men of *l'Echo de Paris*. Mounier concluded his angry attack on Castelnau with a rhetorical question that immediately became a *mot célèbre*. "General, are not three sons enough?," Mounier asked, referring to the sons General de Castelnau had lost in the First World War.[12] After receiving the justifiably violent response from Castelnau, Mounier apologized both privately and in public print for his outburst and further explained his position.[13]

Mounier's explanation clearly revealed that his opposition to General de Castelnau was rooted far less in any consideration of the practical problems of French security in the face of new international developments than in the basic revolutionary position of *Esprit*. The patriotism of the Catholic Right, he argued was nothing more than a mask for "the commercialization of death and of spiritual values by the purveyors of the army." Those who sounded the trumpets of nationalism while they received dividends in the banks of Basel and exported war matériel to Germany were hypocrites, Mounier charged. More important in Mounier's judgment was the "abominable confusion" of *l'Echo de Paris*: the journal's tendency, typified by Castelnau, to link Catholicism to the men of money and of war, to consolidate "the greatest scandal of the century," the abandonment of Christianity by the proletariat. Although he opposed what he called "enervated pacifism" and "parliamentary anti-militarism," Mounier contended that national defense should not be used as a "pretext for a new militarization of consciences and of the resources of the nation." Mounier feared lest increased French armaments would consolidate the unjust status quo and, in the case of General de Castelnau and his supporters, perpetuate the identification of Catholicism with "the established disorder." That increased armaments would have had either result is highly problematical.

At the same time Mounier became involved in another controversy in which he took his first definite stand in an election campaign. Among the men who had supported General de Castelnau in his polemic with Mounier was Jean Chiappe, the former Prefect of Police in Paris. Long hated by the Left which accused him of negligence, if not of outright complicity, in the Stavisky affair, Chiappe was a candidate in Notre-Dame-des-Champs for a seat on the Paris Municipal Council. André

---

[12] Mounier, "Les catholiques et la défense nationale," *Esprit*, No. 31 (April, 1935), 133–134.
[13] Mounier, "Une polémique," *Esprit*, No. 32 (May, 1935), 316–320; and Rémond, *Les catholiques, le communisme et les crises*, 82–83.

Ulmann of *Esprit* accused Chiappe of having used the police for his own political purposes, of having allowed vice to operate openly in Paris, and of cultivating numerous scandalous associations.[14] To contest the candidacy of Chiappe, who was posing as "the Catholic Candidate," the Christian democrats of *l'aube* first approached the *Parti Démocrate Populaire* with the hope that it would provide a candidate. "The type of man needed [in the sixth arrondissement to oppose Chiappe] was a *Démocrate Populaire* of the Right," Mounier noted in his diary in an entirely uncharacteristic display of political calculation.[15] Failing to obtain a *Démocrate Populaire* willing to sacrifice himself in a losing cause, Francisque Gay and his friends persuaded a young collaborator of *Esprit* to run against Chiappe. Jacques Madaule, who joined the *Jeune-République* a year later, was completely innocent of political experience but he was, *Esprit* proclaimed, "the candidate of a Christian conscience." [16]

In the midst of the Chiappe-Madaule campaign, *Esprit* departed from its practice of refusing to oppose or support individual candidates or parties. In May, 1935 a manifesto entitled "Against Chiappe" and signed *"Esprit"* appeared in the journal. The manifesto stated that *Esprit* was uninterested in the electoral game and could not support any particular candidate. But Chiappe was a symbol of the confusions that *Esprit* was founded to denounce. Chiappe's candidacy was a scandal not because he was a man of the Right or disliked by the Left but rather because, after ten years of open association with corruption and vice, he now presented himself as a Catholic candidate of Order, Family, Property, and the Nation. "We ask all our friends of the VIe to block this candidate of Disorder. We ask our Catholic friends in particular," the manifesto stated. Then, after detailing Ulmann's charges against Chiappe, *Esprit* stated that a young Catholic (Madaule) had made the gesture for which *Esprit* had waited.[17] Shortly after the publication of this manifesto a group of men who identified themselves as "Catholic writers, journalists, and publicists" issued a statement in support of Madaule. "In order to permit all the inhabitants of a quarter known for its traditions of honor to participate in the electoral process, they [the signers of the manifesto] have designated as a candidate a man who is a symbol of propriety in his civic, professional and family

---

[14] André Ulmann, "La candidature Chiappe, scandale public," *Esprit*, No. 31 (April, 1935), 126–128.

[15] Mounier, "Entretiens VIII, 17 mai 1935," *O.M.*, IV, 569.

[16] "Contre Chiappe," *Esprit*, No. 32 (May, 1935), 333.

[17] *Ibid.*, 331–333.

life." The signatories of the statement included Paul Archambault, Georges Bidault, Joseph Folliet, Maurice Lacroix of the *Jeune-République*, Jean Soulairol of *la Vie Catholique*, and Pierre-Henri Simon.[18] Only after the election did Mounier formally add his name to these signatories. It was not on the manifesto, he explained, because his controversy with General de Castelnau would have damaged Madaule's campaign.[19]

No doubt, opposing Chiappe's candidacy with that of another Catholic who was a good family man was the most effective political tactic possible; but the obvious religious implications of the appeal suggest that Mounier had played the game he had so consistently condemned. He had perhaps discovered what his Christian democratic allies had already learned in their bitter conflicts with the Catholic Right: the task of dissociating Catholicism from the Right without falling victim to the opposite error was far from easy. Mounier's reasons for associating himself with the Christian democratic campaign in support of Madaule merit further clarification.

A few days before the election, Chiappe and his supporters had distributed a circular in which Madaule was defamed as a "Pharisée" and an "illustrious unknown." Mounier charged that the latter meant that the police did not have a dossier on Madaule and the former that Madaule "is a Catholic who does not separate politics from morality." Those who voted for Chiappe in ignorance of the facts could not be condemned. But the men who responded to the revelations of Ulmann with the crude statement in *l'Echo de Paris* that "we have known about M. Chiappe longer than you have, ... but archbishops do not make good politicians" were the sworn enemies of *Esprit*.[20] In both the Castelnau and Chiappe affairs, Mounier's profoundest antipathies had been aroused by his opponents' failure to comprehend the proper relationship of religion and politics. Castelnau and his supporters had failed to distinguish properly between the two while many of the supporters of Chiappe, who received some 4,000 votes to Madaule's 488, had completely separated the two. It was with these *affaires* in mind that Mounier began a long entry in his diary in mid-May, 1935 with the words: "In a thoroughly *péguyste* position for fifteen days." [21]

In another sense also Mounier recalled the name of Péguy in the same diary entry. Referring to his "abominable insult" to the General, Mounier wrote that the words had come from deep within him, from

---

[18] Reprinted in Mounier, "Leçons d'une campagne," *Esprit*, No. 33 (June, 1935), 458–459.
[19] *Ibid.*, 459.
[20] *Ibid.*, 459–460.
[21] Mounier, "Entretiens VIII, 17 mai 1935," *O.M.*, IV, 567–569

his affection for the dead youths. "How can all of these good, virtuous, honest men who are indignant be made to feel that there was something exceptionally pure in that question? They liked articles from me in which there was a serenity, a kind of happy chastity in ideas and tone." He himself had lulled his readers into a state of self-satisfaction, colorless indolence, and softness, which had made his brutal question all the more shocking. But now, happily, this wrong had been righted. "The idol is broken," Mounier wrote, "the idol of complacent men. The little saint." Mounier's personal reaction to the events of the spring of 1935 led him once more to the secret source of his revolutionary indignation against the soft, petit-bourgeois Christianity he condemned.

Mounier's entrance into the arena of political controversy was *péguyste* in yet another sense, although Mounier himself perhaps did not clearly recognize it. In both controversies Mounier's foremost allies had been the Catholic and Christian democrats of *l'aube, Sept, la Vie intellectuelle,* and the J.O.C. The Catholic Right began to include Mounier and *Esprit* on its Index of Christian democratic and "Red Christian" heretics. Henri Massis accused *Esprit* of justifying German patriotism and condemning French patriotism. The defeatists and false spiritualists of *Esprit*, he was later to write, abandoned themselves to "pious equivocations," to "disastrous aberrations," and to "mournful abdications" in the face of the dangers which confronted France. And he added, of course, that *Esprit*, like so many Catholics in France, had been penetrated by the propaganda of *l'Humanité* and was, in fact, a mouthpiece for the Communists.[22] Because the Communist Party had contended that "the two-years law means war," Massis argued that Mounier and *Esprit* had formed "an ignoble alliance with materialism negating God." [23] Other veterans of *Action Française* accused Mounier of being unrealistic and of submitting to the vague idealism he so abhorred by opposing French rearmament.[24] Although this particular criticism was not entirely without merit, it was strange that it should come from men who less than a year later, when confronted with Mussolini's aggression against Abyssinia, had begun their remarkable about-face with the slogan "Above all, no war." [25]

The Right continued its attacks on Mounier and the Catholic Left throughout the 1930s. A climax was reached in May and June of 1936

---

[22] Massis, *Maurras et notre temps*, I, 111–113.
[23] Quoted in Mounier, "Polémiques," *Esprit*, No. 33 (June, 1935), 470.
[24] Mounier, "Une polémique," 319.
[25] On the about-face of the Right, see Charles Micaud, *The French Right and Nazi Germany, 1933–1939* (Durham, N.C.: Dule University Press, 1943).

when Simon nearly lost his chair in Lille and *Esprit* was rumored to be on the verge of condemnation. In Mounier's view, what had motivated the onslaught on *Esprit, l'aube, Sept,* and their allies was the political line they had adopted. One of the chief agents of this campaign was Robert Havard de la Montagne, a veteran of *Action Française,* who contended that without the salutary influence of *Action Française* French Catholicism was shifting too far to the Left. Havard de la Montagne claimed that both the errors and the expanding influence of such publications as *Sept, Esprit, l'aube,* and, later, *Temps présent* were due to the condemnation of *Action Française* which had removed the right-wing champions of Catholicism and had left such men as Mauriac, Mounier, Maritain, Madaule, Merklen (of *La Croix*), Bidault, and Gay an opportunity to exercise their corrupting activities.[26] The campaign against the Catholic Left claimed one important victim. In August, 1937 *Sept* was forced to discontinue publication. It was shortly replaced, however, by *Temps présent.*

By the mid-1930s Mounier and his allies had begun to dissociate Catholicism and nationalism which, for a half-century, had been identified by friends and foes of Catholicism alike.[27] *Esprit, l'aube,* and *Sept* supported forms of pacifism that clearly separated them from the Catholic Right. In not entirely disparate ways they supported a policy of Franco-German rapprochement; they opposed France's pursuit of security by means of armaments and encircling alliances; and they supported the League of Nations not as a weapon to enforce the unjust status quo of 1919–1920 but as a means of collective security and treaty revision.

The pacifism of *l'aube* has been defined as "the defense of an international policy based on a spirit of confidence and on the condemnation of war." More specifically, the Christian pacifism of *l'aube* included the ideas of "tranquility in order" and "organic order," the latter in particular being a phrase cherished by all Christian democrats.[28] The collaborators of *Sept* were pacifists also but in a somewhat different sense. They supported international dialogue and rapprochement between peoples but they took great care to avoid two errors. The first error, in their judgment, was the belief that only force and armaments could maintain peace; and the second was that of impru-

---

[26] Weber, 248. Weber refers to "Mercklen" which is undoubtedly a misspelling of Père Léon Merklen of *La Croix.*

[27] Rémond, *Les catholiques, le communisme et les crises,* 88.

[28] Mayeur, *l'aube,* 108.

dently responding to German rearmament by "an integral disarmament." [29]

Mounier's pacifism was more akin to that of *Sept* than to that of *l'aube*, for it was positive and so vigorous that the phrase "tranquility in order" was hardly descriptive of it. In June, 1935 Mounier and *Esprit* repudiated "that pacifism which is merely a coalition of the Tranquil against heroism and the last refuge of collective fears ... which leads to the folly of armaments." [30] In a series of articles, special issues, and a collective declaration, Mounier and *Esprit* lashed out at "international lies," the merchants of munitions and death, the idolatrous nationalism of the *bien-pensant* press, the hypocrisy of those who made the League of Nations into a kind of "consortium of the satisfied," the "confused and ambiguous realism" of Maurrasien *raison d'Etat*, and a "certain nationalist press' which accused all those who criticized the two-years conscription law and "the established disorder" of materialism, Marxism, and a lack of patriotism.[31] The most dangerous international lie was the lie of Germany's unilateral responsibility. Those who propagated it believed that France was a paragon of virtue, that a disinterested and chivalric France was confronted by a German nation that consistently acted in bad faith. Time and again Mounier and *Esprit* condemned the press, the munitions makers, war profiteers, and those who used a double standard of truth and justice. On the day after Hitler's proclamation of military conscription, stocks fell on the Paris Bourse with the notable exception of Schneider, which rose thirty-eight points. "What a magnificent client death is!" Mounier proclaimed with *péguyste* anger.

Mounier and *Esprit* did more than denounce what they considered to be the lies and spiritual dangers of the Nationalist Right. They condemned any unilateral violation of a treaty as a warlike act; they admitted that national defense was a measure of necessary prudence; and they condemned the errors of both Weimar and Hitlerian Germany including its "dangerous and insolent militarism," its acts of "intolerable international indiscipline" and its sabotage of efforts for general disarmament. They supported the League but because of its deficiencies they called for "the constitution of an international juridical organization which has authority over national sovereignties on behalf

[29] Coutrot, 114.

[30] "Notre Patrie. Déclaration collective," *Esprit*, No. 33 (June, 1935), 344.

[31] *Ibid.*, 339–348; Mounier, "L'après-guerre. Tableau des responsabilités," *Esprit*, No. 34 (July, 1935), 499–500; and Mounier, "La course à la guerre," *Esprit*, No. 31 (April, 1935), 142–148.

of distributive justice with the express proviso that it be independent of every interest of class, group or regime." Most specifically of all, they called for the nationalization of all war industries. On balance nonetheless, Mounier and *Esprit* were far more vigorous in their condemnations of the Right than in their positive proposals.

There was no more avid proponent of Franco-German reconciliation and international cooperation and arbitration than the little *Jeune-République*. The party declared in the summer of 1934 that the international crisis was a direct result of nationalism. Even after Hitler's proclamation of military conscription, the *Jeune-République* stated that the maintenance of international peace required collaboration between peoples no matter what form of domestic political regime they lived under. The party declared that anti-Fascism was not an adequate basis for French foreign policy; it condemned armaments as one of the principal causes of war and called for both moral and material disarmament; and it was particularly emphatic in demanding the revision of the peace treaties and that Germany be given equal rights.[32] Not surprisingly, in view of its fervent pacifism, the party's two deputies, Guy Menant and Philippe Serre, refused to support the two-years law.[33]

In the controversy over the extension of military conscription, *l'aube* opposed the two-years law although it did so with none of the vehemence exhibited by the men of *Esprit*. Georges Bidault, for example, could not conceal his distaste for lengthening the term of military service but at the same time he denounced "the wastefulness and incapacity" of the general staff which made the new law necessary and called for a reorganization of the army.[34] In the Chamber itself all sixteen members of the *Parti Démocrate Populaire* supported the two-years law.[35]

The general position of the *Parti Démocrate Populaire* was far more moderate than that of the *Jeune-République*. Shortly after Hitler's advent to power Ernest Pezet, the party's leading foreign policy spokesman, admitted the need for treaty revision but he emphasized that the grievances of the neutral and friendly states of eastern Europe were far too often overlooked. Peace treaties, he said, were "imperfect like any

---

[32] See Georges Hoog *et al.*, "Aspects de la crise," *Cahiers de la Démocratie*, No. 14–15 (July-August, 1934), 13–17; and Georges Hoog, "Jeune-République et Rassemblement Populaire," *Cahiers de la Démocratie*, No. 41–42 (October-November, 1936), 28–29.

[33] *J.O.C.*, No. 32 (March 15, 1935), 1060–1061.

[34] Coutrot, 113.

[35] *J.O.C.*, No. 32 (March 15, 1935), 1060–1061.

human work." [36] Later in the same year Raymond-Laurent admitted that the terms of Versailles had never been "integrally executed" but he added that armaments and alliances were not the real solutions to the problem of French security – nor, he added, was disarmament. Rather, like most Christian democrats, Raymond-Laurent called for the juridical organization of peace and security. The alternatives confronting Europe, he said, were either to unite in a community of nations or to risk perishing.[37] Pezet meanwhile persisted in his support of the League as both a safeguard of French security and an instrument of treaty revision and in his defense of the French East European alliance system which he once described as "branches grafted on the trunk" of the Covenant of the League.[38] Austria and Czechoslovakia were to have no better friend in the French Chamber than Pezet.

The Ethiopian crisis was more important than Hitler's initial violation of the Treaty of Versailles in the political evolution of *Esprit* and the Christian democratic Left. Mussolini's aggression against Ethiopia and the resultant questions of voting and applying economic sanctions were decisive factors in moderating the pacifism of Mounier and his Christian democratic allies. The Ethiopian crisis also acted as a catalyst in the Right's abandonment of its traditional nationalism and its movement in the direction of appeasement.[39] Although a pro-sanctionist observer contended that "the Ethiopian War, more than any other event, made a number of Catholics break their traditional ties with the parties of the Right," [40] the ranks of Catholics who opposed Fascism were swelled at this time only by the parliamentary representatives of the *Parti Démocrate Populaire*. The latter increasingly separated themselves from the Right in foreign affairs while they carefully cultivated their conservative electoral clientele in domestic affairs.

The Ethiopian crisis provided a stern test of the Christian democrats' confidence in the League as an effective instrument of international pacification. Moreover, in addition to the maze of complicated problems relating to the security of France and the peace of Europe which confronted all Frenchmen, Mussolini's "defense of the Christian West"

---

[36] "La problème de la revision des traités. Une conversation avec M. Ernest Pezet," *l'Eveil des Peuples*, April 30, 1933.

[37] Raymond-Laurent, *Face à la Crise*, 95–129 *passim*.

[38] See *J.O.C.*, No. 19 (February 25, 1935), 572–576.

[39] Micaud, *The French Right and Nazi Germany*, 65. For a survey of French press opinion concerning Fascist Italy, see Pierre Milza, *L'Italie fasciste devant l'opinion française, 1920–1940* (Paris: Armand Colin, 1967).

[40] Simon, *La grande crise de la République française*, 130. See also Mounier, "Entretiens VIII, 24 octobre 1935," *O.M.*, IV, 576.

posed a special problem for French Catholics. Like all Frenchmen, Catholics had to weigh the risks inherent in opposing Mussolini's aggression: the risk of jeopardizing the relations between France and Italy contained in the Ciano-Laval Agreement of January, 1935 and the Stresa Front of April, 1935; the risk of seriously undermining the future usefulness of the League by applying sanctions against Italy; and perhaps even the risk of a general European war. What made the split between the great mass of French Catholics who supported Mussolini and the little coterie of *Esprit*, *l'aube*, the *Jeune-République*, the *Parti Démocrate Populaire*, and most of the collaborators of *Sept* especially bitter was the religious question.[41] In several statements prior to the Italian attack on Ethiopia, Pope Pius XI had condemned the idea that the demographic and economic needs of Italy constituted in and of themselves the right of military expansion. But the Pope did this with sufficient ambiguity to provide ammunition for the Catholic Right, and the way in which the major French press agencies reported the Papal statements further compounded this ambiguity.[42] For Mounier and many of his Christian democratic allies, the Ethiopian crisis was in large measure less a problem which affected the security of France and the peace of Europe than a clear-cut question of international law and morality.

This particular response to Mussolini's aggression was determined, in part at least, by a defense of Mussolini by Henri Massis and a group of Right-wing intellectuals. On October 4, 1935 a "Manifesto of French intellectuals. For the defense of the West and peace in Europe" appeared. The signatories contended that Italian expansion at the expense of Ethiopia was justified by the superior virtues of the civilization of the Christian West which Italy represented and that the imposition of sanctions upon Italy would seriously endanger the peace of Europe.[43] The initial reaction to the Right's crude attempt to justify aggression by condemning "a false juridical universalism which places on a footing of equality the superior and the inferior, the civilized and the barbarian," was a "Manifesto for the respect of international law" drawn up by a group of anti-Fascist intellectuals who condemned the racism implicit in the Rightist manifesto. Shortly thereafter, a third

---

[41] *Ibid.*, 85.

[42] Rémond, *Les catholiques, le communisme et les crises*, 91–96; Coutrot, 172–173; Mayeur, *l'aube*, 116–119; and Mounier, "L'opinion chrétienne et la guerre d'Ethiopie," *Esprit*, No. 37 (October, 1935), 136–138.

[43] Rémond, *Les catholiques, le communisme et les crises*, 108–110. See the criticism of Yves Simon, *La campagne d'Ethiopie et la pensée politique française* (Lille: S.I.L.C., n.d.), 99–107.

declaration, a "Manifesto for Justice and Peace," appeared almost simultaneously in *l'aube, la Vie Catholique, Sept, le Petit Démocrate,* and *Esprit.*[44] The signatories of the new manifesto included Mounier, Etienne Borne, Pierre-Henri Simon, Jean Lacroix, and other members of *Esprit.* The purpose of the new manifesto was not to add fuel to the already bitter political debate over Ethiopia but rather to clarify the moral issues involved in Mussolini's act of aggression and the Right's defense of this aggression.[45]

The "Manifesto for Justice and Peace" emphasized that neither the need for expansion nor the work of civilization constituted the right to seize the territories of another nation and to bring death to its inhabitants. A new European war would be an irreparable catastrophe, the manifesto stated, but the elementary requirements of justice demanded that an act of aggression be forthrightly condemned. That the benefits of Western civilization should be demonstrated to the people of Ethiopia by the superiority of its means of destruction was a moral disaster. So too, the manifesto declared, was the sophism explicit in the Right's argument concerning the racial superiority of the Italians over the natives of Ethiopia. The manifesto concluded that the League of Nations should act as the organ of those peoples and governments which sincerely desired both justice and peace.

To this defense of Ethiopia on the bases of international law and morality, the Right responded with what they referred to as "political realism." The gist of the most pervasive argument against sanctions was that they would antagonize Italy and thereby weaken or completely break the ties of Franco-Italian friendship. It was argued that sanctions would create the risk of a European war in which France's position in the face of German advances on the continent would be seriously weakened.[46] The friends of Italy among French Catholics expressed their views with their customary virulence in *L'Action Française, la France catholique,* and *l'Echo de Paris.* "*L'aube* is for war," *L'Action Française* stated, after contending that for several years *l'aube* had pursued a policy of weakness and treason by supporting Franco-German rapprochement. Maurras himself published a list of 140 members of Parliament who allegedly favored sanctions and, after adding

---

[44] The manifesto was published on October 18 and 19, 1935 in *la Vie Catholique, l'aube, Sept,* and *le Petit Démocrate,* and in the November issue of *Esprit,* 306–309. The text is reprinted in Rémond, *Les catholiques, le communisme et les crises,* 112–115, and in Mayeur, *l'aube,* 227–228.

[45] Mayeur, *l'aube,* 121.

[46] Micaud, *The French Right and Nazi Germany,* 52–66 *passim.*

the names of Léon Blum and Francisque Gay to his list, called for their punishment by death in the event of French mobilization. Gay, as he so often did, took Maurras seriously and another of the many legal battles between the two men ensued with Maurras ultimately receiving a short prison sentence.[47]

Two of the ablest of the Christian democratic spokesmen on foreign policy opposed the practical principle of the indivisibility of the peace to the "political realism" of the Right. Bidault asked: "Are the friends of Fascist aggression incapable of understanding that all of the liberties that they grant the Transalpine dictator work to the benefit of another dictator?" Even more explicitly he asked if France's allies in eastern Europe might not feel that a European aggressor would receive the same treatment as that proposed by the anti-sanctionists for an African aggressor. If this occurred, Bidault concluded prophetically, Hitler's *Mittel Europa* would be complete.[48] Ernest Pezet also supported the strict application of sanctions against Italy. In the heated debate in the Chamber that followed the Hoare-Laval Agreement to resolve the Abyssinian crisis by granting Italy substantial territorial and economic concessions primarily at the expense of Abyssinia, Pezet contended that if France refused to honor her commitments to the League, her eastern European allies would undoubtedly, and with good reason, conclude that unless the frontiers of France were actually violated, France would not fulfill her commitments in eastern Europe.[49] As he was always to do, Pezet discussed the immediate question confronting French foreign policy-makers in terms of the entire European situation and with special attention to both the possible reactions of France's Little Entente allies and the contractual commitments of France in Europe.[50]

Although the *Parti Démocrate Populaire* and the *Jeune-République* had supported the Ciano-Laval Agreement, they refused to base Franco-Italian reconciliation on acquiescence to Italian aggression. Like the men of *l'aube*, who had supported Laval's quest for Mussolini's friendship as a means of isolating Hitler, they were firmly pro-sanctionist.[51] To sanction Italian aggression, Pezet argued in late December, 1935, would constitute a major and disastrous change in

---

[47] Mayeur, *l'aube*, 122–123; Rémond, *Les catholiques, le communisme et les crises*, 96–102; and Weber, 288–289.
[48] Mayeur, *l'aube*, 121; and Rémond, *Les catholiques, le communisme et lescrises*,106–107.
[49] *J.O.C.*, No. 84 (December 28, 1935), 2845–2849.
[50] *Ibid.*; and *J.O.C.*, No. 50 (June 23, 1936), 1538–1541.
[51] Milza, 256; and *J.O.C.*, No. 50 (June 23, 1936), 1538–1539.

French policy by abandoning the principle of collective security.[52] In the Chamber the deputies of the *Parti Démocrate Populaire* voted against Laval's attempt to appease Italy. The two deputies of the *Jeune-République*, on the other hand, supported Laval but there is little doubt that their support was not rooted in any sympathy for Mussolini. Georges Hoog joined a *Comité d'assistance aux victimes de la guerre en Ethiopie* which was sponsored by the anti-Fascist journal *Vigilance* and which sent an ambulance to Abyssinia.[53]

The collaborators of *Sept* actively participated in drawing up the "Manifesto for Justice and Peace" and were consistent in their opposition to Mussolini and in their support of the League. Among the more prominent collaborators of the weekly, only Etienne Gilson attempted to defend the aggressive intentions of Mussolini and he terminated his association with *Sept* in the summer of 1935.[54] Early in April, 1936 the journal addressed a questionnaire to its readers on the international situation. The results of this "referendum" clearly revealed that *Sept* and its readers were warm supporters of the maintenance of peace by means of international organizations. A large majority supported the revision of the peace treaties and the League, opposed a policy of alliances and, by a rather slim margin, opposed the continuation of sanctions against Italy.[55] Mounier was not in disagreement with the majority of the readers of *Sept*. The *Amis d'Esprit* published an appeal for a peace plebiscite in May, 1936 and Mounier himself assumed the responsibility of representing his journal in this international effort. The plebiscite asked for an end to building up armed forces, the use of existing mechanisms for the pacific resolution of present conflicts, a world treaty providing for immediate arms reduction as a first step toward total and universal disarmament, and an agreement which would put an end to the economic anarchy of the world.[56]

Mounier's assessment of the Abyssinian crisis lacked the realism which characterized the positions of Bidault and Pezet. Like many opponents of Laval, Mounier suspected that the French Foreign Minister had given Mussolini *laissez passer* in Africa during his visit to Rome in January, 1935.[57] Mounier was almost deliberately unconcerned about

[52] *J.O.C.*, No. 84 (December 28, 1935), 2848–2849.

[53] "Comité d'assistance aux victimes de la guerre en Ethiopie," *Vigilance*, No. 33 (February 15, 1936), 13.

[54] Coutrot, 173–175.

[55] *Ibid.*, 176.

[56] "Amis d'Esprit. Plébicitez la Paix," *Esprit*, No. 44 (May, 1936), 259–260.

[57] Mounier, "Déclaration sur un alliance franco-allemande," *Esprit*, No. 39 (December, 1935), 481.

the effects of the Abyssinian crisis upon French security. His approach to the crisis was based entirely upon Mussolini's violation of international law and morality. The manifesto to which he lent his name accurately stated his fundamental position. As always, he was concerned with the moral dimensions of the crisis.

"The Ethiopian conflict," Mounier noted cryptically in his diary, "has continued the work of February 12, especially in Catholic circles." [58] He persisted in condemning the French alliance system to which he attributed the acute encirclement-psychosis of Germany. In December, 1935 he supported some sort of entente between France and Germany[59] and he opposed the Franco-Soviet Pact of May, 1935 because it duplicated France's obligations as a member of the League.[60] The Christian democrats of *l'aube*, the *Parti Démocrate Populaire*, and the *Jeune-République*, on the other hand, supported the Pact when it was finally debated and passed in the Chamber in February, 1936.[61] So far had the *Jeune-République* departed from its extreme pacifism of the 1920s that its secretary-general proposed that the Pact be expanded.[62]

The Chamber's ratification of the Franco-Soviet Pact provided Hitler with an excuse to remilitarize the Rhineland, thereby violating not only the Treaty of Versailles but the Treaty of Locarno of 1925 as well. Although none of the Christian democrats explicitly proposed the use of military force, all of them adopted a "policy of firmness." Once again it was Ernest Pezet who recognized most clearly the consequences of Hitler's latest action. In a lengthy speech in the Chamber, he told his colleagues that the new laws of necessity and expansion had now triumphed over the international law that had governed the relations of the European states since the First World War.[63] He complained that the French government had apparently not yet fully recognized the consequences of the new law of German racism. Pezet proposed that even at this late date the Covenant of the League be strengthened and the treaties of 1919–1920 be readjusted to prevent their alteration by force. As preliminary steps in this direction, Pezet proposed that the new government of Léon Blum should reverse its intention of supporting the withdrawal of sanctions against Italy and that the most

---

[58] Mounier, "Entretiens VIII, 24 octobre 1935," *O.M.*, IV, 576.
[59] Mounier, "Adresse des vivants à quelques survivants," *Esprit*, No. 43 (April, 1936), 5.
[60] *Ibid.*, 2–16 *passim*.
[61] *J.O.C.*, No. 21 (February 27, 1936), 647–648; Micaud, *The French Right and Nazi Germany*, 68, 70–71.
[62] Hoog, "Jeune-République et Rassemblement Populaire," 31–32.
[63] *J.O.C.*, No. 50 (June 23, 1936), 1538–1541.

serious defect in the French alliance system should be corrected. Pezet considered the latter to be the increasingly close economic ties between the Third Reich and France's eastern European allies. As a corrective, Pezet proposed the formation of some sort of Danubian economic pact between France and the latter nations.

Georges Bidault's response to the remilitarization of the Rhineland clearly reflected the dilemma of the Christian democrat who opposed German aggression and yet retained some vestiges of his earlier pacifism. Immediately Bidault expressed his belief that Hitler's "abominable action" would arouse the anger and indignation of everyone and his hope that this anger and indignation would not remain "platonic." But he added that France's position would be much stronger had she expressed her hostility to the violation of treaties more forcefully in the past. Several days later Bidault stated that "the response [to Hilter's remilitarization of the Rhineland] does not depend solely upon France," but upon the League and the peoples of Europe. At the same time he indicated that neither sanctions nor negotiations with Hitler could solve the problem. A week later Bidault reaffirmed his faith in collective security. The restoration of confidence in the treaties was in his judgment, and in that of the men of *l'aube* generally, a prerequisite of any negotiations.[64]

Mounier's response to the remilitarization of the Rhineland was not entirely dissimilar to the responses of both Bidault and Pezet. While he remained consistent in his opposition to strengthening or expanding French alliances, Mounier recognized that the remilitarization of the Rhineland constituted a revolutionary alteration in the diplomatic alignment of the states of Europe.[65] At first glance, however, Mounier's assessment was very similar to the one expressed in the famous leader in *The Times* of London: "... the old structure of European peace, one-sided and unbalanced, is nearly in ruins ... it is the moment, not to despair, but to rebuild." [66] Mounier proposed that the old positions and old treaties be liquidated on the grounds that any policy based upon them would only prolong the humiliation of Germany and consequently consolidate Hitler's position within Germany.[67] Like Pezet, he condemned Hitler's unilateral repudiation of Locarno and proposed that the Covenant of the League should be strenghtened so

---

[64] Mayeur, *l'aube*, 125–126.

[65] Mounier, "Adresse des vivants à quelques survivants," 8.

[66] Quoted in A. L. Rowse, *Appeasement: A Study in Political Decline, 1933–39* (New York: W. W. Norton & Co., Inc., 1963), 39.

[67] Mounier, "Adresse des vivants à quelques survivants," 9–16.

as to facilitate treaty revision. Mounier also proposed that the League should impose sanctions on Germany and that the Rhineland violation be adjudicated by the International Tribunal at the Hague. Mounier's residue of pacifism, however, prevented him from supporting increased armaments, even of the economic variety proposed by Pezet. The best defense against Fascist aggression, he believed, was the negotiation of issues dividing France and Germany.

In one final respect, Mounier and Pezet were in complete agreement. Both of them were aware of what Mounier termed "the dangerous tendency on the part of the French to make foreign policy with the sentiments of domestic politics." [68] Among the reasons for the French Right's support of Mussolini's aggression against Abyssinia, its failure to condemn forthrightly Hitler's violation of Versailles and Locarno, and its opposition to the Franco-Soviet Pact were its sympathies for the authoritarian governments of Italy and Germany and its fear of Communism. These attitudes were accentuated by the Popular Front coalition of Radicals, Socialists, and Communists which won the elections of April and May, 1936 and formed a government under Léon Blum in June of the same year. Mounier, *l'aube, Sept*, and the Christian democratic parties had to take a position on the actual substance of the program of the Popular Front but, in addition, the question of collaborating with the Communist supporters of the Popular Front raised a religious question. The question of collaborating with the Communists bitterly divided French Catholics but it did not raise the old issues of clericalism and anticlericalism. The quarrels within French Catholicism had practically no effect upon the relations between Catholics and the state.[69]

The issue of Catholic-Communist collaboration was raised in an especially acute form by a new tactic adopted by the French Communist Party. In April, 1936 Maurice Thorez offered his famous "outstretched hand" to French Catholics in an address over Radio-Paris.[70] The response of French Catholics to Thorez's appeal was a massive *non possumus*.[71] Only the Catholic members of one organization and a few

[68] Mounier, "Déclaration sur une alliance franco-allemande," 482. For Pezet's views see *J.O.C.*, No. 50 (June 23, 1936), 1538–1539.

[69] For a general assessment of the historical significance of the Popular Front in this context, see René Rémond, "Les catholiques et le Front Populaire (1936–1937)," *Archives de sociologie des religions*, No. 10 (July-December, 1960), 63–69.

[70] *L'Humanité*, April 19, 1936 quoted in Rémond, *Les catholiques, le communisme et les crises*, 218.

[71] See, for example, Gaston Fessard, *La main tendue. Le dialogue catholique-communiste est-il possible?* (Paris: Bernard Grasset, 1937); Gaëtan Bernoville, *La farce de la main tendue du "Frente popular" au "Front populaire"* (Paris: Bernard Grasset, 1937); Marc Scherer,

isolated individuals accepted the proferred alliance with the Communist Party. But because they did, other Catholics like the collaborators of *Esprit, Sept,* and *l'aube,* as well as the members of the *Jeune-République,* who in varying degrees looked with favor upon, welcomed, or supported the program of the Popular Front without actually accepting the "outstretched hand," were invariably tarred as "Red Christians" by the Catholic Right. It was hardly a happenstance that Pierre-Henri Simon's difficulties in Lille and the rumors of a condemnation of *Esprit* coincided with the triumph of the Popular Front, or that Mounier devoted a special section of his report for Cardinal Verdier to Communism.[72]

The Catholic collaborators of the strange "Christian Marxist" journal *Terre Nouvelle* were the only group who accepted the "outstretched hand" forthrightly and without reservations.[73] The first issue of *Terre Nouvelle* caused a sensation as a result of the design of its cover alone: on a green background was a map with Russia and France in red, and on the map was a cross tinted red on which, in turn, a hammer and sickle were superimposed. *Terre Nouvelle* invited all Christians to accept the "outstretched hand." Like the *Chrétiens Progressistes* of the Fourth Republic, the men of *Terre Nouvelle* believed that the Catholic Church was allied with an economic regime which was perverse, especially because it maintained the working classes in bondage, and that the demands of the workers should be satisfied in order to construct a more just and human society. They also identified Communism with the working class as their *Chrétiens Progressistes* successors were to do.

Unlike the later *Chrétiens Progressistes,* however, the "Christian revolutionaries" of *Terre Nouvelle* supported not only the practical collaboration of Christians with the Communist Party in furthering the revolution which, in the words of Maurice Laudrain, would "permit the flowering of Christian and supernatural life through socialism" and would constitute an important step toward St. Augustine's City of God, but they also sought a doctrinal reconciliation between Communism and Christianity. Following a series of remarkable mental gymnastics in which he argued that atheism was not essential to Commu-

---

Catholiques et communistes (Paris: Tournai, 1936); François Mauriac et al·, *Le communisme et les chrétiens* (Paris: Plon, 1937); and Jean le Cour Grandmaison, *Catholiques et communistes.* "*La main tendue*" (Paris: Fédération Nationale Catholique, 1938).

[72] Mounier, "Extraits du rapport privé sur 'Esprit,'" *O.M.,* IV, 580–591.

[73] On *Terre Nouvelle,* see Joseph Dusserre, "L'histoire de la 'main tendue' des origines à 1952," *Chronique sociale de France,* 60e année, No. 4 (May, 1952), 372–377; and "Croix-faucelle-marteau," *Dossiers de l'Action populaire,* No. 346 (July 25, 1935), 1509–1540.

THE BROKEN IDOL 171

nism, a collaborator of *Terre Nouvelle* concluded that "the idea of a Catholic Marxism is by no means the fruit of a cerebral denegation." Moreover, the journal published such material as Laudrain's uncorroborated report that Cardinal Verdier, the well-known "Red Cardinal" of the Paris archdiocese, had told him that "the Church is enchained and so am I. ... Deliver it. Deliver me." In September, 1935, four months after the appearance of the journal, the *Semaine religieuse de Paris* published a warning to *Terre Nouvelle* and on July 23, 1936 the Sacred Congregation of the Holy Office placed *Terre Nouvelle* on the Index.

Of the isolated individuals who welcomed the proferred hand of Maurice Thorez, two merit particular attention. Robert Honnert, a Catholic poet, accepted the "outstretched hand" with an unusual combination of pragmatism and romantic sentimentalism. To the problem of Communist persecution of Christians in Russia and Spain, Honnert responded that "very often believers cover their human positions with a divine veil." There were no religious persecutions, he continued, but only "a terrible settling of accounts among men." With a "lyric enthusiasm reminiscent of the Lamennais of the *Paroles d'un croyant,*" Honnert stated that "more courage and confidence in human grandeur and divine intelligence is required to take this hand ... than to retreat in tears and devote oneself to useless vituperations." [74] More significant than Honnert was Martin-Chauffier, who collaborated with the Popular Front weekly *Vendredi*. *Vendredi* was founded in November, 1935 by Jean Guéhenno, Andrée Viollis and André Chamson and was "specifically designed to embrace all strata of opinion within the Popular Front." [75] In the pages of the new weekly Martin-Chauffier accepted the "outstretched hand" and wrote that "Robert Honnert has magistrally exposed and justified the reasons for such an adherence." [76]

Mounier and other Catholics who supported or were sympathetic to many of the objectives of the Popular Front dissociated themselves from *Terre Nouvelle*, Honnert and Martin-Chauffier. Mounier characteristically first paid tribute to the men of *Terre Nouvelle*. "The generosity and courage of this group is not in doubt. But audacity has its limits." Then he severely criticized *Terre Nouvelle* for the confusion of

---

[74] Rémond, *Les catholiques, le communisme et les crises*, 218; Robert Honnert, "Foi et révolution," *Europe*, No. 161 (May 15, 1936), 45–58; and Dusserre, "L'histoire de la 'main tendue,'" 377–379.

[75] Caute, 120–121.

[76] Dusserre, "L'histoire de la 'main tendue,'" 379.

religion and politics epitomized by the symbols on the cover of the journal, a confusion that he compared to the Right's identification of Catholicism with nationalism.[77] Nevertheless, *Esprit* was consistently accused by the Catholic Right of supporting the positions of *Terre Nouvelle*. When *Terre Nouvelle* was condemned by the French hierarchy Mounier considered the campaign against *Esprit* to be of sufficient importance to publish an appeal asking that the insinuations identifying *Esprit* with *Terre Nouvelle* – and implying that the condemnation of one involved a condemnation of the other – be brought to an end. If the political opponents of the two journals were often the same, Mounier explained, they had nothing else in common, either in organization, methods, or doctrine.[78] Given the Right's inability to distinguish between Communist and non-Communist supporters of the Popular Front, the fact that Mounier himself collaborated with *Vendredi* and that Andrée Viollis was a good friend of Mounier and *Esprit* did nothing to temper the angry attacks against *Esprit*.[79] Mounier's Catholic allies were also subjected to virulent attacks.[80] It took substantial courage for a Catholic to support the Popular Front in such an atmosphere.

The men of the *Jeune-République* had the requisite courage. The party refused to join the *Front commun* because it was a "Marxist front" but it adhered to the Popular Front because it was an "anti-Fascist front." On Bastille Day, 1935 the party declared that to oppose the Fascist Leagues and the power of the Bank of France was not to be Communist. "It is quite simply to be republican. July 14, 1935 will be in the full sense of the word a republican day. . . . The Republic menaced by fascism, enslaved by money, requires the support of all democrats. The *Jeunes Républicains* respond: present!" [81] In their party congresses of November, 1935 and October-November, 1936, the *Jeunes Républicains* drew up voluminous reports justifying their membership in the Popular Front coalition.[82] The problem confronting them was not one of defending the program of the Popular Front. Since its "Pour une Jeune Politique" proposals of early February, 1934, the party had

---

[77] Mounier, "Chrétiens révolutionnaires," *Esprit*, No. 33 (June, 1935), 423–424.

[78] "Terre Nouvelle," *Esprit*, No. 45 (June, 1936), 452–453.

[79] Viollis contributed to *Esprit* in 1934–1935 and Mounier and his family lived with Viollis for a time during the War. J.-M. Domenach, "Mort d'Andrée Viollis," *Esprit*, No. 172 (October, 1950), 549. Mounier contributed to *Vendredi*, April 10, 1936, and April 17, 1936.

[80] See, for example, Marteaux, I, 228–232; Mounier, "Chrétiens dans la Cité," *Esprit*, No. 41 (February, 1936), 797–800; Mayeur, *l'aube*, 99ff.; Coutrot, 272–275; J. Brugerette, *Le Prêtre française et la société contemporaine*. Vol. III: *Sous le régime de la Séparation. La reconstitution catholique (1908–1936)* (Paris: P. Lethielleux, 1938), 675–678.

[81] *La Jeune-République*, July 14, 1935, quoted in Estier, 127–128.

[82] Hoog, "Jeune-République et Rassemblement Populaire," 1–95; and Mayeur, *l'aube*, 79.

consistently worked for the formation of a Leftist front as the only effective instrument of necessary reforms and for combatting the growth of French Fascism. Moreover, the little party supported a program of reforms that went well beyond those included in the official program of the Popular Front. It advocated, for example, not only the nationalization of the munitions industry and the reorganization of the Bank of France, which were part of the Popular Front's program, but the nationalization of railways, large banks, insurance companies, mines, and other large scale economic enterprises as well.[83]

One of the conditions for the adherence of the *Jeune-République* to the Popular Front was that the Radicals, Socialists, and Communists should respect the "spiritual and moral forces" which the *Jeune-République* valued so highly. The mission of the *Jeune-République* in entering the Popular Front was to defend "the greatest human and spiritual values." [84] What the little party demanded, in effect, was that the Popular Front should refrain from anticlericalism in both its program and its campaign. This demand was satisfied, for no mention of the traditional anticlericalism of the Left was contained in the program of the coalition when it was fully published in January, 1936, and during the campaigns of April and May there were only a few minor incidents smacking of anticlericalism.[85]

The additional problem of collaborating with the Communist weighed heavily in the calculations of the *Jeune-République*. The party was anxious to make it clear that it was not being duped by what it believed was simply a tactical maneuver on the part of the Communist Party.[86] It emphasized the incompatibility of the political, economic, and philosophical doctrines of the two parties and, for that matter, of the Communist Party and that of any other truly democratic or republican party. Having ruled out the possibility of doctrinal compromise, the *Jeune-République* contended that agreement with the Communists on a clearly specified and limited program of reforms was possible.[87] Deliberately recalling the argument put forward by Robert Cornilleau in his ill-fated "Pourquoi pas?" of 1929, the *Jeune-République* distinguished between the men and the doctrine of Communism – as Pope Pius XI was to do in the encyclical *Divini Redemptoris* of March,

1937.[88] That the *Jeune-République* succeeded in 1935–1936 in carrying out its policy of collaboration with the Communist Party, while the *Parti Démocrate Populaire* had refused to adopt Cornilleau's proposal to collaborate with the Socialists less than a decade before, was indicative of the changing political orientation of at least a small number of French Catholics during the last decade of the Third Republic. As Armand Hoog of the *Jeune-République* stated in terms that *Esprit* would have found congenial, his generation was no longer interested in the conflicts of its elders, least of all in the religious question; rather, its enemies were capitalism and Fascism.[89]

The men of *l'aube* were confronted by what one of them aptly termed a "dangerous dualism" as a result of the *Jeune-République*'s adherence to the Popular Front and the *Parti Démocrate Populaire*'s vehement opposition to the experiment.[90] No such problem faced the men of *Sept*.[91] From the end of 1935 until its suppression in August, 1937, *Sept* published numerous articles on Communism in both Russia and France and on the policy of the "outstretched hand." Nothing that the journal published justified the epithets "Red Christian" and "Bolshevik" that its enemies on the Right threw at it. It was rigorous in its criticism of Marxism and forthright in its refusal to accept the "outstretched hand." This is not to say that the journal pursued a policy of negative anti-Communism or rejected completely any collaboration with the Communists on certain clearly defined issues.

In late 1935 a declaration signed by "Istina," the Dominican group of Soviet studies which worked closely with *Sept*, made it clear that its rejection of Marxism did not signify support of the economic regimes of the Western democracies. The journal was careful to publish every warning issued by the hierarchy and the Vatican concerning the dangers of the "outstretched hand" and responded with a firm *non possumus* to Thorez, but it was also insistent that opposition to the Communists was a useless exercise unless the social injustices that contributed to the strength of the Communist Party were not attacked at the same time. Marc Scherer wrote a lengthy series of articles in which he explained the reasons for the impossibility of any rapprochement between Catholics and Communists. But Scherer also argued that although Marxist doctrine had been condemned many times and an alliance with the Communists was impossible there still remained cer-

[88] *La Jeune-République*, November 20, 1938, and September 25, 1939.
[89] Quoted in Marteaux, I, 251.
[90] Mayeur, *l'aube*, 78.
[91] The summary of the position of *Sept* is taken from Coutrot, 129–134, 140–143, 181–192.

tain precise points upon which an encounter between Communists and Catholics was legitimate.

The positive, constructive anti-Communism of *Sept* led it to welcome the Matignon Accords, particularly the forty-hour week, and generally to support the rights of the workers against any incursion by the employers. *Sept* was a fervent defender of syndical pluralism; it defended the C.F.T.C. and it called the effort of the C.G.T. to impose a monopoly "syndical fascism." In its articles on the occupation of the factories in June, 1936, and on the question of collective arbitration, however, *Sept*, revealed "an unresolved conflict between its inclination toward order and liberty and the recognition of certain social injustices against which the strike seems to be the only possible weapon." Syndicalism was accepted by *Sept* as conforming to the teachings of the Church, but its value was definitely inferior to the corporative organization that it hopefully prefigured.

On February 19, 1937 *Sept* published an interview with Léon Blum conducted by Maurice Schumann.[92] The publication of the interview immediately became a *cause célèbre*. Schumann's interview consisted of two questions: "What do you think of the social doctrine of the Church, [and] what collaboration do you expect from it in the construction of that new order for which France is working?" Blum's response was brief. The ideals of democratic liberty, social justice, and human peace upon which the Popular Front was based, he said, were compatible with the Catholic faith. He then made reference to two papal encyclicals – undoubtedly *Rerum novarum* and *Quadragesimo anno* – which in his judgment contained formulas for resolving social problems which were similar to those that his government was attempting to give the force of law. Catholics could support and collaborate with the Popular Front, Blum concluded. Appended to Blum's brief statement was a much longer commentary by *Sept* in which a careful distinction was drawn between Blum's position as the premier of the legitimate government of France and as the leader of a party whose doctrine was contrary to the principles of the Catholic Church. It was as the former and not as the latter that Blum's statement was being published. The commentary concluded: "If there is, in fact, a coincidence between certain initiatives of the Popular Front and the reforms demanded by the Social Catholic school, we see no reason for not giving them our

---

[92] On the *affaire* of the Blum interview, see Coutrot, 275–286; Rémond, "Les catholiques et le Front populaire," 67–68; Rémond, *Les catholiques, le communisme et les crises*, 228–238; and Desgranges, *Journal d'un Prêtre député*, 116.

loyal support." Although *Sept* received the support of Cardinal Verdier, the journal was immediately attacked by *L'Action Française, l'Echo de Paris, la France catholique,* and their satellites. "In July," writes the historian of the short-lived journal, "*Sept* was for a segment of Catholic opinion the enemy to be destroyed, the enemy that was flourishing to judge by the increase in the size of its format and its circulation; in August the journal will suddenly disappear."

A year earlier the enemies of *Sept* had concentrated many of their attacks upon *l'aube.* The sympathy with which many of the collaborators of the Christian democratic daily viewed some of the social reforms of the Popular Front had made *l'aube* a particularly convenient target for members of the Catholic Right. At the same time there were rumors that the very existence of *l'aube* was in serious jeopardy. In these circumstances it was perhaps understandable that *l'aube* was doubly careful to distinguish between its sympathy for some parts of the program of the Popular Front and its firm opposition to the "outstretched hand" and any doctrinal conciliation with Communism.[93] The entente of Christian democrats, Christian syndicalists, and Social Catholics which supported *l'aube* was badly split over the Popular Front, however. The completely different policies of the *Jeune-République* and the *Parti Démocrate Populaire* was the most obvious manifestation of the deep division among the Christian democrats. Indicative also of the difficult position in which the collaborators of *l'aube* found themselves was the attempt by Francisque Gay and Georges Bidault to organize a *Tiers Parti* between the Popular Front and the implacable Right.

Gay presented himself as an independent candidate at Cholet in the Maine-et-Loire.[94] Although he did not formally commit his newspaper in his campaign, Gay's chances of victory seemed extremely bright at the outset for he was running in a district which had elected Louis Rolland, a *Démocrate Populaire*, in 1932. Rolland had decided not to seek reelection and the local federation of the *Parti Démocrate Populaire* decided not to present a candidate, thereby further enhancing Gay's chances of success. Initially, the campaign was a classic Christian democratic one with Gay opposing a Communist on his Left and a Conservative on his Right. Much to his dismay, however, Gay was the object of attacks by the powerful Christian democratic daily, *l'Ouest-*

---

[93] Mayeur, *l'aube*, 99–105.

[94] Rémond, *Les catholiques, le communisme et les crises,* 141–142; Mayeur, *l'aube,* 82–86; and Marteaux, I, 256–257. For the position of *l'Ouest-Eclair,* see Louis Bodin and Jean Touchard, *Front populaire 1936* (Paris: Armand Colin, 1961), 30.

Eclair, which accused him of being a member of the *Jeune-République* (which he had been for a brief time in 1919–1920) and thus a supporter of the "Socialist-Communist Popular Front" and perhaps even a Mason. Then Bernard Manceau, a former member of the *Amis de l'aube*, entered the lists against Gay, and Manceau was followed by other centrist candidates. The result was disastrous: Gay received only 412 votes and retired after the first round. Not even Mounier's criticisms of 1934 were prophetic of the Christian democratic fratracide suffered by Gay at Cholet.

Georges Bidault's campaign at Domfort in the Orne was not quite as disastrous; Bidault received some 4800 votes to the victorious candidate's 11,000.[95] Nor was Bidault's position quite the same as Gay's. Bidault was a member of the *Parti Démocrate Populaire* and was particularly influential among the younger members of the party. Moreover, Bidault's chief opponent was Roulleaux-Dugage, a member of General de Castelnau's F.N.C. and the conservative *Union Républicaine Démocratique*, who voted regularly at the Right, was sympathetic to the *Croix de Feu*, and represented, in short, the typical candidate of religious defense. Bidault and Roulleaux-Dugage typified two different generations of Catholics and two entirely different conceptions of the relationship between Catholicism and politics. The most unexpected and least explicable event in the campaign was the candidacy of Charles Serre, a member of the *Jeune-République*. Although Roulleaux-Dugage obtained a majority in the first round, the spectacle of two Christian democrats contesting one another for a seat in the Chamber did little for the cause.

That the *Jeune-République* presented a candidate to oppose Bidault is especially difficult to understand because Bidault, unlike many other *Démocrates Populaires*, was sympathetic to the Popular Front. Bidault's profession of faith when he announced his candidacy was couched in traditional *Démocrate Populaire* terms but he contended that the Christian democrats had nothing to gain and indeed would betray their mission if they opposed "the irresistible and, on so many points, legitimate movement which involves the world and the century in which we live. ... It is in the name of the same tradition that we resist stagnation and egoist or sanctimonious immobility."[96]

Generally, *l'aube* was remarkably open in its assessment of the work

---

[95] Mayeur, *l'aube*, 86–88; Rémond, *Les catholiques, le communisme et les crises*, 138–142; and Marteaux, I, 257.

[96] The summary of *l'aube* and the Popular Front is taken from Mayeur, *l'aube*, 88–99; and Rémond, *Les catholiques, le communisme et les crises*, 143–164 *passim*.

of the Popular Front. It refused to prejudge the reforms of the government on the basis of the argument that these reforms were of Marxist
inspiration. One of its collaborators suggested that there was nothing
to prevent the collaboration of the men of *l'aube* and the Socialists, thus
recalling Robert Cornilleau's "Pourquoi pas?." Gay's journal was particularly sensitive on two issues. One was the question of syndical pluralism; like *Sept*, *l'aube* vigorously opposed the efforts of the C.G.T. to
impose syndical unity at the expense of the C.F.T.C. The other was the
role of the press. This issue was raised in particularly dramatic fashion
by the campaign of slander and calumny waged against Roger Salengro, the Minister of the Interior and Mayor of Lille, by *Gringoire* and
other organs of the extreme Right. The suicide of Salengro in November, 1936 led *l'aube* to reassemble the signatories of its "Manifesto for
Justice and Peace" of the previous year. Among the signatories of the
new manifesto, "For Honor," which condemned the campaign against
Salengro, was Emmanuel Mounier.[97]

Early in 1937 Bidault paid tribute to Blum's government in an
assessment which was a fair summary of the views of the Catholic and
Christian democratic Left of *l'aube*, *Sept*, and the *Jeune-République*.
By refraining from anticlericalism, Blum's government had broken not
only one of the oldest traditions of the Left, Bidault explained, but
also the bloc of Catholic opposition to governments of the Left. The
young professor of history in the Lycée Louis-le-Grand concluded that
"the leagues, party fanaticisms, [and] the great economic interests are
attempting to make life difficult for the Blum experiment. Catholics,
insofar as they are faithful to the exigencies of their faith, can only
desire the success of this experiment so long as it follows the requirements of the common good." [98] Bidault's views were not shared by
many of the elders and parliamentary representatives of his own party.
The *Parti Démocrate Populaire* opposed the Popular Front but its opposition was not entirely consistent.

When Paul Simon, the Benjamin of Christian democratic deputies,
told his fellow deputies that "our opposition ... has never been systematic; it has never been inspired by that partisan spirit which is narrow
and negative," his contention had some substance.[99] In the vote to

[97] See Mayeur, *l'aube*, 92–93; Rémond, *Les catholiques, le communisme et les crises*, 165–
173; Simon, *La grande crise de la République française*, 86–89; and "Pour l'honneur. Un appel
des intellectuels," *Esprit*, No. 51 (December, 1936), 535.
[98] Georges Bidault, "L'Expérience Blum et les catholiques," *Europe Nouvelle*, March 6,
1937. See also Georges Bidault, "Forces religieuses," *Europe Nouvelle*, November 19, 1938.
[99] *J.O.C.*, No. 105 (December 15, 1936), 3797.

disband the Rightist leagues in June, 1936, for example, half of the *Démocrate Populaire* deputies opposed the measure and half abstained.[100] The party consistently supported the government's budgets, it frequently supported Blum's foreign policy, and it did not oppose the government's program of nationalizations en bloc.[101] Even so conservative a member of the parliamentary group of the *Parti Démocrate Populaire* as Abbé Jean Desgranges accepted the proposition that the program of the Popular Front was imprinted in the social teachings of the Church and not in Marx's *Das Kapital*.[102] During a debate in the Chamber on the government's agricultural policy Ernest Pezet noted with tongue in cheek that Blum's policy did not correspond to his own conception of socialism. When Georges Monnet, the government's spokesman, told Pezet that the *Démocrate Populaire* idea of socialism was obviously a caricature of the genuine doctrine, Pezet responded that he and his fellow *Démocrates Populaires* would rejoice in this new knowledge – but that only the future could reveal which was the caricature and which the real doctrine.[103] The conservatism of the *Parti Démocrate Populaire* in domestic affairs thus persisted.

Because of the position of the *Jeunes Républicains* and many of the collaborators of *Sept* and *l'aube*, Mounier's sympathies for the Popular Front were not as original as they would otherwise have been. Nor, because of the new Catholic and Christian democratic Left, was Mounier almost alone among French Catholics in rejecting a purely negative anti-Communism. The position of Mounier and *Esprit*, however, was rooted in a revolutionary opposition to "the established disorder" which was, of course, irreconcilable with the reformism of most other Catholics of the Left. By any conceivable measuring device, Mounier and the Catholic members of *Esprit* constituted a genuine avant-garde in Catholic opinion.

This was especially true of Mounier's position on Communism. No single facet of Mounier's thought and action is more difficult to summarize than his attitude toward Marxism. Mounier made use of the Marxist critique of capitalism, bourgeois idealism, a certain disembodied spiritualism, and other social and economic ills in his own criticism of "the established disorder." He respected Marxism for the ele-

---

[100] *J.O.C.*, No. 53 (June 30, 1936), 1671–1672.
[101] See, for example, *J.O.C.*, No. 60 (July 17, 1936), 2002–2003; Desgranges, *Journal d'un prêtre député*, 156; *J.O.C.*, No. 59 (July 16, 1936), 1981–1982; and *J.O.C.*, No. 40 (June 17, 1936), 1416–1418.
[102] Desgranges, *Journal d'un prêtre député*, 156.
[103] *J.O.C.*, No. 30 (March 16, 1937), 1051.

ment of truth he believed it contained and was clearly attracted by its revolutionary vigor. Indeed, Mounier was disposed to make concessions to the Communists which he refused to make to anyone else, although he ultimately used "a critical arsenal borrowed from Marxism itself" in a general critique of Marxism.[104] It was on the human level, however, on the plane of personal encounters, of human needs and aspirations, that Mounier's attitude toward Communism was explicable. The purely human dimensions of the problem of Communism were to be far more important during the early years of the Fourth Republic than they were during the 1930s, but the first indications of Mounier's well-known "dialogue with the Communists" were apparent during the 1930s.

The key to Mounier's ambivalent attitude toward Communism during the 1930s was his "horror of an anti-Communism which sheltered under religious pretexts an attitude of defense of unjustified privileges, an indifference to proletarian misery." [105] Something of the nature of his position was evident in his report of June, 1936 for the Cardinal-Archbishop of Paris. There he wrote that

The entire future of Christian societies depends upon knowing whether Christianity, or more exactly whether Christians will reject their support of capitalism and an unjust society; whether Christian humanity will finally attempt to realize in the name of God and Christ the truth that the Communists are realizing in the name of an atheistic collectivity, in the name of a paradise on earth.[106]

Slightly more than two years later in an article entitled "Sur le destin spirituel du monde ouvrier," Mounier testified that "we ourselves in *Esprit*," were aided by Marx in becoming aware of "the historic betrayals of a certain spiritualism, of the inevitable servitudes of the spiritual." While Marxism, he continued, had been guilty of serious tactical errors it had at certain times saved the working-class movement from political dangers: from anarchist utopianism and the duperies of liberal democracy. Then Mounier clearly distinguished between an anti-Marxism based upon hatred, indignation and fear and "our anti-Marxism [which] is the desire to save men who call themselves Marxists, with all of the truth that they bring with them; we certainly know that we will not save them *against* that truth, truncated and disfigured though it is, but through it, from it, and by no other means." [107]

[104] Domenach, "Les principes du choix politique," 823.
[105] Rouquette, "Positions et oppositions d'Emmanuel Mounier," 150.
[106] Mounier, "Extraits du rapport privé sur 'Esprit,'" *O.M.*, IV, 591.
[107] Mounier, "Sur le destin spirituel du monde ouvrier," *Cahiers protestants*, September-October, 1938, reprinted in *B.A.E.M.*, No. 18 (December, 1961), 8–9.

In November, 1938 Mounier addressed himself to the frequent charge that *Esprit* had lowered its guard against Communism.[108] Mounier contended that what lent some credence to this criticism was that "for many years we have affirmed a number of primary truths." Among them was a refusal to adopt a purely negative position toward Communism because such a position failed to take into account "the formidable historic élan which is partially and temporarily carried by Communism." Negative anti-Communism was a façade for the defense of economic interests, the world of money, and a totalitarian *mystique* as well as an excuse for refusing to confront the evils of "the established disorder." In sum, "the best 'quartermasters of Communism' are to be found among the defenders of that disorder which Communism claims to remove." After having emphasized the defects of negative anti-Communism with almost *péguyste* repetitiveness, Mounier turned to the relationship between *Esprit* and Communism. There was a total battle on all levels between the two, he explained. "Communism in Europe today is one of the rare sources of asceticism, discipline, and total devotion. But it places the grandeur of man first" and makes man the complete master of nature and himself. Communism was tyrannical and inhuman. It was a form of collectivism which negated personal creativity. And as a political movement Communism, in Mounier's judgment, was a frightening school which deformed and brutalized its members.

The practical consequences of Mounier's attitude toward Communism were becoming clear by the time of the Popular Front. On one hand, his criticism of the negative anti-Communism of the defenders of "the established disorder" made him the target of increasingly venomous attacks by the Right. The stale charge of "Red Christian" continued and even Mounier's old mentor in Grenoble spoke of *Esprit's* "conciliatory attitude" toward Communism. Mounier responded to Chevalier by writing that if "conciliation" meant sympathy for the most suffering and abandoned people "for us it is not a question of 'conciliation' but of total giving, throughout life and to the death." But he added: "if one speaks of Communism as a doctrine and a party, there is not the least particle of conciliation in us." [109] On the other hand Mounier's vigorous opposition to the forces of negative anti-Communism as well as his political options made him the object of

---

[108] Mounier, "Anticommunisme," *le Voltigeur*, No. 4 (November 16, 1938), reprinted in *B.A.E.M.*, No. 23–24 (December, 1964), 14–17.
[109] Mounier, "Lettre à Jacques Chevalier, 26 mai 1937," *O.M.*, IV, 604.

both intermittent courtship and bitter attacks by the Communist Left. Ultimately, his persistent criticism of Communist doctrine and tactics and his refusal to allow *Esprit* to be assimilated by the Communists made the pens of Communist writers flow with ink poisoned by their own disappointment.

As early as late 1934, Mounier's "spiritualism" and his supposed creation of "an association of pseudo-revolutionary writers" were attacked in the pages of *Commune*, the organ of the *Association des Ecrivains et Artistes Révolutionnaires* (A.E.A.R.).[110] Only six months later, the A.E.A.R. proposed an armistice and invited Mounier to participate in its meetings. Mounier accepted but he noted afterwards that, although "intelligence is incontestably at the Left," the meeting had been dominated by "Stalinist conformism." [111] In the pages of *Esprit* Mounier rejoiced over the "detente of Communist dogmatism" apparent in the idea of a Popular Front.[112] He was even receptive to the possibility of some sort of limited tactical alliance with the Communists but he attached such rigid conditions to a doctrinal entente that such an entente was foredoomed to failure. Consequently, a Soviet critic referred to Mounier and *Esprit* as Trotskyites, White Guards, and Fascists.[113] The well-known Stalinist intellectual Ilya Ehrenburg believed Mounier and the *Esprit* group were enthusiastic about Soviet society, but there is reason to question Ehrenburg's powers of observation.[114] Mounier was far more sympathetic to Victor Serge, who had been imprisoned in the Soviet Union for "Trotskyite deviations," and Serge's attack on the Moscow purge trials was published in *Esprit*. Serge himself attended several *Esprit* congresses in the late 1930s and expressed his high regard for Mounier and his friends in terms that no good Stalinist would have used: "Around the review *Esprit* I met left-wing Catholics like Jacques Lefranc [sic] and Emmanuel Mounier, genuine Christians of fine, honest intellect. They sensed sharply that they were living at the end of an era; they loathed all lying, especially if it formed an excuse for murder, and they said so outright. In their simple teaching

---

[110] Vladimir Pozner, "Le congrès des écrivains sovietiques vu à travers la presse française bourgeoise ou étude comparée sur les réflexes de la sèche," *Commune*, No. 15 (November, 1934), 256; and Bartoli, "Esprit (octobre 1934)," *Commune*, No. 16 (December, 1934), 377–378.

[111] Mounier, "Entretiens VIII, 29 juin 1935," *O.M.*, IV, 574.

[112] Mounier, "Journal des témoins. Infiltrations sentimentales?," *Esprit*, No. 34 (July, 1935), 633–634.

[113] Z. V. Pesis, "Fascism and the French Intelligentsia. Notes on the *Esprit* Group," *International Literature*, No. 8 (August, 1935), 54–71 *passim*.

[114] Ilya Ehrenburg, *Memoirs: 1921–1941*, trans. Tatania Shebunia (Cleveland: World Publishing Company, 1964), 305.

of 'reverence for the human person,' I felt immediately at one with them." [115] Similarly, Mounier opened the pages of *Esprit* to a group of young Russian exiles who called themselves the "Post Revolutionaries" and were disciples of Berdiaev.[116] The Communists resumed their attacks on Mounier. *Commune* accused *Esprit* of working for Franco and of being in the hands of Trotskyites.[117] Mounier's personalist revolution was harshly criticized and the Communist intellectual Roger Garaudy accused Mounier of supporting Salazar and linked Mounier with Maurras and *Action Française*.[118]

Such attacks did not in any discernible way alter Mounier's remarkable determination to remain "open" to the Communists. Certainly Communist membership did not in any way inhibit Mounier's assessment of the Popular Front. Mounier's position was characteristically somewhat ambivalent in the period leading up to the electoral triumph of the Popular Front. In the general political ferment of those months, Mounier undertook first to organize what he called a "Center for permanent liaison of movements for the spiritual revolution." The members of the Center constituted what Mounier called "a little entente of sovereign states." [119] Still searching for an effective means of preparing for the future, in May, 1935 Mounier added to his "little entente" those members of Gaston Bergery's *Front Social*, the J.O.C., the *Jeune-République*, and Socialists who sympathized with the personalist aspirations of *Esprit*.[120] But in October, after an article published by another member of *Esprit* had led some readers to conclude that the journal was supporting the Popular Front, Mounier published a note in which he stated cryptically that the Popular Front contained a number of serious ambiguities and *Esprit* still adhered to the old adage: "I am with those who are with me." [121]

---

[115] Victor Serge, *Memoirs of a Revolutionary, 1901–1941*, trans. and ed. by Peter Sedgwick (London: Oxford University Press, 1963), 333–334. Serge's reference is to Mounier's close friend Jacques Lefrancq.

[116] Iswolsky, *Light Before Dusk*, 105–106.

[117] Georges Sadoul, "Droits d'auteur et droits d'éditeur. A propos d'*Esprit* – Au service de Franco," *Commune*, No. 38 (October, 1936), 241–247; and "Revues des revues," *Esprit*, No. 50 (November, 1936), 345.

[118] Eva Metraux, "Trends in French Thought During the Third Republic," *Science and Society*, V, No. 3 (Summer, 1941), 217; and Roger Garaudy, *Lettre à Emmanuel Mounier, homme d'"Esprit"* (Paris: Editions de la Nouvelle Critique, [1950]), 4–11 *passim*.

[119] Mounier, "Vers l'action organique," *Esprit*, No. 29 (February, 1935), 756–767.

[120] "Centre de liaison des mouvements de recherche et d'action pour une cité personnaliste," *Esprit*, No. 32 (May, 1935), 333–334.

[121] Georges Zérapha, "Recherches sur des points communs d'un programme électoral," *Esprit*, No. 35–36 (September, 1935), 677–724; and Mounier, "Mise au point," *Esprit*, No. 37 (October, 1935), 174.

The following month Mounier opened a "Permanent chronicle for a third force." [122] While waiting for the *Troisième force* to materialize, Mounier indicated his tentative support of the Popular Front. "To the extent, and to the exact extent, that the Popular Front corresponds to a living reality and is not a machination or confusion of politicians, it marks a first awareness on the part of the masses of this third way." Then, less ambiguously, he added: "Accept largely, loyally, the human rapprochements that the Popular Front offers us, without allowing it to compromise us in its electoral or partisan positions, simply because we cannot desert the places where the oppressed today place their confidence." When the new government actually assumed power in June, 1936 Mounier's position was more forthright. He welcomed Blum's government with a "fraternal salute." [123] At the same time, however, he issued a warning and emphasized the continued independence of *Esprit*. His warning was not to those for whom the Popular Front was a catastrophe but rather to those for whom it augured something akin to the advent of a golden age. The victory of the Popular Front, Mounier proclaimed prophetically, did not represent "a gratuitous passage to some paradise," but rather the beginning of "a battle and of numerous difficulties." On the other hand, *Esprit* had not actually joined the Popular Front and would not do so even were the Popular Front to adopt all of its program. It had not and would not do so, Mounier stated, again with prophetic insight, because of the possibility of the Communists betraying the cause of the Popular Front. The role of *Esprit* would be to follow, to encourage, and to support the Popular Front, "but to act also as a team of vigilant lookouts." [124]

The experience of the Popular Front turned the attentions of Mounier and *Esprit* to careful examinations of such specific issues as "Grève et arbitrage," "Le problème des nationisations," and, after the fall of the Popular Front, "Le parti politique. Bilan. Avenir." Mounier said that "more attention had to be paid to popular realities." [125] In March, 1938 a special number of *Esprit* was devoted to drawing up a balance sheet in which members of *Esprit* attempted to examine the reasons for which such great hopes had been placed in the experiment, the

[122] Mounier, "Chronique permanente pour une troisième force. I. Faisons le point," *Esprit*, No. 38 (November, 1935), 275–281; and "Chronique permanente pour une troisième force," *Esprit*, No. 38 (November, 1935), 281–302.

[123] Mounier, "Rassemblement populaire," *Esprit*, No. 45 (June, 1936), 441–449.

[124] See Goguel, "Positions politiques," 808; and Pierre Andreu, "'Esprit' (1932–1940)," *Itinéraires*, No. 33 (May, 1959), 46.

[125] Mounier, "Premiers éléments d'une methode réaliste," *Esprit*, No. 51 (December, 1936), 384–385.

causes of its relative failure, and the prospects for the future. In a preface to this examination, Mounier reviewed the positions of the journal.[126] He stated that *Esprit* had affirmed its moral solidarity with the Popular Front primarily because the enemies of the Popular Front were also the enemies of *Esprit*. But if the positions of the journal were solidary with the great causes supported by the Popular Front, they were at the same time both autonomous and independent of any political party. The Popular Front had been at once "a great élan of youthfulness" and the hope of "a French national revival." Its fall from power, Mounier contended, was due as much to its own internal weakness as to the attacks of its enemies. Many of its supporters had hurled anathemas at its imperfections and had succumbed to a kind of utopian romanticism. The experience as a whole had demonstrated once again that social reforms which were not based upon a permanent spiritual revolution become lost in the thickets of political opportunism.[127]

In his preface to the special issue of *Esprit*, Mounier concluded by turning his attention to international affairs. One foreign policy issue had been dominant during Blum's first ministry – the Spanish Civil War. More than any other single event during the 1930s, the Spanish Civil War divided French Catholics into two bitterly opposed camps. The Ethiopian War had been given a certain religious character by many French Catholics, but the Spanish Civil War was immediately looked upon as a religious war by an even greater number of Catholics.[128] The Spanish republican government was a *Frente Popular* similar to Blum's government in France. This in itself was sufficient reason for many French Catholics to oppose the republic. In addition, however, the republican government in Spain had attacked the economic position of the Church and some of its supporters had committed crimes and outrages against the Church. Therefore when General Franco raised his flag of rebellion in the name of the "Christian civilization of Spain" most French Catholics rallied to his "Holy Crusade."

A handful of French Catholics refused to grant the religious character given the Civil War by Franco's supporters.[129] Don Luigi Sturzo spoke for many of these Catholics when he wrote in *l'aube* that "the

---

[126] Mounier, "Le Front Populaire. Bilan – Avenir," *Esprit*, No. 66 (March, 1938), 801–806. See also Mounier, "Les cinq étapes d'*Esprit*," 47.

[127] Mounier, "Bilan spirituel. ...ont traité de la mythique de gauche," (March, 1938), *O.M.*, IV, 40–75.

[128] Paul Vignaux, "Les catholiques français et la politique étrangère de la France," *Politique Etrangère*, 3ᵉ année, No. 5 (October, 1938), 453–454; and Rémond, *Les catholiques, le communisme et les crises*, 189–211 passim.

[129] Micaud, *The French Right and Nazi Germany*, 113; and Marteaux, I, 303.

civil war has two sides: justice demands that the excesses committed by both sides be reproved; that the insurgents not be given a religious character that they do not and cannot have ... and that they use for political advantage." [130] During the Civil War, political ammunition was provided the supporters of the Republic by the loyalty of the Catholic Basques as well as by such atrocities as the bombing of the civilian population of the small Basque town of Guernica by the Heinkels and Junkers of the rebel air force. As in the case of the Ethiopian conflict, the ramifications of the war in Spain in the relations of the European states, even after the intervention of Italy, Germany, and the Soviet Union, were generally subordinated to religious and moral questions in the debate between the Catholic supporters and opponents of the Nationalists.

In the forefront of those French Catholics who refused to enlist in Franco's "Holy Crusade" were Emmanuel Mounier, most of the collaborators of *Sept* and its successor *Temps présent*, the Christian democrats of *l'aube*, the *Jeune-République*, some of the leaders of the *Parti Démocrate Populaire*, and, in addition, Jacques Maritain, François Mauriac, and Georges Bernanos. Somewhat more forthrightly than most of his allies of the Catholic and Christian democratic Left, Mounier immediately proclaimed his support of the Spanish Republic. Mounier wrote in retrospect that the Spanish problem, with Catholics on both sides and crimes committed by both sides, "was yet another of those cases where it seemed that the ideal thing to say would be: I am on neither one side nor the other because basically there is as much evil on one side as on the other." But this position was a false position, Mounier later recalled. The values for which *Esprit* stood, he said, were those defended by the Spanish Republic in the historical juncture of the time. [131]

In his first contemporary commentary on the war in Spain Mounier emphasized the dilemma which confronted *Esprit* and its friends in Spain. [132] He related that he and "the Spanish Maritain," José Bergamin, along with the other collaborators of the Spanish personalist journal *Cruz y Raya*, were supporting the Republic. "Spain," Mounier said, "... is the bloody image of the drama in which personalists, and especially Christian personalists like our friends there, find themselves between two walls of hatred." On one side there was the Church, the

---

[130] Quoted in Rémond, *Les catholiques, le communisme et les crises*, 190–191.
[131] Mounier, "Les cinq étapes d'*Esprit*," 46.
[132] Mounier, "Espagne, signe de contradiction," *Esprit*, No. 49 (October, 1936), 1–3.

certain repression of the people, "a worse consolidation of the established disorder, years of cultural and social regression." On the other side, Mounier continued, there was the legal government which, unfortunately for Catholics, symbolized a violent assault on the Church of Spain, a kind of Red terror. But Spanish Catholics, Mounier reported, had been the victims of false news dispatches and doctored photographs and many of the sacrileges committed by the Republicans were the result of convents and churches being used by the Nationalists and members of the Spanish clergy, the most backward in all of Europe. "Between a Church sheltered under the shadow of the sword by such dangerous protectors and a suffering Church, a handful of Catholics have chosen."

Almost immediately Mounier qualified his support of the Republic. Indeed, Jean-Marie Domenach states that of all of the crises of the 1930s the Spanish Civil War provoked the most characteristic response from Mounier.[133] In answer to a complaint from Chevalier, Mounier admitted that his first statement in *Esprit* had been too brief, elliptical, and lacking in "the nuances toward which all of us are now inclined. ..." [134] But to these qualifications Mounier reiterated that the Church in Spain could gain nothing from the victory of the Nationalists. "Behind them," Mounier wrote Chevalier, "there is the entire feudal apparatus, all of the new industrial feudal system, the bank." The following month *Esprit* published two reports on Spain which, in Mounier's words, comprised a kind of tableau of "the entire drama of the personalist attitude before the opposing fatalities which menace it today." [135] One article was by José-Marie Semprun y Gurrea, a professor of law and *Esprit* correspondent, who forthrightly supported the Republic and the other was by Alfred Mendizabal Vilalba, an eminent professor of law in the University of Oviedo, who refused his unequivocal support to either side.[136] Mounier also qualified his earlier position by stating that he was not yet making a definite commitment to either side in the conflict. More facts were necessary, he said, before "true Catholics" could properly take sides.

Additional information was provided Mounier by Francisque Gay of *l'aube*. After receiving a collection of documents and press commentaries on the Civil War from Gay, Mounier wrote the editor of *l'aube* that

---

[133] Domenach, "L'Evénement politique," 11.
[134] Mounier, "Lettre à Jacques Chevalier, 24 octobre 1936," *O.M.*, IV, 597.
[135] Mounier, "Terre libre," *Esprit*, No. 50 (November, 1936), 286–290.
[136] J. M. de Semprun y Gurrea, "La question d'Espagne inconnue," and A. M. V. [Alfred Mendizabal Vilalba], "Double refus," *Esprit*, No. 50 (November, 1936), 291–330.

he was prepared to associate himself with anything that could be done "to aid our suffering brothers and to prevent new crimes." But this had to be done without political partisanship and the documents had to be rigorously examined so that Catholics did not too easily regard themselves as martyrs.[137] The materials Gay had sent Mounier were almost certainly the contents of a book entitled *Dans les flammes et dans le sang*.[138] To the casual reader, particularly because the book contained neither a preface nor an introduction to explain its purpose, *Dans les flammes et dans le sang* appeared to be an attack on the Spanish Republicans for the outrages they had committed against the Church. To the careful reader of the French press, however, Gay's book was intended to mark out the position of *l'aube* between the extreme Left and the extreme Right. Included in *Dans les flammes et dans le sang* was not only a dossier on the crimes committed by the Spanish Republicans but a collection of declarations by the Holy See which condemned all excesses in Spain, whatever their source, and supplementary documents which were intended to demonstrate that not all of the Spanish clergy had joined the rebellion and that most Spanish Catholics supported the Republic. Mounier praised Gay's work but at the same time he indicated that it lacked the balanced judgment required by the Spanish dilemma.[139]

In the first months of 1937 the position of *Esprit* was more forthright in its support of the Spanish Republic. The friends of *Esprit* in Spain, an unsigned note declared, "have defended the Spanish Republic not in order to deliver it to Communism or anarchy but in order to save it from Fascism and to try to develop within it all of the promises of personalism." There followed a series of articles and documents which, taken together, clearly opposed the idea of a "Holy War" and supported the Republican cause.[140] Late in the spring of 1937 Mounier vehemently condemned the bombing of the Basque town of Guernica and the way in which the pro-Nationalist press had reported this atrocity.[141] At the same time he was called upon to respond to another

[137] Mounier, "Lettre à Francisque Gay, novembre 1936," *O.M.*, IV, 602–603.

[138] Francisque Gay, *Dans les flammes et dans le sang* (Paris: Bloud & Gay, 1936). For a summary see Mayeur, *l'aube*, 129–134.

[139] Mounier, "Encore l'Espagne. Francisque Gay: Dans les flammes et dans le sang," *Esprit*, No. 51 (December, 1936), 529–532.

[140] See J. M. de Semprun y Gurrea, "Un programme de reconstruction des amis d'*Esprit* en Espagne," G. R., "Réflexions d'un prêtre catholique sur la guerre d'Espagne," "Les prêtres basques persecutés par les militaires," and "Documents annexes," *Esprit*, No. 52 (January, 1937), 605–625; and "Espagne: un nouveau dossier," *Esprit*, No. 53 (February, 1937), 854–857.

[141] Mounier, "Guernica," *Esprit*, No. 56 (May, 1937), 327; Mounier, "Guernica ou la

critical letter from Chevalier in Grenoble.[142] "I do not believe," he told Chevalier, "that there is something wrong in our attitude, but rather that the tragic historical antinomy, in which 'Catholic' Spain shares responsibility with evil forces, makes only bastard positions possible today." To Chevalier's obvious concern about the problem of Communism and his reference to the recent Papal condemnation of Communism, Mounier responded that he was waiting for the Pope to condemn the Basque clergy, the Catholic members of the Spanish Republican government, and the Catholic supporters of the Popular Front in France. Moreover, he told Chevalier that there was also an encyclical against Hitlerism: "is the situation of Franco supported by Nazi Germany different from that of his adversaries supported by the Communists?"

In May 1938 Semprun y Gurrea addressed an open letter to Mounier in which he protested Mounier's consistent facility for finding fault with both sides in the conflict and, perhaps more important, Mounier's tendency to believe that he, as an outsider, could somehow maintain both "solidarity" with the Republicans and "distance" from their crimes.[143] In his response, Mounier attempted to delineate the extent of both his agreement and disagreement with Semprun's unqualified support of the Republic. Mounier agreed with Semprun's condemnation of non-intervention by the Western democracies. Ideally, Mounier told Semprun, non-intervention should allow a people to determine their own destiny free of external interference. But when non-intervention was violated by one side, it became a kind of de facto intervention by the other side: "the irresolute 'great democracies' participate, in a real though negative act of war, in the attack against the Spanish Republic." Unlike Semprun and certain other friends of *Esprit*, Mounier did not support military intervention by France, but he agreed with Semprun's denunciation of a "kind of monstrous mediation between good and evil" in Spain. There could be no compromise with men who paid homage to Hitler, who bombed Barcelona, and who supported the program of the Falange. In Mounier's judgment it would seem this did not contradict his earlier support of mediation efforts undertaken by the *Comité français pour paix civile et religieuse en Espagne*

---

technique du mensonge," *Esprit*, No. 57 (June, 1937), 449–473; and Iswolsky, *Light Before Dusk*, 192–196.

[142] Mounier, "Lettre à Jacques Chevalier, 26 mai 1937," *O.M.*, IV, 604–605.

[143] J. M. de Semprun y Gurrea, "Lettre ouverte à Emmanuel Mounier et aux amis d'Esprit," *Esprit*, No. 68 (May, 1938), 235–243; and Mounier, "Réponse à Semprun" (May, 1938), *O.M.*, IV, 31–39.

which was led by Claude Bourdet and supported by Alfred Mendizabal Vilalba.[144]

In spite of these areas of agreement between Mounier and Semprun, events had conspired to separate the two men by an "incommensurable distance," Mounier told his Spanish friend. Semprun was already confronted by a fatal fissure in his native land but France had not yet reached this tragic point. "A way is open for us – which is closed for you." It was natural that a Frenchman should choose different tactics, different languages, and divergents battles, Mounier said. Semprun, unhappily, had had to make decisions which had been simplified by "the urgency of death." Mounier concluded his response to Semprun on a characteristic note. Confronted with the Spanish War, "the personalist can only be in a tragic situation, in a state of watchful vigilance."

If Semprun was offended by Mounier's response, his feelings must certainly have been soothed the following month. In June, 1938 Mounier welcomed Georges Bernanos's famous indictment of Franco, the conservative Right, and the Spanish hierarchy.[145] *Les grands cimetières sous la lune*, Mounier proclaimed, could not possibly be read as a political tract in view of Bernanos's traditionalist sympathies and earlier membership in *Action Française*. Rather, Mounier said, Bernanos had now joined Péguy and Bloy as the author of a book which belonged to the literature of "the apocalypses of an agonized Christendom." Later still, Semprun may well have welcomed Mounier's criticism of Pope Pius XII's position on the Spanish Civil War.[146] The article which contained Mounier's criticism was reportedly widely distributed among the Basques in Franco's prisons.[147]

As Gay's *Dans les flammes et dans le sang* indicated, *l'aube* approached the Spanish Civil War as a Catholic journal and did not hesitate to condemn the crimes committed by the supporters of the Republic.[148] Throughout 1936 the journal refused to condemn or to support systematically either side in the conflict. Bidault opposed French intervention in July, 1936 and as early as October of the same year Don Sturzo announced his support of international mediation. Bidault

---

[144] "Déclaration du Comité pour la paix civile et religieuse en Espagne," *Esprit*, No. 58 (July, 1937), 651; and Coutrot, 215.

[145] Mounier, "Georges Bernanos: Les grands cimetières sous la lune," *Esprit*, No. 69 (June, 1938), 435–441.

[146] Mounier, "En interrogeant les silences de Pie XII," *le Voltigeur*, May 5, 1939, reprinted in *B.A.E.M.*, No. 23–24 (December, 1964), 28–33.

[147] Editor's note in *ibid.*, 28.

[148] The summary of the position of *l'aube* is taken from Mayeur, *l'aube*, 127–136.

tended to examine the Spanish War in the context of international affairs; after the intervention of Italian volunteers, he reconsidered the possibility of French intervention but he immediately drew back by declaring that France's ties to England were vital and should not be jeopardized. *L'aube* did not consider the Nationalists' *Pronunciamiento* legitimate. Nor, in spite of its condemnation of the crimes of the Republicans, did it ever accept the thesis of a "Holy War." Gay himself was a particularly close friend of a number of Basques and the headquarters of *l'aube* became something of a foyer for Basque refugees in France.[149]

If Mounier and the Christian democrats of *l'aube* had an eloquent spokesman in Georges Bernanos, the pro-Nationalists in France had an equally renowned man of letters in Paul Claudel. In 1937 Claudel published a poetic eulogy of the martyrdom of the Spanish Church and of Franco's cause in *Sept*.[150] *Sept* also published a collective letter of support for Franco by the Spanish hierarchy which was addressed to the Catholic bishops of the entire world. Neither Claudel's "lyrical adherence to Franco" nor the declaration of the Spanish bishops accurately reflected the position of *Sept*, however. The first was published in all probability in an effort to retain Claudel's collaboration with the journal and the second in an effort to demonstrate the objectivity of the journal or, perhaps, as the result of a directive from ecclesiastical authority. The fact that *Sept* was published by a religious order had some effect upon the journal's position. In 1934 *Sept* had expressed the hope that Catholics in Spain would separate themselves from the Right and support the construction of a more just social order. With the election of the *Frente Popular*, the journal was obviously concerned about the consequences of the shift to the Left; but when the Civil War broke out *Sept* almost immediately opposed the idea that the conflict could be reduced to a battle between the forces of goodness and the forces of evil. François Mauriac began his collaboration with *Sept* at this time and, like the journal, he wanted to take a stand without being overly partisan. In May, 1937 Mauriac joined Jacques Maritain, Gabriel Marcel, and other Catholic intellectuals in signing a manifesto, "For the Basque people." The collaborators of *Sept* also supported nonintervention by the major powers, deplored the aid given the conflicting forces by both Russian and the Fascist powers, and later, largely

---

[149] Articles in *l'aube* on the Basques were collected in Pierre Dumas, *Euzkadi, les Basques devant la guerre d'Espagne* (Paris: Editions de l'aube, 1939).

[150] The following summary of the position of *Sept* is taken from Coutrot, 193–217, and Rémond, *Les catholiques, le communisme et les crises*, 175–211 *passim*.

through the efforts of Alfred Mendizabal Vilalba, supported various mediation efforts.

The *Jeune-République* faithfully supported Blum's policy of non-intervention.[151] In a speech to the party congress in Lyons in early November, 1936, Georges Hoog pledged the support of his party for Blum's policy. He admitted that crimes had been committed by both sides but insisted that if the rebels won the war the rights of the Spanish people would quickly be destroyed by a Fascist dictatorship. Far more than the men of *Esprit*, *l'aube*, and *Sept*, the *Jeune-République* was concerned with the European implications of the Spanish conflict. The party believed that the French government had a right to sell arms and munitions to another government provided that government was "regular" and not insurrectional. The Republican regime in Spain was, of course, "regular" in this sense, but the *Jeune-République* argued rather weakly that French intervention would only widen the Spanish conflict in spite of the fact that other governments had provided aid for both sides in Spain.

Even more emphatically than the *Jeune-République*, the *Parti Démocrate Populaire* took into account the international context of the war in Spain. In the parliamentary debate on the government's policy of non-intervention in December, 1936, Ernest Pezet supported non-intervention but in doing so he emphasized the need for Franco-Italian reconciliation and indicated that he opposed French intervention in support of the Republic because he feared that it would further exacerbate Franco-Italian relations. Pezet was mistakenly convinced that Italy would never tolerate the expansion of German influence in the area of the Danube and that Franco-Italian relations might still be shored up.[152] As he later demonstrated, however, Pezet was no friend of Franco.[153] At least one of the leaders of Pezet's party followed in the path of the Catholic supporters of the Spanish republic. On January 26, 1939 Jean Raymond-Laurent reported to the Chamber on a trip he had taken to Catalonia as a member of a parliamentary investigating committee.[154] He told his fellow deputies that the Catholic religion was being openly practiced in Catalonia and that this was the official policy of the Republican government. At that point, he was interrupted by applause from the banks on the left, and much of the remainder of

---

[151] Hoog, "Jeune-République et Rassemblement Populaire," 30–31, 87–89.
[152] *J.O.C.*, No. 97 (December 4, 1936), 3362–3364.
[153] See, for example, *J.O.C.*, No. 7 (January 20, 1939), 130–131.
[154] *J.O.C.*, No. 9 (January 27, 1939), 220–225.

his speech received similar response. For his efforts, Raymond-Laurent was accused by *Gringoire* and *Je suis partout* of accepting the hands of the "Red disinterrers of the Carmelites" and of being the "Host of the murderers of priests." [155]

By the time of Raymond-Laurent's speech in the Chamber, the Spanish Civil War had subsided into the background of the final crises of the Third Republic and the Europe of Versailles. The *Anschluss* and Munich once again found Mounier in general accord with the men of *l'aube*, the new journal *Temps présent*, the *Jeune-République*, and the leaders of the *Parti Démocrate Populaire*. To his condemnation of both the *Anschluss* and the Munich Agreement Mounier brought all of the resources of the revolutionary indignation which had led him to found his journal and organize his movement. To it also he brought some of the ambivalence which characterized his approach to the great historical events through which he lived. In his first major article after the *Anschluss*, Mounier addressed himself to the significance of Germany's annexation of Austria.[156] In Mounier's judgment, the real tragedy of the *Anschluss* was less that it signified the passing of the Europe of Versailles and the Europe of French hegemony than that it extended Nazi dominance and with that dominance fear and hatred of every civilized regime based upon spiritual liberty. "A Christendom which shows such signs of weakness, at Vienna as at Madrid ... is a dying Christendom," Mounier proclaimed. What was required was a total regeneration of French life and institutions. "Never have the terms French revolution, national renovation, if they are more than mere slogans, taken on a more precise and more urgent meaning." In an analogy worthy of Péguy, Mounier concluded by comparing France with a rich man who had lost his money: he could now make a new start.

On September 22, 1938 Mounier began a lengthy commentary on Munich on much the same note.[157] "For six years," he said, "we have waited for France to receive some salutary wound. ... In March, we thought the time had come." Unfortunately a century of mediocrity had prevented this from happening and now "the men, a regime, a country which have for twenty years made themselves the champions of their given word and of the rights of small nations have disavowed their commitment. ..." In a statement which was *péguyste* in its tone

---

[155] *Ibid.*, 221; and Raymond-Laurent, *Figures de militants*, 54–55.
[156] Mounier, "Dernières cartouches," *Esprit*, No. 67 (April, 1938), 1–4.
[157] Mounier, "Lendemains d'un trahison," *Esprit*, No. 73 (October, 1938), 1–15.

of moral indignation, Mounier complained that the streets and villages of France swarmed with men sweating with fear, men who were not interested in justice for the Sudetans or the Czechs, Germany, Europe or France, not even in the injustice of war, but men who were concerned only with a "moratorium of tranquility" which was only "the tranquility of disorder." In other commentaries on Munich, Mounier addressed himself to the problems of French domestic and foreign affairs. France was not dead, he said, but she was dying.[158] France was dying of doubt, hatred and lies. "This winter," Mounier proclaimed, "France has a humiliation to atone for: September 20; a danger to avoid: internal Fascism; a catastrophe to avert: war and its long shadow, armed peace; a task to recommence: its regeneration." [159]

Mounier's forthright, almost bellicose, condemnation of what he referred to as "the Daladier-Chamberlain felony" and the "gesture of Pilate" brought immediate dissent from some members of Esprit. Maurice de Gandillac, Roger Labrousse, Marcel Moré, and François Goguel vehemently opposed Mounier's firm stand.[160] A collaborator of Esprit recalls that those who did not share Mounier's view

said that everything should be sacrificed to peace; it should be bought at any cost, because it was only in a peaceful world that social reconstruction could be pursued. And social reconstruction, they asserted, was essential; it should be the chief aim of the present generation. We held a special congress to discuss these questions; its atmosphere was exceptionally troubled and confused.... Everyone looked worried and unsettled. Mounier tried to bring the dissenting parties to an understanding, but even his skill at conducting a debate failed to appease them.[161]

A majority of the journal's collaborators supported Mounier, however, and there was no real schism within the Esprit movement.[162]

Among Mounier's allies of the Catholic and Christian democratic Left there was almost complete unanimity on the Anschluss. There was, in fact, a strange quasi-unanimity among all French Catholics in February, 1938.[163] With its characteristic nostalgia for things past the Catholic Right had looked with favor upon the corporative, authoritarian regime of Dollfuss, with horror upon his assassination, and with

158 Mounier, "La France est-elle finie?," le Voltigeur, September 29, 1938, reprinted in B.A.E.M., No. 23–24 (December, 1964), 3–5.

159 Mounier, "Europe contre les hégémonies," Esprit, No. 74 (November, 1938), 147–165; and Mounier, "De l'Europe à la France," Esprit, No. 74 (November, 1938), 228–230.

160 Mounier, "Lettre à un ami, 10 octobre 1938," O.M., IV, 621; and "Carnets d'un mobilisation (suite)," Esprit, No. 74 (November, 1938), 293–301. See also Marrou, "L'action politique d'Emmanuel Mounier," 92.

161 Iswolsky, Light Before Dusk, 200–201.

162 Mounier, "Les cinq étapes d'Esprit," 19.

163 Vignaux, "Les catholiques français et la politque étrangère," 450–453.

general sympathy upon Schussnigg and his Catholic compatriots. The Catholic and Christian democratic Left adopted similar positions but for different reasons. The Christian democrats were consistent in their ideological opposition to Fascist expansion and their defense of French interests in central and eastern Europe.[164] No such unanimity, even among the Christian democrats, obtained during the Munich crisis. Like the men of *Esprit* the Christian democrats were divided, but like *Esprit* also there was no major break within any Christian democratic group and the great majority of Christian democrats opposed Munich. The Christian democrat did not necessarily fit Mounier's portrait of the indecisive man who proposed "a moratorium of tranquility."

The collaborators of *l'aube* demonstrated a consistent interest in Austrian affairs from the beginning of the publication of the journal.[165] They preached resistance to Hitler and expressed the hope that Schussnigg would display firmness in his dealings with Hitler. Following the *Anschluss*, there was some difference of opinion among the men of *l'aube* concerning the question of French armaments, but the journal was firmly anti-Munich. The men of *l'aube* condemned the Munich Agreement largely on moral grounds, assessing its international ramifications only secondarily. Like Mounier, after forthrightly condemning Munich with a series of *mea culpas* for France's part in the crime, *l'aube* returned to such familiar themes as disarmament, Franco-German reconciliation, and the regeneration of France. But, like Mounier also, the entire thrust of *l'aube*'s assessment was in the direction of resistance to Hitler, and the references to disarmament and Franco-German reconciliation appeared to be little more than the recitation of a well-memorized but somewhat meaningless litany of past commitments. Late in 1938 Gay published a collective work, *La Tchécoslovaquie devant notre conscience et devant l'Histoire*, which contained reprints of articles by a number of the collaborators of *l'aube* as well as texts on Munich originally published in such "friendly" journals as *Esprit*, *Temps présent, le Petit Démocrate, la Vie intellectuelle*, and *Politique*.[166] Significantly, the book contained not a single article defending Hitler's aggression.

Among the articles reprinted in the *l'aube* publication was one by

---

[164] See, for example, Ernest Pezet, *Fin de l'Autriche, fin d'une Europe* (Paris: F. Sorlot, 1938).

[165] The summary of *l'aube* is taken from Mayeur, *l'aube*, 142–155.

[166] Francisque Gay *et al.*, *La Tchécoslovaquie devant notre conscience et devant l'Histoire* (Paris: Editions de l'aube [1938]).

Ernest Pezet.[167] In it Pezet denounced Munich by angrily rebutting a number of widely circulated arguments used by the Catholic Right in defense of Munich: that the Sudetan Germans were oppressed and tortured; that Czechoslovakia was the carrier of the Bolshevik virus; that President Beneš was a Freemason and Czechoslovakia the country *par excellence* of integral *laïcisme* and omnipotent Freemasonry. In the Chamber Pezet had clearly recognized the threat that Hitler posed to the independence of both Austria and Czechoslovakia as early as June, 1936.[168] In February, 1938 Pezet explained that the continued independence of Austria was crucial for the economic and political organization of a new Europe. As a personal friend of Schussnigg, Pezet refused to believe that Austria would succumb to Hitler's threats and he argued that French inaction would result in the surrender of all of Danubian Europe. He went so far as to suggest that the hesitation or inaction of Great Britain should not deter France from fullfilling her obligations to the Austrian David against the German Goliath.[169] Following the Munich Agreement, Pezet concluded a devastating attack on the government with the statement: "Gentlemen, we want peace, but the peace of free men and not that of slaves." [170]

The parliamentary representatives of both the *Parti Démocrate Populaire* and the *Jeune-République* supported the government in a vote of confidence after the *Anschluss*, and again in October, 1938 by ratifying the Munich Agreement.[171] In the first vote, the deputies were led to understand that the government was committed to collective security and to the defense of Czechoslovakia. In the second, François Saudubray of the *Parti Démocrate Populaire* protested being presented with a *fait accompli*, but every group in the Chamber, with the sole exception of the Communists, voted for the government on the grounds that a rejection of Munich would provoke serious international repercussions.[172]

The prolonged crisis of 1938 provoked similar responses from Mounier and his Christian democratic allies. All of them agreed that the crisis was primarily a moral crisis and that the solution was the moral or spiritual regeneration of France. At the *Esprit* congress of July, 1938

---

[167] Ernest Pezet, "A la Bohême victime de la calonmie," *la Vie intellectuelle*, Vol 59 (October 25, 1938), 221–228, reprinted in part in *ibid.*, 93–94.

[168] *J.O.C.*, No. 50 (June 23, 1936), 1539.

[169] *J.O.C.*, No. 19 (February 25, 1938), 572–576.

[170] *J.O.C.*, No. 7 (January 20, 1939), 130–138.

[171] *J.O.C.*, No. 20 (February 26, 1938), 660–662; and *J.O.C.*, No. 52 (October 4, 1938), 1346–1349.

[172] Raymond-Laurent, *Le Parti Démocrate Populaire*, 85.

Mounier re-examined the means by which the *Esprit* movement might undertake a more immediate and effective form of action. At the same time a decision was made to begin publication of a political action journal subsidiary to *Esprit* called *le Voltigeur* (and somewhat ironically plans to publish a separate poetry review called *Droit de Survivre* were also completed).[173] The quest of the Christian democrats for a means of bringing about the regeneration of France took the form of an organization called the *Nouvelles équipes françaises* (N.E.F.). Although there was much about the spirit and activities of the N.E.F. which lent substance to Mounier's fundamental criticism of Christian democracy and its adherents, Mounier was sympathetic to the N.E.F.; and the N.E.F., in turn, carried with it traces of the influence of Mounier and *Esprit*.

Mounier began his report to the *Esprit* congress of 1938 by asking if *Esprit* should participate in political activity and, if it did, should such activity be undertaken within existent organizations or should *Esprit* organize its own political movement?[174] To the first question, Mounier gave an affirmative reply and in the process he reverted once again to a discussion of the dangers of a-politicism and of "thinking politically as moralists" which he believed to be especially acute among some members of *Esprit*. Once again also, Mounier revealed the fundamental a-politicism of his own métier as well as of the function he had assigned *Esprit*. The function of *Esprit*, Mounier reiterated, would be seriously endangered, if not entirely perverted, were the movement to join any political party en bloc. Political activity within a party would ultimately sterilize the action of *Esprit*, for no existing party "can promise us in the foreseeable future ... the total recovery that our situation requires." Mounier thus ruled out any formal collaboration between *Esprit* and existing political parties, but he remained equally consistent in not ruling out collaboration of individual members of the group with political parties.

The precise form that the political action of *Esprit* itself would take was provided by Mounier's suggestion that the *Esprit* groups throughout France should form "camps volants" or "volitigeurs." Each of these little action cells was to examine specific political problems and local situations and to undertake the kind of independent political activities that its members believed consonant with the principles of *Esprit*. Mounier regarded these cells as a means of bringing the voice of

---

[173] On *Droit de Survivre*, see "Adrian Miatlev tel qu'en nous autres," *La Tour de Feu*, No. 90-91 (June, 1966), especially 13ff.

[174] Mounier, "'Esprit' et l'action politique," *Esprit*, No. 73 (October, 1938), 34-64.

Esprit to bear more immediately and effectively upon the course of political events.[175] This new departure was apparently in large part the result of pressure exerted by other members or friends of *Esprit* upon Mounier.[176] Left to himself, Mounier might have devoted his energies almost exclusively to another project in 1938. Beginning in the spring of that year, Mounier and three of his closest friends, Jacques Lefrancq, Emile-Albert Niklaus, and Paul Fraisse, carried on lengthy conversations and a voluminous correspondence concerning the establishment of an *Esprit* center and school.[177]

Although Mounier actively collaborated in the new enterprise, it was Pierre-Aimé Touchard, who had joined *Esprit* as a drama critic in 1933, who assumed the task of coordinating the activities of the "voltigeurs." [178] In explaining the genesis and purpose of the new bimonthly journal, *le Voltigeur*, Touchard indicated that many friends of *Esprit* wanted to undertake a form of action which was more directly involved "at once in actuality and in political life than the Review and the *Esprit* groups could be." [179] The creation of *le Voltigeur* alone would not suffice, however, and the action groups were to become more and more independent of the journal and were ultimately to undertake autonomous political action. As a good disciple of Mounier, Touchard warned of the dangers inherent in political activity and expressed his concern that the positive accomplishments of *Esprit* not be compromised by the new journal or by the activities of its groups. The first issue of *le Voltigeur* appeared on September 29, 1938 and it was published twice monthly until July 15, 1939 when it merged with the parent journal.

The N.E.F. of *l'aube* and its *Journal de bord* were primarily the results of the personal labors of Francisque Gay.[180] When *l'aube* was founded in 1932, Gay's purpose was clearly to provide a kind of forum or meeting place for all of the members of the badly fragmented "democrats of Christian inspiration." As early as 1935 in his confidential memoir *Pour*

---

[175] Mounier, "Les cinq étapes d'*Esprit*," 19.

[176] See, for example, Mounier, "'Esprit' et l'action politique," 34–64 *passim*.; Marrou, "L'action politique d'Emmanuel Mounier," 92; and P.-A. Touchard, "Le Voltigeur français," *Esprit*, No. 73 (October, 1938), 65.

[177] Béguin, "Une vie," 1002, 1005; Mounier, "Lettres à Emile-Albert Niklaus, 10 janvier 1938, 7 mai 1938, 8 septembre 1938, 29 septembre 1938, 3 janvier 1939," *O.M.*, IV, 612–627 *passim*.; and Jacques Lefrancq, *Oser penser* (Neuchâtel: Editions de la Baconnière, 1961), 204–206.

[178] Mounier's contributions to *le Voltigeur*, consisting of eight articles, are reprinted in *B.A.E.M.*, No. 23–24 (December, 1964), 3–33.

[179] Touchard, "Le Voltigeur français," 65–67.

[180] Unless otherwise indicated, the account of the N.E.F. is taken from Mayeur, *l'aube*, 186–211, and Carité, 95–109.

un rassemblement des forces démocratiques d'inspiration chrétienne, Gay denounced the weaknesses and divisive activities of the various organizations and organs of his "spiritual family." Clearly, *l'aube* was not effectively fulfilling the purpose for which it had been founded. In spite of the reputation the journal earned for its forthright commentaries and analyses of contemporary events, the history of *l'aube* was increasingly the continued story of dissension within the Christian democratic movement. The *Parti Démocrate Populaire* was reserved if not actually hostile to *l'aube*, in spite of the active collaboration of such *Démocrates Populaires* as Georges Bidault and Robert Cornilleau. The great Christian democratic provincial daily *l'Ouest-Eclair* followed a political line well to the right of *l'aube*, as Gay's own painful experience in the election campaign of 1936 demonstrated. The *Jeune-République* was also initially cool towards *l'aube* but the Abyssinian affair served to make the relations between the little party and Gay's journal far more cordial. Edmond Bloud, of the publishing house of Bloud et Gay, severed his connection with *l'aube* at the time of the Chiappe-Madaule controversy and he took with him the rest of the *Group Républicain et Social*. Gaston Tessier resigned from the editorial board in October, 1936 and at the same time Georges Pernot and his Social Catholic followers quit the journal.

In the face of these schisms, Gay personally undertook almost heroic efforts to increase the journal's subscribers and to coordinate the work of the *Amis de l'aube*. He made a number of tours of the provinces and received encouragement from the younger readers of *l'aube*. In May, June, and July of 1937 a series of articles calling for "the rejuvenation of the democratic *mystique*" and emphasizing the dynamism of the younger generation and their criticism of the fragmented status of the Christian democratic movement appeared in *l'aube*. In November, 1937 the first congress of the *Amis de l'aube* was held in Paris. In the course of the congress special attention was paid to the younger generation's desire for unity of action, but Georges Bidault made specific reference to the serious problem of the relationship between the *Parti Démocrate Populaire* and the *Jeune-République* in his report to the congress.

In January, 1938 the executive commission of the *Parti Démocrate Populaire* issued a statement in which it reaffirmed the autonomy of *l'aube* and the *Parti Démocrate Populaire* but at the same time supported the development of closer and more friendly contacts between the journal and the party. Gay received additional encouragement as a result of a number of meetings of the *Amis de l'aube* in Paris. The ener-

gies and attentions of Gay and his friends were diverted by the international crisis until the end of the summer of 1938, but the *Anschluss*
and particularly the Munich Agreement gave a new urgency to the work
of the *Amis de l'aube*. On November 9, 1938 some 1500 representatives
of the more than 200 groups of *Amis de l'aube* throughout France
gathered in a second congress. "We have made our choice of an expression," the assemblage was told, "which evokes at once our desire
for renovation, well-disciplined action, and national recovery: the
Nouvelles équipes françaises."

The character and purpose of the N.E.F. were far from clear. From
the congress of November, 1938 until the early fall of 1939, enthusiasm
prevailed over all else as time after time the old parties were charged
with being useless and as the need for moral and political renovation was
emphasized. During the founding congress of the N.E.F., one by one,
Gay, Jacques Madaule, Georges Bidault, Etienne Borne, Georges Hoog,
and, among many others and as was mandatory on such occasions,
Marc Sangnier himself went to the rostrum. The manifesto of the
N.E.F. was a brochure of sixteen pages written mainly by Bidault with
the help of Charles Blondel and entitled in good Christian democratic
fashion "To men of our spirit." Intended as a point of departure rather
than as a doctrinal synthesis or specific statement of purpose, the manifesto omitted any matters upon which there might have been serious
differences of opinion among the leaders of the *Parti Démocrate Populaire*, the *Jeune-République*, the Christian trade unionists. *Temps présent*, and even *Esprit*. Bidault condemned the old parties, the old formulas, the old routines, and "the regime in which the government cannot govern and in which the Parliament cannot control." Echoing the
substance, if not the precise language Mounier had used in his debate
with Archambault in 1934, the slogan of the congress and the N.E.F.
was: "It is no longer a question of defending democracy. It is a question of establishing it."

Other declarations by members of the N.E.F. were equally diffuse.
"The *raison d'être* and the strength of a movement like the N.E.F.,"
said one, "is that it can, and must, serve as a center of ralliement for
men belonging to all parties, to all social milieux, to all confessions, for
all those animated by the common ideal of French restoration." [181]
Charles d'Aragon declared that the new movement refused to be seduced by what he termed "the oratorial debauchery or verbal specula-

[181] Max André, "Chronique du reveil français," *Politique*, 12e année, No. 2 (February,
1939), 162.

tions" of the Parliament and yet refused "to play, like irresponsible witnesses, the role of Greek choruses before the events of our times." [182] Gay's son-in-law, Louis Terrenoire, reiterated the traditional Christian democratic opposition to the "two blocs" by stating that the mission of the N.E.F. was to bridge the meaningless dichotomy between Right and Left as "sons of the Christian tradition and pioneers of a new order." [183] Indicative of the real nature of the N.E.F. were the positions of the *Parti Démocrate Populaire* and the *Jeune-République*. At the time of the first congress of the *Amis de l'aube* both parties denied that they were participating in the organization of an assemblage of "democrats of Christian inspiration." [184] In November, 1938, however, they both welcomed the N.E.F. because it was not a political party in any meaningful sense of the term.[185]

Symptomatic also of the character of the N.E.F. was a statement made at the closing banquet of the founding congress. A man rose from his place at a table alongside Stanislas Fumet, the editor of *Temps présent*, and expressed his pleasure with the formation of the N.E.F. He then stated that the diversity of those present "is a gauge of good order and this convergence is a gauge of the French unity that we seek." [186] Whatever Emmanuel Mounier meant by this toast to the N.E.F., it was well received by the congress. The final crises of the Third Republic brought forth roughly parallel responses from *Esprit* and the *Amis d'Esprit*, on one hand, and *l'aube* and the *Amis de l'aube*, on the other. The crises also made the Christian democrats receptive to Mounier's revolutionary message. Time and again in the course of the speeches delivered at the congress, references were made to the human person, personalism, Mounier and *Esprit*. Paul Archambault, for example, placed the N.E.F. within the tradition of personalist democracy being carried forward by Mounier and Maritain.[187] Many members of *Esprit* were present at the congress and several of them took an active part in its proceedings.[188] The following month, in an "Appel à un rassemblement pour une démocratie personnaliste," Mounier recognized this convergence by including the N.E.F. and the

---

[182] *l'aube*, February 19, 1939.
[183] *l'aube*, June 16, 1939.
[184] *La Jeune-République*, November 14, 1937.
[185] *l'aube*, November 20, 1938, and November 18, 1939; and *La Jeune-République*, November 20, 1938.
[186] *l'aube*, November 15, 1938.
[187] *l'aube*, November 13, 1938.
[188] *l'aube*, November 17, 1938.

Christian democrats in his appeal.[189] A volume in Archambault's *La Nouvelle Journée* entitled *Options sur demain, tâches nouvelles, nouvelles équipes*, which was recognized by the N.E.F. as expressing their *raison d'être* and ideal, bore the stamp of Mounier's influence throughout its pages.[190] The three authors of *Options sur demain* were Jean Lacroix, Etienne Borne, and Marc Scherer, the young Christian democrat whose contribution was an almost *mouniériste* critique of social and political Catholicism in France.

In his contribution to *Options sur demain*, Borne called for the reconciliation of all of the old intellectual differences within French Catholicism as a prerequisite to a common and concerted effort of practical action. Like Mounier, he contended that democracy in France had been compromised in serious equivocations since its birth and that the only viable political system was one that was based upon the communitarian sense of the people and served the human person. But when Borne addressed himself to the problem of the relationship between Christianity and democracy his solution was a typically Christian democratic one. "An immense misunderstanding has led to the belief that the democrats of *l'Avenir* or the *Sillon* made democracy the necessary political expression of Christianity," he said. Just the opposite was true: "it is not democracy that is necessary to Christianity but Christianity that is necessary to democracy, or at least the moral climate which in France can only be a Christian climate." Democracy and its allied institutions had to be entirely reconstructed. "On all of these questions," Borne stated with excessive optimism, "from the *Semaines sociales* to the young *Esprit* movement, from Jacques Maritain to Paul Archambault, the accord grows more and more profound." [191]

The subject of Jean Lacroix's contribution to the same volume was "Mystique et politique." After discussing the relationship between Péguy's *mystique* and *politique*, Lacroix addressed himself to the problem examined by Borne. One of the fundamental differences between *Esprit* and Christian democracy became immediately clear. "To wish to construct the City solely and directly by means of the Christian *mystique*," Lacroix charged, "would ... be as dangerous for Christianity as for the country." Rather, the *mystique* necessary for a total re-

[189] Mounier, "Appel à un rassemblement pour un démocratie personnaliste," *Esprit*, No. 75 (December, 1938), 424–434.
[190] Etienne Borne, Jean Lacroix, and Marc Scherer, *Options sur demain, tâches nouvelles, nouvelles équipes* ("La Nouvelle Journee," No. 6; Paris: Bloud & Gay, 1939).
[191] Borne, "Rencontres et convergences," in *ibid.*, 15–61.

novation of France was a *mystique* of liberty, a *mystique* of the human person. Lacroix concluded by stating that "we are among those who believe with St. Paul that piety is useful to everyone, but that piety does not suffice for everyone and that, while being always animated by the Christian spirit, it is necessary to deal with political problems in political terms and with economic problems in economic terms." [192]

The apparent convergence of the efforts of *Esprit* and Christian democracy did not have immediate results. Mounier himself did not abandon or even moderate his basic criticisms of Christian democracy and its adherents. He was particularly insistent upon guarding the independence of *Esprit* and balancing the similarities between *Esprit* and the N.E.F. with their important differences. Only a week after he attended the closing banquet of the N.E.F. congress, he re-emphasized the differing missions of *Esprit* and the N.E.F. In an article in *l'aube* Mounier paid tribute to the N.E.F. for recognizing that French unity and regeneration could not be achieved through political parties that no longer truly represented France. He added, however, that the seeds of French unity were being sown by the individual efforts of many men, including a small group of men who had gathered in a Paris suburb at the very time the N.E.F. was being organized. Mounier's reference was obviously to the *Esprit* congress of 1938. He concluded by saying that each group should work to reform and transform its particular milieu: "you the Christian democrats, we the intellectuals, others the various political and working-class elites." [193]

In February, 1939 Mounier again lectured the Christian democrats of *l'aube*. He admitted that a member of *Esprit* could write in *l'aube*, that there ought to be intermediaries between the two journals because their political positions were not dissimilar. But then Mounier warned the Christian democrats of the dangers inherent in their conception of a "Third party." Too often, he said, a third way resulted in impotence and abstention. Then Mounier repeated many of his old criticisms of the Christian democrats.[194] On the occasion of the publication of the 2,000th issue of *l'aube*, Mounier again stressed the differing functions of *Esprit* and *l'aube*. "There are political temperaments just as there are spiritual temperaments and philosophical temperaments," he explain-

---

[192] Lacroix, "Mystique et politique," in *ibid.*, 63–92.

[193] Mounier, "Thérapeutique de nos divisions," *l'aube*, November 22, 1938, reprinted in *B.A.E.M.*, No. 23–24 (December, 1964), 40–42.

[194] Mounier, "Troisième voie," *l'aube*, February 1, 1939, reprinted in *B.A.E.M.*, No. 23–24 (December, 1964), 43–46, and, as a posthumous tribute, in *l'aube*, March 25–26, 1950.

ed. The *Esprit* team approached problems with different attitudes, perspectives, and methods from those of the men of *l'aube*.[195]

In view of the foregoing, there is some doubt that the influence of Mounier and *Esprit* upon the Christian democrats would have borne fruit even in different historical circumstances. Admittedly, some of the younger members of the N.E.F. believed that the battles against the Catholic Right were "out of date, useless, even injurious to the extent that they maintained the confusion between religion and politics." [196] The fact remains, however, that the very crisis which had made the Christian democrats partially receptive to Mounier's revolutionary message foreclosed such a possibility, slight though it may have been. What François Goguel has said of the failure of *le Voltigeur* applies in large measure to the N.E.F. of the Christian democrats:

This temptation to political action failed. Basically, it seems to me, because the international situation of the winter of 38–39 allowed no opportunity for domestic political action of a new kind: for what purpose if the future was to be obstructed by war? But also because the vocations of responsible leaders which were necessary around Mounier were not produced, and it was not Mounier's nature for him to become the central inspiration of a political movement. Finally, because the vacuum left behind by the Popular Front was not conducive to a new political venture, the lassitude and skepticism of the masses rendering them, on the contrary, very difficult to stir up in a new outburst.[197]

This first indication of the growing influence of Mounier and *Esprit* among some of the Christian democrats was not to be entirely without results, however. Six years after the organization of the N.E.F. many of the same men gathered in Paris to found the Christian democratic M.R.P. The seeds planted by the N.E.F., as Christian democrats were fond of saying, thus ultimately bore fruit.[198] In the process of their maturation, Mounier and *Esprit* were to make important contributions for, in the conversations and meetings which preceded the decision to found a great Christian democratic movement, the influence of Mounier and *Esprit* was felt once again by the men who had been in many respects his political allies while they remained his doctrinal adversaries.

---

[195] *l'aube*, February 19, 1939.
[196] Mayeur, *l'aube*, 162.
[197] Goguel, "Positions politiques," 811.
[198] On the significance of the N.E.F. in the genesis of the M.R.P., see Pezet, *Chrétiens au service de la cité*, 124–125; Raymond-Laurent, *Le Parti Démocrate Populaire*, 89–92; Mayeur, *l'aube*, 213–216; and "Origines et mission du M.R.P.," *Forces Nouvelles* (Special issue, n.d.), 20–21.

CHAPTER V

RESISTANCE AND REVOLUTION:
MOUNIER AND THE FOUNDING OF THE
MOUVEMENT RÉPUBLICAIN POPULAIRE, 1940–1944

> Je peux mesurer aussi la brusque explosion d'influence qui
> nous a fait silencieusement, depuis la guerre, un point de
> ralliement de ceux qui voulaient maintenir unis la fidélité
> spirituelle, l'honneur français et l'attention révolutionnaire.
>
> Mounier, "Entretiens XIII, 17 novembre 1941."

On June 1, 1940, with the Germans only several hours outside of the city, the *Comédie française* presented an "evening with Péguy." This performance opened a "Péguy season" which was to last for four years. The use and abuse of Charles Péguy by both the men of Vichy and those of the Resistance was symbolic of the profound and complex divisions which rent France between the defeat of 1940 and the Liberation of 1944. For some, Péguy was a Christian racist who devoted his life to combatting the Republic, modern industrial civilization, and the evils of the University. For others, the poet-patriot was a source of hope and national resistance to the collaborationists of Vichy and the material and spiritual dangers of Nazism. Even before the radio appeal of Charles de Gaulle and the signing of the Armistice, a veteran of *Sept* and *Temps présent* published what was very probably the first Resistance tract; Edmond Michelet placed a citation from Péguy at the head of his appeal. Later, in 1941, a book entitled *Le Destin de Charles Péguy* depicted Péguy as a kind of French National Socialist.[1] Its author was Marcel Péguy who had collaborated with Emmanuel Mounier and Georges Izard in *La Pensée de Charles Péguy* in 1931. Mounier himself recalled a few months after the Liberation that Péguy had suffered two deaths: "The first time was a glorious death: on the Marne in 1914. The second, an ignominious death, a spiritual death: his utilization and disfiguration by the propaganda of Vichy in 1940." The intellectual and spiritual heir of Péguy continued:

What Péguy was able to sustain in us during those months! His criticism of the politicians of the Republic was eagerly underscored; that he had dedicated whole books to praising a republican *mystique*... as he had known it during

---

[1] Jacques Duquesne, *Les Catholiques français sous l'occupation* (Paris: Editions Bernard Grasset, 1966), 120–121.

its infancy was forgotten. His traditional patriotism was exalted; that he had written pages of cutting contemporary relevance against the proponents of "peace at any price," against those retreating generals who had discouraged respect by losing their own self-respect was forgotten. For good reason, neither the long, inspiring eulogy he had paid the Jewish people..., nor the consistent connection he had established between the Jewish *mystique* and the Christian *mystique*, nor his definitive pages against anti-Semitism were cited. A good parishioner of the established order, a respectable servant of moral hypocrisy was made of this sturdy peasant whose hard stare could ill-conceal his constant and obstinate revolt against the least bit of injustice, against the least shadow of a lie. A patron of the most unfortunate clericalism and of passive submission to tyrannical authority was made of this total and slightly anarchistic Christian....[2]

Mounier's retrospective assessment of the disparate uses made of Péguy suggests that the political bifurcation of France which followed the defeat of 1940 was accompanied by a far more complex moral and spiritual crisis. The outbreak of war in September, 1939, the defeat of the following June, and the establishment of the Vichy regime provoked a variety of responses from Frenchmen. Some members of the Right welcomed the defeat of France with a series of *mea culpas* which hardly concealed their rejoicing over the fall of the Republic. And those old enemies of Mounier and the Christian democrats, Charles Maurras and his disciples, looked upon Marshal Pétain's political ability as a "divine surprise."[3] The defeat offered some of them the opportunity to become the theoreticians of Pétain's National Revolution. Most of the veterans of the prewar Christian democratic parties and the N.E.F., on the other hand, regarded the defeat as the ultimate outcome of the policies they had condemned during the 1930s and the Vichy regime as the triumph of all they detested in their old opponents of *Action Française* and the *Fédération Nationale Catholique*. André Colin of the N.E.F. broadcast an appeal on Radio-Beyrouth on June 22, 1940 asking his fellow countrymen to continue the struggle; and in occupied France a group of *Jeunes Républicains* published *Valmy*, one of the first Resistance journals, and for their efforts a number of them were arrested, tried, and eventually executed.[4]

The response of Mounier to both the defeat of France and the establishment of the Vichy regime was at once more complex and more typical of the time than that of either many members of the Right or many of the leaders of Christian democracy. Neither the supporters nor the

[2] Mounier, "Péguy ressuscité," *B.A.E.M.*, No. 12 (June, 1958), 4-7. See also Mounier, "Panthéon," *B.A.E.M.*, No. 12 (June, 1958), 3.

[3] Duquesne, 74, and Weber, 447.

[4] Duquesne, 122; Pezet, *Chrétiens au service de la cité*, 127; and Claude Bellanger, *Presse clandestine, 1940-1944* (Paris: Armand Colin, 1961), 58-63.

opponents of Vichy were a bloc, and like many Frenchmen Mounier's position was initially ambivalent.[5] Shortly after the "phoney war" began, Mounier wrote Nicolas Berdiaev that "we are, perhaps, at the beginning of the 'New Middle Ages,'" and he expressed his intention of working for the new France he was certain would emerge after the war.[6] The defeat of 1940 and the advent of Pétain made Mounier's position even more complex. His consistent battle against "the established disorder" of the Third Republic predisposed him to welcome its downfall, but his equally consistent opposition to any form of Fascism precluded his acceptance of the National Revolution. As a result, Mounier worked within the apparatus of the new regime for a little more than a year; he resumed publication of *Esprit* and collaborated with such organizations as the *Compagnons de France*, the *Chantiers de Jeunesse, Jeune France*, and the *Ecole nationale des cadres d'Uriage*. But, on the other hand, as early as the fall of 1940, Mounier began to meet with a number of future leaders of the Resistance, *Uriage* became an important center of Resistance, *Esprit* was suppressed and Mounier was excluded from *Uriage*, the *Compagnons*, the *Chantiers*, and *Jeune France*. In January, 1942 Mounier was arrested and imprisoned as a Resistance leader.

The sudden revival of the fame of Péguy in almost every sector of French opinion which followed the crisis of 1940 brought with it a remarkable expansion of the influence of the man who had sought since 1932 to continue the work of Péguy and the *Cahiers de la Quinzaine*. The influence of Mounier, like that of Péguy, penetrated both the men of Vichy, some of whom were self-styled personalists, and the men of the Resistance, many of whom regarded Mounier as their *spiritus rector*. Among the latter were the young men who began the publication of the *Cahiers de notre jeunesse* in June, 1941. "Notre Jeunesse," wrote one of its collaborators, "Péguy is there. He is our master." [7] And so too was Mounier. The secretary of the *Cahiers de notre jeunesse* was a young student in the University of Lyons named Gilbert Dru. Inspired by the example and ideas of Mounier, young Dru drew up a declaration which was to be the basis of a great personalist "Mouvement" and this "Mouvement," in turn, was to become first the *Mouve-*

[5] For suggestive reinterpretations of Vichy and the Resistance, see Stanley Hoffmann, "Aspects du régime de Vichy," *Revue française de science politique*, VI, No. 1 (January-March, 1956), 44–69; and Gordon Wright, "Reflections on the French Resistance (1940–1944)," *Political Science Quarterly*, LXXVII, No. 3 (September, 1962), 336–349.

[6] Mounier, "Lettre à Nicolas Berdiaeff, 13 novembre 1939," *O.M.*, IV, 646.

[7] Domenach, *Gilbert Dru*, 37.

ment de Libération Nationale and then the M.R.P. Ironically, albeit indirectly and in the most extraordinary circumstances, the great critic of Christian democracy became a *parrain* of the largest Christian democratic party in the history of France.

In September, 1939 Emmanuel Mounier was mobilized as a second-class infantry-man in the Auxiliary Service of the Army. Because of the injury he had suffered to his eye as a youth, he was assigned duty as a headquarters clerk. Always a far from humorless man, in a letter to a friend Mounier wrote that "my *argot* is improving daily. It is my principal cultural acquisition. ..." [8] In addition to his new facility with the language of his fellow soldiers, Mounier's military service also afforded him an opportunity to renew his ties with the countryside of his native Grenoble. His military unit, *Dépôt* 143, was stationed near Grenoble where he sent his wife and daughter to live with his parents in March, 1940. Meanwhile, the publication of *Esprit* continued in spite of Mounier's absence, the dispersion of his collaborators and readers, and Mounier's own recognition that sooner or later the voice of *Esprit* would be silent.[9] Pierre-Aimé Touchard and his wife assumed the primary editorial duties of the journal in Paris, but the clerk in *Dépôt* 143 continued to contribute to *Esprit*. Mounier remained faithful to his vocation: the enemy was Hitler and not Germany; the facile slogans of war were denounced in "Gardons nous de notre ennemi, l'Ennemi"; the element of international civil war contained in the Second World War was emphasized; the brutalizing effects of war were fought against. Mounier contributed a long, anonymous essay on Catholic personalism to a volume commemorating the centennial of the Catholic University of America; and, when the final prewar issue of *Esprit* was published in June, 1940, plans were underway for a special issue on "l'Avant et l'Arrière," the serious divorce between the war and home fronts that had occurred in 1914–1918.[10]

The winter of 1939–1940 was a time of profound personal anguish for Mounier and his wife Paulette. In November, 1937, seven months after her birth, the Mouniers' first child, Françoise, had become ill after being vaccinated for small-pox. Slowly, the illness became more serious until finally, at less than two years of age, Françoise's malady

8 Mounier, "Lettre à Jacques Lefrancq, 6 septembre 1939," *O.M.*, IV, 634.
9 Mounier, "Lettre à Jacques Lefrancq, 7 janvier 1940," *O.M.*, IV, 654.
10 Béguin, "Une vie," 1009–1010; Mounier, "Les cinq étapes d'*Esprit*," 19–20; and Mounier, "L'enjeu des valeurs judéo-chrétiennes: Personnalisme catholique," *Esprit*, No. 89, 90, 91 (February, March, April, 1940), 220–246, 395–409, 57–72.

was diagnosed as incurable encephalitis. As their little child slipped into "a mysterious night of the spirit," Mounier and his wife reconciled themselves to what Mounier told his wife were "days filled with an unknown grace." [11] Until Mounier's death (Françoise died four years after her father), there was always the "presence of Françoise. The story of our little Françoise who seems to slip away on days without a history." [12] Mounier accepted this suffering with an extraordinary sense of spirituality and his letters to his wife at this time undoubtedly belong to the great spiritual literature of his generation. No one who reads Mounier's letters can doubt the profound and unquestioning character of his religious faith.[13]

In July, 1940 after spending three weeks as a prisoner of war near Saintes in the Charente, Mounier was demobilized in Orange, returned to Grenoble for his wife and child and then went to Lyons. First in a single room at 5 rue Pizay and then in a small apartment, Mounier undertook to resume the publication of *Esprit* and to provide for his family. To support his family, he taught philosophy in the Ecole Robin in Vienne and in a school run by the Lazarists in Lyons. Mounier supplemented his meager income through his work for *Jeune France* and other organizations, and later, after his arrest, imprisonment, and release, he received a small weekly stipend from the Resistance movement *Combat* which he supplemented by writing for several publishers in Switzerland.[14] The financial circumstances of the Mouniers, particularly during the terrible winter of 1940–1941, were almost equalled in their difficulty by Mounier's decision to resume publication of *Esprit* with the approval of Vichy officials and under the surveillance of their censor in Lyons.

The reappearance of *Esprit* in November, 1940, and what Mounier referred to as the period of "open clandestineness" in the history of *Esprit*, came only after a series of debates among the members of *Esprit* in the unoccupied zone and a good deal of soul-searching by Mounier himself.[15] Early in August, 1940 Mounier met with Charles Blondel, a veteran Christian democrat who had just returned from Vichy, and Jean Lacroix in the home of Lacroix in Lyons. The three men agreed almost spontaneously that since the Third Republic was

---

[11] Mounier, "Lettre à Paulette Mounier, 20 mars 1940," *O.M.*, IV, 661.

[12] Mounier, "Entretiens X, 29 août 1940," *O.M.*, IV, 670.

[13] See the letters in *O.M.*, IV, 660–664. A second daughter, Annette, was born in August, 1941, and a third daughter, Martine, in 1947.

[14] Béguin, "Une vie," 1017.

[15] Mounier, "Les cinq étapes d'*Esprit*," 20. For a general assessment of the "hesitations" of *Esprit*, see Duquesne, 131–137.

dead and the new visage of history was an authoritarian one, "nothing remains but to assure the same fidelities, with new forms and actions, within the new materials [of history]." [16] The dominant feature of these new circumstances, Mounier wrote, was "that our defeat is a defeat for France rather than for the French army; at least for a certain France, and behind her of a certain form of Western civilization." [17] What Mounier meant, of course, was that the bourgeois spirit and all that he associated with it – the "international of comfort and personal selfishness," the "world of money," the individualism of the "self-seeking and the irresponsible," French parliamentarianism, all of those who were not "willing to die for anything: neither for God, nor for the revolution, nor for France, nor for a friend" – all of this had suffered a massive and perhaps fatal blow. [18]

In retrospect, Mounier explained that "we were divided not only among ourselves but within ourselves" over the question of resuming publication of *Esprit*. Some members of the group wanted to cease publication of the journal purely and simply while others wanted it to reappear and die on the field of battle. "I must say," Mounier admitted, "that I was inclined in the latter direction, after having hesitated myself." But Mounier believed that to cease publication of *Esprit* would signify a retreat, and it was preferable to fight openly and to bring about the suppression of the journal in a clear and plain manner. [19] In retrospect also, the subscribers of *Esprit* were told that the journal had resumed publication on two conditions: that a positive order from the censor would never be accepted without a battle; and that little by little the chord of opposition would be stretched until the inevitable break between *Esprit* and Vichy occurred. [20]

Typical of the reaction of some friends of *Esprit* was that of Hélène Iswolsky:

After the Armistice I met several members of *Esprit*, and often heard from Mounier himself. He had resumed the publication of his review in spite of the innumerable technical and psychological difficulties he encountered. His aim was to contribute to the task of national reconstruction so urgently needed. He still believed that it was possible to spread his ideas and to preserve his spiritual independence.

[16] Mounier, "Entretiens X, Lyon, 4 août 1940," *O.M.*, IV, 668.
[17] Mounier, "Letter from France," *The Commonweal*, XXXIII, No. 1 (October 25, 1940), 8.
[18] *Ibid.*, 8–9.
[19] Mounier, "Les cinq étapes d'*Esprit*," 20.
[20] "Esprit 40–41," *Esprit*, No. 106 (January, 1945), 303.

I must admit that I felt extremely sceptical as to the fate of *Esprit* and its friends. They were champions of a personalist and pluralist society which was exactly the opposite of the regime which victorious Germany was enforcing in France. I listened with sadness and foreboding to these young men when they spoke enthusiastically about their work. How many months, I wondered, would they be allowed to survive; for the order they defended was a defiance of the "order" made in Berlin.[21]

Similar, if not stronger, reservations were expressed by Pierre-Aimé Touchard, Marcel Moré, and other collaborators and friends of *Esprit* who had remained in the occupied zone.[22] In March, 1941 the entire question of continuing publication was reopened when Daniel Villey, a veteran of *Esprit*, was released from prison and arrived in Lyons.[23] In retrospect, several of Mounier's closest friends faulted his jugdment and Mounier himself expressed increasingly grave reservations concerning the efficacy of his venture in spite of certain triumphs over the Vichy censor.[24]

Whatever misgivings Mounier may have had were no doubt initially mitigated by the response he received after the reappearance of *Esprit*. A great majority of the many letters he received from his readers welcomed the reappearance of the journal. "*Esprit* reappears. *Resurrexit. Alleluia*," wrote Roger Martin du Gard.[25] Mounier's intention was clear even though his method and ultimately his success were the subject of debate and criticism. His primary intention was contained in a formula enunciated by Charles Blondel whom Mounier characterized as "one of the rare men of Christian democratic background who has some sense of history." The formula was "to undertake a clandestine spiritual battle," that is, to take advantage of the similarity of the terms used for the values of *Esprit* and those used by the Vichy regime by introducing the proper content into the latter.[26] Mounier recognized that his venture was a modest gesture but he hoped that it would be a creative one. He was determined to maintain his *présence* within the new regime in order to moderate or thwart the internal influences acting upon it. In a rather curious line of argument, he believed that "one does not base one's presence in history on either a future which is independent of us or on a negation." To refuse all confidence to "a mixed regime," Mounier believed, was tantamount to abandoning that re-

---

[21] Iswolsky, *Light Before Dusk*, 118.
[22] Mounier, "Entretiens XI, 20 décembre 1940," *O.M.*, IV, 683.
[23] Mounier, "Entretiens XI, 30 mars 1941," *O.M.*, IV, 699–703.
[24] See, for example, Goguel, "Postitions politiques," 815; and Béguin, "Une vie," 1020.
[25] Mounier, "Entretiens XI, 20 décembre 1940," *O.M.*, IV, 684.
[26] Mounier, "Entretiens X, Lyon, 4 août 1940," *O.M.*, IV, 668.

gime to what he termed its "internal determinisms." [27] At the same
time, however, while waiting for official authorization to resume
publication of *Esprit*, he made it clear that he would not jeopar-
dize his freedom by asking for any official post in the new regime.[28]

The success of the ten issues of *Esprit* published between November,
1940, and August, 1941 is highly dubious. If, on one hand, Mounier
succeeded at times in giving a different content to certain official
themes and catch-words of the Vichy regime, it is not at all certain that
some of his own readers were any more perceptive in reading between
the lines than were the censors who approved the publication of
Esprit. The devices to which Mounier resorted were sometimes so
subtle that a number of his own friends became genuinely alarmed and
Mounier himself carried on a private debate over the efficacy of his
undertaking.[29] In the first issue of the resurrected journal, no mention was made of the new regime at all.[30] When a censor rejected an
article, Mounier substituted some material by Georges Zérapha. "A
good trick," Mounier exulted, "to call anonymously upon a Jew in this
first issue." Mounier was amused by the fact that of the four lines deleted by the censor in Zérapha's article, two had been taken from the
words of the Marshal himself. In the November issue also, Mounier
praised those Frenchmen who, with Péguy, had resisted "peace at any
price"; and there was a long review of an issue of *Etudes Carmélitaines*
on the spiritual equality of all men and all races.

Mounier was not pleased with what he believed had been a rather
unskillful exercise in his new technique and he was determined to be
more forthright in the next issue. Warned by a friend that *Esprit* might
well suffer the fate of *Marianne*, a weekly that had been suppressed,
Mounier nonetheless was determined to take the risk. He had already
confessed that half-truths could result in confusion and was aware that
many of his sympathetic critics believed that "a half-truth is a counter-
truth." After a lengthy, almost comic-tragic, encounter with the censors, Mounier's articles for the December number of *Esprit*, "Sur l'intelligence en temps de crise" and "Charles Péguy et le problème juif,"
were rejected by the censors. All in all, some fifty per cent of the original December issue was rejected and the published journal consisted

[27] Mounier, "Entretiens X, 10 novembre 1940," *O.M.*, IV, 677.
[28] Mounier, "Lettre à Xavier Schorderet, 15 octobre 1940," *O.M.*, IV, 674.
[29] Béguin, "Une vie," 1025; and Mounier, "Entretiens XI, 20 décembre 1940," *O.M.*, IV, 683.
[30] The following summary of *Esprit* under Vichy is taken from "Esprit 40-41," *Esprit*, No. 106 (January, 1945), 303-306; Mounier, "Les cinq étapes d'*Esprit*," 20-21; and Mounier, "Lettres" and "Entretiens," *O.M.*, IV, 679-714 *passim*.

almost entirely of articles on music, medicine, and other non-political subjects. "They have cut its beak and claws," Mounier lamented, "and we did not have time to prepare secondary lines of defense." In an attempt to defend his failure, Mounier argued that the number of blank pages in *Esprit* had had a great effect upon its readers and that at least, unlike *La Croix*, *Esprit* had not published propaganda provided it by the government. The next issue of *Esprit* was to be an "attack," Mounier said, and he dedicated it to a problem that was assuming increasing importance in his own battle against the ideological and spiritual contagions of Vichy and Nazism. In two articles, Mounier attacked the monolithic and totalitarian character that the Vichy regime was attempting to impose upon the many youth movements in unoccupied France. The February issue was possibly the most successful issue of the journal published under the eyes of the Vichy censors. In it appeared the two articles by Mounier which had been rejected for publication in December. In one of them, Mounier denounced the dangers of imperceptibly slipping into an intellectual betrayal of the values for which France stood; and in the other, he clearly demonstrated that Charles Péguy could not be made the patron of official anti-Semitism without doing violence to the truth.

"Finally," Mounier exulted, "I know that *Esprit* can receive a visage which is not unfaithful." Then, however, he expressed his recognition of the fact that he had scored only a temporary victory. Early in March he admitted that "for five months, I have been alone in having all of the ideas for series of articles, new themes, methods of passing the censor. What strength we would have were each of us to contribute a little of himself!" He had been, Mounier continued, a victim of Blondel's formula, "to undertake a clandestine spiritual battle" and this technique was now in question. The next day, however, his confidence had been restored. He wrote Georges Zérapha that "in *Esprit*, outside *Esprit*, I am working wherever I think it possible to arm the French soul against Nazi contamination." Zérapha's apparent concern over Mounier's methods was shared by many of the collaborators of *Esprit*, judging from a letter Mounier sent to a number of them on March 18, 1941. The last two numbers of *Esprit*, Mounier wrote, proved that possibilities still remained open to the journal in spite of the difficult circumstances of the time. Mounier then complained about the unwillingness of many of the journal's prewar collaborators to help the journal, leaving the burden of publishing *Esprit* almost entirely upon Mounier and three or four others.[31] Admittedly, about three-quarters of the collaborators of *Esprit* were either prisoners or isolated in the occupied zone, Mounier said, but if others did not help *"Esprit* is dead." "We are no longer taking part in the war of guns," he told his readers, "but we have not signed an armistice in the spiritual war that we began in 1932."

Something of a climax in the debate concerning the continued publication of the journal occurred in the last week of March, 1941, when Daniel Villey arrived in Lyons. The debate centered on the question of "the legitimacy of an action of *présence*" within the Vichy regime. Villey told Mounier that the impression *Esprit* had made in the occupied zone was a good one but that this sentiment had changed almost immediately upon reaching the unoccupied zone. The question then became a simple one: "What is this, this operetta in the face of the enemy?" Villey's position evoked in Mounier a return to the source of his vocation, a reaffirmation of his profound belief in the efficacy of his *témoignage*, and a restatement of the essentially a-political character of his *engagement*. Mounier's more specific response to Villey was that the situation in Vichy France was not completely closed, that there was still an opportunity to prevent the infiltration of Nazi values, and that *Esprit* was working for this purpose. Mounier concluded, however, that "the Review is only a springboard. Our activity at *Uriage*, in the *Chantiers*, in the [youth] Movements is ten times more important," he said, making reference to his many other activities of the time.

And so Mounier persisted in his enterprise. In future issues of *Esprit* he assailed the "ambiguous values" of Vichy and celebrated such dubious triumphs over the censor as the juxta-positioning of an announcement that the Germans had given the Paris Zoo a number of wild animals with a report that a number of writers had been released from political imprisonment and allowed to resume their work with certain collaborationist journals. In June, 1941 a "Supplément aux Mémoires d'un Âne" was published. Under the guise of a fable, the essay was in fact a parody of collaboration in which any number of men, including Marshal Pétain himself, could recognize themselves with any measure of perception. The censor allowed such material to be published, "but Vichy," Mounier later recalled, "had seen more clearly and we were suppressed for our general tendency in September, 1941." In the judgment of one of Mounier's closest friends, "'Esprit'

---

[31] For a recollection of this period by one of the mainstays of *Esprit*, see "Notes de Jean-Marie Soutou," *E.M., 1905–1950*, 1026–1026.

was widely read especially by the youths in the camps of the *Chantiers* [*de Jeunesse*], and played an essential role in education as 'the organ of independence and resistance.'" [32] Several young men later testified to the influence of Mounier and "Emile," as Mounier called *Esprit* during this period of open clandestineness. "He was our conscience," one of them said. Confronted with any decision, many young men habitually asked themselves what Mounier's views were. "But in the night of Occupation, after the suppression of *Esprit*, we would no longer say: what does he think? We would say: what is he doing?" [33] Another young devotée of *Esprit* testified that the journal served as an indispensable guide during the difficult months of 1940–1941. He received copies of *Esprit* while he was in a German prison camp, and Mounier, in this way, saved him from the "mirage" of the National Revolution.[34] Such testimonies are rare, however, and Mounier himself admitted that *Esprit* had not accomplished anything of great note during the period of its publication in Vichy France.

Mounier's position was further complicated by the fact that the doctrinaires of the National Revolution included not only some of the men of *Action Française* but a small number of self-styled personalists. A historian of the Vichy regime, who was himself an original member of *Esprit* before he joined the team of *l'Ordre Nouveau*, states that at least three important men at Vichy had frequented personalist milieux during the 1930s and that they "exercised an episodical but certain influence in the doctrinal elaboration of the National Revolution." [35] Their use of personalism as a prop for Pétain's "new order" and "intellectual and moral recovery" was, without a doubt, a complete perversion of Mounier's use of the term, but Mounier was forced to defend himself against the charge that "Vichy paternalism sought to incarnate itself in a new 'personalism' . . ." [36] Symptomatic of the confusion that this unfortunate coincidence created was a curious episode in the history of *Esprit*. In February, 1942 the first issue of a new journal was received by the former subscribers of *Esprit*. Entitled *Demain* and edited by Jean de Fabrègues, the journal apparently had access to the subscription list of *Esprit* and sought to profit from both the prestige of Mounier and his recent ambiguous *présence* within the regime. Al-

[32] Marrou, "L'action politique d'Emmanuel Mounier," 95.

[33] Duméry, "Hommage à Mounier," 10.

[34] Jean Baboulène, "Emmanuel Mounier et le mouvement catholique," *La Revue Nouvelle*, XI, No. 5 (May, 1950), 524.

[35] Robert Aron, *Histoire de Vichy, 1940–1944* (Paris: Librairie Arthème Fayard, 1954), 204.

[36] Mounier, "'Personnalisme' à tout faire," *Esprit*, No. 105 (December, 1944), 158.

though the editor of *Demain* had recently been repatriated from a German prison camp, the purpose of the new journal was to win over to the support of Vichy many Catholics who had hitherto opposed the regime.[37]

The friends and collaborators of *Esprit* were not the only men to express grave reservations concerning Mounier's decision to maintain his *présence* within the new regime. From the outset, several of the leaders of Christian democracy and Christian syndicalism were among the most vociferous critics of Mounier's position. When Charles Blondel and Jean Lacroix had originally proposed the formula, "to undertake a clandestine spiritual battle," their Christian democratic friends were, in Mounier's words, "overwhelmed and sensed some sort of betrayal in such a project." "They looked askance at everything from their private retreats" Mounier complained.[38] Early in November, 1940 Lacroix saw Marcel Prélot and Paul Vignaux. Both men had adopted an "attitude of absolute opposition" to Vichy and Nazism and believed that the only possible course of action was to support the victory of England. Mounier judged this position to be "dangerously abstentionist." "Yes," he confessed, "if possible the success of England. No, no compromise with Nazism." But Mounier was equally insistent in his efforts to alter the course of events by working within the Vichy regime.[39] Later still, in February, 1941, Mounier responded to a letter from his old friend Etienne Borne who had challenged his action of *présence*. Mounier criticized Borne and his friends of the recently defunct *l'aube* for "involving themselves dangerously again in the formula 'defense of democracy.'" The growing inflexibility of their anti-Fascism, he told Borne, was "a dangerous stigma of the Christian democrats." "Defensive positions," Mounier continued, "even heroically defensive positions, are bad and kill the spirit of creativity." He then added somewhat gratuitously that he had been taken aback by the lamentations of these same Christian democrats after the armistice – "as if the *Parti démocrate populaire* had contributed something great to France for twenty years." Mounier once again accused the Christian democrats of taking refuge in the "absolute." The mere suppression of a journal did not necessarily testify to the honor of its editors, Mounier said.

---

[37] The foregoing has been pieced together from Béguin, "Une vie," 1025; Michel François, "La revue qui a formé une génération chrétienne," 13; Mounier, "De l'usage du mot catholique" (May, 1949), *O.M.*, III, 653; Hoffmann, "Aspects du régime de Vichy," 46–47; and Duquesne, 78.
[38] Mounier, "Entretiens X, Lyon, 4 août 1940," *O.M.*, IV, 668.
[39] Mounier, "Entretiens X, 10 novembre 1940," *O.M.*, IV, 677–678.

"Pornographic brochures have also disappeared from the shop-windows. *L'aube* was not suppressed for its opposition to Nazi values, otherwise *Esprit* would have been suppressed at the same time, but because it was for the new political circles 'the journal of Champetier de Ribes,' who [with only two other *Démocrates Populaires*] had voted against the government [in July, 1940]." [40] If Borne had responded to Mounier's criticism, he might well have asked if the "all or nothing" position of the Christian democrats toward Vichy was less justified than Mounier's own "all or nothing" opposition to the Third Republic, a position which had not only led Mounier to welcome the fall of the Republic but to his short-lived ambivalence toward the new regime of Marshal Pétain.

With Borne and with many of the veterans of "the journal of Champetier de Ribes," on the other hand, Mounier shared one profound conviction. He believed that the future of France rested upon the shoulders of the younger generation.[41] This belief was shared by both the men of Vichy and the future leaders of the Resistance and resulted in the collaboration within the same youth movements of men of radically opposed political views. As early as October, 1940, Mounier associated himself with the *Compagnons de France*, a semi-official youth organiza-tion, and, under the pseudonym of Bussy-Robin, contributed to the movement's weekly journal.[42] The initiative for the organization of the *Compagnons* was taken by Henry Dhavernas, an Inspector of Finances and a leader of the *Scouts de France*, who had ready access to such influential government officials as Paul Baudouin, the Minister of Foreign Affairs, and Jean Ybarnegaray, the head of the newly organ-ized Ministry of Youth.[43] With the support of an extraordinarily varied group of men, Dhavernas's enterprise met with immediate though somewhat deceptive success.

At Randan, near Vichy, in August, 1940, a statement of purpose of the *Compagnons* was drafted. The "Charter of Randan" reflected both the diversity of the movement's membership and its leaders' desire to maintain the autonomy of all existing youth movements. The Charter

---

[40] Mounier, "Lettre à Etienne Borne, 22 février 1941," *O.M.*, IV, 694–695.

[41] See, for example, Mounier, "Aux jeunes françaises," *Esprit*, No. 96 (January, 1941), 129–131.

[42] Mounier, "Lettre à Xavier Schorderet, 15 octobre 1940," *O.M.*, IV, 674; and Joseph Folliet, "Histoire et souvenirs. La vie secrète de la Chronique pendant la guerre et sous l'oc-cupation," *Chronique sociale de France*, 70e année, No. 8 (August, 1962), 637.

[43] On the *Compagnons*, see Robert Hervet's overly sympathetic *Les Compagnons de France* (Paris: Editions France-Empire, 1965); Duquesne, 201–205; Benigno Cacéres, *Histoire de l'éducation populaire* (Paris: Editions du Seuil, 1964), 125–128.

also presaged the future evolution of some of the members of the *Compagnons*. It specifically affirmed the autonomy of the *Compagnons* and that of other youth movements but called upon the latter to support the new organization. The essential purpose of the *Compagnons* was the training or formation of the personality of each of its members with complete respect for his individual convictions. Especially after Dhavernas was replaced by Colonel Guillaume de Touremire, a young officer and devotée of Marshal Pétain, the *Compagnons* adopted a style which derived not only from the Scout movement but from the military as well. Financed by the Vichy regime which intervened in the selection of its leaders, the *Compagnons* cultivated the *mystique* of the chief and betrayed a certain nostalgia for the Middle Ages which were characteristic of all Vichy youth movements. In their quest for a doctrine upon which to base their educational program, the leaders of the *Compagnons* accepted many of the negative features of the National Revolution: its opposition to capitalism, liberal democracy and the individualism they held responsible for the defeat of 1940. More positively, they found the communitarianism of Vichy particularly attractive. When the *Compagnons* were forced to take a stand on such crucial issues as the Jewish question and the *Service du Travail Obligatoire* (S.T.O.), however, the unreal unity of the movement was shattered. Some of the *Compagnons* continued to collaborate with the regime until the organization was formally disbanded by Pierre Laval and Abel Bonnard in January, 1944. Others had already entered into Resistance activities.

Mounier's attitude toward the *Compagnons* reflected the ambivalence of his *présence* in the new regime. "At Vichy," he wrote in October, 1940, "'the Youth' (Ministry and *Compagnons*) is certainly what is best down there, with sane and clear intentions, but a bit overly burdened with ideas." He was prepared, he said, to contribute an article on an important topic each week to the journal of the movement.[44] Only a few weeks later, however, Mounier expressed his first misgivings concerning the *Compagnons*. Not only had the journal failed to publish all of the articles he had submitted to it but there were differences within the movement between those of its leaders "who wish to make the *Compagnons* the great movement of French youth and those who look upon it as only a means of observation and surveillance [by Vichy authorities]."[45] Mounier supported neither faction; he was a vigorous

[44] Mounier, "Lettre à Xavier Schorderet, 15 octobre 1940," *O.M.*, IV, 674.
[45] Mounier, "Entretiens X, 9 novembre 1940," *O.M.*, IV, 676–677.

defender of pluralism among the youth movements and a vehement critic of Vichy's efforts to erect a monolithic youth organization under strict governmental supervision.[46] When his good friend Msgr. Guerry complained of the treatment members of the J.O.C. received at the hands of the *Compagnons*, Mounier explained that he too defended the independence of the J.O.C. but that Catholic movements had missed a great opportunity by not offering their collaboration to the *Compagnons* more freely and openly. Reiterating a familiar theme, Mounier charged that Catholic youths were victims of their habit of working within narrowly Catholic milieux and that when they were afforded the opportunity to work on an equal footing with non-Catholics in an organization like the *Compagnons* they immediately drew back and retreated to more familiar surroundings.[47] In January, 1941 Mounier expressed even graver reservations concerning the *Compagnons*. "The *Compagnons* are dragging themselves toward their own ruin," he lamented. Some of their members had acquired reputations as playboys, and a climate of political intrigue and mistrust pervaded the entire movement.[48] Shortly afterwards Mounier feared that a severe crisis was about to split the *Compagnons*. One of their leaders had spent a month in Paris where he had frequented the circles of Laval and Abetz and "will return even more collaborationist than before." [49] In fact, Mounier had already mourned the passing of the early and "pure" days of the *Compagnons de France*, although as late as August, 1941 he praised the *Compagnons* for their courage in asking him to contribute an article to their journal.[50]

Mounier's influence within the *Compagnons de France* was substantial, particularly among its Catholic members. Many of the latter adopted the communitarianism of Père Maurice Montuclard, whose *Jeunesse de l'Eglise* was to be one of the pillars of the postwar *Chrétien Progressiste* movement, and with whom Mounier and some members of the *Compagnons* worked during the war.[51] Some Catholic *Compagnons* adopted Mounier's own communitarian personalism, and in the process abandoned their narrow and sectarian outlook.[52] This was but one instance of the new strength given Left-wing Catholicism by

[46] Mounier, "Les devoirs du pluralisme," *Esprit*, No. 99 (April, 1941), 361–367.
[47] Mounier, "Entretiens XI, 14 janvier 1941," *O.M.*, IV, 688–689.
[48] Mounier, "Entretiens XI, 28 janvier 1941," *O.M.*, IV, 692.
[49] Mounier, "Entretiens XI, 12 février 1941," *O.M.*, IV, 693.
[50] Mounier, "Entretiens XII, 10 septembre 1941," *O.M.*, IV, 714–715.
[51] Duquesne, 205.
[52] Folliet, "La vie secrète de la Chronique," 641; and Mounier, "Entretiens X, 20 août 1940," *O.M.*, IV, 668–670.

the experiences and trials of the period of Vichy and the Resistance.[53]

Mounier was also associated, and encountered similar difficulties, with two other youth movements. One was *Jeune France* which was organized in January, 1941 independently of Vichy but which was partially subsidized by the government.[54] Pierre Schaeffer, one of *Jeune France*'s founders, asked Mounier to join its Bureau of Studies, but Mounier refused on the grounds that he wished to remain free of formal ties to Vichy. Nonetheless, Mounier agreed, out of his great personal regard for Schaeffer, to assist Schaeffer informally in planning courses of instruction and "maisons de culture." [55] He lectured to meetings of *Jeune France*, as well as to many other organizations, on such topics as "Fin du bourgeois français," "Positions actuelles du personnalisme," "Notre révolution culturelle," and "Le sens chrétien de la communauté." [56] *Jeune France*, Mounier told Etienne Borne in the course of justifying his *présence* and attacking the "all or nothing" position of Borne and his fellow Christian democrats, was one of the "real isles of health, the corners of truly free France." [57] And similarly, in the course of his debate with Daniel Villey concerning continuing the publication of *Esprit*, Mounier spoke of "the total independence of a circle like that of *Jeune France*. ..." [58] Undoubtedly because of its relative independence of the government, Mounier was permitted to collaborate with *Jeune France* until late September, 1941.[59]

Unlike *Jeune France* and the *Compagnons de France*, the *Chantiers de Jeunesse* was created by a Vichy law of July 30, 1940.[60] In associating himself with the *Chantiers*, therefore, Mounier jeopardized his independence far more than he had by collaborating with *Jeune France*, although he held no official position in the *Chantiers*. The task assigned General Joseph de la Porte du Theil, the head of the *Chantiers*, was to restore the morale of the young Frenchmen of the military class

---

[53] *Ibid.*, 393. See also H. I. Marrou, "Ideas in France: 1939 to 1945," *The Review of Politics*, VIII, No. 1 (January, 1946), 112.

[54] On *Jeune France*, see Mounier, "Jeune France," *Esprit*, No. 97 (February, 1941), 261–263; Pierre Schaeffer, "Jeune France," *Confluences*, No. 1 (July, 1941), 127–129.

[55] Mounier, "Entretiens XI, 28 janvier 1941," *O.M.*, IV, 690–691.

[56] Mounier, "Entretiens XI, 17 février 1941," *O.M.*, IV, 693.

[57] Mounier, "Lettre à Etienne Borne, 22 fevrier 1941," *O.M.*, IV, 695.

[58] Mounier, "Entretiens XI, 30 mars 1941," *O.M.*, IV, 702.

[59] Mounier, "Entretiens XII, 25 septembre 1941," *O.M.*, IV, 715–716.

[60] On the *Chantiers*, see the partisan works of Jean Délage, *Espoir de la France, les Chantiers de la Jeunesse* (Paris: A Quillet, 1942), and *Grandeurs et servitudes des Chantiers de Jeunesse* (Paris: Editions André Bonne, 1950); Robert Hervet, *Les Chantiers de la Jeunesse* (Paris: Editions France-Empire, 1962); Raymond Josse, "Les Chantiers de la Jeunesse," *Revue d'histoire de la deuxième guerre mondiale*, 4e année, No. 56 (October, 1964), 5–42; and Duquesne, 196–200.

of 1940 which had been mobilized in June of that year only to take part in the military disaster. For this purpose and also to fit the members of this class into their assigned places in Pétain's new France, the young men were sent to camps for six months of training. On the advice of Père Forestier, the National Chaplain of the Scouts, General de la Porte du Theil deliberately avoided the use of a name which smacked of the military and modeled the *Chantiers* upon the style and organization of the Scouts. Unofficially, however, General de la Porte du Theil regarded the *Chantiers de Jeunesse*, which was expanded in January, 1941 to include all men of twenty years of age, as a trained reserve force which could be drawn upon in the event of a resumption of hostilities.[61] Until late 1943 the head of the *Chantiers* was a faithful supporter of Pétain. The turning point in the history of the *Chantiers* occurred when the government demobilized the *Chantiers* and asked that its members volunteer for labor service in Germany. Initially General de la Porte du Theil urged the *Chantiers* to obey the government but he reversed his position after a personal meeting with the German Consul, Krug von Nidda, who demanded that the *Chantiers* provide 100,000 youths for the S.T.O. On January 4, 1944 the General was arrested and sent to prison in Germany; and in June of the same year the *Chantiers de Jeunesse* were formally disbanded.

Like the other youth movements with which Mounier worked, the *Chantiers de Jeunesse* drew upon both military and Scout styles of living; they tended to conform, in varying degrees and for varying lengths of time, to Vichy, the *mystique* of the leader, and the vogues of Joan of Arc and of Charles Péguy; they encountered serious difficulties over the question of the S.T.O.; and they underwent internal crises which brought to the surface the latent divergencies of their membership. Some members of the *Chantiers* remained faithful to Pétain and became collaborationists, while for others the *Chantiers* were a foyer to the Resistance. Mounier was a leader of the latter group and among the *Chantiers* his influence was extensive. "From all sides," he exulted in early April, 1941, "the *Chantiers* are subscribing to *Esprit*." [62] In early August of the same year Mounier noted that "some *Chantiers* are now subscribing [to *Esprit*] in packets of ten and fifteen for each one of their groups." At the same time Mounier received a report that the *Chantiers* and other youth movements were seeking a doctrine as a

---

[61] Aron, *Histoire de Vichy*, 242–243.
[62] Mounier, "Entretiens XI, 4 avril 1941," *O.M.*, IV, 704.

basis for their work. "They are searching; two [doctrines] alone are being considered: *l'Action Française* and *Esprit.*" [63]

Of all of Mounier's work during the period of "open clandestineness," the most important took place under the auspices of the *Ecole nationale des cadres d'Uriage*, an institution created and financed by Vichy at Uriage-les-bains only a few miles from Mounier's native Grenoble.[64] Established as a training school first for the *Chantiers de Jeunesse* and then for Vichy's Ministry of Youth, *Uriage* transformed itself under the eyes of Vichy into a school for the Resistance. Few ironies exceed this curious phenomenon in which the leaders and students of a school created to train cadres for the National Revolution emerged almost en bloc as members of the Resistance. And no single facet of Mounier's *présence* was more successful, for in the evolution of *Uriage* the influence of Mounier and *Esprit* was an important and perhaps even a decisive factor.

Uriage was established in August, 1940 on the initiative of Captain Dunoyer de Segonzac, a thirty-four year old graduate of Saint Cyr. Its first headquarters was the Chateau de la Faulconnière, near Gannat in the Allier. In November, 1940 Dunoyer de Segonzac, along with about a dozen young officers and Abbé de Naurois, the school's chaplain, moved the school to the medieval Chateau de Murinet at Uriage in a determined effort to maintain the school as far as possible from the atmosphere of intrigue and mistrust that pervaded Vichy. It was there that the school was given official status by the Vichy law of December 7, 1940. The atmosphere of *Uriage* was described by a visitor in March, 1941: "Men who met for the first time could speak to each other in confidence and could converse in the same spirit: the spirit of enthusiasm and youthful fervour. The German conqueror ceased to exist; his physical rule was spiritually overcome." [65] Initially, *Uriage* trained young officers who had been demobilized in order to work with the *Chantiers de Jeunesse*. When General de la Porte du Theil established his own schools for the *Chantiers*, *Uriage* received youths from other Vichy institutions. Dunoyer de Segonzac and the other young officers

[63] Mounier, "Entretiens XII, 11 août 1941," *O.M.*, IV, 712.

[64] On *Uriage*, see Janine Bourdin, "Des intellectuels à la recherche d'un style de vie: l'Ecole nationale des cadres d'Uriage," *Revue française de science politique*, IX, No. 4 (December, 1959), 1029–1045; Raymond Josse, "L'Ecole des cadres d'Uriage (1940–1942)," *Revue d'histoire de la deuxième guerre mondiale*, 6e année, No. 61 (January, 1966), 49–74; Mounier, "L'Ecole nationale des cadres d'Uriage," *Esprit*, No. 99 (April, 1941), 429–431; Duquesne, 206–211; and Benigno Cacéres' novel *L'Espoir au coeur* (Paris: Editions du Seuil, 1967).

[65] Iswolsky, *Light Before Dusk*, 227.

who had established the school opposed collaboration and were influenced to some extent by Marshal Lyautey's conception of the social role of the officer as well as by Albert de Mun's Social Catholicism. With these possible exceptions, however, the men of *Uriage* were unencumbered by any doctrinal or ideological preconceptions. They regarded their task as simply the training of the future leaders of France. With the advent of a large number of intellectuals, both on the staff of the school and as lecturers, a turning point in the history of the militarily-oriented school occurred.

Especially numerous among the newcomers at *Uriage* were professors and teachers from nearby schools. Among the first to offer his services was Mounier, and among his associates at the school were Jean Lacroix, Hubert Beuve-Méry, who became *Uriage's* director of studies, Paul Claudel, Msgr. Bruno de Solages, the rector of the Catholic Institute of Toulouse, Père Henri de Lubac, the Jesuit historian and theologian, Jean-Marie Domenach, Henri Massis, and many others. These men did not share precisely the same political and spiritual convictions. They ultimately provided *Uriage* not so much with a doctrine or an ideology as with what the leaders of the school were to call "the style of the twentieth century" or "the spirit of *Uriage*." [66] The common bond which united the men of *Uriage* and provided the school with both its unique character and its extraordinary influence was its "search for a new type of man" for which "a new pedagogy" was to be the method.

The men of *Uriage* shared the same reaction to a particularly dramatic series of events. The "spirit of *Uriage*," as it developed under the aegis of Mounier, Lacroix, Beuve-Méry, and their colleagues, was in total opposition to both the National Revolution and the men and institutions of the Third Republic. In many respects, it was a revival of the search for a *troisième voie* which had first developed among the *Jeunes équipes* of the late 1920s and early 1930s. A sense of revolutionary crisis pervaded the school and all of its members regarded the defeat of France as a part of the larger crisis of the modern world. The men of *Uriage* regarded the defeat as the result of a long series of errors and capitulations by the men and institutions of the Third Republic. They condemned liberal capitalism, liberal democracy, National Socialism, and Communism. They also refused to allow Vichy to make

[66] See Gilbert Gadoffre [*Equipe d'Uriage*], *Vers le style du XXe siècle* (Paris: Editions du Seuil, 1945); Bernard d'Astorg, "Sur le style du XXe siècle," *Esprit*, No. 120 (March, 1946), 482–487; and Gilles Ferry, *Une expérience de formation de chefs. Le stage de six mois à Uriage* (Paris: Editions du Seuil, 1945).

Uriage the docile agent of the propaganda and doctrine of the National Revolution and they condemned the new regime for its clericalism, its Labor Charter, and the S.T.O. They condemned, in fact, nearly all of those things that Mounier had included under the label, "the established disorder," a decade before. Calling for a complete break with the prewar regime and its habits, they contended that "Liberation and revolution are inseparable." [67]

The "new type of man" sought by *Uriage* was not viewed as a merely theoretical or abstract endeavor. Rather, "it is a search in which each participates to the extent that he *commits himself.*" [68] The fundamental crisis was a crisis of man and the first eight weeks of the twenty-five week program of work and study at *Uriage* were devoted to remaking men; one session was devoted entirely to the personal revolution; "more virile and more honest" men were to be trained at *Uriage;* and Dunoyer de Segonzac himself echoed Mounier in calling for a more virile and aggressive Christianity.[69] The men of *Uriage* also believed that there could be "no new man without new social and economic structures." [70] Eleven weeks at *Uriage* were devoted to remaking society and a great deal of attention was given to the organization of various communities and to the elaboration of the principles of a new economy. The directive principle of the new economy was to be the satisfaction of human needs rather than the pursuit of profit.[71] Finally, a member of the *Uriage* staff explained, the *Ecole des cadres* attempted to find a solution to "the difficult problem of the relationships between action and contemplation." [72]

There is little reason to challenge the verdicts concerning the influence of Mounier at *Uriage* reached by two students of the short history of the school. "The influence of his thought is readily discernible behind the definition of the person and its ties with various communities adopted by the team of *Uriage,*" one of them writes.[73] And the other states that "one influence among others played a great role in education at *Uriage:* this was that of Emmanel Mounier and the

[67] "Libération et révolution sont inséparables. Texte de l'Ecole d'Uriage," in Henri Michel and Boris Mirkine-Guetzévitch, *Les idées politiques et sociales de la Résistance (Documents clandestins – (1940-1944)* (Paris: Presses universitaires de France, 1954), 170-174.
[68] Ferry, 127.
[69] *Ibid.,* 74-77; and P. Dunoyer de Segonzac, "Réponse. Le christianisme a-t-il dévirilise l'homme?," *Jeunesse de l'Eglise,* Cahier 2 (1943), 78-82.
[70] Gadoffre, 211.
[71] *Ibid.,* 217.
[72] Ferry, 133.
[73] Bourdin, 1042.

review *Esprit* ... Personalism was the doctrine most frequently referred to at *Uriage*." [74] It was perhaps in *Uriage's* attempt to elaborate a new pedagogy which would encompass every dimension of human activity – intellectual, physical, manual, artistic, moral, and spiritual – that the mark of Mounier was most clearly discernible. Certainly Mounier's own interests were tending in this direction. The idea of an *Esprit* Center and School was still undoubtedly in Mounier's mind and his *Traité du caractère* was shortly to be written. With some justification, therefore, Mounier noted in his personal journal that *"Uriage* is *Esprit*, it is said with irritation in certain quarters." [75]

In November, 1941 after an extensive trip through the unoccupied zone, Mounier noted in his diary: "Possibly I can measure ... the sudden explosion of the influence we have had since the war: a rallying place for those who wished to maintain at once their spiritual fidelity, French honor, and revolutionary vigilance." [76] The extent of the influence exerted by Mounier and *Esprit* during the period of "open clandestineness" cannot be measured with any degree of accuracy. Many of Mounier's opponents recognized him as the "spiritual master of the Resistance," [77] and at the time of the Liberation he was regarded as a spiritual director of the *chrétiens engagés*.[78] It is entirely possible, however, that Mounier himself tended to exaggerate the success of his *présence* within Vichy. If he had almost absolute confidence in his *témoignage*, he was also impatient for the changes he wished to bring about in France. Moreover, the nature of his work was such that it cannot be described easily or concretely. It was at once profound and long-lasting in the realm of personal relationships and elusive and often abstract in the sphere of attitudes and ideas. Finally, the extent to which the ideas which were taken up by such groups as the *Chantiers*, the *Compagnons*, *Jeune France*, and *Uriage* were a reaction to the great crisis and intellectual malaise of the time; or, rather, a direct result of the growing influence and prestige of Mounier and *Esprit* cannot be definitely ascertained. What seems clear is that the great crisis of Western civilization about which Mounier had written and spoken so consistently since 1932 had, in the judgment of many Frenchmen,

---

[74] Josse, "L'Ecole des cadres d'Uriage," 60.
[75] Mounier, "Entretiens XII, 28 juillet 1941," *O.M.*, IV, 711.
[76] Mounier, "Entretiens, 17 novembre 1941," *O.M.*, IV, 720.
[77] Alban-Vistel, "Fondements spirituels de la Résistance," *Esprit*, No. 195 (October, 1952), 489. See also the same author's *L'Héritage spirituel de la Résistance* (Lyons: Editions LUG, 1955).
[78] Pierre de Boisdeffre, *Une histoire vivante de la littérature d'aujourd'hui (1939–1964)* (Paris: Librairie Académique Perrin, 1964), 129.

come to pass. The events of 1940–1941 created a climate which made many men receptive to the message of Mounier and *Esprit*.

There is yet another reason for questioning the extent of Mounier's influence during the period of "open clandestineness." Mounier himself expressed increasingly serious misgivings about the validity and effectiveness of his *présence* within Vichy. And these misgivings combined with a train of events to terminate his *présence*. With the accession to power of Admiral Darlan in February, 1941, Mounier was subjected to increasingly close surveillance by such men as Paul Marion who "wanted to save France by adopting a totalitarian ideology." [79] Early in April an unidentified Vichy official informally advised Dunoyer de Segonzac to dispense with Mounier's services at *Uriage*.[80] Without consulting Mounier beforehand, Dunoyer de Segonzac had put Mounier's name on a list of members of the new Bureau of Studies of *Uriage* and had submitted the project to Henri Massis in the Ministry of Youth for approval. Mounier's old antagonist refused to approve the new Bureau, specifically because of the inclusion of Mounier. In reporting the affair to Mounier, Dunoyer de Segonzac expressed his belief that *Uriage* could expect the worst from Vichy in the near future.[81]

By July, 1941 several of Mounier's friends had been forbidden to lecture at *Uriage* and Mounier himself was convinced that his name was at the head of Massis' list of those who were to be excluded from the school.[82] The following month these fears were fulfilled. Not only was Dunoyer de Segonzac ordered not to allow Mounier to lecture at *Uriage* but Mounier received a letter from Marion informing him that *Esprit* was to be suppressed. The same month Mounier was eliminated from the *Compagnons* and the *Chantiers*, and when his name was placed on a list comprising the governing committee of a new Institute of Psychology and Pedagogy in Lyons, an official of Vichy struck it out with a pencil with the statement, "At no price." [83] With his exclusion from *Jeune France* in September, 1941, Mounier's *présence* was brought to its final, and perhaps inevitable, conclusion. Events at *Uriage*, meanwhile, ran their course as "*Uriage* passed from the National Revolution to the Resistance and relations with Vichy degenerated." [84] After Pierre Laval's return to power in April, 1942, Dunoyer de Segon-

[79] Aron, *Histoire de Vichy*, 383–384.
[80] Mounier, "Entretiens XI, 4 avril 1941," *O.M.*, IV, 704.
[81] Mounier, "Entretiens XI, Pâques, 13 avril 1941," *O.M.*, IV, 705.
[82] Mounier, "Entretiens XII, 28 juillet 1941," *O.M.*, IV, 705.
[83] Mounier, "Entretiens XII, 11 août 1941," *O.M.*, IV, 712.
[84] Duquesne, 209.

zac was placed under increasing pressure to conform to Laval's policies. After the entrance of the Germans into the southern zone, Laval
signed a decree disbanding *Uriage*. Almost immediately, Dunoyer de
Segonzac, Jean-Marie Domenach, Gilbert Gadoffre, and a number of
their colleagues established a clandestine school at the Chateau de
Murinet which they called "La Thébaïde." [85] The new school trained
cadres for the *maquis* until it was attacked by the police and the Germans in December, 1943 and its members were forced to disperse.

Mounier welcomed the freedom which the events of August and
September, 1941 provided him.[86] He immediately began several
writing projects. The first was a book tentatively entitled *La tradition
ouvrière française* which Mounier expected to complete by the following spring and to publish in the Swiss *Cahiers du Rhône*, an important
collection of works in the history of the intellectual and spiritual
Resistance.[87] The second was what he called "un grand machin
sur *le christianisme et l'époque*." [88] It was eventually published as
L'Affrontement chrétien in the *Cahiers du Rhône* in place of *La tradition
ouvrière française* which Mounier abandoned. Finally, Mounier began
work at this time on his most scholarly book, the *Traité du caractère*
which he tentatively entitled *Connaissance du caractère*.

The year of intensive work Mounier hoped for was not granted in
quite the circumstances he had envisaged. On January 15, 1942 at
three o'clock in the afternoon, the police rang the bell at the door of
Mounier's residence in Lyons. They arrested him and sent him, without
any preliminary explanation, to a prison in Lyons.[89] On January 21
he was sent to prison at Clermont-Ferrand where he was charged with
being a leader of the Resistance movement *Combat*. While he was imprisoned at Clermont-Ferrand in the spring of 1942 and later, while he
was awaiting trial in the Prison Saint-Paul in Lyons, he made
substantial progress on two of the writing projects he had begun the
preceding year.[90] In later years Mounier was fond of saying that his
year in prison was the only time during which he had any rest; and
Jean-Marie Domenach suggests that the three years during which the

---

[85] *Ibid.*, 210; and Cacéres, *passim.*
[86] Mounier, "Entretiens XII, 27 septembre 1941," *O.M.*, IV, 717.
[87] Mounier, "Lettre à Xavier Schorderet, 5 octobre 1941," *O.M.*, IV, 717; Mounier, "Lettre à Albert Béguin, 21 septembre 1941," *E.M.*, *1905–1950*, 1030–1031; and Duquesne, 181.
[88] Mounier, "Lettre à Jacques Lefrancq, 28 novembre 1941," *O.M.*, IV, 720–722.
[89] Mounier, "Lettre à Jéromine Martinaggi, février 1945," *O.M.*, IV, 725.
[90] Mounier, "Journaux de Prison d'Emmanuel Mounier. Prison Saint-Paul, Lyon, 27 octobre 1942," *E.M.*, *1905–1950*, 769.

publication of the journal was suspended were the most important from the point of view of the influence of Mounier.[91]

The activities which led to Mounier's arrest in January, 1942 began as early as November, 1940. At that time Mounier began to meet fairly regularly with representatives of innumerable organizations and publications, many of whom were to be leaders of various Resistance movements. So numerous were Mounier's contacts with other men and movements in Lyons, the future capital of the Resistance in the South, that it is difficult to enumerate them all. He met with Stanislas Fumet and the *Amis de Temps Nouveau;* with Joseph Vialatoux, Joseph Folliet and other collaborators of the venerable *Chronique sociale de France;* with Marcel Poimbeuf and Maurice Guérin of the C.F.T.C.; with François de Menthon and P. H. Teitgen, veterans of the *Parti Démocrate Populaire* and founders of the Resistance movement *Liberté;* with the Jesuit Pères Gaston Fessard, Henri de Lubac and Pierre Chaillet, who founded the important *Cahiers du Témoignage Chrétien;* with Joseph Hours and many other veterans of Francisque Gay's *l'aube;* with leaders of the A.C.J.F. and its specialized branches, the J.O.C. and J.E.C.; and with many other men whose position on collaboration was unequivocal.[92] Mounier himself organized a meeting of a number of important leaders in Lyons on the evening of November 30, 1940.[93] There was no agreement among the members of Mounier's group concerning a specific position regarding Vichy but there was general opposition to the *mea culpisme* and resigned acceptance of defeat current in Lyons.[94]

Early in 1941 Mounier met with Henri Frenay, one of the foremost leaders produced by the Resistance. A career military officer, Frenay escaped from a prison camp and arrived in the unoccupied zone in mid-July, 1940. While assigned to military duty first in Marseilles and then in Vichy itself, Frenay began to organize the *Mouvement de Libération Nationale* (M.L.N.). He resigned from the army in January, 1941 and took up residence in Lyons. Shortly thereafter, as a contemporary has recalled, Mounier met Frenay for the first time:

[91] Jean-Marie Domenach, "Emmanuel Mounier," *Psyché*, 5ᵉ année, No. 4 (June, 1950), 500.

[92] See, for example, Folliet, "La vie secrète de la Chronique," 636; François and Renée Bedarida, "Une résistance spirituelle, aux origines de 'Témoignage chrétien,'" *Revue d'histoire de la deuxième guerre mondiale*, No. 61 (January, 1966), 20; Jean-Pierre Gault, *Histoire d'une fidélité. Témoignage Chrétien, 1944–1956* (Paris: Editions Témoignage Chrétien, n.d.), 35; Iswolsky, *Light Before Dusk*, 245; Duquesne, 143–144; Mounier, "Entretiens XI, 28 janvier 1941," *O.M.*, IV, 690–693; and Mounier, "Entretiens XI, 4 avril 1941," *O.M.*, IV, 703–704.

[93] Mounier, "Entretiens X, 30 novembre," *O.M.*, IV, 680.

[94] *Ibid.*; and Duquesne, 143–144.

Frenay contacted Mounier. He explained his plans to him. The ideological resistance should be doubled by resistance by means of sabotage and the organization of a secret army. A few days later, a clandestine meeting took place in a back room of the Café de la Marine in Lyons. I attended along with Mounier.... I think that this meeting was the beginning of the Lyons Resistance as we knew it.[95]

Not long after this meeting Frenay's M.L.N. merged with the Christian democratic dominated *Liberté* and Emmanuel d'Astier de la Vigerie's *Libération* to form the *Mouvement de Libération Française*. The latter, in turn, began publication of a clandestine journal called *Combat* in December, 1941 and it was by this name that Frenay's organization was known.[96] One of Frenay's first actions was to ask Mounier to organize a clandestine study center for the *Combat* movement; and with the aid of his old friend André Philip and François de Menthon, Mounier entered actively into the Resistance.[97]

It would appear that Mounier regarded the new study center as a means of resurrecting or continuing the work of the prewar *Esprit* study groups.[98] The leaders of *Combat*, on the other hand, looked upon the new center as an organization which could conveniently make use of the existing *Esprit* organization in making plans for the future constitution of France.[99] Indicative, perhaps, of these differing conceptions of the purpose of the clandestine meetings was the first project upon which its members worked. It was a "Déclaration des droits de la personne" for which Mounier drew up a preliminary draft.[100] Mounier later claimed that his declaration had some effect upon the Declaration of Rights which was subjected to long, heated, and ultimately fruitless debate in the First Constituent Assembly in January, 1946. François de Menthon was highly critical of Mounier's project. The future leader of the M.R.P. said that

Besides the manifest inadaptability of its vocabulary, it presents us with a pretention that is foredoomed to failure. A document of this kind cannot and ought not to philosophize, but rather should set forth, without any philosophical

---

[95] "Notes de Jean-Marie Soutou," *E.M.*, *1905–1950*, 1027.

[96] See Marie Granet and Henri Michel, *Combat. Histoire d'un mouvement de résistance* (Paris: Presses universitaires de France, 1957), especially, 26–68.

[97] Mounier, "Lettre à Jéromine Martinaggi, février 1945," *O.M.*, IV, 726; and Duquesne, 150.

[98] Editor's note to Mounier, "Entretiens XIII, 23 décembre 1941," *O.M.*, IV, 722.

[99] Granet and Michel, 201; and René Hostache, *Le Conseil National de la Résistance* (Paris: Presses universitaires de France, 1958), 221.

[100] Mounier, "Entretiens XIII, 23 décembre 1941," *O.M.*, IV, 722–723; and Duquesne, 144.

reference, some essential political principles which have a clear juridical meaning and on which men of various outlooks can agree.[101]

These differences between Mounier the *agrégé* in philosophy and François de Menthon the law professor did not prevent the prosecuting attorney from using Mounier's draft declaration as evidence in his trial in October, 1942, although there is some possibility that Mounier was mistaken for de Menthon when he was originally arrested.[102] Mounier's name and address – or those of de Menthon – were found among the papers of André Koehl, a young man arrested for distributing clandestine journals in January, 1942.[103] Along with forty-seven other members of *Combat*, Mounier was charged with disobeying the Vichy decrees which prohibited the distribution of "foreign" (Gaullist) tracts, the publication of information which might undermine the morale of the population and the army, and membership in any organization whose "aim has a subversive character." [104]

Mounier's arrest and trial on the charge of being a leader of *Combat* surprised him greatly, and he believed that his acquittal on October 30, 1942 was entirely justified.[105] That he believed this is striking evidence of his deep-seated a-politicism. He was genuinely convinced that because his motives in associating himself with *Combat* had been largely non-political the results of his activities were necessarily non-political also. In spite of Mounier's disclaimer and tendency to equivocate, there can be little doubt that his clandestine spiritual battle was as contrary, and possibly as dangerous, to the purposes of Vichy as were the more overt activities of many of his friends. If the Resistance is viewed not as a position of static defense or even as the negligible military movement that it was, but rather as "the revolt of man against tyrannies," as "a revolt of conscience, a desire for revolution," then Mounier was a dangerous member of the Resistance.[106]

Mounier characterized the charges brought against him as stupifying, generally ambiguous in nature, and as being motivated by stupidity. Initially at least, he seems to have distinguished between the letter of the law and its spirit. "I have not violated articles *n* and *n* of the laws prohibiting the distribution of clandestine literature and propaganda activity in the service of a foreign power tending to undermine

[101] François de Menthon, "Vers une nouvelle déclaration des droits," *Politique*, New Series, I, No. 3–4 (August-September, 1945), 264.
[102] Granet and Michel, 267–268; and Hostache, 221.
[103] Granet and Michel, 267–268.
[104] *Ibid.*
[105] Mounier, "Lettre à Emile-Albert Niklaus, 30 octobre 1942," *O.M.*, IV, 765.
[106] Alban-Vistel, "Fondements spirituels de la Résistance," 480–481.

the morale of the civilian population and the army." On the other hand, Mounier recognized that his position of opposition to what he termed "those who surrender their dignity to force, their country to tranquility, the sacred to the prestigious" implied certain "consequences." [107] When more specific charges were brought against him, Mounier's reaction was different. Among these charges were that he opposed the government and certain of its ministers, that he had planned for the establishment of a new government, and that he was a regional leader of *Combat*.[108] In advising his lawyer Emmanuel Gounot on his defense, Mounier dismissed the last of these charges completely out of hand. As to the others, he told Gounot that "my activity has never been of a political nature, but spiritual and cultural" and that "my [writing] projects testify to my activities." Referring to the *Traité du caractère* and *La tradition ouvrière française*, he asked rhetorically: "Are ministers overthrown by such as these?" [109] Unless Mounier intended such a project as his "Déclaration des droits de la personne" to be a philosophical tract without practical consequences, however, he was guilty of at least one of the charges brought against him. For him to have had this intention would have constituted a major change in the purpose of his life and work, for which there is no evidence whatsoever.[110]

Mounier's journey to his trial was long and complicated. After spending a month in prison at Clermont-Ferrand, he was released and placed in forced residence in Clermont until April, when he was granted provisional liberty to return to Lyons. There on April 29, 1942 he was again arrested for administrative confinement in the Chateau de Vals-les-bains. Early in July he was sent to the Prison Saint-Paul in Lyons where he remained until his trial on October 19, 1942.[111] The trial ended on October 26, and four days later the verdict was handed down. The verdict was that

in that which concerns Mounier, whereas there exist against this accused some troubling presumptions of guilt, etc.

Whereas no formal proof of the participation of Mounier in the *Combat* movement has been brought by the public prosecutor;

[107] Mounier, "Journaux de prison. Prison de Clermont, janvier-février 1942," *E.M.*, *1905–1950*, 721–722.

[108] Mounier, "Lettre à son père, 6 octobre 1942," *O.M.*, IV, 762; and Mounier "Lettre à Me Gounot, 7 mai 1942," *O.M.*, IV, 740–741.

[109] Mounier, "Lettre à Me Gounot, 7 mai 1942," *O.M.*, IV, 741.

[110] See Mounier, "Lettre à Monsieur le Secrétaire général à la police, 19 juin 1942," *O.M.*, IV, 745–750.

[111] Béguin, "Une vie," 1032–1035 *passim*.

As the presumptions of guilt existing against him are insufficient to bring conviction by the tribunal;

As it is therefore agreed, with the benefit of doubt, to release Mounier from the proceedings of the prosecution;

For these reasons:

the tribunal rules that the evidence of the prosecution has not been sufficiently established in that which concerns Mounier; as a consequence, it releases this accused from the proceedings of the prosecution without penalty or costs.[112]

After his acquittal Mounier went to the old Protestant town of Dieulefit in the Drôme. He resumed his writing and other activities until the Liberation under the assumed name of Leclercq.[113] But with him into the final and somewhat anticlimactic phase of his Resistance activities, Mounier carried the marks of the physical hardships and the memory of the spiritual anguish he had suffered in the prisons of Vichy.

The physical suffering resulted primarily from a hunger strike which Mounier and three of his fellow prisoners undertook at Vals-les-bains in June, 1942.[114] The strike was a protest against the confinement of one of Mounier's friends who was gravely ill and, in fact, died shortly after his release, as well as against the actual confinement of the strikers. After twelve days, Mounier and his fellow strikers succeeded in gaining the release of their friend, but their belief that they had also succeeded in obtaining their own release was illusory for they were sent to the Prison Saint-Paul shortly afterwards. This protest left Mounier almost on the verge of death, and one of his friends contends that "his death at forty-five can be explained in large part by the sufferings he [endured] . . . in the prisons of Vichy." [115] Characteristically Mounier discerned a bit of humor in the situation, for he wrote a friend several days after ending his fast that he had lost "eleven kilos of personalist substance!" [116] The reaction of a number of his friends to what Mounier belittled as his "fragile action," however, was understandably not only void of humor but mixed. "For the last two years of the Occupation," one man testified, "it was this exemplary act, this fragile action . . . which aided us in living, in fighting." [117] On the other hand, even some of Mounier's closest friends found his action incomprehensible. One of them writes:

[112] Quoted in "Notes de Jean Perrin," *E.M.*, *1905–1950*, 1037–1038.
[113] Mounier, "Lettre à Jéromine Martinaggi, février 1945," *O.M.*, IV, 769; Béguin "Une vie," 1038; and Cacéres, 120–121.
[114] Mounier, "Journal d'un acte fragile (Grève de la faim)," *E.M.*, *1905–1950*, 731–764.
[115] Goguel, "Positions politiques," 815. See also J. B. Coates, "The Personalism of Emmanuel Mounier," *The Fortnightly*, CLXXII (August, 1952), 109.
[116] Mounier, "Lettre à Raymond Vincent, 2 juillet 1942," *E.M.*, *1905–1950*, 1035.
[117] Duméry, "Hommage à Mounier," 11.

I recall that one of the most serious misunderstandings which separated us on the level of action... took place during the occupation, at the time when, detained illegally in prison by Vichy, he decided to undertake a hunger strike.... Remaining in the occupied zone where each day we impotently helped in the execution of our comrades in battle, it seemed to me puerile that Mounier should risk his life in order to protest against a delay of a few weeks in bringing about his trial. Politically, this action seemed useless and even dangerous to me for it risked diverting efforts and desires toward an infinitely secondary objective – discrediting the government of Vichy – while the essential objective was to expel the invader.[118]

As this friend admits, had he known all of the details of Mounier's action he might well have altered his judgment.[119] Another man recalls that he learned the details of Mounier's hunger strike:

Finding himself, after a number of days, at the extreme limit of his strength and fearing that he would lose his life, he had a country priest come to him in order to receive absolution and communion. The priest – that he would be a "saintly man" would not surprise me! – refused him absolution for having "disobeyed legitimate authority and not repenting for it!" The bestiality of men, even of men of the Church, is truly without limits. All of the strength and purity of faith of an Emmanuel Mounier is necessary to avoid discouragement, to remain faithful to the Church in spite of it.[120]

Even this man did not know that prior to beginning his hunger strike Mounier had given written authorization to the prison doctor to force him to end his fast if it seriously endangered his life or his faculties.[121] Nor did Mounier's friend know that he had written Père Henri de Lubac from his hospital bed: "You and two or three around me are my secret tie with my Church." [122] Mounier's religious faith prevented him from taking his own life.

The sentiments expressed by Mounier's friend and explicit in Mounier's letter reflected the fact that a majority of French Catholics, bishops, ordinary clergy and laity alike, had rallied to the Vichy regime. "With the exception of youths trained in the movements of Catholic Action and the spiritual descendancy of the *Sillon* of Marc Sangnier, with the exception of a certain number of young priests in close touch with the militants of A.C. [Catholic Action], the quasi-totality of my coreligionists have adhered with enthusiasm and disinterestedness to the national revolution," a progressive priest observed in his journal in late 1942.[123] The reasons for the adherence of

---

[118] Touchard, "Dernier dialogue," 782.
[119] *Ibid.*, 782–783.
[120] Ignace Lepp, *Le monde chrétien et ses malfaçons* (Paris: Aubier, 1956), 41.
[121] Mounier, "Journal d'un acte fragile," 736.
[122] Mounier, "Lettre à P. de Lubac, 1er juillet 1942," *O.M.*, IV, 754.
[123] Lepp, *Le monde chrétien et ses malfaçons*, 43.

most Catholics to Vichy varied widely.[124] For some Catholics Vichy's claim of legitimacy was sufficient. For others the defeat was a kind of providential punishment for the Third Republic they had hated and for the lack of moral fiber which they believed had resulted from the absence of religion in that regime. Many Catholics were favorably impressed by the policies of the Vichy regime: the abrogation of that part of the Law of 1904 which had suppressed all teaching orders (although this law had not been enforced since 1914); the dissolution of that *bête noire* of so many Catholics, Free-Masonry; a series of decrees providing for religious instruction in public schools and subsidies for the Catholic schools; a decree which facilitated the return of Church properties to the diocesan associations created by the Church in 1924; and even such decrees as that of August 24, 1940 which instituted a campaign against alcoholism. Indeed, the traditionalist and counter-revolutionary spirit of Pétain's National Revolution, with its device "Work, Family, Country," had a special appeal for many Catholics. And the fact that most members of the French hierarchy actively supported the new regime gave added force to the adherence of French Catholics to the new regime.

Mounier was especially concerned about the resurgence of clericalism and anticlericalism. In January, 1941 he encountered a public school teacher whom he had known before the war and was told that "a great occasion has been lost." The teacher had abandoned his anticlericalism and had been ready to cooperate with the Catholic schools. But because of Vichy's school policies, "now it is finished, confidence is broken." [125] Mounier also complained with ill-concealed anger that the local curé was now telling his catechism classes that "the war was lost by their teachers." Anticlericalism, which was almost dead in 1939, "has already indistinctly assumed its old virulence, as always through the good work of the clericals. ... Modern Christendom continues to prepare its own death." [126] In a radio address after the Liberation Mounier stated that in 1939, "if the French remained by temperament, even by conviction, opposed to any political interference by the clergy, aggressive anticlericalism subsisted as no more than an artifact in a museum." But the Vichy regime had jeopardized all this. "It took on a paternalistic, clerical and moralizing look which is perfectly designed to irritate the French temperament. A part of the clergy, and notably

---

[124] See Rémond, "Catholicisme de droite et catholicisme de gauche," 191–192; and Duquesne, 17–108 *passim*.
[125] Mounier, "Entretiens XI, 9 janvier 1941," *O.M.*, IV, 686–687.
[126] *Ibid.*, 687.

of the higher clergy, allowed itself once more to become intoxicated by official support." Mounier believed that had things continued, "the anticlerical flame would have burst forth out of its ashes with increased intensity." [127]

"Happily for religious peace," Mounier added, "the Laval-Darnand regime substituted teams of killers for teams of *bien-pensants*, and numerous Catholics entered the Resistance." [128] There were, of course, many other reasons for the gradual withdrawal of Catholic support from the Vichy regime.[129] Among the most important was Vichy's policy towards youth movements. Although, unlike the specialized movements of the A.C.J.F., such Catholic organizations as the *Scouts de France* and the *Guides de France* were active in several of the Vichy youth movements with which Mounier worked, all Catholic youth organizations were suspicious of the efforts of the Ministry of Youth to create a monolithic youth movement. Many Catholic leaders, lay and clerical alike, opposed the totalitarian spirit implicit in this policy. In addition, many members of the French hierarchy were jealous of their jurisdiction over Catholic youth movements. When the Vichy *Equipes nationales* were organized in 1942, the A.C.J.F. and its specialized branches refused to join the new movement in spite of the urgings of many French bishops. In addition, to the credit of the French Church as a whole, the racial policy of Vichy was vigorously opposed. Finally, although it was the occasion of violent debate within Catholic circles, the labor policies of Vichy led to the break between many Catholics and the Vichy regime. The Labor Charter of October, 1941 caused a split within the C.F.T.C., although a majority of its members refused to cooperate in the new enterprise.[130] The institution of the S.T.O. in 1943 brought the rupture of many more Catholics with the Vichy regime. With the support of many priests and bishops, French Catholics refused to leave France for forced labor in Germany.

This disaffection and opposition led many Catholics into the Resistance. There they provided added strength to the Resistance of those Catholics who did not need the youth, racial or labor policies of

[127] Mounier, "Cléricalisme et anticléricalisme," *B.A.E.M.*, No. 9–10 (December, 1956), 14–15.
[128] *Ibid.*, 15.
[129] Rémond, "Catholicisme de droite et catholicisme de gauche," 193–195; Msgr. Guerry, *L'Eglise catholique en France sous l'occupation* (Paris: Flammarion, 1947), 31–79, 147–184; and Duquesne, 190–223, 250–316.
[130] See Gérard Adam, *La C.F.T.C., 1940–1958. Histoire politique et idéologique* (Cahier 134, "Cahiers de la Fondation nationale des sciences plitiques"; Paris: Armand Colin, 1964), 15–36.

the Vichy regime to convince them of the necessity of Resistance. Like their fellow Catholics who had supported Vichy, their motives were various.[131] Some of them opposed the Vichy regime on patriotic grounds: they refused to support a government that had resigned itself to defeat. Others based their opposition on ideological and religious grounds, refusing to support a regime that was in league with the National Socialism condemned by the Pope in 1938. Still others joined the Resistance for political reasons: in spite of the disastrous end of the Third Republic, their faith in democracy remained unimpaired. Most often, however, motives were complex. August Champetier de Ribes, for example, voted against giving full powers to Pétain; but this veteran leader of the *Parti Démocrate Populaire* explained that he had not voted against the Marshal but rather against the armistice because of his conviction that the battle against Germany should be continued. And conversely, three other *Démocrates Populaires* who had voted to give full powers to the Marshal signed a manifesto on July 9, 1940 which opposed the new government because of its similarity to the Third Republic.[132]

Present among the first members of the Resistance were a remarkably large number of Christian democrats and members of the traditionally ancillary movements, the A.C.J.F. and C.F.T.C. Indeed, few of the leaders of Christian democracy failed to play important roles in the Resistance. As early as September, 1940 the press of Francisque Gay began to distribute *La France continue*.[133] In 1940 also François de Menthon and P.-H. Teitgen organized the Resistance movement *Liberté*.[134] The men of the *Jeune-République* published the Resistance journal *Valmy* from January, 1941 until October, 1942, when many of them were arrested. Those who escaped and did not go to London to join General de Gaulle worked with the clandestine journals *Demain* and *Résistance*.[135] In Paris, innumerable Resistance tracts came off the press of Marc Sangnier on the boulevard Raspail until the press was

---

[131] Rémond, "Catholicisme de droite et catholicisme de gauche," 192–193; Henri Michel, *Les courants de pensée de la Résistance* (Paris: Presses universitaires de France, 1962), 127–144, 208–221, 351–384; and Duquesne, 111–137.

[132] Duquesne, 125–126.

[133] Carité, 111–113; *Francisque Gay. Témoignages*, 59–68; Pezet, *Chrétiens au service de la cité*, 128.

[134] Pezet, *Chrétiens au service de la cité*, 128; Duquesne, 145–150; and Granet and Michel, 58–64.

[135] Of the abundant literature on *Valmy*, see Granet and Michel, 47–51; Bellanger, 57–63; Paul Simon, *Un seul ennemi: l'envahisseur* (London: Continental Publishers and Distributors, Ltd., 1942); and Paul Petit, *Résistance spirituelle, 1940–1942* (Paris: Gallimard, 1947). On *Résistance*, see Françoise Bruneau, *Essai d'histoire du mouvement né autour du journal clandestin "Résistance"* (Paris: S.E.D.E.S., 1951).

seized and Sangnier was arrested in February, 1944. One *Jeune Répu-blicain* gained especially great renown; he was Maurice Schumann who was the voice of Free France on the B.B.C. and the first president of the M.R.P.[136] Among the founders of *Libération Nord* in late 1940 was the secretary-general of the C.F.T.C., Gaston Tessier.[137] In Lyons, Père Pierre Chaillet founded the most important Catholic Resistance jour-nal, *Cahiers du Témoignage Chrétien*, in November, 1941.[138] Albert Gortais, the secretary-general of the A.C.J.F., founded *Cahiers de notre jeunesse* in June, 1941.[139] The Christian democrats played im-portant roles in innumerable Resistance organizations but there was no specifically Christian democratic Resistance organization.[140] One movement, however, ultimately included most of the future leaders of the M.R.P. This was *Combat*, the movement with which Mounier was associated.

Combat numbered Georges Bidault, François de Menthon, and Pierre-Henri Teitgen among the members of its executive committee; Mou-nier's prison-mate Maurice Guérin, Champetier de Ribes, Reille-Soult, and other veteran Christian democrats among its regional leaders; and Gaston Tessier, Francisque Gay, and Etienne Borne in positions of importance. Because of their previous roles in various Resistance organizations, when the *Mouvements unis de la Résistance* (M.U.R.) and the *Conseil National de la Résistance* (C.N.R.) were organized in 1942–1943, the Christian democrats naturally assumed positions of leader-ship. Both Tessier, representing the C.F.T.C., and Bidault, represent-ing the Christian democrats, were members of the C.N.R.; and when Jean Moulin was arrested in June, 1943 Bidault replaced him as presi-dent of the C.N.R. Of particular importance was the new *Comité Général d'Etudes* (C.G.E.) which included an unusually large number of Christian democrats.

The C.G.E. was an expanded version of the center of clandestine studies of *Combat*. It was organized in 1942 by Georges Bidault, Fran-çois de Menthon, Robert Lacoste, and André Philip, and included Gay

[136] See J.-L. Crémieux-Brilhac, "Les émissions à la B.B.C. pendant la guerre," *Revue d'histoire de la deuxième guerre mondiale*. No. 1 (November, 1950), 75–76.

[137] Adam, *La C.F.T.C.*, 37–45; and Bellanger, 49–50.

[138] Gault, 27–35; Bedarida, "Une résistance spirituelle," 3–33; Paul Vignaux (ed.), *France prends garde de perdre ton âme (Cahiers du Témoignage Chrétien)* (New York: Editions de la Maison Française, Inc., 1943); "Histoire d'un journal: Témoignage Chrétien," *Infor-mations catholiques internationales*, No. 50 (June 15, 1957), 13–16; and Duquesne, 150–160.

[139] Duquesne, 140–142; Maurice-René Simonnet, *Sept ans d'histoire au service de la France (1939–1946)* (Paris: Editions de l'Epi, n.d.), 10–20; and Vergnet, 16ff.

[140] Francisque Gay, "Le temps des grandes espérances reviendra," *L'Observateur*, No. 129 (August 31, 1952), 10. See also Michel, *Les courants de pensée de la Résistance*, 12–13.

and Teitgen among its members. The purpose of the C.G.E. was to elaborate proposals for the future constitutional, economic and social organization of France; and the results of its work appeared in its journal *Les cahiers politiques*. In April, 1943 when the C.G.E. moved to Paris, it used the facilities of the Librairie Bloud et Gay and often held its meetings in the home of Francisque Gay. From his residence in Dieulefit, Mounier collaborated with the C.G.E. by contributing a number of articles to *Les cahiers politiques*.[141] He had continued his association with his old friends in Lyons after his trial and acquittal, and now many of them held positions of leadership in the organizations which were formulating plans for the new France which they believed would emerge after the end of the war.

The precise nature of the role that the Christian democrats envisaged for themselves in the new France was far from clear. As early as 1941, particularly in the South, there was talk of a "renewal" or an "enlargement" among Christian democrats.[142] Henri Frenay recollects that in 1942 he had lengthy conversations with Georges Bidault, François de Menthon, Pierre-Henri Teitgen, and other leaders of the old *Parti Démocrate Populaire* concerning postwar plans. "At no time," Frenay says, "did the veterans of the P.D.P. broach the idea of reconstituting their old party, even under another form and another name." [143] Some of the Christian democratic members of the Resistance, however, began to consider the possibility of a separate Christian or Christian democratic organization in late 1942 and 1943. Late in 1942 a group of Christian democrats gathered in a restaurant in Lyons to honor the memory of Robert Cornilleau who had died ministering to the victims of a typhus epidemic in Algeria.[144] Various proposals for future action were discussed but most of those in attendance tended to think in terms of reviving or enlarging the old *Parti Démocrate Populaire*. That a pro-

---

[141] The editor of *O.M.*, IV, 863, attributes the following unsigned articles in *Les cahiers politiques* to Mounier: "Problèmes sociaux de demain," No. 1 (April, 1943), 24–30; "Pourquoi je suis républicain. Réponse d'un catholique," No. 2 (July, 1943), 4–9, reprinted in Michel and Guetzévitch, 88–94; "Vers l'avenir dans la clarté," No. 4 (November, 1943), 1–2; and "Pour la France de demain. Libres réflexions d'un catholique de la Résistance," No. 5 (January, 1944), 1–15. Duquesne, 368–369, attributes the second of these articles to François de Menthon, but uses the incorrect date of 1942. François de Menthon did, in fact, write "Pourquoi je suis républicain. Réponse d'un chef de Mouvement de Résistance," *Les cahiers politiques*, No. 1 (April, 1943). Duquesne also attributes the fourth article to Joseph Hours, as does Michel, *Les courants de pensée de la Résistance*, 361. This article is reprinted in Joseph Hours, *Mouvement Républicain Populaire. Directions. Libres propos pour action politique* (Lyon, n.d.), 9–23.

[142] "La naissance d'un grand Mouvement," *Forces Nouvelles*, No. 19 (June 16, 1945).

[143] Henri Frenay, "Le travaillisme enfant mort-né de la Résistance," *Preuves*, No. 73 (March, 1957), 47.

[144] Duquesne, 370.

gressive organization similar to the old *Jeune-République* might form the nucleus of a new movement seems not to have entered into their calculations, probably because the *Jeune Républicains* were notably absent from the councils of the newly unified Resistance movement.[145] In the spring of 1943 three additional clandestine meetings were held by the Christian democrats in Lyons. Veterans of the *Parti Démocrate Populaire* were dominant in all of them. In the last of these meetings in April, 1943, Georges Bidault expressed his preference for a kind of cartel of prewar Christian democratic groups and parties as a preliminary step towards the organization of a large political movement.[146] By the spring of 1943 the Christian democrats were separating themselves from their fellow members of the Resistance. No definite decision concerning the nature of what was called "the Movement" had been reached, however, when Bidault left Lyons for Paris in July, 1943 to replace Jean Moulin as head of the C.N.R.[147]

Meanwhile Mounier was devoting most of his energies to his writing and to his postwar plans for *Esprit*. Late in the spring of 1943 he wrote a friend that he was already thinking of "evoking, next month for the first time, the memories of Jouy [-en-Josas]," where a number of the prewar congresses of *Esprit* had been held.[148] A number of his friends believed that Mounier should devote himself entirely to the scholarly work to which he had turned at almost every opportunity since the suppression of *Esprit*.[149] Mounier, however, gave no serious thought to the possibility that *Esprit* would not be revived. Twice in 1943 and once again in 1944 little congresses of *Esprit* were held in Dieulefit.[150] Certainly, Mounier did not envisage an active political role for either himself or the *Esprit* movement in postwar France. When he was asked to attend the Consultative Assembly in Algiers in January, 1944,

---

[145] A search of the membership of *Combat*, the M.U.R., and the C.N.R. in Granet and Michel, *Combat*, and in Hostache, *Le Conseil national de la Résistance* reveals only a handful of *Jeunes Républicains*. See also *La Jeune-République*, May 31, 1945.

[146] "Origines et mission du M.R.P.," 25; Raymond-Laurent, *Le Parti Démocrate Populaire*, 92–93; and Duquesne, 370.

[147] Raymond-Laurent, *Le Parti Démocrate Populaire*, 93; and Duquesne, 370ff. Frenay, "Le travaillisme enfant mort-né," 47, argues that the Christian democrats began to think in terms of a separate organization because Bidault represented the Christian democrats and not *Combat* on the C.N.R. and because the Christian democrats were excluded from positions of real authority in the M.U.R.

[148] Mounier, "Lettre à Jacques Lefrancq, 20 mai 1943," *O.M.*, IV, 781.

[149] Béguin, "Une vie," 1045.

[150] "Nos Journées de juillet," *Esprit*, No. 111 (June, 1945), 152, makes reference to two *Esprit* meetings in the Drôme in 1943. Beguin, "Une vie," 1045, refers to two *Esprit* meetings, one in 1943 and one in 1944.

Mounier's response was brief and to the point: "... no vocation as a deputy." [151]

In a letter to Jacques Lefrancq in November, 1943, Mounier reported that his *Traité du caractère* was finished and that he was now compelled to turn to other problems. Characteristically, the first problems to which he made reference were "the imminence of the Sedan of our Latin, Constantinian, and bourgeois Christendom," the certainty that a new City would be constructed, and the necessity of ultimately implanting the seeds of Christianity in the future edifice. In the meanwhile, he told Lefrancq, more modest tasks had to be undertaken.[152] Mounier addressed himself to "the France of tomorrow" and to the role of Catholics in that France in the pages of *Les cahiers politiques*. He emphasized that the disorders of the Third Republic precluded its restoration; that a Catholic, simply because he was a Catholic, brought no special competence to the solution of political problems. If anything, the Catholic was faced with the special danger of allowing himself to slip from "an imprecise spiritual affirmation to a nebulous politics." It was necessary, Mounier said, reiterating his criticism of Christian democracy, to deal with politics in political terms. He concluded with a typical lack of concern with specific political institutions that whatever the political structure of the new France the only true measure of that regime would be the extent to which it provided "the permanent conditions of a humanity open to all the sumptuous promises of man." [153] Certainly Mounier did not foresee the formation of a new Christian democratic party. He believed that the entry of so many French Catholics into various Resistance organizations would stifle their "ghetto complex" and contribute to ending their historical predisposition to enclose themselves in confessional organizations.[154]

"I believe a ground-swell carries the young towards personalism. ..." Mounier added in his letter to Lefrancq in November, 1943.[155] One such young man was Gilbert Dru. Dru provided an important link between Dieulefit, where he attended a clandestine meeting of *Esprit* in September, 1943, and Lyons and Paris, where the Christian democrats were discussing their plans for the future.[156] Inspired by the ideas and

[151] Mounier, "Lettre à Jéromine Martinaggi, février, 1945," *O.M.*, IV, 769.
[152] Mounier, "Lettre à Jacques Lefrancq, 21 novembre 1943," *O.M.*, IV, 786.
[153] "Pourquoi je suis républicain. Réponse d'un catholique," 88–94 *passim*.
[154] See, for example, Mounier, "La religion et la France nouvelle," *B.A.E.M.*, Nos. 9–10 (December, 1956), 4–5.
[155] Mounier, "Lettre à Jacques Lefrancq, 21 novembre 1943," *O.M.*, IV, 786–787.
[156] "Mémento," *Esprit*, No. 107 (February, 1945), 623.

example of Mounier, Dru formulated a project which acted as a catalyst upon the Christian democrats.

Gilbert Dru was a member of the J.E.C. and a classmate of Jean-Marie Domenach at the University of Lyons.[157] Educated by the Jesuits in Lyons, young Dru had often scandalized his fellow students, the heavy preponderance of whom were *bien-pensants*, with his political and religious views. He read *Sept, Temps présent* and *Esprit*. He believed he was of "the socialist race of Péguy." When the war began Dru viewed the conflict as something more than merely a battle for the defense of France. It was, rather, "a war for Justice, for Liberty, for the City of Christ." Dru joined the *Chantiers de Jeunesse* in the summer of 1940 and then he returned to his studies at the University of Lyons where he was profoundly disturbed by the complacency of his fellow students and his teachers. He was determined to take an active part in the battle against *mea culpisme*. Dru then joined Albert Gortais, the secretary-general of the A.C.J.F., in founding the *Cahiers de notre jeunesse* in June, 1941. As a member of the team of this journal, young Dru worked with Jean-Marie Domenach, Rémy Montagne, the Jesuit Pères Fraisse, Chambre and de Lubac, and later with André Mandouze who succeeded Gortais as the editor of the journal.

References to and citations from Péguy abounded in the pages of the *Cahiers de notre jeunesse*. Dru and his colleagues undertook the same *présence* and attempted to use the same strategy that Mounier practiced in *Esprit*. In an article on one of the patron saints of the Vichy regime, Dru discussed the mission of Joan of Arc in a way that was completely contrary to the intentions of the government's propagandists.[158] Young Dru also regarded the example of Péguy as an inspiration for Resistance rather than as a source of the National Revolution's "return to the land" and the glorification of the "ancient virtues" of France.[159] He derived from Péguy a number of ideas which were, in substance, identical to those that Mounier had enunciated a decade before: the idea that exercising intelligence was an important form of action; that no man could remain neutral in a time of crisis; that a true revolution was necessary in order to reconstruct a France in which the values of the human person would be protected and nourished in com-

---

[157] On Dru, see Domenach, *Gilbert Dru*; Duquesne, 138–141; and Vergnet, 199–200.
[158] Gilbert Dru, "Jeanne d'Arc," reprinted in Annex I of Domenach, *Gilbert Dru*, 143–147.
[159] Gilbert Dru, "De l'intelligence en temps de crise," *Cahiers de notre jeunesse*, No. 3, 6–11.

munitarian organizations.[160] In discussing Nicolas Berdiaev's *Un nouveau Moyen Age*, Dru responded to the Russian philosopher's criticism of modern civilization in precisely the same fashion that Mounier had in his manifesto, "Refaire la Renaissance." [161] Dru also referred to Jean Lacroix as "a philosopher of that personalist school which has meant so much in the French spiritual renewal begun before the defeat, and which marks out a sure path to the restoration of our country." [162]

Dru's collaboration with the *Cahiers de notre Jeunesse* ended in June, 1943 when the journal was suppressed because of its opposition to the S.T.O. By this time, his activities had extended from the pen to active association with various Resistance organizations. He had become a collaborator of the *Cahiers du Témoignage Chrétien*, and the representative of the *Jeunes chrétiens combattants* in the *Forces unies de la jeunesse patriotiques* in Lyons.[163] He worked with Joseph Hours and Maurice Guérin on the *Comité chrétien d'action civique*.[164] In the course of these activities, Dru slowly came to the conclusion that "Resistance and politics can only be one and the same thing, that Resistance was the only form of political action possible at the time, and the mother, the teacher of future political action." [165]

At this particularly decisive time in Gilbert Dru's short life, he attended a meeting of *Esprit* in Dieulefit. Jean-Marie Domenach recalls that

decisive at this time was the influence of *Esprit*, the review of Emmanuel Mounier, which represented much more than an abstract publication for the young intellectuals of the years 1930–40. *Esprit* was always a living center of attraction and discoveries.... For Gilbert, *Esprit* and personalism were the essential basis, the point of departure finally found. He adopted directly from them his fundamental postulates and essential views that, consequently, he did nothing but specify and formulate in a way that better suited the particular form of his own thought.... Such is the evolution which led him... to dream of a great political party constructed on the basis of personalism.[166]

The concrete results of this influence were evident in two manifestoes drawn up by Dru in August, 1943. The first was "Notre jeunesse vers

[160] *Ibid.*; and Gilbert Dru, "Les étudiants et la Cité," *Cahiers de notre jeunesse*, No. 8, 28–35.
[161] Gilbert Dru, "Lumières sur notre crise: Bardiaeff," *Cahiers de notre jeunesse*, No. 6, 27–30.
[162] Gilbert Dru, "Jean Lacroix: Conscience et amour," *Cahiers de notre jeunesse*, No. 11, 30.
[163] Gault, 31; and Hostache, 352.
[164] Pezet, *Chrétiens au service de la cité*, 128.
[165] Domenach, *Gilbert Dru*, 65.
[166] *Ibid.*, 73–75.

la politique. Introduction à une action des jeunesse française." [167] It
opened with an outburst against the sufferings and humiliations which
all faithful Frenchmen, but especially the young men of Dru's generation, had been forced to endure. Dru held not only the Fascist powers,
the Vichy regime, and its coterie of practitioners of *Politique d'abord*
responsible for these experiences but the old men, the habits and institutions of the Third Republic as well. He condemned "the false democratic mythology." the "political morality," the "decadent and en-
croaching parliamentarianism," the "rotten press," the "unjustified
privileges," and the "economic institutions" of the old regime. Dru
believed that the condemnation of Vichy and the Third Republic constituted, in itself, a political decision for the future. Dru noted that
politics had unclean connotations because of the use to which politics
had been put. Moreover, he continued in a statement echoing Mounier's
convictions, "our education . . . contributed to turning us away from
[politics] . . . as a dangerous and corrupting game." Dru saw the key to
the future in political activity, however. "Politics is worth precisely
what those who conceive of it and practice it are worth." A revolution
was necessary, he believed, and this revolution would have to be not
only a profound and *péguyste* transformation of consciences and morality, but a revolutionary change in every area of life.

In undertaking the necessary work of revolution, Dru recognized
that he would encounter opposition from the "old men" and their
ideas, habits, and parties. Although they were not to be entirely excluded from the revolutionary tasks taken on by the new generation,
their habits would have to be uprooted and their "system" not be
allowed to revive. The instrument of this revolution and renewal
was to be the "Mouvement." What this "Mouvement" might become
was delineated in broad terms by Dru in his second manifesto.[168] While
there can be little doubt that this declaration was inspired, in part at
least, by the Christian democratic tradition into which Dru's J.E.C.
had moved in the late 1920s and 1930s, there is equally little doubt that
its central affirmations included many of those of Mounier and *Esprit*.
There was the same basis of revolutionism, the same desire for a complete rupture with the old habits and old political organizations, the
same willingness to collaborate fraternally with all other Frenchmen,
even the Communists, in the pursuit of common aims, and, perhaps

[167] Gilbert Dru, "Notre jeunesse vers la politique," reprinted as Annex 3 of Domenach,
Gilbert Dru, 153–166.
[168] Gilbert Dru, "Déclaration," reprinted in Domenach, *Gilbert Dru*, 78–80.

most important, the same openness of spirit. Nowhere in his manifesto did Dru mention a test of religious belief or even the stereotyped "respect for moral and religious forces" of the Christian democratic tradition.

Dru envisaged three great political organization in postwar France. On one side, he saw a new movement regrouping the traditional forces of the Right which had been "purified" by the removal of the "pernicious ascendancy of *Action Française* and the trusts." On the other side, he saw the Communists who had earned their "rights in the City" as a result of their Resistance activities. In both instances, Dru's hopes were identical to those expressed by Mounier in 1945.[169] Finally, acting as a counter-weight to the Communists, was the revolutionary "Mouvement." Discounting the possibility of a resurrection of the other old parties, notably the Socialist and Radical parties, Dru saw the "Mouvement" as a kind of "republican assemblage" which would unite the heirs of the Christian democratic tradition and those of the lay tradition of the Rights of Man. Together they would undertake a complete renovation of French life and institutions in fraternal cooperation with the new party of the Right and the Communists. Beyond this, however, Dru's manifesto was remarkable for its absence of practical proposals. He believed that the "Mouvement" would derive its dynamism from its youth but he was not oblivious to the problems inherent in the collaboration of the younger and older generations in the "Mouvement." In the "practical sections" which concluded his manifesto, Dru called only for a course in political education and the organization of working teams to elaborate the program of the "Mouvement."

The initial reaction of some of Dru's friends to his project was a very natural one. They believed Dru was a visionary and dreamer.[170] Consequently, the fact that a large number of men – lawyers, trade union leaders, politicians, journalists, professors of law and history – welcomed Dru's project and used it as a point of departure for their own plans requires explanation. Part of the answer is to be found in the intellectual climate of France in 1943 and 1944: during the last years of the Resistance, grandiose plans for the future of France were commonplace.[171] In addition, Gilbert Dru lived, worked, and died for his dream. By his words and by the tremendous flurry of activity in the last year

---

[169] See Mounier, "The Structures of Liberation," *The Commonweal*, XLII, No. 5 (May 18, 1945), 114.

[170] Domenach, *Gilbert Dru*, 81.

[171] For surveys of these plans, see Michel, *Les courants de pensée de la Résistance*, 351–410; and Michel and Guetzévitch, 193–249.

of his life, he demonstrated such a deep sense of mission and such profound convictions that he succeeded in convincing others of the feasibility of his project and the practicality of his vision. Moreover the veterans of the *Parti Démocrate Populaire*, the N.E.F., the C.F.T.C., and the A.C.J.F. and its specialized branches – all of these men were receptive to a project that would enable them to organize themselves for the work of constructing a new France. The meetings in Lyons in the spring of 1943, after all, had been relatively inconclusive.

The first man to whom Dru with turned his project was André Mandouze, who was then an editor of the *Cahiers du Témoignage Chrétien*. Although Mandouze agreed to support Dru, he was too actively involved in organizing a movement of "Christian renewal," which coincided, at best, only in part with Dru's project, to devote his time to the plan.[172] That Mandouze's work would lead him to a position of leadership in the *Chrétien Progressiste* movement was an irony hidden by the future. Dru next turned to Père Chaillet, the founder of *Témoignage Chrétien*, and Rémy Montagne, a leader of the A.C.J.F. Both men gave their support to Dru.[173] Montagne offered to send Dru to Paris as a member of the staff of the A.C.J.F., thereby affording him the opportunity to enter into conversations with Catholic leaders in the capital.

Dru also approached Joseph Hours, a former *Démocrate Populaire* who taught history in the University of Lyons. Young Dru was on particularly good terms with Hours, having worked with him on the *Comité chrétien d'action civique* and other Resistance projects. Dru hoped to meet another history professor who "symbolized in the eyes of Gilbert the properly 'political' side of his preoccupations." [174] Before he could leave for Paris to meet Georges Bidault, however, Dru was informed that he was to attend the Consultative Assembly at Algiers. In late August, 1943 Dru met with Maurice Guérin, who was so receptive to Dru's project that he helped the young man revise a section of his original declaration.[175] Finally, late in October, 1943 after several further delays, the young missionary arrived in Paris. He first attended a meeting of the A.C.J.F. and collaborated in drawing up a manifesto aimed at encouraging and coordinating the Resistance activities of Catholic youths.[176] Dru then began to meet with various Catholic leaders. He met Marc Sangnier; he conferred with Pères

---

[172] Domenach, *Gilbert Dru*, 82–84.
[173] *Ibid.*, 84–88; and Duquesne, 371–372.
[174] *Ibid.*, 88.
[175] *Ibid.*, 92–93.
[176] *Ibid.*, 98–101.

Fessard and Daniélou, two of Mounier's friends from the Jesuit school of Fourvières; and he met with Francisque Gay. Gay welcomed Dru's project because it corresponded to his old views of a "broadly based movement supported by new cadres." [177] It was Gay who finally took Dru and a young friend, Jean Gilibert, to meet Georges Bidault.

The prestige of Bidault's new office as president of the C.N.R. coupled with the reputation he had acquired as the editorialist of *l'aube* before the war, made him the most obvious candidate for the leadership of what was called the "Mouvement d'Avenir." Moreover, Bidault belonged to a generation of Christian democrats which could provide a link between the young visionaries of Dru's age and such veterans as Gay, Guérin, and Raymond-Laurent. Bidault accepted Dru's plans and in doing so he and the other founders of the party expressed their belief that the liberation of France was to be not only a liberation from the German occupation "but from money, from the centralized State, from outmoded political formulas." [178] They agreed with Dru that "fighting France" had to become "revolutionary France" by prolonging the fraternity born of the Resistance.[179] The "Mouvement" which was to assist in this liberation was to be different from any political party of Third Republic vintage; it was to be something more than an ordinary political party and its activities were to go beyond the realm of politics and parliamentary activity. It was to be based upon "a conception of the world" and, as "a school of thought," it was to perform "an educational role." [180] These latter conceptions were, of course, clearly of Third Republic vintage. It is entirely possible that the spirit of Dru's project was dampened from the outset by the old Christian democratic preconceptions of many of the founders of the M.R.P.

After welcoming Dru, Bidault sent him to André Colin, a leader of the A.C.J.F. and the future secretary-general of the M.R.P. Colin was given the responsibility of setting up the organizational structure of the "Mouvement" and there followed a series of meetings at which the general structure of the new organization was formulated. One of these meetings was held in January, 1944 in the home of Jean Letourneau, a veteran of the *Parti Démocrate Populaire*. Dru and Gilibert attended this gathering along with a number of veterans of Christian democracy and Social Catholicism. A Bureau of Studies under Charles Flory and

---

[177] "Origines et mission du M.R.P.," 26.
[178] *Ibid.*
[179] "La naissance d'un grand Mouvement."
[180] "Origines et mission du M.R.P.," 26.

Charles Blondel was organized, Alphonse Juge was placed in charge of the Secretariate, and Dru and Colin were charged with forming the first cadres of the "Mouvement."

On January 16, 1944 a decisive meeting was held in the home of Jean Raymond-Laurent on the rue de Furstenberg in Paris.[181] In the very room in which the editorial board of *le Petit Démocrate* had assembled every Friday before the war, the future "Mouvement" was discussed by veteran Christian democrats. There were few, if any, young men of Dru's generation present. Dru himself had already left Paris to begin his organizational work in Lyons. Various points of view concerning the nature and composition of the "Mouvement" were voiced in the meeting. Generally, however, two tendencies had already crystallized among the organizers of the future M.R.P. On one hand, there were those who "saw in [the future party] . . . a kind of 'Christian democrat' party which, while remaining free of any attachment [to the Church], would take on a clearly 'confessional' character." [182] On the other hand, there were those who supported the youthful *tabula rasa* project of Dru in most of its essentials. The latter wanted to organize a vast "republican assemblage" which would embrace Christians and non-Christians alike on the basis of a program of revolutionary reform.[183] Joseph Hours was particularly insistent that the "Mouvement" should be open to all, whatever their origins or convictions, but he also emphasized the need of excluding many Catholics from the organization because of their association with Vichy and their responsibility for many of the errors of the Third Republic.[184] Several men supported the formation of a kind of Labor Party of Christian inspiration. Indeed, the idea of a French Labor Party was widely and loosely advocated by many members of the Resistance ranging from Henri Frenay and Mounier's long-time friend Georges Izard to the men of the *Jeune-République* and of the Christian democratic (and largely *Démocrate Populaire*) *Groupe Lille* which published the *Cahiers du Travaillisme français*.[185]

[181] Descriptions of this meeting are contained in Raymond-Laurent, *Figures de militants*, 67–69; "La naissance d'un grand Mouvement"; and Duquesne, 374.

[182] Domenach, *Gilbert Dru*, 119. See also Frenay, "Le travaillisme enfant mort-né de la Résistance," 47; Claude Bourdet, "La politique intérieure de la Résistance," *Les Temps Modernes*, 10e année, No. 112–113 (May, 1955), 1861; and Lepp, *Espoirs et déboires du progressisme*, 84–85.

[183] *Ibid.*, 119–120.

[184] Hours, *Mouvement Républicain Populaire. Directions*, 20–22.

[185] Bourdet, "La politique intérieure de la Résistance," 1861; Frenay, "Le travaillisme enfant mort-né de la Résistance," 43–48; Duquesne, 373; Izard, "Et maintenant?," 5–10; *La Jeune-République*, February, 1945; and Bellanger, 196–197.

These differences of opinion were patched over in the meeting of January 16, 1944. Raymond-Laurent later recalled that "it was decided to create 'the Mouvement' (it still had no name) which would associate veterans and youths, but in which the leadership, by common consent, would belong to the leaders of the new generation so that members of the latter would better understand our appeal – and particularly the *Jeunesse Catholique* created at the time when François de Menthon was its general president." [186] Most of the organizers of the Movement were joined not only by the bonds of the Resistance but by their training and experience in the A.C.J.F. and its specialized branches.[187] But, as Mounier pointed out shortly after the Liberation, the real problems of postwar France were not confronted during the Resistance for fear of creating political divisions within the Resistance. And, he added sarcastically: "Patriotism, heroism, civic-mindedness are not badges of political ability." [188] As the future of the M.R.P. was to demonstrate, past or present membership in the A.C.J.F. or its specialized branches was no guarantee of political ability or a convergence of political views.[189] The agreement reached on January 16, 1944, therefore, may well have been little more than a tactic adopted by veteran Christian democrats to obtain the support of the new generation for a renewal and enlargement of the old *Parti Démocrate Populaire* under a new name rather than a genuine effort to incorporate the new spirit of Dru's generation. Indeed, Georges Bidault clearly intended to seek electoral support primarily in the confessional milieux from which the youths of the *Jeunesse Catholique* issued. His critics were fond of placing much of the responsibility for stifling the spirit of Gilbert Dru upon the president of the C.N.R. Claude Bourdet, for example, states that Bidault opted for great and rapid success. "We will build the M.R.P.," Bourdet quotes Bidault as having said, "with women and curés." [190] And, in an often-cited incident, Bidault reportedly encountered a friend in July, 1944 and told him: "Don't forget that tomorrow women are going to vote. Then, when you do your electoral campaigning, don't forget: In the name of the Father, of the Son, and of the Holy Spirit." Bidault then blessed himself a number of times and added: "Thus, we will gain a hundred deputies." [191]

[186] Raymond-Laurent, *Figures de militants*, 68.
[187] Duquesne, 374.
[188] Mounier, "Pas de politique. Pas de problèmes," *Esprit*, No. 106 (January, 1945), 284.
[189] See, for example, Mounier, "La jeunesse comme mythe et la jeunesse comme réalité – bilan 1940–1944," *Esprit*, No. 105 (December, 1944), 146–147.
[190] Bourdet, "La politique intérieure de la Résistance," 1861.
[191] Quoted in Duquesne, 377–378.

Whether or not the presence of Gilbert Dru at the meetings of the organizers of the new Movement would have altered the direction of its development is, of course, problematical. Dru himself did nothing further to specify or elaborate more concretely his manifestoes of August, 1943. After his return to Lyons, he worked energetically organizing the first teams of the Movement in the Southeast while other men organized similar cadres in the Rhône, the Southwest and the North.[192] Dru was aided by both Maurice Guérin and a young friend named Francis Chirat. Chirat was a dedicated member of the J.O.C. and he, along with Guérin, worked to provide the Movement with working-class support. On July 17 Dru and Chirat were arrested in Lyons as they were leaving a meeting in Guérin's home. Ten days later Dru, Chirat, and three other young men were struck down by their German captors in a terrible display of brutality in the Place Bellecour in Lyons. In the words of Dru's good friend Jean-Marie Domenach,

he was trained in the J.E.C. less as a militant than as a leader. But he was also educated in the best of the Christian democratic tradition. He had, to aid him, the advice of a [Henri Marrou-] Davenson, the lessons of a [Jean] Lacroix, of a Joseph Hours, the writings, so often reread and meditated upon, of Emmanuel Mounier.... He had Péguy whom we often read and who provided the permanent basis of our friendship in those *Cahiers de notre jeunesse* whose very title was intended to bring to mind his presence.

Dru contributed importantly to the formation of what was to become the M.R.P., Domenach maintained, but then Domenach asked rhetorically: "Can it be worthy of the blood out of which it was born?" [193] More clearly still, Joseph Folliet later said that "I have often thought that death took [Dru and Chirat] while their dream was intact, sparing them the sight of the diminuations and distortions that reality was to inflict upon their ideal – upon our ideal." [194] Similarly, Mounier is said to have warned young Dru at the congress of *Esprit* in Dieulefit in September, 1943: "You are going to inherit the Catholic masses who tend to be conservative and you will be their prisoners." [195]

While Dru labored and was ultimately martyred in Lyons, the organizers of the newly christened *Mouvement Républicain de Libération* (M.R.L.) in Paris continued their work. There were meetings every Sunday of the provisional executive committee. The task of drawing up a manifesto for the M.R.L. was assigned to two younger leaders

[192] Domenach, *Gilbert Dru*, 109–118; and "La naissance d'un grand Mouvement."
[193] Domenach, *Gilbert Dru*, 135–138.
[194] Folliet, "La vie secrète de la Chronique," 651.
[195] Quoted in Duquesne, 375–376. The author gives no source for the statement he attributes to Mounier.

of the Movement, both of whom were veterans of the A.C.J.F. In April, 1944 André Colin and Maurice-René Simonnet retired to Vernoux, a little village in the Ardèche, and prepared a seven page declaration entitled "Lignes d'action pour la libération." [196] The declaration opened with a call for the liberation of France not only from the German invaders and the men of Vichy but from the prewar "disorder" as well. Colin and Simonnet believed that a new France could be constructed thanks to the fraternity born of the Resistance between men who had hitherto been divided by vain political and religious quarrels. The declaration did not, however, call for the creation of a new political party. Rather, in an apparent effort to enlarge the M.R.L., it called for the creation of "a current, a *Mystique* in the service of the total liberation of France." The new Movement was to work for the liberation of man "from all oppressions, servitudes which impede his full development and his free spiritual, moral, and material ascent." Liberation and revolution were inseparable, the authors continued in language reminiscent of Dru's manifestoes. "It is essential to free man from the tyranny of money. ... A complete break with the capitalist system is necessary." More specifically, the declaration called for the re-establishment of a republican regime; a family policy not dissimilar to that of the *Parti Démocrate Populaire*; the establishment of a plan for economic development in which various syndical organizations would participate; the nationalization of certain enterprises including gas, electricity, transport, mines, and insurance; the socialization of credit; and the establishment of a cooperative agricultural system.

Perhaps most significantly, the new Movement which was to accomplish these revolutionary tasks was not to base its membership upon a religious test. Then, however, Colin and Simonnet added that the purpose of the Movement was to build a new France on *"the basic principles of Christian civilization."* It is difficult to believe that Colin and Simonnet, as well as their colleagues, failed to discern the important contradiction implicit in their manifesto or that they had violated the spirit of Dru's project. On September 3, 1944 some fifty members of the M.R.L. met in the former quarters of the collaborationist *Je suis partout* at 186 rue de Rivoli and adopted the substance of the declaration.[197] Most of the revisions made in the original decla-

---

[196] Duquesne, 379–381, quotes the declaration extensively. *Mouvement Républicain Populaire. Lignes d'action pour la libération* (Paris: Centre National, n.d.) is the later revised version of this declaration.

[197] Duquesne, 381; Raymond-Laurent, *Le Parti Démocrate Populaire*, 37; "La naissance d'un grand Mouvement"; and "Origines et mission du M.R.P.", 27–28.

ration merely reflected the changed time and circumstances in which the Christian democrats found themselves. Included in the declaration now was the Charter of the Resistance, but the economic and social program of the M.R.L. did not differ substantially from the Charter.[198] The revised declaration omitted the original reference to the Movement as being not a new party but rather "a current, a *Mystique* in the service of the total liberation of France." Bidault and the other leaders of the future M.R.P. may well have already decided that the prospect of expanding the M.R.L. was already dim. The original reference to *"the basic principles of Christian civilization"* remained in the revised declaration, however. If the M.R.L. (and M.R.P.) was not technically a confessional organization, it laid itself open to Mounier's later charge that the Christian democrats were dispensing the "tasteless pap" of a Christian civilization.

In the euphoria of the Liberation, the Constituent Assembly of the M.R.P. on November 24 and 25, 1944 was a great, though in many ways, deceptive success. Just prior to the Assembly, a brief gathering of *Démocrates Populaires* decided not to resurrect the old party but shortly after the official formation of the M.R.P., the *Jeune-République* passed a motion to maintain the independence of the progressive little party.[199] Out of the experience of 1940–1944 added strength was provided the *Jeune-République* and the Catholic Left by such movements and journals as *Jeunesse de l'Eglise, Témoignage Chrétien, Economie et Humanisme,* the priest-worker *Mission de France* and *Mission de Paris,* and the *Mouvement Populaire des Familles.*[200] Many French Catholics had abandoned the historical predispositions which had marked and hampered the labors of the Christian democrats. These Catholics carried forward the work of Gilbert Dru far more faithfully than did the M.R.P. And many of them also bore the mark of the extraordinary influence of Mounier.[201]

Several weeks after the meeting of the M.R.L. on the rue de Rivoli, the man who had provided much of the inspiration for Gilbert Dru's enterprise arrived in Paris to resume the publication of *Esprit.* Mounier had worked with the *maquis* and had collaborated with *Le Résistant de la Drôme* and *La France intérieure,* but he took far greater pride in

[198] Compare *Mouvement Républicain Populaire. Lignes d'action pour la libération* and *M.R.P. Lignes directrices d'un programme économique et social* with the "Programme du C.N.R." in Michel and Guetzévitch, 215–218.

[199] *La Jeune-République,* February, 1945.

[200] Duquesne, 382–395.

[201] Mounier, "Lettre à Jéromine Martinaggi, février 1945," *O.M.,* IV, 769; and Béguin, "Une vie," 1047.

the fact that *Esprit* was the first journal to be published in Paris after the Liberation. In the pages of *Esprit*, he soon began his criticism of his deformed offspring. In doing so, however, he was no longer criticizing a number of little "chapels," but one of the largest political parties in postwar France. And the experience of the War, the Vichy regime, and the Resistance added a new dimension to his opposition to Christian democracy and "ghetto" Catholicism: "the temptation of Communism," he wrote, "has become our household demon." [202]

[202] Mounier, "Débat à haute voix" (February, 1946), *O.M.*, IV, 114.

CHAPTER VI

THE DILEMMA OF COMMUNISM:
MOUNIER AND THE MOUVEMENT RÉPUBLICAIN
POPULAIRE, 1944–1950

> Plus que jamais, il nous faut reprendre la révolte de nos
> vingt ans, les ruptures de nos vingt-cinq ans. Le chrétien ne
> quitte pas le pauvre, le socialiste n'abandonne pas le pro-
> létariat, ou ils parjurent leur nom.
>
> Mounier, "Fidélité," February, 1950.

The Communist poet and novelist Louis Aragon greeted the Liberation
of France with an outburst of good will and fraternal feeling typical of
the time. He dedicated a poem to Gilbert Dru and three other young
martyrs of the Resistance and in it voiced the widespread belief that
the events through which his nation had just passed had forged a new
sense of unity among the French people, even between Catholics and
Communists:

> Celui qui croyait au ciel
> Celui qui n'y croyait pas
> Tous deux adoraient la belle
> Prisonnière des soldats
> Lequel montait à l'échelle
> Et lequel guettait en bas
> Celui qui croyait au ciel
> Celui qui n'y croyait pas
> Qu'importe comment s'appelle
> Cette clarté sur leur pas
> Que l'un fût de la chapelle
> Et l'autre s'y derobât
> Celui qui croyait au ciel
> Celui qui n'y croyait pas
> ....[1]

Less than two years later, Aragon repeated the refrain of his poem but
robbed it of its original spirit. In a speech to an assemblage of Communist youths, he explained that "celui qui croyait au ciel" and "celui qui
n'y croyait pas" had undertaken the same battle only against a

[1] Aragon, "La Rose et le Réséda," in La Diane française (Paris: Editions Seghers, n.d.), 24.

common enemy and that this unity did not extend to their views on education and particularly on the question of state subsidies to the Catholic schools.[2]

On the floor of the National Constituent Assembly, at the same time, another man repeated the refrain of Aragon's paean to the unity of the Resistance. Pierre-Henri Teitgen, a leader of the new M.R.P., concluded a speech in which he advocated the inclusion of freedom of education in the new Declaration of Rights by appealing with Aragon's words to those who did not believe in heaven.[3] Joined by their Socialist allies, the Communist deputies refused to support Teitgen's obvious intention of protecting the status of the Catholic schools. Consequently, freedom of education was not included in the Declaration.[4]

Here in capsule, and admittedly oversimplified, form was one of the major issues which divided the political heirs of Gilbert Dru and the members of Aragon's party. That the old question of the Catholic schools had become a matter of importance symbolized the failure of the hopes born of the Resistance and, in a larger sense, the resurrection of the old regime with many of its parties, problems, and habits. No single party, of course, was solely responsible for this but the new M.R.P. played an important role in this turn of events. At the time of Teitgen's speech, it was the second largest party in France and it had supported the continuation of the Vichy subsidies to the Catholic schools early in 1945.[5] To this extent, the M.R.P. had either abandoned or found it impossible to fulfill the inspiration provided its founders by Gilbert Dru.

It is possible, but uncertain, that the leaders of the M.R.P. knew how far Dru's *mystique* had degenerated into a *politique* by the late 1940s. In early 1947 Dru's former schoolmate, Jean-Marie Domenach, reacted angrily to an M.R.P. political circular which stated that to fail to vote for the M.R.P. was to vote for an anti-French Marxist government. This unconscionable tactic was a desecration of the spirit of Gilbert Dru, Domenach declared.[6] In September, 1948 the government, of which the M.R.P. was a member, erected a monument to the young martyrs of the Place Bellecour in Lyons where the Germans had earlier

2 Louis Aragon, *L'homme communiste* (Paris: Gallimard, 1946), 37.

3 *J.O.C.*, No. 25 (March 15, 1946), 780.

4 Gordon Wright, *The Reshaping of French Democracy* (New York: Reynal & Hitchcock, 1948), 159.

5 Mario Einaudi and François Goguel, *Christian Democracy in Italy and France* (Notre Dame, Indiana: University of Notre Dame Press, 1952), 192.

6 J.–M. D. [Domenach], "Chronique du fascisme," *Esprit*, No. 129 (January, 1947), 157–158.

constructed "an atrocious statue in the purest Nazi style of Arno Brekker." [7] At least one man discerned the irony implicit in this little ceremony. Emmanuel Mounier reacted angrily to what he regarded as an act of hypocrisy. One could not help but wonder, Mounier said, what the minds and hearts of these martyrs would hold had they overheard the whispered comment of one government official to another: "No majority is possible in this Chamber, my good man." [8]

The reasons for the failure of the spirit of the Resistance to effect more substantial changes were much debated in France during the early years of the Fourth Republic.[9] To Mounier, a man not given to simple explanations, one cause took precedence over, and in many ways determined, all other causes. He explained in his last editorial in *Esprit* that "the union of the Resistance offered a chance to the unexpected. ... The Resistance bequeathed the promise of a Communism reintegrated in the French tradition." [10] In Mounier's estimation, that so many Frenchmen disregarded this was the major reason for the failure of the Resistance to carry out its proclaimed revolution. The problem of Communism was foremost among Mounier's concerns during the last six years of his life. His attitude towards it was determined largely by his keen sense of injustice. Rightly or wrongly, he was convinced that the Communist Party had the confidence of the oppressed, the suffering, and the disinherited; and, as he told his friend Abbé André Depierre of the priest-worker *Mission de Paris* only two days before his death, he wanted "to enter into the sufferings and struggles of the workers." [11] It was, ultimately, Mounier's refusal to separate himself from those who suffered most from injustice that led him to declare that Communism was his "household demon." [12]

The practical consequences of this position posed a serious dilemma for Mounier. He refused to give his support to any political party or movement which had neither broad popular support nor the prospect of obtaining such support. On the other hand, he refused without the slightest ambiguity, his numerous critics to the contrary, to accept either the doctrinal bases or the political deficiencies of the only party that, in his view, had the requisite popular support. "It is difficult, in

---

[7] Folliet, "La vie secrète de la Chronique," 651.
[8] Mounier, "Une majorité," *Esprit*, No. 149 (October, 1948), 569.
[9] See especially "Un rendez-vous: la Résistance," *France-Forum* (July-August, 1964); "Huit ans après," *L'Observateur*, No. 119 (August 21, 1952); and Claude Jamet (ed.), *Le Rendez-Vous manqué de 1944* (Paris: Editions France-Empire, 1964).
[10] Mounier, "Fidélité" (February, 1950), *O.M.*, IV, 17.
[11] Mounier, "Lettre à l'abbé Depierre, 20 mars 1950," *O.M.*, IV, 830.
[12] Mounier, "Débat à haute voix" (February, 1946), *O.M.*, IV, 114.

1946," he wrote, "not to be a Communist, and it is still more difficult to be one. ...." [13]

This position conditioned Mounier's attitude toward the Christian democrats. That Christian democracy was a "weak" idea which engendered "soft" politics unsuitable to the harsh realities of postwar France and to Mounier's own virile and aggressive Christianity received fresh verification, in Mounier's judgment, between 1944 and 1950. It was during the winter of 1943–1944 in Dieulefit that Mounier had written his *L'Affrontement chrétien*, in which he vehemently attacked contemporary Christianity as a "coalition of the feeble and the timorous"; it was in May, 1946 in his "L'Agonie du christianisme?," that he described the Christian democratic parties of postwar Europe as "an oedema on the sick body of Christendom"; and it was in an address to the *Semaine des intellectuels catholiques* in May, 1949 that he accused the Christian democrats of submitting to "the last fervors of romanticism," of "indiscriminately intermingling politics, religion, and impulses of the heart," and of attempting to solve political and economic problems by means of "good will and moral approximations." [14] Supported by the bourgeoisie, the new M.R.P., Mounier charged, could not possibly be the instrument for fulfilling the aspirations of the popular classes.[15]

As the sole survivors of the revolutionary *Jeunes équipes* of the 1930s, Mounier and *Esprit* remained faithful to their initial rebellion against "the established disorder" of which Christian democracy was a part. A man of lesser conviction than Mounier might well have tempered his revolutionary zeal or perhaps have abandoned it entirely. In the years from 1944 to 1950 the fame and, albeit to a lesser extent, even the material fortunes of Mounier increased substantially. The winter of 1944–1945 was an extraordinarily difficult time for Mounier and his family; they were forced to live in a small apartment on the avenue Emile-Zola and their finances were minimal. In the course of 1945, however, the offices of the journal were established on the third floor of the Editions du Seuil at 27 rue Jacob, and the "Murs Blancs," the house in Châtenay-Malabry purchased on the eve of the war, was made habitable. The *Esprit* community, consisting of the Mouniers, Paul and

[13] Mounier, "Post-scriptum" (February, 1946), *O.M.*, IV, 138.
[14] Mounier, *L'Affrontement chrétien, O.M.*, III, 11; Mounier, "L'agonie du christianisme?," *O.M.*, III, 531; and Mounier, "Feu la chrétienté," *O.M.*, III, 705–706.
[15] Mounier, "Cléricalisme et anticléricalisme," *B.A.E.M.*, No. 9–10 (December, 1956), 16. See also Mounier, "Bilan spirituel français 1946," *Cahiers du libre examen*, February, 1946, reprinted in *B.A.E.M.*, No. 19 (October, 1962), 21.

Simone Fraisse, Jean-Marie and Nicole Domenach, Henri and Jeanne Marrou, and Jean and Jacqueline Baboulène, was organized. One Sunday a month, the *Amis d'Esprit* gathered for discussion and to greet friends from the provinces and abroad.[16]

Although the ranks of the original *Esprit* team had been decimated by the war and other members pursued new interests, many of the veterans – Jean Lacroix, François Goguel, Bertrand d'Astorg, and the inhabitants of the "Murs Blancs" – resumed their collaboration with the journal. Members of the generation of Gilbert Dru and Jean-Marie Domenach also joined *Esprit*. "A great number of young Frenchmen found in personalism the doctrine which impelled them into activity in the heart of the Resistance," Domenach recalled. "When *Esprit* reappeared, the juncture with the young generation was effected." [17] Mounier believed that the first task confronting *Esprit* in 1944 was to effect the union of the generation of 1930 and that of the 1940s.[18] Among the latter were Chris Marker, Jean Cayrol, Paul Ricoeur, Marc Beigbeder, and many others. A year before Mounier's death, Domenach joined Mounier as co-editor of the journal.[19]

Mounier's personal activities might well have exhausted even the young newcomers to *Esprit*. He travelled often in the provinces and frequently abroad: to Belgium in 1944; to Switzerland and Poland in 1945; to Austria and Belgium in 1946; to Germany, French Equatorial Africa, Geneva, and Italy in 1947; to Germany and Austria in 1948; and to England and Scandinavia in 1949.[20] But if such activities indicated an improvement in the material situation of Mounier and his journal – and the growing international reputation of both of them – Mounier did not surrender to any of the bourgeois comforts and satisfactions that often come with fame and fortune. As Jean Lacroix states, "more and more, he was convinced that his vocation required an integral poverty of him." [21]

The pages of *Esprit* once again reflected the unusual breadth and depth of Mounier's interests. There were articles or special issues devoted to subjects ranging from the Marshal Plan, the Communist revolutions of Eastern Europe, and the Atlantic Pact, to existentialism, Marxism,

---

[16] Béguin, "Une vie," 1047–1048.
[17] Domenach, "Emmanuel Mounier," *Psyché*, 5ᵉ année, No. 4 (June, 1950), 500.
[18] "Enquête sur la revue Esprit," *Les Revues européennes*, November, 1946, reprinted in *B.A.E.M.*, No. 15 (March, 1960), 5. See also "Aux jeunes français," *Esprit*, No. 96 (January, 1941), 129–131.
[19] "Note," *Esprit*, No. 153 (February, 1949), 161.
[20] Béguin, "Une vie," 1048.
[21] Lacroix, "Un témoin et un guide," 27.

and the work of Père Teilhard de Chardin. Mounier's friendship with Teilhard de Chardin, whose posthumous fame was far to exceed that of Mounier, was but a striking example of Mounier's association with an extraordinarily large number of the elite of French intellectual life.[22] His correspondence during the last five years of his life unhappily was much less voluminous than before, primarily because Mounier was in close personal contact with his principal friends and collaborators either in Paris or through his frequent travels. Moereover, *Esprit* was a true "Revue internationale." Although its circulation remained relatively small, the journal was widely read, *Esprit* groups were organized, and Mounier's writings were translated in every continent of the globe.[23] And *Esprit* was still regarded as a somewhat subversive publication in certain Catholic circles both in France and elsewhere. As late as 1947–1948, for example, a French Canadian was warned by a Jesuit priest in Montreal that *Esprit* was "dangerous."[24]

Mounier continued to reflect upon the events of his time. Among these events were the effects of the travail of France between 1940 and 1944. "Beneath the French realities of today," he wrote in early 1945, "you can still see this past, just as when you look at the profile of a landscape you can trace the lines of its geological history." [25] As he had been convinced after the fall of France, Mounier maintained that "the rule of the French bourgeoisie as the directing class of the country is over. Its treason at Munich and at Vichy comprised only the final result of a long failure to take due responsibility." [26] In Mounier's estimation even the fact that many members of the bourgeoisie had served France well during the War and the Occupation did not alter this almost elemental fact. Because some of the sons of the bourgeoisie had given their lives for France, he argued, did not mean that their fathers were qualified for the great tasks of the new France.[27] Mounier recognized, nonetheless, that certain elements of the bourgeoisie and also the

[22] On the personal and intellectual relationship of Mounier and Teilhard de Chardin, see Madeleine Barthélemy-Madaule, *La Personne et le drame chez Teilhard de Chardin* (Paris: Editions du Seuil, 1967), 302–322; and "Teilhard de Chardin et le personnalisme," *Esprit*, No. 315 (March, 1963) and No. 326 (March, 1964).

[23] On the international fame of Mounier, see especially *B.A.E.M.*, No. 21 (December, 1963), and *B.A.E.M.*, No. 22 (June, 1964).

[24] *Cité libre* (Montreal), I, No. 1 (June, 1950), 29.

[25] Mounier, "France in the Catacombs," *The Commonweal*, XLII, No. 4 (May 11, 1945), 86.

[26] Mounier, "The Structures of Liberation," *The Commonweal*, XLII, No. 5 (May 18, 1945), 113.

[27] Mounier, "Bourgeoisie," *Esprit*, No. 107 (February, 1945), 451–452.

attitudes, habits, and values which he called the bourgeois spirit would weigh heavily upon the efforts to construct the new France.[28]

If Mounier's major premise is accepted, the next step in his rather merciless assessment of the condition of France at the time of the Liberation is a logical one. Since the bourgeoisie had been the governing class in the old France, the problem confronting Frenchmen in 1944–45 was to find a new governing class.[29] Mounier firmly believed that this new class would necessarily have to be drawn from the popular classes. At this point, however, Mounier encountered a major difficulty. Whereas the old bourgeoisie had been prepared for its accession to power in 1789 by two centuries of training, the bourgeoisie had not offered the popular classes a similar opportunity, Mounier contended in a distorted interpretation of the French Revolution. In France at the time of the Liberation a revolutionary situation analogous to that of 1789 was present, but the men necessary to carry out the revolution were lacking.[30] The most obvious solution to this problem was a program of political education of the masses,[31] perhaps in the manner of the Christian democrats of the 1890s or of the *Sillon*. This answer, however, did not occur to Mounier.

Mounier's inventory of the forces available for building the new France ended on the debit side of the ledger, with the notable exception of the Communist Party. The major trade unions, the C.G.T. and C.F.T.C., offered no immediate prospect of providing the new elite desired by Mounier, for both of them were in a state of disarray at the time of the Liberation.[32] The French peasantry, for whom Mounier, like Charles Péguy, always had great affection, was badly in need of re-education after its long attachment to the Radical-Socialist Party. The latter was nothing more than a "cadaver" dominated by "social unintelligence and economic interests" in Mounier's analysis.[33] Similarly the Socialist Party had shared in the defeat of France: "It satisfied in the petit bourgeois, especially in the petit bourgeois of the South, the need for verbal courage without great practical consequences." [34] Mounier was convinced that without a complete renewal

[28] Mounier, "France in the Catacombs," 86.
[29] Mounier, "Bourgeoisie," 452; and Mounier, "The Structures of Liberation," 112.
[30] Mounier, "The Structures of Liberation," 112; and Mounier, "Suite française aux maladies infantiles des révolutions" (November, 1944), O.M., IV, 76–90 *passim*.
[31] Rouquette, "Positions et oppositions d'Emmanuel Mounier," 54.
[32] Mounier, "The Structures of Liberation," 112.
[33] *Ibid.*, 114.
[34] *Ibid.* See also Mounier, "Personnalisme et socialisme," *Cité Soir*, August 4, 1945, reprinted in *B.A.E.M.*, No. 29 (March, 1967), 31–32.

of its membership and its spirit it was doomed to beat "a peaceful retreat into the storerooms of history, a retreat perhaps subsidized by a few electoral victories, but a retreat leading to death." [35] The old parties of the Right, finally, were not only completely disorganized but discredited by their collaborationist activities. Here, however, Mounier, like Gilbert Dru, expressed the hope that a new French Right would be reconstituted embodying "a conservatism which is at the same time generous and traditional the way France has always manifested that temper." [36]

Significantly, Mounier failed to discuss the new-born M.R.P. in his inventory of available forces in early 1945. It is possible, but unlikely, that he hoped that the new party would support the revolution because he paid tribute to the non-sectarian efforts of its leaders during the Resistance in a talk on *Radiodiffusion française* early in January, 1945.[37] Toward the end of the same year, again in a talk on *Radiodiffusion française*, he praised the fraternal collaboration of Catholics and Communists during the Resistance and stated his overly optimistic belief that "great and terrible debates between the Christian conception and non-Christian conception of life will continue, but they will no longer be poisoned by mixing them with economic interests and political prejudices." [38]

Whatever illusions Mounier may have had concerning what has been called "the myth of the durable reconciliation between those who believe in heaven and those who do not, as sung by Aragon," [39] had definitely disappeared by late spring of 1946. He reasserted his former criticism of the Christian democrats when he told his radio audience that the M.R.P. was

generous in inspiration and language, [but] it belongs by its reflexes to the moderate petite and moyenne bourgeoisie. Part of the electors of the Right have even voted for it in the Constituent elections. Moreover, bold in language and timid in deeds, it has voted more often with the Right than with the Left. . . . It represents the point of view of numerous French Catholics. The danger is not this, but that it will appear to the public as *the* position of Catholicism, which ought not to be attached to a centrist democratic position or to any other political position.[40]

[35] Mounier, "The Resistance," *The Commonweal*, XLII, No. 6 (May 25, 1945), 138.
[36] Mounier, "The Structures of Liberation," 114.
[37] Mounier, "La religion et la France nouvelle," *B.A.E.M.*, No. 9–10 (December, 1956), 4.
[38] Mounier, "Catholiques et communistes," *B.A.E.M.*, No. 9–10 (December, 1956), 11.
[39] Michel, *Les courants de pensée de la Résistance*, 768.
[40] Mounier, "Cléricalisme et anticléricalisme," 15–16.

The very success of the M.R.P. in the elections for the First Constituent Assembly in October, 1945, when it received one out of every four votes cast, and again in the referendum of May, 1946, when it succeeded in defeating the draft constitution with the help of the Moderates and Radicals, caused Mounier to add a new facet to his criticism of the Christian democrats. Neither the old *Parti Démocrate Populaire* nor the *Jeune-République* had ever been successful in creating the new danger feared by Mounier: that the political positions of the Christian democrats would be interpreted as the positions of all French Catholics. The question of the supposed Rightist tendencies of the M.R.P. aside, it is clear that Mounier prejudged the new Christian democratic party. He looked elsewhere for the men who were to fulfill his hopes.

As the only party that had not sunk in the general shipwreck of 1940 – but for reasons which Mounier neglected to emphasize – the Communist Party claimed for itself the title, "le parti des Fusillés." Mounier believed that the Occupation and Resistance had made the party a genuinely French party, thus fulfilling the hopes expressed by Gilbert Dru in 1943. Mounier argued that "one can be opposed to it. But this return of the people to the sentiment of a common destiny with that of the nation, this end of a long exile is a sociological fact of prime importance." [41] It was clearly to the cadres of the Communist Party that Mounier tended to look for the new elite which was to rebuild France. "Any form of political anti-Communism," he concluded in late 1944, "today works against France. ..." [42]

Mounier's assessment of the condition of France in early 1945 was further complicated by a major deficiency that he discerned in the Resistance movements. What had been a source of strength in these movements prior to the Liberation was, in Mounier's view, a serious shortcoming after 1944:

In order to avoid resurrecting the old politicians' squabbles, men drew back from all forms of political thinking [during the Resistance]. Thus were maintained misunderstandings and over-facile agreement as well as unity, and there was serious risk that when the negative purpose of the whole movement – the liberation of French soil – had been attained, the Resistance movement would find itself somewhat hollow and baffled. [43]

[41] Mounier, "The Structures of Liberation," 113.
[42] Mounier, "Délivrons-nous des peurs," *Combat*, December 8, 1944.
[43] Mounier, "The Resistance," 136. See also Mounier, "Pas de politique. Pas de problèmes," *Esprit*, No. 106 (January, 1945), 282; and Mounier, "L'intelligence qui rassemble. Texte inédit" (October, 1945), *B.A.E.M.*, No. 28 (August, 1966), 4.

Mounier therefore concluded his survey on a note of uncertainty. France, he stated, was undergoing a profound crisis and "you do not remake a country with ideas, enthusiasm, or little clubs of reformers." [44] "Ideas" Mounier declared, "are nothing without men who alone can nourish them." [45]

Of the many ideas to which the Resistance movements gave birth, one was particularly pervasive in 1944–1945. Mounier gave it his tentative support and his personalism was one source of its inspiration. This was a new socialism for which various terms were imprecisely used: "travaillisme," "République du Travail," "socialisme humaniste," "socialisme libéral." [46] Mounier believed that this new socialism ". . . would seek to join to the revolutionary enthusiasm of the old [socialism] a youthful dynamism which the latter has lost, as well as a desire to forestall the tyranny which we have all seen develop among partisans of collectivization." [47] Somewhat more specifically, its aim was "the expulsion of the powers of money, the suppression of the proletarian condition, the installation of a republic of labor, the formation and accession [to power] of new popular elites." [48] In this sense, Mounier could argue that the revolution for which *Esprit* labored was "at once personalist and communitarian, or, if one wishes, personalist and socialist, the two terms being almost synonymous in the great French tradition." [49] A critic of *Esprit* suggested only half facetiously that had the French Socialist and Communist Parties united on the basis of a "humanist socialism" Mounier would have been a member of the Châtenay-Malabry section. [50]

"The whole world is today socialist," Mounier complained in December, 1944, and he went on to issue a warning against the widespread use of the word as a label to cover the most confused and divergent positions. [51] In opening the pages of *Esprit* to an inquiry on "Un 'socialisme humaniste'? " several months later, Mounier stated that "the phrase is à la mode," and the editors of *l'aube* said even more sarcastically that just as all of the parties of the Third Republic called themselves republicans, so all of those of the Fourth Republic called themselves

---

[44] Mounier, "The Structures of Liberation," 112.
[45] Mounier, *Qu'est-ce que le personnalisme?*, *O.M.*, III, 245.
[46] Mounier, "The Resistance," 137; Michel, *Les courants de pensée de la Résistance*, 387–389; and Jean Lacroix, *Socialisme?* (Paris: Editions du Livre Français, 1945), 22–47.
[47] Mounier, "The Resistance," 137.
[48] Mounier, "Suite française aux maladies infantiles des révolutions," 89.
[49] Mounier, "Personnalisme et socialisme," 31–32.
[50] Pierre Andreu in "Qu'as-tu fait de ta jeunesse?"
[51] Mounier, "Les cinq étapes d'*Esprit*," 52.

socialists.[52] The most important attempts to define the new socialism were contained in books by Léon Blum, André Hauriou, and Jean Lacroix.[53] These attempts to elaborate a new socialism reflected the moralism and messianic hopes typical of Resistance thinking. Emphasis was placed on the moral or humanist content of French socialism and on the purely human ends of the hoped-for socialist republic. The new socialism, Jean Lacroix aptly concluded, was less a new technique or a statement of new solutions than "a new social and psychological climate, another style of life, a larger, more comprehensive and more human philosophy." [54] Because of the uncertain practical application of such ideas the most disparate men and political organizations could call themselves "socialist."

The new "travaillisme français" which was to embody this new socialism meant entirely different things to different men once the negative bond of Resistance unity was broken. Even within the *Mouvement de Libération Nationale*, which included many of the leading proponents of the new socialism, there was a split between a minority led by the young Marxist intellectual Pierre Hervé and a majority led by André Malraux and Philippe Viannay.[55] To Robert Verdier, a secretary-general of the Socialist Party, the "travaillisme français" meant little more than the union of the resurrected Socialist Party with various Resistance groups.[56] To Pierre Stibbe, a member of the Resistance movement *Ceux de la Résistance* and the editor of *Volontés*, the new socialism was little more than the Charter of the Resistance put into practice by the Socialist and Communist Parties.[57] To Mounier's old friends Henri Frenay and Georges Izard, the new movement was to be a union of all political forces between the Communist Party on the Left and the most extreme Conservatives on the Right.[58] To a majority of the members of the reconstituted little *Jeune-République*, it was to consist of "all democrats and all socialists of rationalist or Christian

---

[52] "Un 'socialisme humaniste'?," *Esprit*, No. 107 (February, 1945), 408; and *l'aube*, December 26, 1945.
[53] Léon Blum, *A l'échelle humaine* in *L'Oeuvre de Léon Blum* (Paris: Editions Albin Michel, 1955), IV, 405–495; André Hauriou, *Vers une doctrine de la Résistance: le socialisme humaniste* (Algiers: Editions Fontaine, 1944); Lacroix, *Socialisme?*; and Mounier, "Vers une doctrine de la Résistance," *Esprit*, No. 107 (February, 1945), 461–464.
[54] Lacroix, *Socialisme?*, 84.
[55] "Un 'socialisme humaniste'?," 408–414. See also *1er Congrès national. Mouvement de Libération Nationale. Janvier 1945* (Paris: Imp. de Sceaux, n.d.).
[56] "Socialisme humaniste?," *Esprit*, No. 109 (April, 1945), 687–691.
[57] *Ibid.*, 692–695.
[58] Frenay, "Le travaillisme enfant mort-né," 43–48; and Izard, "Et maintenant?," 5–10.

inspiration."[59] And to some of the young members of the nascent
M.R.P., it meant an entente between progressive Catholics and Socialists of the Blum variety.[60]

The difficulties implicit in this unreal semantic or verbal agreement
were compounded by the resurrection of many of the old parties.
Mounier himself wrote in late 1946 that "very quickly, the old organizations have taken over, and humanist socialism has been lost in the
puny fibre of some small centrist groups, deserted by everyone, and has
ended up being fitted into the classic parliamentary game."[61] Foremost among the former was the Communist Party which regarded a
new political movement as a serious challenge to its pretentions of representing the popular classes. Similarly, the Socialist Party, although
it flirted with the idea of a "travaillisme français" on one hand and
hesitantly accepted the unity-of-action pact proferred it by the Communist Party on the other, preserved its identity.[62]

A final and controversial barrier to the constitution of a "travaillisme français" was the nascent M.R.P. That the relatively formless
Christian democratic movement might have formed the core of a Left-
Center Labor Party in late 1944 or early 1945 was a possibility that
Mounier did not consider. This possibility was not discussed by the
leaders of Christian democracy in the Constituent Assembly of the
M.R.P.[63] In a left-handed tribute to the M.R.P. in 1946, Mounier suggested that the M.R.P. was an unacknowledged recipient of the heritage of humanist socialism. "But," he added, "if it in truth constitutes
one of the most Leftist of the Christian democratic parties of Europe,
much more clearly 'advanced,' at least in one wing, than for example
the Christian democrats of Austria or Italy, it nonetheless owes its
success to a heavy ballast of old conservative-oriented votes which
cause it sometimes (not always) to defend liberty in the manner of
traditional liberalism more than in the manner of socialism."[64] Several
of the leading advocates of a French Labor Party were in agreement
with Mounier's unspoken, but nonetheless clear, original assumption.
Henri Frenay, for example, had opposed the slowly germinating plans

[59] *La Jeune-République*, February, 1945.

[60] See, for example, Claude Julien, "Christian Democracy in France," *The Commonweal*,
XLV, No. 47 (October 1, 1948), 590.

[61] Mounier, "L'Inquiétude de la liberté dans la France contemporaine," *Suisse contemporaine*, October, 1946, reprinted in *B.A.E.M.*, No. 19 (October, 1962), 10.

[62] Hoffmann, "Paradoxes of the French Political Community," 47; and Wright, *The
Reshaping of French Democracy*, 70–72.

[63] *Mouvement républicain populaire. Compte-rendu sténographique des congrès nationaux.*
1er *Congrès national* (Paris: Fondation nationale des sciences politiques, n.d.), 1–81 *passim*.

[64] Mounier, "L'Inquiétude de la liberté dans la France contemporaine," 10.

of Georges Bidault, François de Menthon, and their friends in the last years of the Resistance. Frenay stated well after the event that "the creation of the M.R.P. could have no other effect than to revive the old quarrel over *laïcité*, and as a consequence render impossible the creation of the great political regrouping that we had begun [in 1943] to call the French Labor Party and about which we had dreamed so much." [65] Abbé Ignace Lepp, one of Mounier's greatest admirers, also recalled that "we were convinced that what we called at that time *travaillisme français* had a chance of becoming at least as powerful as English laborism." [66] This hope was shattered, however, when the Christian democrats refused to cooperate ". . . with all these men of other metaphysical opinions – or even without any. . . ." [67] And finally, implicitly at least, even Francisque Gay, who was to be quickly disillusioned by the M.R.P., expressed a similar criticism. Gay lamented that the M.R.P. had placed itself in "the paternalist tradition of La Tour du Pin, Albert de Mun, Henri Bazire or Jacques Piou." [68]

The organization of the M.R.P., therefore, was a decisive setback to the plans of men like Frenay, Bourdet, and Lepp. In a more general sense also, the new Christian democratic party was a notable example of what Mounier called the "hollow and baffled" hopes of the Resistance. These were the hopes voiced by young Gilbert Dru; and the failure of the new party to translate them into an effective political program marked the end of Dru's inspiration. Without a program that could win the support of the popular classes, the M.R.P. was destined to remain the object of Mounier's bitterest criticism. The new party was but one example of Mounier's conviction that "any *travaillisme* which would refashion socialism . . . without the ballast and strength of the proletariat is doomed to sink into the morass: failure of the post-Resistance." [69]

Like Dru, the founders of the party regarded their organization as an extension of their Resistance activities. They often said that their party had been "forged in the Resistance" or "born in clandestineness," and its organization was simply an effort to give substance to what one of them called the *mystique* of the Resistance.[70] But this conception

---

[65] Frenay, "Le travaillisme enfant mort-né," 47.
[66] Lepp, *Espoirs et déboires du progressisme*, 85.
[67] *Ibid.*, 84.
[68] Francisque Gay, "Le temps des grandes espérances reviendra," *l'Observateur*, No. 119 (August 21, 1952), 11.
[69] Mounier, "Fidélité," *O.M.*, IV, 19.
[70] Guérin, "Nous sommes en marche vers une révolution totale"; and Albert Gortais, "La ligne du M.R.P.," *l'aube*, October 2, 1945.

was spiritual or moral before it was political. Just as Gilbert Dru had believed that the war and the Resistance were essentially battles for the principles of justice and liberty and for the City of Christ rather than merely for the defense of France, the founders of the M.R.P. regarded their activities during the Resistance as a struggle to free both the "body" and the "soul" of France.[71] The secretary-general of the new party described the Christian democratic Resistance in the following terms:

The occupation forced us to experience a regime based upon a misconception of man: forced labor, deportations, torture, massacres were only the logical application of this absolute misconception which identified man with the charcoal that one burns, with the animal one kills according to the whim of a monstrous power. The insurrection against this inhuman dictatorship, in the profound sense of the word, had to join in the same cause the liberation of France and the liberation of man. It was necessary to regain the country's total independence and to build a society in which man would finally be respected, delivered from injustice and social oppression in all of their forms.[72]

The manifesto approved by the Constituent Assembly of the M.R.P. in November 1944 was no more specific. Reflecting typical Christian democratic sentiments, it was filled with completely unobjectionable references to "the requirements of the human person and the necessities of national grandeur," "a Revolution which will permit ... a moral and spiritual elevation of all men," and "a Revolution which will make political and social democracy a complete reality." [73] Even making allowances for the kind of platitudes and generous appeals normally voiced on such occasions, it is clear that the initial bonds of the new Christian democratic party were common sentiments or aspirations of a moral and spiritual nature rather than any precise conception of the political program and action necessary to fulfill such aspirations.

This was the judgment of one of the founders of the M.R.P. and his criticism was seconded by the men of *Esprit*.[74] Joseph Hours, Gilbert Dru's history professor at Lyons and the original director of the political study circles of the "Mouvement," analyzed the weakness of the party largely in terms of the circumstances of its founding:

Unfortunately, the Resistance allowed little leisure time. It did not permit meditation on the aims and conditions of political action. It was above all a

---

[71] Marc Sangnier, "Il faut que l'âme de la France soit liberée," *l'aube*, November 28, 1944.
[72] Gortais, "La ligne du M.R.P."
[73] "Le manifeste du M.R.P.," *l'aube*, November 28, 1944.
[74] Joseph Hours, "Les Chrétiens dans la politique. L'Expérience du M.R.P.," *la Vie intellectuelle*, (May, 1948), 62–77; and "Enquête sur la France disorientée," *Esprit*, No. 146 (July, 1948), 42.

generous élan whose motives cannot be analyzed. If they could be, doubtless the Resistance of Christians would be understood as having prepared them badly for political action because its motives were not political at all. They were primarily religious.... The men of the M.R.P. imagined that generous yearnings of a philosophical or religious nature were sufficient for politics. They thought that with this meager equipment they were prepared to grapple with the perils of government under exceptionally difficult circumstances. Lacking any comprehensive grasp of the major constitutional, economic, military, or colonial problems, they tackled each one separately; is it any wonder that they were overwhelmed? [75]

Another critic summarized this basic difficulty more succinctly. "Christian democracy," he said, "was a 'spiritual family' [which] believed it could become a 'governmental party.'" [76]

Other traditional Christian democratic factors entered into the relative political vacuum at the center of the new movement. Chief among them were those characteristics previously condemned by Mounier during the 1930s and repeated in the study he had written in Dieulefit in 1943–1944: "a tendency to confuse evengelical fraternity with a taste for little coteries and to carry with them into political groups, under the pretext of giving them a familial atmosphere, a domestic sentimentalism which is as embarassing spiritually as it is aesthetically." [77] The symbol of this deficiency was the Christian democratic sentiment of "friendship" which, ironically, could only have been strengthened by the widespread feeling of fraternity which developed during the Resistance.

At the Constituent Assembly of the party, the Movement was frequently referred to as the "fraternal party." [78] The high point of the proceedings occurred when the call of "Marc Sangnier to the rostrum" went up. The grand old man of French Christian democracy went slowly up to the rostrum looking, according to one observer, "very noble, very great, almost from another world." [79] Then in a short extemporaneous speech of the kind in which he had long excelled, the founder of the *Sillon* evoked the old conception of "friendship" and told his listeners: "Do not renounce your spirit of Christian fraternity, but address yourselves to all of France in order to achieve the great republican reconciliation." [80] The audience rose spontaneously and sang the "Marseil-

---

[75] Hours, "Les Chrétiens dans la politique," 70.
[76] Bernard Georges, "Le role politique des catholiques français depuis la Libération," *La Nef*, 11e année, No. 5 (January, 1954), 148.
[77] Mounier, *L'Affrontement chrétien*, O.M., III, 55.
[78] Pierre Corval, "Né dans la clandestinité. Le Mouvement républicain populaire a tenu son premier congrès," *l'aube*, November 28, 1944.
[79] "Introduction" to Sangnier, "Il faut que l'âme de la France soit liberée."
[80] Sangnier, "Il faut que l'âme de la France soit liberée."

laise," and offered "the apostle Marc" the honorary presidency of the new organization. Sangnier accepted his new office after consulting with his old friends of the *Jeune-République*.[81]

In later years this religious or moral sentiment was manifested in party affairs. In 1945 a young leader of the party defined its program in terms of respect for "loyalty, truth, love." [82] In 1947 a party philosopher stated that the two principles which inspired the action of the M.R.P. were justice and friendship.[83] A year later Maurice Schumann, the party's president, who had declared shortly after the founding of the M.R.P. that "it is time that love became a force," [84] demonstrated the persistence of this religious sensibility when he stated: "The country stronger than egoisms; the law stronger than violence; the spirit stronger than matter; love stronger than hate. These are the ideas that we will not debase." [85] A friendly critic asked somewhat rhetorically: "At the origins of the M.R.P. is there a system of thought or only a certain state of spirit which made one of my friends say one day that a Catholic will never feel at ease if he is not among other Catholics?" [86]

Another less friendly critic of the M.R.P. elaborated upon what Mounier had identified as the Christian democratic temperament. Jean-Marie Domenach stated:

The Christian democrat is attached to his Movement by an inexpressible union of the heart. The doctrine and action of his leaders are only of secondary concern to him: he has a religious veneration for them which, when deceived, can change into hatred, but even in this hatred there remains a kind of loving attachment. Thus it is that within his party he is like an infant within his family: he does not even imagine that he could live in a world other than his own, which is a universe of the heart, ...an aquarium of moral sentiment.... Even when betrayed by his chiefs, the Christian democrat gives them credit for having a conscience that he supposes does not exist in the men of other parties, of the Right or the Left.[87]

Even its dissidents of the years after 1946–1947 continued to attend the party congresses, Domenach contended. Whatever the policy over

---

[81] *La Jeune-République*, Special Number (October, 1944-September, 1945), and *La Jeune-République*, February, 1945.

[82] *l'aube*, January 14–15, 1945.

[83] Etienne Gilson, "Le Mouvement et le parti," in *M.R.P. Vers une démocratie nouvelle* (Paris: S.E.R.P., 1947), 11–12.

[84] *l'aube*, January 10, 1945.

[85] *l'aube*, January 1, 1948.

[86] Louis Le Saulnier, "Brèves questions sur la démocratie chrétienne," *Cahiers de la République*, No. 4 (December, 1956), 111.

[87] J.-M. Domenach, "Petite psychologie du M.R.P.," *Esprit*, No. 207–208 (October-November, 1953), 659.

which they had split from the M.R.P. – its increasingly rigid anti-Communism, its opposition to Charles de Gaulle, its European or colonial policies – these men still came to hear "Georges" or "Maurice." Domenach recounted that

I know an old believer, one of those to whom the Movement owes its birth. . . . Deceived in his dream, almost abandoned, he is seen reappearing at every congress, trembling with lyrical reproofs. His is the voice of the Left; it is the echo of Lacordaire, of Sangnier. There is only one heart and one tradition. Then, in the happy atmosphere thus created, Maurice [Schumann], or Georges [Bidault], or Pierre-Henri [Teitgen] have only to take this hero by the shoulder to persuade him that his motion was generous but inopportune and that the task of those who have "the responsibility of power" should not be complicated.[88]

As Domenach's account suggests, the political uncertainty of the M.R.P. was also reflected in the emphasis it placed upon its past tradition. In this regard, however, the party tended to be both ambiguous and excessive. Its leaders stressed, one one hand, that the party was not "a chance event" and, on the other hand, that it had been "forged in the Resistance." [89] In their emphasis upon the historical antecedents of the party, the leaders betrayed their religious certitudes and their political uncertainty by including men who were Christians but hardly Christian democrats. In his speech to the Constituent Assembly, for example, Maurice Guérin included not only Lamennais, Lacordaire, Montalembert, and the men of the *Sillon* in his list of Christian democratic pioneers, but Albert de Mun as well. Guérin also paid tribute to the *Parti Démocrate Populaire*, the *Jeune-République*, and the N.E.F., but more than one veteran of the *Parti Démocrate Populaire* complained that the M.R.P. did not welcome some of the old *Démocrates Populaires* and refused to recognize the labors of the Christian democrats of the years between 1910 and 1939.[90]

Maurice Schumann argued that historically the Christian democrats had allowed their *mystique* to be degraded into one or the other of two *politiques*: the formation of "the fervent little group," or the fruitless attempt to make "the great breach" among the conservative *bien-pensants*. To escape these past errors, Schumann said, the new party had to bridge the great "chasm" between Right and Left in French

---

[88] *Ibid.*, 660.
[89] Guérin, "Nous sommes en marche vers une révolution totale." See also Max André, "Forces," *l'aube*, September 10, 1944; and Jacques Fauvet, *The Cockpit of France*, trans. Nancy Pearson (London: The Harvill Press, 1960), 49.
[90] See, for example, Pezet, *Chrétiens au service de la cité*, 132ff.; and Vaussard, *Histoire de la démocratie chrétienne*, 110.

political life.[91] Even the language used to express the purpose of the
M.R.P. in the party's official account of its origins and mission was
painfully familiar. The purpose of the Christian democratic movement
"has always been to end the disastrous split between Right and Left,
to put an end to the foolish opposition between social justice and spiritual liberty, to reconcile the one and the other in the Republic, to rejoin
respect for spiritual values with service on behalf of the people. ..." [92]
The M.R.P. was a prisoner of its Christian democratic past. It intended
to locate itself at the center of the political spectrum and its program,
accordingly, was determined, in some measure, by this pre-determined
position.[93]

The political uncertainty and the religious sentimentality of the
M.R.P. also reflected the background of the new generation of Christian democrats. With the important exceptions of such veterans as
François de Menthon, Maurice Schumann, Maurice Guérin, and a few
others, the new generation was entirely without political experience.
Most of them had "been together" in the A.C.J.F. and its various
specialized branches. It is far from certain that the young veterans of
these organizations did not suffer the effects of this religiously oriented
training.[94] One of their critics pointed out that the religious character
of their previous training prepared them badly for the harsh realities of
building the new France.[95]

The A.C.J.F. and its specialized branches had emerged in liberated
France with considerably increased prestige because of their opposition to the Vichy Labor Charter, to the S.T.O., and to Vichy's youth
policies as well as because of the role many of their members had played
in the Resistance. During the Resistance many members of the
A.C.J.F. had discovered that their activities had a temporal dimension
which had not been clear during the early years of specialized Catholic
Action.[96] As a consequence, a controversy developed both within the
A.C.J.F. and between the A.C.J.F. and the French hierarchy which resulted in the dissolution of the venerable organization in 1956. The
controversy centered in large part on the relationship between the

[91] l'aube, January 10, 1945.
[92] "Origines et mission du M.R.P.," 34–35.
[93] Rémond, "Les partis catholiques," 180.
[94] See "Table 7. Previous Catholic Action Affiliation of M.R.P. Leaders, 1959," in William
Bosworth, Catholicism and Crisis in Modern France. French Catholic Groups at the Threshold
of the Fifth Republic (Princeton: Princeton University Press, 1962), 254–255; and "Origines
et mission du M.R.P.," 24.
[95] Hours, "Les Chrétiens dans la politique," 71.
[96] A.C.J.F. Signification d'une crise, 35.

temporal and the spiritual, on the question of whether the A.C.J.F. was more involved in temporal than religious activities.[97]

Meanwhile, the translation of the moral principles and imperatives learned in the A.C.J.F. and its specialized branches into concrete political terms by the youthful members of the new M.R.P. was a difficult and relatively new experience for them. In the work of infusing political action with moral and spiritual principles, it was far too easy to succumb to the deformations and distortions delineated by Mounier before the war. It was often said that no one ever questioned the good faith or intentions of the men of the M.R.P., but their uncertainty and hesitation in the give and take of everyday politics could be interpreted all too easily as duplicity or opportunism.[98] Often also, the religious propensities of the M.R.P. parliamentary representatives led them to speak a language that was not always comprehensible to their fellow deputies.[99]

The Catholic Action training of the new leaders of the Christian democratic movement also predisposed them to a certain form of clericalism. The M.R.P. was not in the strict sense a confessional party – as even Mounier admitted – but the "hothouse" atmosphere of Catholic Action in which members of the clergy provided religious guidance led many of its veterans to continue to look to priests and bishops for guidance and support. That members of the clergy occasionally issued appeals to the faithful calling upon them to support the M.R.P. as the party which applied the social teachings of the Church and defended the Catholic schools did nothing to lessen this difficulty.[100]

The M.R.P. adopted two strategies in an attempt to compensate for these shortcomings. First, it modelled its organization on a conception of the monolithic party in which decisions were made by members of the party hierarchy working in committees and were rarely debated in the party congresses.[101] The highly centralized and highly disciplined party

[97] Jean-Marie Domenach and Robert de Montvalon (eds.), *The Catholic Avant-Garde. French Catholicism Since World War II*, trans. Brigid Elson *et al.* (New York: Holt, Rinehart and Winston, Inc., 1967), 93–95.

[98] See, for example, Pierre Dournes, "Difficultés de la démocratie chrétienne," *Terre humaine*, No. 2 (February, 1951), 35–37; François Goguel, "Destin du M.R.P.," *Terre humaine* No. 6 (June, 1951), 92–96; *La Jeune-République*, June 21–27, 1946; and Elié Beaussart, "Responsabilités des démocrates chrétiens," *Esprit*, No. 162 (December, 1947), 919.

[99] See, for example, *J.O.C.*, No. 25 (March 15, 1946), 777–780.

[100] See, for example, *M.R.P. – Un groupe des prêtres du diocèse Laval, 14 octobre 1945* (n.d.).

[101] Marc Scherer, "Réflexions sur le congrès du Mouvement républicain populaire," *Politique*, New Series, III, No. 7 (January, 1946), 80–84; and Philip Williams, *Crisis and Compromise. Politics in The Fourth Republic* (Garden City, N.Y.: Doubleday & Company, Inc., 1966), 113–115.

thus found one substitute for the political doctrine that bound together most other parties. As with nearly every other facet of the
development and politics of the M.R.P., however, this too brought
criticism. In 1947 a group of dissidents accused the leaders of the party
of being "sheepdogs" and of stifling debate over party policy in "closed
door" proceedings.[102] Bound together less by shared political opinions
than by common religious sentiments, the Christian democratic party
required some measure of authoritarian control to prevent the centri-
fugal forces of its membership from shattering its unity.

The second distinctive characteristic of the M.R.P. was its doctrine.
This doctrine was intended to recruit the greatest electoral support
from Left to Right in the political spectrum. Etienne Gilson argued
that the M.R.P. had no doctrine at all and that this was in keeping
with the spirit of Christian democracy – indeed, that this was one of
the movement's chief advantages.[103] Gilson stated that no political
system could possibly provide ready-made solutions for every conceivable problem. The M.R.P. had, instead, Gilson proclaimed, a set
of principles which its members could apply to any given situation:
"In this sense, one can go so far as to say that there is a doctrine, but
this doctrine is of the simplest kind for it consists in always applying
the same principles to the study of various political, social, and economic problems . . ." [104] But Gilson warned that these principles were
justice and charity and that they could not be monopolized by any
single political party. The M.R.P. was a movement and not a party: it
was not an entente or union of representatives of a social class or set of
economic interests and was not organized against anything or anyone; rather, it was a union of all who wanted to work for the welfare of
all Frenchmen.[105] "The first duty of a Movement is to keep its liberty
of movement which, in addition, expresses only the flexibility of practical reason, and is concerned with moving itself with ease in the complexity of facts that it has the task of regulating," the Christian democratic philosopher explained in a statement that must have left many
of his readers completely baffled.[106]

The early programs of the M.R.P. were both vague and eclectic. The
party accepted the famous Charter of the Resistance which called for

---

[102] *Pour votre information. "Livre blanc" sur la crise du M.R.P.* (Angers, 1948), 3–5.
[103] Etienne Gilson, "Le système et l'esprit," *Politique*, New Series, IV, No. 27 (October,
1947), 676–678.
[104] *Ibid.*, 675.
[105] Etienne Gilson, "Le Mouvement et le parti," 8–10.
[106] *Ibid.*, 11.

radical economic, social, and political reforms and used it as one of the bases for its proclaimed revolution by legal means.[107] In one of the first statements of its program, the party called for extensive nationalizations, economic reforms which would give the workers a greater role in the management of their own affairs, and a new constitution which would avoid resurrecting the old parliamentarianism and the old electoral and political habits. At the same time, however, it gathered together all of those remnants of the program of the *Parti Démocrate Populaire* which seemed applicable in the France of 1944–1945. The M.R.P. supported an upper chamber representing local, professional, and family interests; proportional representation; liberty of trade unionism (to protect the C.F.T.C.), and of education (to protect the Catholic schools); a place within the new structure of France for the natural communities dear to all Social Catholics and Christian democrats; and similar reforms.[108]

The M.R.P. found the place in the center of the Chamber that it sought. Its policy was largely empirical, a kind of extemporaneous reaction to political problems as they developed. As long as those problems could be met within the atmosphere created by the *mystique* of Resistance unity and as long as none of them created decisive divisions within the political fabric of France, the M.R.P. met with considerable success. In the elections for the First Constituent Assembly in October, 1945 the new party received over four and a half million votes and 145 seats and was second only to the Communist Party.[109] In the referendum on the draft constitution of May, 1946 the M.R.P. succeeded in defeating the constitution which was supported by the Socialists and Communists; and in the elections of June, 1946 for the Second Constituent Assembly, the M.R.P. became the premier party of France with more than five and a half million votes and 162 seats.

With the referendum of October, 1946, however, the decline of the M.R.P. began. The party's losses in that month were relatively slight, but in the municipal elections of October, 1947, the party suffered disastrous setbacks. In Paris it lost about three-fourths of its 1946 votes and in other cities more than half of its voters deserted the party. By

---

[107] For an excellent discussion of the Resistance Charter, see Michel, *Les courants de pensée de la Résistance*, 400–405.

[108] See *Mouvement Républicain Populaire. Notre Programme* (Lyons: Imp. commerciale, 1945); and *M.R.P. Lignes directrices d'un programme économique et social* (n.d.). The fullest statment of the program is Albert Gortais *et al.*, "Le M.R.P., Parti de la IVᵉ République," *l'aube*, October 2, 1945 through October 19, 1945.

[109] These and the following figures are taken from Einaudi and Goguel, *Christian Democracy*, 173ff.

June, 1951 the M.R.P. had lost almost exactly half of its electoral support and a slightly smaller proportion of its parliamentary seats. Commenting on the early successes of the M.R.P., an historian aptly states that "for the first time in their history, the Christian democrats were too numerous!" [110] The new party had benefitted from the growing fear of Communism, from its often frank appeal to Catholic voters, from the popularity of General de Gaulle, which it retained for a short time after the General's sudden resignation in January, 1946 by labelling itself "the party of fidelity," and from the widespread desire for "a new party," "new men," and "new politics." Its electoral success was due largely, however, to an equivocation. The party was supported by many voters who were really conservative in their political propensities and who voted for it for lack of something better since the old conservative parties had not been revived. Once a genuine conservative party appeared on the political horizon – as was the case in October, 1947 with the newly organized Gaullist *Rassemblement du Peuple Français* – many of the supporters of the M.R.P. returned to their natural political habitat.[111]

The M.R.P. had partially fulfilled Emmanuel Mounier's prophetic judgment of June, 1934. To unite a large number of Catholics in a political party, he had written, was "to condemn oneself to [political] impotence through eclecticism." [112] Less kindly, a contemporary observer suggested that the M.R.P. should become a "spirit" so that the old Radical-Socialist Party might take the place for which the former could no longer compete.[113]

Coincident with the formation of the *Rassemblement du Peuple Français* and the resultant electoral setbacks of the M.R.P. were two other important events. The M.R.P. completed its break with the Communist Party and ended the period of tripartite government by Christian democrats, Socialists, and Communists; and an attempt was made to organize a Third Force between the Gaullists on one hand and the Communists on the other.[114] With the beginning of what has been

---

[110] Louis Biton, *La démocratie chrétienne dans la politique française. Sa grandeur, ses servitudes* (Angers: H. Siraudeau, 1955), 66.

[111] Einaudi and Goguel, *Christian Democracy*, 172–187. This generally accepted explanation of the electoral decline of the M.R.P. is based upon Goguel's *Géographie des élections françaises de 1870 à 1951* (Cahier 27; "Cahiers de la Fondation nationale des sciences politiques"; Paris: Armand Colin, 1951).

[112] Mounier, "Y a-t-il une politique chrétienne?," 405.

[113] Jacques Fauvet, "Le M.R.P. doit-il disparaitre?," *Une Semaine dans la monde*, August 7, 1948.

[114] Einaudi and Goguel, *Christian Democracy*, 199ff.

called in a classic phrase, "the great schism," [115] the problem of Communism in all of its ramifications came clearly to the fore among the many issues which divided Mounier and the men of the M.R.P. Mounier's position on Communism and his refusal to support the Third Force against the Communists contributed to further defections in the ranks of the M.R.P.

No single facet of Mounier's life and influence in postwar France was subject to greater criticism and misunderstanding than his attitude towards Communism and its adherents. To his enemies on the Right, he was the central influence in a sinister movement to subvert the men and organizations of French Catholicism.[116] To the philosopher Père Gaston Fessard, Mounier's good faith and intentions were not in doubt, but the objective results of Mounier's position were to aid the Communists and endanger the liberty of France.[117] From the Communist side came angry charges. In April, 1949 at the National Congress of the Communist Party in Montreuil, Maurice Thorez asked Mounier to join with the Communists.[118] When Mounier refused, he was subjected to bitter attacks not only by the intellectuals of the French Communist Party but in the pages of *Pravda* as well. These attacks ranged from the charge that *Esprit* was a brigade of anti-Communism to the accusation that Mounier was playing a Machiavellian double game.[119] In the pages of the M.R.P. paper *l'aube*, Mounier was accused by his old friend Etienne Borne of deforming the spirit of Charles Péguy into a "Leninist personalism." [120] On one point, perhaps, almost all of Mounier's critics would have agreed: "It is always necessary to turn to *Esprit* if one wishes to study, at this time, the great Christian temptation of Communism." [121]

[115] Raymond Aron, *Le grand schisme* (Paris: Gallimard, 1948). On the resultant problem of the French intellectuals and Communism, see Aron's *The Opium of the Intellectuals*, trans. Terence Kilmartin (New York: Doubleday and Company, Inc., 1957).

[116] See, for example, Jean Calbrette, *Mounier, le mauvais esprit* (Paris: Nouvelles Editions Latines, 1957); François Ducaud-Bourget, *Faux Témoignage Chrétien* (Paris: Editions du XXe Siècle, 1952); and Michaël, *Les responsables catholiques de la collaboration rouge* (Paris: Les Actes des Apôtres, 1947).

[117] See, for example, Gaston Fessard, *Le communisme va-t-il dans le sens de l'Histoire?* (Paris: Psyché, 1948).

[118] "Le discours de clôture de Maurice Thorez à la Conférence Nationale du Parti Communiste Français (Montreuil le 10 avril 1949)," *l'Humanité*, April 12, 1949.

[119] See, for example, Garaudy, *Lettre à Emmanuel Mounier, homme d'"Esprit"; Pravda*, September 29, 1951, quoted in J.-M. Domenach, "'Esprit' démasqué par le 'Pravda,'" *Esprit*, No. 186 (January, 1952), 68–70; and Mounier, "L'avillissement ne rend pas" (March, 1950), *O.M.*, IV, 180–189.

[120] Etienne Borne, "Le parti intellectuel contre la Troisième force," *l'aube*, January 11–12, 1948.

[121] Pierre Andreu, *Grandeurs et erreurs des prêtres ouvriers* (Paris: Amiot-Dumont, 1955), 70.

Since the first years of *Esprit,* Mounier had attempted to delineate both the common ground shared by personalism and Marxism and their major differences. He partially accepted certain facets of the Marxist critique of bourgeois capitalism. "Marxism," he wrote, "is an acute description of the social and technical status of man. ..." [122] Mounier believed that Marxism was a useful, but ultimately inadequate, corrective to bourgeois idealism: "Against an inhuman spiritualism [Marx] ... has recalled great truths: the spirit has its servitudes, man is largely conditioned by his social and economic situation." [123] And Mounier also believed that "the Marxist critique of alienation and the life of the worker movement is impregnated by personalism. ..."[124] Mounier therefore was able to say that "our philosophy ... owes part of its soundness to Marxist water." [125]

On the other hand, Mounier pointed out one of the essential differences between personalism and Marxism in the prospectus announcing the publication of *Esprit* in 1932. "Marxism," he explained, "is the rebellious son of capitalism from which it received its faith in the material. Revolting against an evil society, it carries with it some justice, *but only until it triumphs.*" [126] Two years later he explained that Marxism and personalism were ultimately incompatible because Marxism denied the conception of human transcendence basic to personalism.[127] "There remains, in fact, at the base of Marxism, a fundamental negation of the spiritual as a creative, primary, and autonomous reality." [128] Mounier never dissociated Marxism and atheism, and, in the words of one of the foremost French students of Marxism, "It is the radical imminence of Marxist anthropology which remained for him the major obstacle to an acceptance of Communist theses." [129]

The doctrinal problems relating to Christianity and Marxism were always of great importance to Mounier. There can be little doubt that Mounier would have welcomed the post-Vatican II dialogue between Catholics and Marxists – and particularly the work of Rober Garaudy,

---

122 Mounier, "Débat à haute voix," 121. For a comprehensive survey of Mounier's position, see Lucien Pelissier, "Mounier et les communistes," in *Emmanuel Mounier ou le combat du juste,* 65–117.

123 Moix, 216–217.

124 Mounier, *Qu'est-ce que le personnalisme?*, *O.M.*, III, 203; and Mounier, "Tâches actuelles d'une pensée d'inspiration personnaliste," *Esprit,* No. 150 (November, 1948), 686–691.

125 Mounier, "Fidélité," 17.

126 Mounier, "Extrait du prospectus annonçant le publication d'‘Esprit,'" 489.

127 Mounier, "Tentation du communisme," 234.

128 Mounier, *Manifeste au service du personnalisme,* *O.M.*, I, 513.

129 Jean-Yves Calvez, *La pensée de Karl Marx* (Paris: Editions du Seuil, 1956), 574.

one of his foremost Marxist antagonists.[130] But ultimately of far greater concern to Mounier were the purely human dimensions of the problem of Communism. As early as 1935 he had written that

Marxism has the confidence of the world of misery. Although its roots there are not deep, ...it is the symbol of liberation for this world at the present time; it gives to the most legitimate demands, to the greatest human richness of these times, a form that [the poor] believe is intimately linked with their hopes. Any arrow shot against [the Marxist parties]... wounds, behind them, men who are justly in revolt.[131]

The greatest event in the history of the French Communist Party between the Popular Front and 1944–45, in Mounier's estimation, was the new prestige and strength acquired by the party as a result of the Resistance records of its members. Mounier believed that "the best French youths coming from the Resistance or returning from deportation camps are joining in greater and greater numbers the only party in which they believe they can find at once a virile discipline, the sense of history, grandeur and efficacy." [132]

Because the Communist Party had the confidence and support of the immense majority of the working class, to speak of a revolution in post-Liberation France without the support of this party was, in Mounier's view, empty verbalism.[133] Any group, including what Mounier referred to as the "progressive wing" of the M.R.P., which failed to take this into account was doomed to an ineffectual "workerism without workers" and an unrealistic "humanism without men." [134] Mounier himself refused either to abandon his support of the necessary revolution or to separate himself from the world of misery inhabited by the working class. In his last testament, he wrote:

It is necessary to know what is meant by Communism. Seen from Chaillot, it is a horrible beast; from the Sorbonne, an erroneous system; from the Hotel Matignon, a plot against the security of the State. Seen from Montreuil or Clichy, it is the armor of the outcasts, the only one that counts in their eyes. Montreuil is not infallible, but Montreuil is at the heart of the problem: we refuse the abstraction which omits the point of view of Montreuil.[135]

Mounier's practical position was neither one of pro-Communism nor one of anti-Communism. It was, rather, what he termed a position of

[130] Roger Garaudy, *From Anathema to Dialogue. A Marxist Challenge to the Christian Churches*, trans. Luke O'Neill (New York: Herder and Herder, 1966).
[131] Mounier, *Manifeste au service du personnalisme, O.M.*, I, 509.
[132] Mounier, "Débat à haute voix," 118–119.
[133] *Ibid.*, 115–116.
[134] *Ibid.*, 118.
[135] Mounier, "Fidélité," 17.

"combative discernment." [136] He condemned anti-Communism for a number of practical reasons: it invariably hurt the cause of "the outcasts"; it was all too often only a façade or defense mechanism for those who defended "the established disorder"; and it opened the door to Fascism by isolating the democratic electorate of the largest political party in France. Mounier could praise a dissident from the M.R.P., even though this man had entered the *Rassemblement du Peuple Fran-çais*, for his refusal to make anti-Communism a kind of "fourth theological virtue." [137] On the other hand, he equally condemned every kind of para-Communist or crypto-Communist activity. Such activity was based upon confusion and "social syncretism" and resulted in either the formation of a subservient appendage of the Communist Party or complete political impotence because of a lack of popular support.

Mounier was forced to do battle on three fronts. He attempted to carry on an intermittent dialogue with the Communists. After 1947 he fought against the Third Force organized by the Socialists and Christian democrats against both the Communists and the Gaullists. And, finally, he opposed the crypto-Communist *Union des Chrétiens Progressistes* which he was accused of having fathered.

Mounier's dialogue with the Communists was ultimately a monologue carried on by the editor of *Esprit* and a few of his colleagues. From the beginning of the post-Liberation period, Mounier looked to the new generation of young Communists to respond to his entreaties. Referring to *La Pensée*, a Marxist journal founded in 1939 by Georges Cogniot and Paul Langevin and resurrected in the winter of 1944,[138] Mounier wrote: "Of all French journals, it is with this one that our dialogue is most necessary. For if we seek to establish through our writings and our actions that Marxist thought is an indispensable element in the spiritual life of twentieth-century man, even if – or more precisely because – the conciliation of Marxist positions with the exigencies of interior experience encounters so many difficulties, *La Pensée* tries to build in its various issues an encyclopedia of the Marxist method applied to all branches of human knowledge." [139] Receiving no response from *La Pensée* save for a biting attack on a special issue of *Esprit* three years later,[140] Mounier turned to Pierre Hervé of the Communist

---

[136] *Ibid.*, 19.
[137] Mounier, "'Temps présent' disparait," *Esprit*, No. 130 (February, 1947), 323.
[138] Caute, 268.
[139] Mounier, "Autour du marxisme," *Esprit*, No. 117 (December, 1945), 964.
[140] See Jeanne Gaillard, "Esprit," *La Pensée*, New Series, No. 19 (July-August, 1948), 125–128.

journal *Action*. In a letter to Hervé in late January, Mounier attempted to clarify his position and to lay down the general guidelines of his proposed dialogue with the Communists. Mounier told Hervé that the minimal requirement for any dialogue was that the positions of the participants not be distorted or misrepresented. As examples of this, Mounier responded to a number of criticisms voiced by the Marxists. He denied the charge that he was attempting "to go beyond Marxism" and weaken the position of the laboring classes; he denied that he was proposing an artificial dissection of Marxism and contended that he was simply pointing out that Marxism took insufficient account of the riches and genius of the proletariat; and he complained that to contend that Marxism was a completed and "acquired" system which could not for this reason be commented upon was to negate the very character of dialectical thought. Mounier told Hervé that truth and honesty and not lies and caricatures should govern a true dialogue.[141]

The following month *Esprit* published a special inquiry on the attitude of young intellectuals towards Communism. In this issue Mounier proposed a "fraternal" dialogue with the Communists based upon his obvious hope that both Marxist doctrine and party discipline were sufficiently flexible for such an endeavor to have concrete results.[142] Such optimism was not only distinctly characteristic of Mounier himself but was undoubtedly also based on the responses to the inquiry which he summarized in the same issue of *Esprit*. Mounier's conclusions were that the attraction exerted by Communism on many young French intellectuals was more than a passing fancy; that the attraction of Communism was opposed by an equally impressive Christian sense of man and an acceptance of the Western tradition of liberty shared by many of these young intellectuals; that a kind of "lyric illusion" concerning the power and efficacy of Communism was responsible for the adherence of many young men to the Communist Party; that the Communists had justifiable fears of heresy and schism which, in turn, stifled both their ideas and their recruitment possibilities; and that, finally, non-Communists should not allow their refusal to join the party to be used either against the Communists or to justify "the established disorder."[143]

In the same issue of his journal, Mounier published his most widely

---

[141] Mounier, "Lettre à Pierre Hervé, 28 janvier 1948," *O.M.*, IV, 802–803. This letter was first published in *Action*, No. 76 (February 15, 1946) in response to Daniel Biegel, "Le marxisme est-il dépassé?," *Action*, No. 73 (January 25, 1946).

[142] "Le communisme devant nous," *Esprit*, No. 119 (February, 1946).

[143] Mounier, "Post-scriptum" (February, 1946), *O.M.*, IV, 137–141.

read examination of Communism, "Débat à haute voix." In many respects the conclusions he drew from the responses to the *Esprit* inquiry reflected his own position on Communism. "There may be a hundred good reasons for anti-Communism, but in the France of 1946," Mounier wrote, "they do not prevent anti-Communism from consolidating all that is dying, all that is poisoning the country in its long agony, nor, above all, do they prevent it from being the necessary and sufficient crystallizing force for a revival of fascism." One should be *non*-Communist without being *anti*-Communist.[144]

Mounier believed that there was only one viable solution to this dilemma. It was to work within the elite of the working class, to use it as a base of action in order to prevent the exploitation of the worker movement. Between Mounier and the working-class elite, however, was the insurmountable barrier posed by the rigid dogmatism of the Communist Party. Responding to Maurice Thorez, who had attacked those who affirmed "the primacy of the spirit over the material" while at the same time he had offered an "outstretched hand" to Catholics and all men of good will, Mounier attempted to deal with the question which ultimately foredoomed any dialogue with the Communists to failure. In an article aptly entitled "La mauvaise querelle de l''esprit,'" Mounier declared: "I do not ignore the fact that the spirit, the human person, liberty, civilization serve to conceal the most base coalitions of interests beneath a clear conscience." Thorez would be right in attacking, with Marx – and also, Mounier added sarcastically, with Nietzsche, La Rochefoucault, Pascal, and the Gospels – the way in which "the spirit," "the spiritual," and "the ideal" have been historically subverted to support the worst of causes. The great merit of Marxism was that it belonged to this current of criticism of idealism. In a sense materialism was an historical necessity, Mounier said. Then he asked that revolutionaries be judged on the basis of their political position. Mounier demanded: "let there be, with regard to this new position, new reactions rather than an outpouring of off-hand and vague excommunications." [145]

It was on the latter note that Mounier opened the pages of *Esprit* to a special inquiry on "marxisme ouvert contre marxisme scolatique" two years later.[146] In return for the criticism explicit in the title of the

144 Mounier, "Débat à haute voix" trans. as "A Dialogue with Communism," *Cross Currents*, III, No. 2 (Winter, 1953), 118–141.
145 Mounier, "La mauvaise querelle de l''esprit,'" *Le Populaire*, July 19, 1947.
146 "Marxisme ouvert contre marxisme scolastique," *Esprit*, No. 134 (June, 1948).

special issue, Mounier was abused in the pages of *l'Humanité, Action, Cahiers du communisme*, and *La Pensée.* "Who are the obscurantists?" Victor Leduc asked rhetorically in *Action*.[147] A writer in *La Pensée* said sarcastically that "while [*Esprit*] accuses the Communist Party of 'sclerosis' and of 'opportunism,' it is however the Marxists of the Communist Party who give proof of creative imagination and it is the personalists of *Esprit* who are deadened by the exigencies of human persons." [148] Mounier responded to such criticisms by denying that he had meant to begin a dialogue with the Communists. But he added that "we will refuse to believe – and this is the reason for our untiring efforts – that one can ever lose hope in man's power of renewal." He concluded by challenging the Communists to do as *Esprit* had already done in its special issues on the "Rupture du christianisme avec la désordre établi" and the more recent – and equally shocking in some Catholic quarters – "Monde chrétien. Monde moderne." [149] The Marxists should publish a special issue of *Action* devoted to "Marxisme ouvert contre marxisme scolastique." [150] No one, of course, responded to Mounier's challenge although Jean Kanapa examined the possibility of a dialogue with Mounier and *Esprit* at great length in the pages of *Cahiers du communisme*. His conclusion was that Mounier would have to see the error of his ways before such a dialogue could take place.[151]

In April, 1949 the almost still-born dialogue between Mounier and the Communists came briefly to life and then expired in a not unexpected manner. In the course of his speech to the National Congress of the French Communist Party at Montreuil on April 10, 1949, Maurice Thorez addressed himself to "men like Emmanuel Mounier and Claude Bourdet" who refused to join the forces of anti-Communism and anti-Sovietism and yet persisted in speaking of "our faults, of our errors." Thorez was willing to admit that the Communists were not infallible and even went so far as to declare that "we are ready to make many concessions" so long as one thing was recognized as being impossible. "Do not ask us to be Communists no longer." He then paid further tribute to Mounier and Bourdet for their opposition to the Atlantic Pact, the war in Vietnam, "anti-Communist provocations," the Third Force and the grave dangers which menaced "France, the Republic,

---

[147] V. Leduc, "Qui sont les obscurantistes?," *Action*, June 22–28, 1948.
[148] Gaillard, "Esprit," 128.
[149] "Monde chrétien. Monde moderne," *Esprit*, No. 125 (August-September, 1946).
[150] Mounier, "Main ouverte et marxisme ferme," *Esprit*, No. 146 (July, 1948), 214–217.
[151] Jean Kanapa, "Avec les catholiques le dialogue est possible... Mais il y faut une vigilance réciproque," *Cahiers du communisme*, No. 8 (August, 1948), 814–831.

the Peace." How, Thorez asked, could such men refuse "the indispensable union" with the Communist Party?[152] Mounier's final response was a succinct paraphrasing of one of Thorez's statements: "Do not ask us not to be ourselves." [153]

Later Mounier was accused by such literary agents of Stalinism as Victor Leduc, Roger Garaudy, Jean Kanapa, and Jean Desanti of being a disguised supporter of "American imperialism" and a confused "byzantinism." [154] He and *Esprit* were taken to task particularly for their support of Tito. Wrote Roger Garaudy: "After Pétain, it is Tito. The bourgeoisie calls you: *Esprit*, are you there? And twice *Esprit* responds: Marshal, here I am!" [155] Another writer in the Communist *La Nouvelle Critique* concluded an attack on *Esprit*'s Titoism with the statement: "But for *Esprit*, Tito is the savior of Communism, the purifier of the worker movement, a kind of Saint Theresa or Saint Ignatius of socialism." [156] Shortly after his death *Pravda* branded Mounier as an idealistic mystic who was in league with "fascist traitors, spies, and Titoist assassins" and whose personalism was a form of "aggressive obscurantism," "a philosophy of the Middle Ages," and an atrophied bourgeois philosophy.[157] Even Mounier's critics on the extreme Right did not match the vehemence of the Communists. What particularly angered the Communists was Mounier's increasingly critical appraisal of international Communism in the last years of his life. In this respect also, Mounier adopted a position of "combative discernment" between East and West. He partook of the anti-Americanism which was widespread in French Left-wing intellectual circles during this time, although he did not live to see its culmination in the vigorous neutralism of the early 1950s.[158] Mounier spoke out honestly

---

[152] "Le discours de clôture de Maurice Thorez à la Conférence Nationale du Parti Communiste Française."

[153] Mounier, "Ne nous demandez pas de ne pas être nous-mêmes" (June, 1949), *O.M.*, IV, 172–176.

[154] See Victor Leduc, "Esprit et une certaine manière de tromper le peuple," *Cahiers du communisme*, No. 12 (January, 1950), 112–114; Jean Kanapa, "Gendarmes et sirènes ou Violences et ruses des Versaillais," *La Nouvelle Critique*, No. 12 (January, 1950), 19–41; and Jean-T. Desanti, "Scruples et ruses d'Emmanuel Mounier," *La Nouvelle Critique*, No. 9 (October, 1949), 56–70.

[155] Roger Garaudy, "Nouvelle lettre à 'Esprit'" *La Nouvelle Critique*, No. 15 (April, 1950), 24.

[156] "Le jeu d''Esprit,'" *La Nouvelle Critique*, No. 15 (April, 1950), 30.

[157] *Pravda*, September 29, 1951, quoted in "'Esprit' et 'les Temps Modernes' vus par la 'Pravda,'" *Prevues*, No. 9 (November, 1951), 21; and, with a reply by the editor of *Esprit*, in J.-M. Domenach, "'Esprit' démasqué par la 'Pravda,'" *Esprit*, No. 186 (January, 1952), 68–70.

[158] See, for example, Mounier, "Le plan Marshal et l'avenir de la France," *Esprit*, No. 144 (April, 1948), 513; Mounier, "Déclaration de guerre," (November, 1948), *O.M.*, IV, 254–258;

and forthrightly against the Communists: the coup in Prague, the Rajk affair, Tito, and other events. In February, 1948 he asked: "is what is happening in Prague, in Bucharest, or in Sophia a form of liberation, of progress, of hope? A step toward social democracy?" His answer was an unequivocal no.[159]

Doubtless, what had contributed to the Communists' belief that they could enlist the support of men like Mounier and Bourdet was the latters' vigorous opposition to the anti-Communism of the Third Force. Mounier's reaction to the formation of the Third Force was consistent with his other political options. He failed to appreciate the difficulties the partners of the Communist Party had encountered during the period of tripartite government.[160] Instead, he emphasized the dire consequences that he believed would result from the exclusion of the Communists from the government.[161] More important still, he regarded the threat of Fascism which he discerned in the nascent *Rassemblement du Peuple Français* as more dangerous than that of Communist totalitarianism.[162] One of Mounier's critics has suggested that Mounier's early experience with the threat of both domestic and international Fascism during the 1930s may well have given him a life-long predisposition to exaggerate the menace of Fascism.[163]

Mounier's primary criticism of the Third Force was that its anti-Communism weakened the most effective anti-Fascist force in France. "As long as Communism in France receives so largely the confidence of the working class," Mounier contended, "as long as Socialism is so inconsistent and unfaithful, as long as the M.R.P. remains dominated by its conservative Right, to speak of effectively resisting Fascism without the Communists is foolishness." [164] Mounier's attack on the Third Force provoked a variety of responses. The most significant and well-reasoned response came from Etienne Borne.

In the exchange between Borne and Mounier that followed, Borne

Mounier, "Lettre à Constance Hyslop, 26 octobre 1948," *O.M.*, IV, 813–814; and Mounier, "Le mois des pacifiques," *Esprit*, No. 156 (June, 1949), 852–854.

[159] Mounier, "Prague" (February, 1948), *O.M.*, IV, 154.

[160] On these difficulties, see Einaudi and Goguel, *Christian Democracy*, 189–205.

[161] Mounier, "Faire-part de presse: séparation de corps," *Esprit*, No. 150 (November, 1948), 735–736.

[162] Mounier, "La pause des fascismes est terminée," *Esprit*, No. 140 (December, 1947), 797–799.

[163] Pierre de Boisdeffre, "Le drame d' 'Esprit,'" *Liberté de l'Esprit*, March, 1949, reprinted in Pierre de Boisdeffre, *Des vivants et des morts. Témoignages, 1948–1953* (Paris: Editions universitaires, 1954), 14–15.

[164] Mounier, "Réponse à quelques critiques," *Esprit*, No. 143 (March, 1948), 460. See also Mounier, "Devant nous," *Esprit*, No. 140 (December, 1947), 940–942; Mounier, "Troisième force (fin)," *Esprit*, No. 141 (January, 1948), 113–114.

scored a number of telling points against his adversary. He convicted Mounier of illogically proposing the idea of "no anti-totalitarianism without the collaboration of totalitarians" and of regarding only Fascism as an absolute evil.[165] He accused Mounier of accepting the Marxist explanation of Fascism as a defensive reflex of a moribund capitalist society and of sacrificing "purity for efficacy" by implicitly accepting Communist methods.[166] Finally, with obvious relish, the editor of l'aube pointed out that since the idea of a Third Force had originated with Mounier, Izard, and Déléage in 1932, Mounier had now placed himself in the strange position of the prophet who refuses the fulfillment of his prophecies.[167]

Mounier's response did not meet the most serious of Borne's charges. He objected to the perverted use to which the supporters of the Third Force had put the term. It was meant to denote a "Liaison des avant-gardes" and not a center or intermediary between the camps of the reactionaries and progressives, Mounier complained.[168] He denied that he accepted totalitarian methods, whether they were Fascist or Communist, and argued that Esprit wished to prepare "a new way" which was both anti-Fascist and non-Communist in order to construct a socialist order.[169] But he refused to recognize the Third Force defended by Borne as the instrument of this "new way." Although he suggested that he and Borne initiate a "creative dialogue," Borne correctly discerned that the dialogue Mounier had offered the Communists was not possible in the case of the men of the Third Force.[170]

Once again, as had happened in the past history of Esprit, Mounier refused to allow his journal to become a cadre of any organized political force, least of all a Christian democratic party. The members of Esprit could work ". . . in the M.R.P. to liberate it from its reactionary mortgages; in the Socialist Party to renew its virility; in the Communist Party in an attempt to graft on to it a new spirit which will uproot its scleroses and its fanaticisms," but Mounier himself believed that there was no political movement which was not being "stifled by the forces of inertia or foundering in the parliamentary morass." [171] Mouniei recognized that the absence of a movement which expressed the political

[165] Etienne Borne, "Pour un dialogue créateur," l'aube, January 18–19, 1948.
[166] Borne, "Le parti intellectuel contre la Troisième force."
[167] Ibid.
[168] Mounier, "Troisième force (fin)," 114.
[169] Mounier, "Délivrez-vous" (January, 1948), O.M., III, 631–632.
[170] Borne, "Pour un dialogue créateur."
[171] Mounier, "Premier signe: ie R.D.R.," Esprit, No. 143 (March, 1948), 462–463.

incidence of *Esprit* created a sense of malaise among his readers.[172] The kind of political dead-end that he invariably reached in his analyses of French political affairs understandably left his readers with the alternative of either abstaining from organized political activity altogether or forming their own political group. Coincident with the organization of the Third Force, a number of its opponents sought an outlet for their stifled political energies by organizing the *Union des Chrétiens Progressistes*. It was this group that provided the final and climatic chapter in Mounier's encounter with his "household demon" and in his relationship with the M.R.P.

The affaire of the *Chrétiens Progressistes* and Mounier's part in it are explicable only in the context of the general development of a current of *progressisme* within French Catholicism in the years immediately after the Liberation. The cases of Mounier and the *Chrétiens Progressistes* were but two instances – albeit probably the most important – of the attraction that Communism held for many Catholics during this period. In this respect, the words of an historian of French Catholicism cannot be improved upon. René Rémond writes that

the conviction that the Communist Party works in the direction of history, the generous desire to remain bound to the working class, a sincere desire to assure a Christian *présence* among the workers were at the origins of the progressivist adventure. Christian progressivism touched only a very limited number of Catholics, but it is undeniable that a much greater number of Catholics expressed illusory hopes of a conciliation between Communism and Christianity.[173]

The collaboration of Catholics and Communists in the Resistance, and the discovery of "the other" by Catholics in the same enterprise, predisposed many Catholics to continue to work with the Communists for a better City.[174] The term *progressiste* was used imprecisely and often in a purely polemical way. Many Catholics, like the men of *Témoignage Chrétien* and *Esprit*, were accused of being *progressiste*. But if the term *Chrétien Progressiste* was used widely and loosely, the most important men and organizations that were genuinely *progressiste* can be fairly clearly identified. Of the latter, the most significant during Mounier's life-time were an organization called *Jeunesse de l'Eglise*, led by Père Maurice Montuclard, a Dominican priest; Père Henri Desroches, another member of the Order of Saint Dominic; a number of the members

---

[172] Mounier, "Premier signe: 1e R.D.R.," 463.
[173] Latreille *et al.*, *Histoire du catholicisme*, III, 636.
[174] Duquesne, 382–391.

of the well-known priest-worker experiment; and the *Union des Chrétiens Progressistes* itself.

As early as 1936 Paul and Maurice Montuclard began to work with a small group of people and to concern themselves with the problem of the Church's abandonment of its tradition of communitarianism. It was, however, in the climate of Catholic-Communist collaboration during the Resistance that *Jeunesse de l'Eglise* was formally organized as both a community of religious and laymen, and a research center which began publishing a series of brochures in Lyons in 1942.[175] Like the other occupants of the *Chrétien Progressiste* current, the members of *Jeunesse de l'Eglise* based their activities on a far-reaching criticism of the sociological content of contemporary Christianity and a desire to construct a new and virile Christianity, both of which bore a marked resemblance to the general criticism and intentions of Mounier. Its founders stated that the group was organized "in reaction against a religion dehumanized by individualism" and intended to search for "a more communitarian Christianity and a new type of Christian man" in an effort to bring about a "Christian restoration." [176] Like Mounier also, the members of *Jeunesse de l'Eglise* looked to the working class to provide the creative energy necessary to build the virile Christianity for which they worked.

Mounier supported the early efforts of Montuclard's group. In 1940 he worked for over a week with Montuclard in Montverdun on the latter's project "to restore Christianity as a communitarian reality." [177] After the Liberation, Mounier praised *Jeunesse de l'Eglise* as "a powerful intellectual avant-garde" of French Catholicism and himself contributed to the group's journal.[178] In *Les événements et la foi*, a book published shortly after Mounier's death, Montuclard went well beyond the limits Mounier had maintained in his encounter with the Communists.[179] Confronted by the confidence that a large part of the working class demonstrated in the Communist Party, and at the same time attracted by that party's revolutionary *mystique*, Montuclard concluded that the Church should welcome both the working class and

175 On *Jeunesse de l'Eglise*, see Dansette, *Destin du catholicisme français*, 234–246; Robert Rouquette, "French Catholicism Confronts Communism," *Thought*, XXVIII, No. 110 (Autumn, 1953), 371–377; Rémond, "Catholicisme de droite et catholicisme de gauche," 215–216; and Duquesne, 391–393.

176 "Tâches d'aujourd'hui," *Jeunesse de l'Eglise*, No. 1 (1942), 7.

177 Mounier, "Entretiens X, 20 août 1940," *O.M.*, IV, 668–670.

178 Mounier, "Deux débats dans l'Eglise de France," *B.A.E.M.*, No. 9–10 (December, 1956), 26–28; and Mounier, "La place du philosophe," *Jeunesse de l'Eglise*, No. 10 (1949), 129–134.

179 Maurice Montuclard, *Les événements et la foi* (Paris: Editions du Seuil, 1951).

its Marxist ideology as the only means of reviving a sterile and moribund Christianity.[180] The Church, Montuclard contended, should return to "the time of St. John the Baptist":

> The human grandeur of Communism shows us that we need to relearn the proper grandeur of Christianity. The historical mission of Communism shows us that we must rediscover the real *raison d'être* of faith. Otherwise, we will never again feel the indispensable pride of being Christians. After we recognize what Communism brings to humanity, we need to be told clearly what Christ will bring to men who will owe their first liberation to Communism! [181]

Should not Christians wait for the Communist revolution to create the structures of a just City which the Church could then baptize?[182] As even two progressive – but not *progressiste* – French Catholics state, "by assuming that Communism was the exclusive instrument of history, the *Jeunesse de l'Eglise* group was led to make concessions to dialectical materialism which are hardly compatible with Christian theology." [183]

In a more forthright fashion, Montuclard's fellow Dominican Père Henri Desroches, of the social and economic study group *Economie et Humanisme*, attempted "to Christianize the Marxist synthesis." [184] In *Signification du marxisme*, Desroches attempted to discover what in Marxism could be absorbed into Christianity, basing this endeavor on the premise that atheism is accidental and not essential in the Marxist system.[185] In reviewing the book, Mounier was quick to point out the error in the author's primary assumption.[186] Although Desroches was involved in many *progressiste* activities, most notably the Communist-inspired *Mouvement de la paix* and the *Appel de Stockholm*, his ideas were far too complex to have more than limited influence. It was Montuclard who exercised a considerable influence on a number of the priest-workers.

Like the entire *Chrétien Progressiste* adventure, the priest-worker experiment was in large measure a result of the experience of the War and the Resistance.[187] The first priest-workers were chaplains sent by

---

[180] Rouquette, "French Catholicism Confronts Communism," 372.

[181] Montuclard, 71–72, quoted in Domenach and Montvalon, 72.

[182] Domenach and Montvalon, 70.

[183] *Ibid.*, 72. For an excellent critique of Montuclard, see Daniélou, *Lord of History*, 85–95.

[184] Henri Desroches, *Signification du marxisme* (Paris: Editions ouvrières, 1949).

[185] Rouquette, "French Catholicism Confronts Communism," 371.

[186] Mounier, "H.-C. Desroches: Signification du marxisme," *Esprit*, No. 159 (September, 1949), 464–466.

[187] Of the massive literature on the priest-worker experiment, the following works are of particular value: Pierre Andreu, *Grandeurs et erreurs des prêtres ouvriers*; Gregor Siefer, *The

the French hierarchy to attend the religious needs of the S.T.O. The contact made with the "de-Christianized" workers in the S.T.O., doubled by the results of a study by Abbés Henri Godin and Yvan Daniel entitled *La France pays de mission?*, led a number of priests to organize the *Mission de Paris* under the patronage of Emmanuel Cardinal Suhard, the Archbishop of Paris. These men and an increasingly large number of other priests from both the *Mission de France*, the missionary organization for metropolitan France, and the religious orders became workers in an effort to bridge the historic chasm between the Church and the working classes.[188] A number of the priest-workers deviated from their initial practice of *témoignage* and, in doing so, demonstrated the difficulty, if not the inherent ambiguity, involved in joining this practice with the a-politicism characteristic of Mounier. Some of them adopted the political positions of many of their fellow workers, joined the Communist-led *Confédération Générale du Travail*, supported Communist-inspired demonstrations and peace movements, attacked the C.F.T.C. and M.R.P., and accused the Church of supporting capitalism to the detriment of the "disinherited masses." Ultimately, some of them allowed their action of *présence* and their desire to ameliorate the social and economic conditions of the workers to take precedence over their purely sacerdotal duty of spiritual redemption – although the complex relationship between temporal progress and spiritual redemption was not clearly faced until the latter stages of the priest-worker experience. In this development the ideas of Montuclard's *Jeunesse de l'Eglise* were clearly in evidence.[189]

A student of the priest-workers points out that Mounier was "among the authors who may be regarded as having blazed a trail intellectually" for them.[190] Mounier's sympathies were obviously with these men of limitless charity and good will. He was a life-long friend of Bishop Guerry, one of the leading supporters in the French hierarchy of the priest-workers, and he was also an especially close friend of Abbé

Church and Industrial Society. A survey of the Worker-Priest Movement and its implications for the Christian Mission, trans. Isabel and Florence McHugh (London: Darton, Longman and Todd, 1964); Emile Poulat, *Naissance des prêtres ouvriers* (Paris: Casterman, 1965); *The Worker-Priests. A Collective Documentation*, trans. John Petrie (London: Routledge and Kegan Paul, 1956); and *Priest and Worker. The Autobiography of Henri Perrin*, trans. with a introduction by Bernard Wall (New York: Holt, Rinehart and Winston, 1964).

[188] On the *Mission de France*, see Jacques Faupin, *La Mission de France* (Paris: Casterman, 1960); and Jean-François Six, *Cheminements de la Mission de France, 1941–1966* (Paris: Editions du Seuil, 1967). There are no comparable studies of the *Mission de Paris*.

[189] See Dansette, *Destin du catholicisme français*, 238ff; and Andreu, *Grandeurs et erreurs des prêtres ouvriers*, 105ff.

[190] Siefer, 12.

André Depierre, a member of the *Mission de Paris*. To the special issue of *Esprit* devoted to "Monde moderne. Monde chrétien," Abbé Depierre contributed "an astonishing article which could be considered a sort of prophetic manifesto for the encounter between the Christian and modern worlds." [191] Although he could illafford it, two days before his death, Mounier sent a small contribution to Depierre to signify his complete support of the work of the *Mission de Paris*.[192]

Mounier also had friends among the members of the *Union des Chrétiens Progressistes* and he opened the pages of *Esprit* to them.[193] It was widely held that Mounier was the spiritual and intellectual parent of this crypto-Communist organization. The *Union des Chrétiens Progressistes* was organized in 1947 by a group of intellectuals led by André Mandouze, Henri Denis, Jean Verlhac, and others.[194] As related by Verlhac, its history

is the drama of a generation of students who believed in Christian democracy without really understanding it, who accepted the "revolutionary" slogans of the M.R.P. literally and, most important, who discovered the Communists and Communism during the Resistance. A brutal awakening took place in 1947 when the great "break" occurred; the return of the Communists to opposition, the Marshall Plan....

For them, the victory of the Resistance remained unfulfilled, "the Liberation had been betrayed," "the new and young force that the M.R.P. should have become was associated with this failure, thus forgetting its origins and its dead."

For them, "the same battle continues," a new battle resumed with the same allies or at least the only ones who have not betrayed it: the Communists.[195]

The *Union des Chrétiens Progressistes* was not a political party although four of its members sat in the National Assembly. In one sense it was "a slightly undisciplined branch of 'Christian democracy,'" in that its members demonstrated a certain "nostalgia for the projects of [Gilbert] Dru." [196] More properly, however, it represented a "state of spirit," a "sentimental disposition." Basic to the reflexes of the *Chrétiens Pro-*

---

[191] Domenach and Montvalon, 26.

[192] Mounier, "Lettre à l'abbé Depierre, 20 mars 1950," *O.M.*, IV,830–831.

[193] See, for example, Henri Denis, "Réponse. Y a-t-il une scolastique marxisme?," *Esprit*, No. 145 (May-June, 1948), 740–743; and Maurice Caveing, "Matérialisme classique et matérialisme dialectique," *Esprit*, No. 145 (May-June, 1948), 831–851.

[194] See Joseph Dusserre, "Réflexions sur l'affaire des 'Chrétiens progressistes,'" *Chronique sociale de France*, 59ᵉ année, No. 6 (November-December, 1949), 493–505; Dusserre, "L'histoire de la 'main tendue,'" 403–413; P. Bigo, "Le progressisme en France," *Revue de l'Action Populaire*, No. 88 (May, 1955), 513–528; and J.-P. Dubois-Dumée, "Les chrétiens progressistes vont-ils sortir de l'équivoque?," *Témoignage Chrétien*, December 15, 1950. J. M. Simon, *L'Impossible alliance. Communisme et progressisme en face de la foi chrétienne* (Paris: Librairie Arthème Fayard, 1954) contains much valuable information on the *Chrétiens Progressistes* in spite of its polemical tone.

[195] Verlhac summarized and quoted in Georges, "Le role politique des catholiques français," 150–151.

[196] *Ibid.*, 150, 153.

gressistes were a number of attitudes similar to those of Mounier and *Esprit:* a deep-rooted anti-capitalism and a condemnation of all institutions, parties, social classes, and nations which were thought to represent capitalism; a tendency towards "workerism," that is, to accept as just and sacrosanct all of the demands of the proletariat and to condemn whatever the proletariat condemned; a refusal to enter into the camp of the anti-Communists, based on the belief that to do so would injure the cause of the workers; and a conviction that the Church was intimately allied with capitalism and the bourgeoisie.[197]

Mounier forthrightly recognized the similarities between these positions and those of *Esprit.* He admitted that the economic and social positions adopted by the *Chrétiens Progressistes* were based upon *Esprit's* critique of the social and economic regime.[198] He agreed with two of the consequences that the *Chrétiens Progressistes* drew from these common positions: that revolutionary *engagement* was a necessity and that such *engagement* could not be carried on in separate or isolated Christian political or social groupings.[199] Beyond this, however, Mounier refused to accept the *Chrétien Progressiste* solution to the political dilemma that he himself had largely posed. The *Chrétien Progressiste* answer was practical collaboration with the Communist Party as the only means of defending the working class, of building a new popular democracy, and of dissociating the Church from the capitalist regime.[200] Rarely did a *Chrétien Progressiste* attempt to justify this position from a doctrinal point of view. André Mandouze adopted the motto, "to be *of* the Church, *in* progressivism, *with* the Communists," in an effort to justify *progressisme*,[201] He encountered numerous difficulties in attempting to validity this strange mélange, however, and failed to find a solution to at least one essential inconsistency. While he separated his religion from his politics, he attempted to justify the use of a term which linked the two together. He argued that

the spiritual belongs essentially, in a strict sense, to Christianity, as the political belongs, in a strict sense, to Marxism; and the Communist Party can no more quarrel with Christianity over the last ends of man, to the extent that religion is above all a *mystique* of ends, than the Church can contest Marxism's choice of its means of action, to the extent that politics is merely a discipline of means.[202]

---

[197] Dusserre, "L'histoire de la 'main tendue,'" 403–405.

[198] Mounier, "Les chrétiens progressistes" (November, 1948), *O.M.*, III, 636.

[199] Mounier, "Communistes chrétiens?" (July, 1947), *O.M.*, III, 620.

[200] "Manifeste de l'Union des Chrétiens progressistes, 15 novembre 1948," *la Vie intellectuelle* (February, 1949), 278–279.

[201] André Mandouze, "Prendre la main tendue," in Henri Guillemin *et al.*, *Les Chrétiens et la Politique* (Paris: Editions du Temps Présent, 1948), 58.

[202] *Ibid.*, 55.

Mandouze went on to argue that the very *raison d'être* of the term *Chrétien Progressiste* indicated that he and his friends did not separate their religion and their politics: they had Christian reasons for pursuing *progressiste* ends, Mandouze explained.[203]

Mounier's reaction to the *Chrétiens Progressistes* was immediate and unequivocal. When Henri Denis stated that he and his fellow *Chrétiens Progressistes* differed from their friends of *Esprit* only in proposing immediate revolutionary action, Mounier quickly replied.[204] He explained that "we do not think that the only revolutionary *engagement* is in the Communist Party, nor that the only revolutionary action is political action."[205] To use the term *Chrétien Progressiste*, Mounier said, "is to expose oneself to the politico-religious contaminations that we have fought against. . . . Christian progressivist or Communist, from this point of view, is the same as Christian democrat or Christian monarchist."[206] Coming from Mounier, few criticisms were more severe. In return, Mounier was attacked in *Des Chrétiens prennent position*, the journal of the *Union des Chrétiens Progressistes*, for a variety of supposed errors, among them for joining in the battle against Communism.[207]

In spite of his disclaimer, Mounier was immediately charged with being the progenitor of the *Chrétiens Progressistes*. *La France catholique*, *Epoque*, *Aurore*, and innumerable other journals and pamphlets identified *Esprit* as a *Chrétien Progressiste* journal and referred to Mounier as one of the movement's intellectual leaders. One critic asked rhetorically: "can a Christian attempt a spiritual rapprochement of Marxism and Communism?"[208] Another critic, who hid behind a *nom de plume*, attacked Mounier and Maritain as "the Catholics responsible for the Red collaboration" of French Catholics in general and the M.R.P. in particular."[209] One of the sources of many of the less vitriolic charges and insinuations against Mounier and *Esprit* was a series of articles on the relationship of Mounier and the *Chrétiens Progressistes* by Père Gaston Fessard, the Jesuit philosopher who was one of the foremost students of Marxism in France.

Fessard criticized Mounier in a lecture given at the *Centre catholique des intellectuels français*, and a lengthy debate between the Jesuit priest

[203] *Ibid.*, 58ff. See also Lacroix, "Un témoin et un guide," 36–43.
[204] Henri Denis, "Que doivent faire les catholiques?," *Action*, May 23, 1947, cited and discussed in Mounier, "Communistes chrétiens?," 620–625.
[205] Mounier, "Communistes chrétiens?," 621.
[206] Mounier, "Les chrétiens progressistes," 634.
[207] Mounier, "Lettre à Jean Verlhac, dans *Positions*, Mars 1950," *O.M.*, IV, 829.
[208] Pierre de Boisdeffre, "Le drame d''Esprit,'" 15.
[209] Michaël, 7 and 59–73 *passim*.

and Mounier ensued.[210] The gist of Fessard's criticism of Mounier may be briefly and simply summarized. First and foremost, Fessard charged that Mounier accepted the Marxist view of history. Even Mounier's friend Jean Daniélou criticized him for his tendency to define the "progress of the Church exclusively in terms of 'sanctifying the new shapes of the [history of the] world.'"[211] Fessard also charged that Mounier's inconsistent and erroneous doctrinal position on Marxism was responsible for the development of the *Chrétien Progressiste* movement itself. Mounier, Fessard complained, was creating "a little schism of the *Action française* variety." [212]

Mounier denied Fessard's charges and dissociated himself from both the theoretical and practical positions held by the *Chrétiens Progressistes*. Further suspicion was cast upon the orthodoxy of his attitude toward Communism, however, by ecclesiastical actions against the *Chrétiens Progressistes* in 1949. As a formal organization, the *Union des Chrétiens Progressistes* did not survive these blows although some of its members founded the short-lived bi-monthly *La Quinzaine* which, in turn, was condemned in 1955. During this period also, ecclesiastical measures were taken against Montuclard (who left the priesthood) and Desroches (who left the Church), the priest-worker experiment, and even against a number of prominent Jesuit and Dominican philosophers and theologians.

A key event in this general suppression of the more adventurous elements of the new Catholic Left was the issuance of the Papal encyclical *Humani Generis* of 1950. In a well-balanced examination of the encyclical, Henri Marrou "reminded the French Catholics that the generosity of Christians was no guarantee that they would not make mistakes, and that the faith of the Church should not be taken lightly by impatient innovators or supercilious integralists." [213] "What is under attack," Marrou said, "is not an original movement of thought so much as obvious deviations (often caricatured) that hasty popularization has engendered. We are in the paradoxial situation of having heresies with-

---

[210] This debate took place in: Gaston Fessard, *Le communisme va-t-il dans le sens de l'Histoire?*; Mounier, "Lettre à R. P. Fessard, mars 1948," *O.M.*, III, 637–643; Gaston Fessard, "Le christianisme des chrétiens progressistes," *Etudes*, CCLIX (January, 1949), 65–93; Mounier, "Lettre à R. P. Fessard, 22 janvier 1949," *O.M.*, III, 644–649; Mounier, "Les chrétiens progressistes," 650–651; Gaston Fessard, "Lettre à Emmanuel Mounier, 3 avril 1949," in Gaston Fessard, *De l'actualité historique* (Paris: Desclée de Brouwer, 1960), II, 419–429; and Gaston Fessard, "Réponse à E. Mounier," *Etudes*, CCLX (March, 1950), 394–399.

[211] Daniélou, *The Lord of History*, 94.

[212] Fessard, "Le christianisme des chrétiens progressistes," 93.

[213] Domenach and Montvalon, 98.

out heresiarchs." Marrou continued, however, by admitting that "it is we who bear the responsibility for the errors that have been condemned [by the encyclical] ... We must be honest enough to analyze our generation without flattery." Then Marrou made reference to the fact that

There are too many frightened spirits in Catholic circles who cannot seem to understand that error – or, if one insists, heresy – is an inevitable by-product of any creative doctrinal speculation.... These people confuse orthodoxy and lazy-mindedness, doctrinal accuracy and the memorizing of formulas, and, in order to avoid error, are glad to give up thinking and would like others to do the same.[214]

In the climate created by these events, *Esprit* itself was once again rumored to be on the verge of condemnation.[215]

In commenting on a decree of the Holy Office in July, 1949 which prohibited Catholics from joining Communist and Communist-dominated organizations, Mounier discerned no reason to repudiate his earlier views on Communism.[216] Indeed, he reaffirmed them and said simply that Church officials would determine whether or not they conformed to the spirit of the decree. In his judgment, the decree prohibited Catholics from freely and clearly adhering to the Communist Party and from collaborating with the Communists in such a way as to contribute to the construction of a "materialist and atheist" Communist regime. He complained of "the politico-religious phariseeism" which used the decree for its own economic and political purposes. And he concluded by affirming: "We have never refused, and we will never refuse, to say that white is white, even when the Communists are the only ones to say so in a given situation. We have never refused to join our action to that of the Communists for a just peace in Vietnam, for justice in Madagascar." On the other hand, however, Mounier refused to accept any responsibility for the excesses of the *Chrétiens Progressistes*. He wrote: "We are not tutors and they are not infants. If some of them, starting with our common positions, follow paths that we ourselves refuse, they do so on their own responsibility." [217]

Nonetheless, the charges levelled against Mounier by several of his most astute and sympathetic critics were not without substance. Père

---

[214] Henri Marrou, "Humani Generis," *Esprit*, No. 172 (October, 1950), 562–570, trans. in *ibid.*, 98–101. See also Robert Barrat, "Reaction to the Encyclical," *The Commonweal*, LII, No. 26 (October 6, 1950), 628–630.

[215] Latreille *et al.*, *Histoire du catholicisme*, III, 637; Lepp, *Espoirs et déboires du progressisme*, 292–293; and François, "La revue qui a formé une génération chrétienne," 13.

[216] Mounier, "Le décret du Saint-Office" (August, 1949), *O.M.*, III, 654–663. See also Pelissier, "Mounier et les communistes," 105–109.

[217] Mounier, "Les chrétiens progressistes," 636.

Jean Daniélou described the malaise created by certain issues of *Esprit* and the *Chrétien Progressiste* journal *Positions* among many young Christians:

Having broken decisively with the capitalist world, desirous of a revolution which will install a new human order, having moreover acquired a taste for direct action in the Resistance, they have experienced for some time a growing lassitude in the face of the impotence of the old parties in undertaking that revolution and in freeing themselves from the compromises – or the scruples – which paralyze them. Only the Communist Party appears at the present time to represent a force sufficiently revolutionary to undertake the transformation to which they aspire. Certainly, the Marxist vision of things is far from satisfying to them. They are spiritualist, Marxism is materialist. Moreover, they are clear-headed enough to perceive the dangers of servitude that Communism carries with it. . . . [But] they believe it more urgent to battle against reaction than to battle against materialism. They place the revolution of man before bearing witness to God.[218]

Similarly, Père Robert Rouquette wrote that

Mounier, the pedagogue of action, has no concrete action to propose. He does not wish to be a tribune, a political leader. But most of those who are instilled with his revolutionary ardor cannot content themselves with an action of purification, of orientation, of demystification like that of the editor of *Esprit*. It is necessary for them to act more concretely and politically. . . . What ways are offered them? The Christian democrats? Mounier has only sarcasm [for them] . . . . Not the S.F.I.O., certainly, an old hack that survives, saddled with moth-eaten old dogmatisms, a party of little bureaucrats cut off from the proletarian masses. What remained? How could these youths not turn to the Communist Party that had been presented to them [by Mounier] as a generous and rich élan. . . . Immediately Mounier cried hold up. . . . But it is he who, without wanting to, has led these young Christians to opt for Communism.[219]

Logically these analyses of the political choice of the disciples of Mounier seem unassailable. At the very least, Mounier's insistence on the need for action combined with his opposition to all political parties, except for his reserved friendliness for the Marxists, posed a dilemma for his followers. For those who believed political action necessary, collaboration with or even membership in the Communist Party seemed a logical choice. There is remarkably little evidence, in spite of widespread criticism similar to that of Daniélou and Rouquette, that any significant number of young Catholics in France adopted a Communist or crypto-Communist position as a result of Mounier's influence.[220] In

218 Daniélou, *Dialogues avec Les Marxistes, Les Existentialistes, Les Protestants, Les Juifs, L'Hindouisme*, 30–32.

219 Rouquette, "Positions et oppositions d'Emmanuel Mounier," 152–153. See also Frederick C. Copleston, "Mounier, Marxism and Man," *The Month*, CXCII, No. 1010 (October, 1951), 207; and Archambault, "Du personnalisme au marxisme: une aventure spirituelle," 481–489.

220 See, for example, Pierre de Boisdeffre, "Le drame d'*Esprit*," 16; Borne, "Emmanuel

one instance, the poet Marc Beigbeder attributed his membership in the Communist Party to his association with *Esprit* and the influence of Mounier. In the words of a critic of *Esprit*, Beigbeder's *Lettre à "Esprit"* "describes the progress of a Christian conscience towards the Communist religion." [221] This accusation was immediately denied by Albert Béguin, Mounier's successor as editor of *Esprit*, in much the same terms that Mounier himself used.[222] Even granting Beigbeder's case, the evidence is much too fragmentary to convict Mounier of providing the impetus for many young Catholics to join or work closely with the Communist Party. Indeed, there is evidence of precisely the opposite – of a young Communist becoming a Christian as the result Mounier's influence.[223] Similarly, Ignace Lepp, a Marxist intellectual, joined the Catholic Church because of the "intellectual excellence" and "philosophical and historical erudition" of a man like Emmanuel Mounier.[224]

This is not to say, of course, that the *Chrétiens Progressistes* did not owe a debt to Mounier and *Esprit*. They borrowed his criticism of "the established disorder" and included the Christian democrats in it. In this respect, Mounier's influence weakened the M.R.P. in a very concrete manner. Even Ignace Lepp admits that

if the Mouniers, the Mandouzes, and certain others had joined [the Christian democrats]... I, for my part, am persuaded that most of the deceptions with which we have charged the M.R.P. would never have had occasion to appear. Instead of this, since 1945, *Esprit* undertook, with reference to the M.R.P., a purely negative criticism.... The practical result of this attitude has been the estrangement from the M.R.P. of numerous progressives who had originally belonged to it, while the position of those who remained faithful to it has become more difficult and their influence within the Movement smaller and smaller.... These Leftist elements, by quitting the party not only condemned themselves to political ineffectiveness, but assumed equally a large part of the responsibility for the M.R.P.'s movement to the Right.[225]

The heightening crescendo of criticism of his supposed leadership of the entire *Chrétien Progressiste* movement and its debilitating effects upon

Mounier juge de la démocratie chrétienne," 70–71; and Gaëtan Bernoville, "Catholic Thought in France," *The Dublin Review*, No. 450 (Fourth Quarter, 1950), 19.

[221] Louis Salleron, "The Temptation to Marxism. 'Esprit' without Mounier," *The Tablet* (London) (October 27, 1951), 288.

[222] See Beigbeder, *Lettre à "Esprit"* and *Les vendeurs du temple*; Albert Béguin, "Temptation to Marxism," *The Tablet* (London), December 15, 1951; Albert Béguin, "Réponse à une 'Lettre,'" *Esprit*, No. 185 (December, 1951), 792–797; and "Réponse de Marc Beigbeder," *Les Lettres Nouvelles*, 4ᵉ année, No. 41 (September, 1956), 342–351.

[223] P.-R. Régamey, *Portrait spirituel du chrétien* (Paris: Editions du Cerf, 1963), 451.

[224] Ignace Lepp, *Atheism in Our Time*, trans. Bernard Murchland (New York: The Macmillan Company, 1963), 25; and Ignace Lepp, *From Karl Marx to Jesus Christ*, (New York: Sheed & Ward, 1958), xi-xii, 212.

[225] Lepp, *Espoirs et déboires du progressisme*, 100–101.

the M.R.P. did not cause Mounier to alter his position in any way. In February, 1950 Mounier told the *Esprit* groups in their *Journal intérieur* that they should make every effort to maintain contact "with what is living among the Communists" and to prevent "the fatal break between Communism and the rest of the country." [226] In this effort, he said, they should sacrifice "*all* save honor." Mounier himself gave substance to his words by remaining accessible, as he had always been, both in his person and intellect, to all those who sought his aid or advice.[227] In spite of two heart attacks, the first in September, 1949 and the second in February 1950, Mounier's exhausting round of activities never slackened.

On March 20, 1950 Mounier performed a characteristic act when he wrote Abbé André Depierre of the *Mission de Paris*:

I am very concerned that, together, we discover a means of entering into the sufferings and struggles of the workers.... We have vainly tried to work for Truth and Justice, but we are not entirely with Christ so long as we do not take our place along side these outcasts.... With *Esprit*, I must in some way be near you if I am to achieve this end. Do not think that in asking this of you I want to make a token payment for a clear conscience; but I would like, with my wife, to give at least a little, and to prepare myself for the day on which events will perhaps impel us to give everything....[228]

Four days later the recipient of this letter celebrated a Mass for the repose of the soul of Emmanuel Mounier in the little church at Châtenay-Malabry. Two days after writing his last letter to Abbé Depierre and enclosing a small contribution, Mounier suffered a fatal heart attack.

In that little church on March 24, 1950 a number of eminent men gathered to pay their last respects to Mounier. In addition to Mounier's personal friends from *Esprit*, there were, among others, a Nobel Prize winner, a Senator, and a former Minister of State.[229] In the cemetery afterwards, at least one of those present turned his thoughts to a man who had died and was buried in far different circumstances and yet for the same cause. Mounier's old friend Pierre-Henri Simon later recalled that

When, some weeks ago in front of Emmanuel Mounier's tomb, we wanted to address to our admirable friend what would have been his own highest form of praise, the thought that came forth most readily from the bottom of our hearts

[226] Quoted in Goguel, "Positions politiques," 818.
[227] Quoted in *ibid*.
[228] Mounier, "Lettre à l'abbé Depierre, 20 mars 1950," *O.M.*, IV, 830–831.
[229] "La mort d'Emmanuel Mounier," *Esprit*, No. 167 (May, 1950), 894–896.

was that Mounier was the only man of our times who deservedly occupied, with the nuances peculiar to this own temperament and intelligence, the place of Péguy.[230]

It is only with an eye cast on the far-off figure of Lieutenant Charles Péguy lying face up in the mud of the Marne – on the man who had also condemned the Catholic party of his day in the name of truth and justice – that any assessment of the heritage of Mounier and the effect of his example and criticism upon the Christian democrats may be made. In his "Heureux ceux," Péguy had written his epitaph and Mounier's as well:

Blessed are those who died in great battles,
Stretched out on the ground in the face of God.[231]

[230] l'aube, May 8, 1950.
[231] Péguy, Basic Verities, 203.

CHAPTER VII

THE HERITAGE OF MOUNIER:
THE CHRISTIAN LEFT AND THE DEATH OF
CHRISTIAN DEMOCRACY

> Le monde est silloné d'influences. De vastes jeux s'y jouent
> qui se joueront de nous si nous ne les maitrisons pas. Nous
> ne donnerons, il est vrai, que ce que l'on acceptera. Nous ne
> choisirons que ce que nous désirons déjà au trefonds de
> nous-mêmes. Mais dans l'humble tâtonnement comme dans
> la maitrise virile s'affirme la même vocation humaine:
> discerner, choisir, transfigurer.
>
> Mounier, "L'Action intellectuelle ou de l'Influence," 1931–
> 1932.

The death of Emmanuel Mounier brought an outpouring of tributes to
the man and his work that equalled or surpassed those paid to Léon
Blum and Marc Sangnier, both of whom died within a short time of
Mounier. In the judgment of one of his friends, Mounier's death was a
far greater loss than that of Blum, for, unlike the grand old man of
French Socialism, Mounier died when he was comparatively young and
at the height of his power. "No one, alas, will be able to take Mounier's place," he said.[1] Typical of the heartfelt reaction of the veterans
of *Esprit* was that of Hélène Iswolsky. "How soon he has left us!" she
wrote.[2] In a similar vein, a friend of thirty years standing complained
that "Mounier seems to have left us at the moment when a generation
had the greatest need of him." [3] And Adrian Miatlev, the Russian-
born poet, confessed in a letter to a friend that although he had never
been especially close to Mounier, he had cried for a day following Mounier's funeral. "It began," Miatlev wrote, "at Châtenay-Malabry where
we accompanied Emmanuel Mounier to the cemetery after the funeral
mass. Inconceivable, an inconceivable thing! I am surprised at my own
grief, and many others are also. I cried like an old woman who finds
peace through tears. ... I have never missed anyone so much." [4]

The tributes given Mounier were unusual. Rare were those like a
writer in *La Croix* of Langres who suggested that "it is time to put an

---

[1] Claude Bourdet, "Two Costly Deaths," *The Nation*, 170, No. 15 (April 15, 1950), 348.

[2] Hélène Iswolsky, "Emmanuel Mounier," *The Commonweal*, LII, No. 4 (May 5, 1950), 92.

[3] Daniélou, "La mort d'Emmanuel Mounier," 250.

[4] Adrian Miatlev, letter dated March 24, 1950, quoted in Pierre Boujut, "Les lettres de
l'être," *La Tour de Feu*, No. 90–91 (June, 1966), 38.

end to the eulogies received by the editor of *Esprit*"; or like Roger Garaudy who accused Mounier of having been an agent of anti-Communism.[5] From other Communist spokesmen, on one hand, to a writer in *La Croix*, on the other, there was unanimity with regard to the integrity and good will of the founder of *Esprit*. In *l'Humanité*, Mounier was criticized for having refused the hand offered him by the Party, and *Esprit* was invited to leave the impasse created by its founder; but the same writer praised Mounier for his genuine attachment to the working class and to the cause of peace and national independence.[6] With similar reservations, the men of *La Nouvelle Critique* paid tribute to Mounier's sincerity and good will.[7] In *La Croix* Luc Estang wrote that he believed some of the practical positions of Mounier were debatable, but he added: "Even when one was not in agreement with him, one could not but render homage to his scrupulous intellectual honesty and to his respect for his adversary." [8]

Similar convictions were expressed in the pages of *Le Monde, Le Figaro, la France catholique, Epoque, La Jeune-République, l'aube, Franc-Tireur*, and dozens of other newspapers and journals.[9] The editors of *Les Temps Modernes* paid tribute to Mounier as the first practitioner of that *pensée engagée* which they themselves later recognized.[10] Even in *La Revue Socialiste*, there were kind words for the man who had few such words for the Socialist Party. Jacques Bois declared that Mounier was "a very noble individual." While he denied any intention of "annexing" Mounier, Bois contended that "Mounier was basically a socialist." [11] Then, after a short but extremely sympathetic review of Mounier's last book on personalism, Bois concluded:

There is in France, independent of organized parties, an opinion attracted to the great cause of social and economic justice at the same time that it is firmly attached to the values of liberty, of political liberty and liberty of conscience particularly. Men like Mounier have done much to extend and improve the clarity, vigor and efficacy of this opinion. To this cause of human emancipation and human advancement, Mounier gave all of his efforts. *He gave his life for it.* Can a more beautiful eulogy be conceived of? [12]

---

[5] Quoted in "La mort d'Emmanuel Mounier," 895, and in J.-M. D. [Domenach], "Le vieux langage," *Esprit*, New Series, No. 2 (February, 1968), 343.

[6] *L'Humanité*, March 23, 1950, cited in "La mort d'Emmanuel Mounier," 895.

[7] "'Esprit' jette le masque," *La Nouvelle Critique*, No. 15 (April, 1950), 18–19.

[8] *La Croix*, March 24, 1950, reprinted in "Deux hommes sont morts," *La documentation catholique*, No. 1069 (May 21, 1950).

[9] For a survey of press tributes to Mounier, see Georges Bouyx, "Hommages à Emmanuel Mounier," *l'aube*, March 24, 1950.

[10] "Mort d'Emmanuel Mounier," *Les Temps Modernes*, No. 54 (April, 1950), 1906.

[11] Jacques Bois, "Le personnalisme d'Emmanuel Mounier," *La Revue Socialiste*, New Series, No. 37 (May, 1950), 459.

[12] *Ibid.*, 462. See also Philippe Luc-Verbon, "Emmanuel Mounier," *La Revue Socialiste*, New Series, No. 44 (February, 1951), 240–243.

Although such hymns of praise were not, by any means, louder in the Catholic press than elsewhere, in the former the consensus was that, for better or worse, Mounier had been the intellectual master of a generation of French Catholics. Joseph Folliet expressed his belief that with Mounier's death, the Péguy of his generation was gone.[13] Mounier's friend and adversary, Etienne Borne, made reference to the deep-rooted "misunderstanding" that had separated Mounier from the M.R.P., but Borne admitted that he and many of the militants of Christian democracy "owe the best in themselves to the pre-war *Esprit* groups." [14] Louis Terrenoire, a Gaullist dissident from the M.R.P., said that *Esprit* was the intellectual center of Left-wing Catholicism and that "the pioneers of *Esprit* have become intellectual masters whose students are numberless, even among theologians." [15]

The leaders of the Catholic Left were even more generous in paying homage to Mounier. One of the leaders of the *Chrétiens Progressistes* recorded his contention that "for Catholics of the generations after the Liberation, the example of Emmanuel Mounier is even more important [than that of Marc Sangnier] and without doubt he represents one of the first Christians who was a man of the Left and was recognized as such by the Left." [16] In the judgment of Georges Suffert, who was too progressive even for *Témoignage Chrétien*, "without the perseverance of a man like Mounier, the movement [of Left-wing Catholicism] in its entirety would never have discovered its key ideas, its justifications, its hopes." [17] In his autobiography, Père Ignace Lepp, who was to be best known for his study of the modern varieties of unbelief, also paid tribute to Mounier.[18]

For entirely different reasons, but with equal emphasis, the opponents of Mounier among Catholics of the Right testified to the decisive role *Esprit* had played in reorienting the social and political complexion of Catholicism in France. One polemicist wrote that the "role in the front rank of French Catholicism assumed [by Mounier] at the time of

---

[13] Fr. Geniève [Joseph Folliet], "Emmanuel Mounier," *Témoignage Chrétien*, March 31, 1950.

[14] Etienne Borne, "Une philosophie ouverte: le personnalisme," *l'aube*, March 25–26, 1950.

[15] Louis Terrenoire, "Réponse. Catholiques de droite? Catholiques de gauche?," *Chronique sociale de France*, 64ᵉ année, No. 7–8 (December, 1956), 724–726.

[16] Jacques Chatagner, "Réponse. Catholiques de droite? Catholiques de gauche?," *Chronique sociale de France*, 64ᵉ année, No. 7–8 (December, 1956), 707.

[17] Georges Suffert, *Les catholiques et la gauche* (Paris: François Maspero, 1960), 125, 121.

[18] Lepp, *Atheism in Our Time*, 158. See also Lepp, *From Karl Marx to Jesus Christ*, xi-xii, 212.

the Liberation was conserved and kept even from
ism acted like a microbe which spreads in the bl
poisoning. Our infection can be measured by th
tributed to the preparer of this bouillon of gern
critic wrote that "*Esprit* is the most important r
one, the 'center of ralliement' whose ideas, bro
belong to the censored theories [of the *Chrétiens Progress....*
in Jacques Madiran's Integralist journal *Itinéraires,* one of the doctrinaires of his school said that "our justifiable opposition to the work of
Mounier is one thing. Our respect for his person and his memory, our
admiration for the example of Christian life that he gave to his neighbor, that he still gives from beyond the grave, is something else." [21]

To this chorus, veterans of *Action Française* added their refrains.
Robert Havard de la Montagne lashed out at the pernicious influence
of Mounier and *Esprit.*[22] Henri Massis, another and better-known
devotée of Maurras, interspersed his account of *Maurras et notre temps*
with attacks on Mounier, whom he associated with the Christian democrats.[23] But even from this quarter came words of praise for Mounier.
Shortly after Mounier's death, Thierry Maulnier praised him as a
man who loved justice "with the passion and imprudence, and perhaps
the injustice of love." "Emmanuel Mounier," Maulnier continued,
"was a man worthy of esteem: one of the most disinterested of our
time: neither ambition, the desire to build a career, money, honors, nor
literary glory had a hold over him. ..." [24]

That Mounier meant different things to different men is a point
which is too obvious to belabor. Mounier's friends and associates, nonetheless, cast light upon one of the most important sources of his influence and prestige. In their recollections, certain descriptions of
Mounier's character appear and reappear. Ignace Lepp, for example,
referred to "dear" Mounier, as did Georges Bernanos in a far less favorable way.[25] In recounting an interesting and revealing incident in

[19] Calbrette, 32.

[20] Ducaud-Bourget, 128.

[21] Marcel Clément, "Emmanuel Mounier (II)," *Itinéraires,* No. 36 (September-October, 1959), 76.

[22] Robert Havard de la Montagne, *Histoire de "l'Action Française"* (Paris: Amiot-Du-mont, 1955), 125–126, 174.

[23] Massis, *Maurras et notre temps,* 88, 295–297, 350.

[24] Thierry Maulnier, "L'esprit d'Emmanuel Mounier," *Hommes et Mondes* (May, 1950), 125.

[25] Lepp, *From Karl Marx to Jesus Christ,* 212; and Georges Bernanos, "Une exposition Charles de Foucauld," *La Bataille,* May 29, 1946, reprinted in Georges Bernanos, *Français, si vous saviez* (Paris: Gallimard, 1961), 165.

...nier's life, François Mauriac used the same adjective:

...read in *Combat* that Mrs. Clare Booth Luce is to be named ambassador from ...the United States to Rome. Not without great distress, I asked myself if this is the same Catholic woman who invited Emmanual Mounier and myself to breakfast, Saturday, November 12, 1949, to sound us out on the preventive use of the atomic bomb. To be truthful, she did not tell us whether she would approve of it, but she saw at first glance our amazement that a Christian would even pose the question. *If dear Mounier had not been there, and if I had not been afraid of shocking him,* I would have pretended to lean in the direction of half-approval to see how far the woman would go. Mounier and I had been cool towards one another, but during this grim breakfast we realized how close to one another we had remained.[26]

Mauriac's fear of offending or shocking Mounier was an understandable reaction to one of the most deceptive facets of Mounier's complex character. In a curious but superficial way, Mounier seems to have possessed some of the traits that he condemned so vigorously in the "Christian democratic temperament." In his case, however, what appeared to be a certain timidity was, in fact, an intellectual honesty which made him recognize the part of truth inherent in the most disparate or conflicting of views; what appeared to be a certain docility was an ability and willingness to listen to another point of view, to take into account new facts and to adjust his own position accordingly; and what appeared to be a certain naïveté was a remarkable openness when confronting new people and new ideas.

A personal meeting with Mounier was often an extraordinary and memorable experience. A French Canadian recollects meeting Mounier in the little office of *Esprit* while he was a student visiting Paris in 1936. "The first greeting was reserved," he recalls, "he had no physical warmth, but his eyes disseminated intelligence. I tried to talk to him about his books. The great philosopher possessed an unbelievable modesty. He was too preoccupied with his work to be preoccupied with his books." Later, on the eve of his departure from Paris and tired and depressed by the impersonal nature of the contacts he had made, the young man invited Mounier to dine with him. To his surprise, Mounier accepted. "There was no physical exuberance about him, but a profound sincerity, the private source of recognizing in the visiting student a man with his own personal problems." [27] When Mounier returned briefly to teaching after the fall of France, one of his students remem-

---

[26] François Mauriac, "9 fevrier 1953," *Bloc-Notes, 1952–1957* (Paris: Gallimard, 1958), 13. Italics added. See also Duméry, "Hommage à Mounier," 17. Duméry does not identify Mrs. Luce by name but rather as "an American woman, a convert to Catholicism, very powerful in the press, destined for high diplomatic responsibilities."

[27] André Laudrendau, "Mounier, 1936," *Le Devoir* (Montreal), April 15, 1950.

bers that "much more than his method of teaching, it was his example which impressed us. For it was a beautiful sight to see this man face and 'confront' an idea. No bias, no subterfuge: an honest contest, an unsparing lucidity for himself as for the other. ...." [28] During the same period, a priest met Mounier and later recalled that

He seemed to cultivate especially the art of listening. But the manner of his attention was very special. He leaned a little, his head slightly forward; his eyes followed the presentation of a problem from afar.... Occasionally a rapid flick of the eyelids, a wrinkled brow, and then he fixed his eyes upon the eyes of the speaker in a way that was not in the least disconcerting. The other person then knew that Mounier had understood and, above all, that he had understood him with his moral or intellectual difficulty, his very personal little drama.[29]

When Mounier's eyes looked away, however, it was a clear sign that his visitor had drifted off into matters of only literary or philosophical interest. "When his eyes were fixed upon those of the other person, the human had been reached and everything was different." Mounier was then, this man recalled, "a friend forever." [30]

Gabriel Germain, a professor in the University of Rabat who had followed *Esprit* since its founding, was struck by Mounier's receptiveness to the ideas and inquiries of others – "it is so rare among our intellectuals!" [31] Germain met Mounier only once, in June, 1948, and spoke with him about Morocco:

I approached him, I confess, with the kind of apprehension that one always experiences when confronting someone to whom one is close and yet separated by the experience of a very different life.... I am now reviewing that conversation we had in the park at Châtenay in which we walked round and round among the wild flowers and tall grass. My apprehension was vain. The entente was immediate.... When one had known Mounier only through his articles or his doctrinal works, one could be apprehensive of seeing the *agrégé* in philosophy reappear in him occasionally. Now I found before me a man who feared no reality, who welcomed even strangers and made friends of them.... One perceived in his eyes, in the movement of his curled brow, that great effort of the loyal worker who wants to know in order to understand, and to understand in order to act.[32]

Yet another man, who was obviously prepared to be intimidated by the mere presence of Mounier, recalls that

the youngest generation of *Esprit*, those who knew Mounier only after the war, is perhaps in the best position to testify to his simplicity and to his extraordinary receptiveness. Here was a man whose influence and audience were international,

---

[28] "Notes de l'abbé Jacques Gallay," *E.M.*, *1905–1950*, 1018.
[29] "Souvenirs de l'abbé Henri Perrin," *E.M.*, *1905–1950*, 1018.
[30] *Ibid.*
[31] Gabriel Germain, *Le regard intérieur* (Paris: Editions du Seuil, 1968), 181.
[32] "Témoignage de Gabriel Germain," *E.M.*, *1905–1950*, 1055–1056.

whose thought, action, and responses served as beacons for tens of thousands of consciences, and whom one could approach like a person of no importance. . . . This complete absence of pose, this unique modesty always amazed me. The spirit of camaraderie with the young was natural to him. No effort was required. . . . This invincible youthfulness of character was expressed on occasion in conversation by boyish pleasantries of gentle irony, even by ordinary puns which perhaps would have astonished readers accustomed to his seriousness. And how he could smile.[33]

There is little doubt that Mounier possessed a rare capacity for friendship in the strict and very best sense of the word.[34] In his own person, he manifested those convictions, that ability for genuine dialogue, and that consistent willingness to confront men, ideas, and events which enabled his journal and movement to survive and increase their prestige and influence. Occasionally, however, his printed words aroused misgivings and even antagonism among readers who did not know him personally. "Emmanuel Mounier had never been for me anything other than a translucent being, rather vapid and remote," one man confesses. But he adds parenthetically that "this is one of those false ideas that one conjures up in the absence of meaningful encounters."[35] Another veteran of *Esprit* has recalled his first contact with both Mounier and his journal. While a young teacher in the Lycée Henri-IV, Pierre-Aimé Touchard was introduced to the first issue of *Esprit* by a fellow teacher who was extremely enthusiastic about the new journal. Touchard found Mounier's style and frame of reference somewhat irritating; and later he accused Mounier of conceit and overweening pride. After a meeting with the young editor of *Esprit*, however, Touchard became a life-long friend, colleague, and, by his own admission, pupil of Mounier.[36]

Mounier was, of course, an extraordinarily prolific writer, but whether or not he was a great writer has been questioned even by his admirers. Joseph Folliet, for example, believes that "Mounier sacrificed the writer that he could have been to the man of action that he would like to have been. This is one of his dramas – and perhaps that of his entire generation. He similarly sacrificed the writer that he could have been to the journalist that the requirements of a review obliged him to be. . . ."[37]

[33] "Témoignage de Jean Guichard-Meili," *E.M.*, *1905–1950*, 1054–1055. See also Duméry, "Hommage à Mounier," 11–12.

[34] Ignace Lepp, *The Psychology of Loving*, trans. Bernard B. Gilligan (Baltimore, Md.: Helicon, 1963), 201.

[35] Pierre Boujut, "Les lettres de l'être," 25.

[36] Touchard, "Dernier dialogue," 777–779. See also Jean Baboulène, "Emmanuel Mounier et le mouvement catholique," *La Revue Nouvelle*, XI, No. 5 (May 15, 1950), 524ff.

[37] Folliet, "Emmanuel Monier," 355–356.

In recounting a trip from Paris to Lille that he and Mounier once took, Pierre-Henri Simon casts light upon Mounier's remarkable dedication to his journal. Simon and Mounier had hardly settled in the third class compartment of their train than Mounier sat forward on the edge of his seat, took a notebook and pencil from his large black briefcase, and then began to write. Scarcely making any corrections, Mounier did not so much as raise his head until the train approached its destination, and then he said to his companion: "It is finished." [38]

The posthumous publication of many of Mounier's letters and personal journals, first in a special commemorative issue of *Esprit* in December, 1950, and then more extensively in *Mounier et sa génération* in 1956 leaves little doubt that Mounier was one of the great spiritual writers of his generation. The reception given *Mounier et sa génération* was one of almost unanimous praise.[39] Albert Béguin, the eminent literary critic, said that he knew Mounier best after his death.[40] Making reference primarily to Mounier's letters and journals, another man writes simply that "personally, the more I frequent his work, the greater is my admiration for it." [41] And Jean-Marie Domenach thinks it fortunate that members of the new generations often first encounter Mounier through the medium of his letters and personal journals – in the pages of *Mounier et sa génération* "which is a book of life much more than of thought." [42]

Fragmentary and sympathetic though it is, such testimony suggests that Mounier's influence was intensive and personal, as Mounier intended it to be. The circulation of *Esprit* also lends support to this conclusion. During the 1930s, the circulation of *Esprit* never exceeded 3,000 to 4,000; during the immediate postwar period, it was between 12,000 and 15,000; and, as late as 1964, the circulation ranged between 15,000 and 19,000.[43] Even allowing for the probability that a single copy of *Esprit*, especially of the special issues, was often read by more than one subscriber or one purchaser at the corner kiosk, this was not a large circulation. One estimate places the total readership of the journal at

---

[38] Simon, "Emmanuel Mounier et le personnalisme d'*Esprit*," 24–25.

[39] A bibliography of the reviews of *Mounier et sa génération* is contained in *B.A.E.M.*, No. 9–10 (December, 1956), 30–32.

[40] Albert Béguin, "Lettre à Collete Paulet, le 22 avril 1954," *Esprit*, No. 268 (December, 1958), 899–900.

[41] Régamey, 446.

[42] Domenach, "Présence de Mounier," 218. See also Folliet, "Emmanuel Mounier," 355–356; and Moix, 326.

[43] *Ibid.*, 220; Lacroix, "Un témoin et un guide," 34–35; and Touchard, "La gauche non communiste," 315.

40,000 to 50,000.[44] But the caliber of both the collaborators and the readers of *Esprit* was unusually high. The graduates and faculty of such lycées as Henri-IV and Louis-le-Grand assume positions of leadership in many areas of French life. The early companions of Mounier pursued careers in administration, diplomacy, literature, and teaching, although the bulk of both the collaborators and readership of the journal was composed largely of academicians.[45] After Mounier's death, Albert Béguin became editor of *Esprit*, although some of Mounier's older friends expressed misgivings about continuing publication of the journal.[46] During Béguin's editorship, literary preoccupations were ascendant in the pages of *Esprit*, although, of course, literature had always been among Mounier's wide-ranging interests. With the death of Béguin in 1957 and his replacement by Jean-Marie Domenach, the *Esprit* team was reorganized.[47] At this juncture "the center of gravity of *Esprit* moved from the University to Administration and to journalism," and increasingly young Counsellors of State, Inspectors of Finance, and other men who possessed technical skills joined *Esprit*.[48]

The continued importance of *Esprit* and the remarkable posthumous fame of its founder might easily lend themselves to the conclusion that Mounier's fear that his journal might become "the *Revue des Deux Mondes* of personalism" was fully justified. At the time of Mounier's death, there were *Esprit* or personalist groups which admitted their debt to Mounier not only in France but in Belgium, Switzerland, Holland, Canada, Africa, Poland, Spain, and elsewhere.[49] Of some significance, perhaps, is the fact that there has been comparatively little interest in Mounier among English-speaking peoples and truly extraordinary interest in him in the countries of Eastern Europe and the Iberian peninsula.[50] Mounier's profound sense of a total crises of

---

[44] Lacroix, "Un témoin et un guide," 35.

[45] François, "La revue qui a formé une génération chrétienne," 13.

[46] Jean Lacroix, "Albert Béguin et 'Esprit,'" in *Albert Béguin. Essais et témoignages* (Neuchâtel: Editions de la Baconnière, 1957), 55–61; J.-M. Domenach, "Albert Béguin," *Esprit*, No. 258 (February, 1958), 311–313; and Albert Béguin, "Fidélité et imagination," *Esprit*, No. 173 (November, 1950), 593–606.

[47] François, "La revue qui a formé une génération chrétienne," 13; and the following articles in *Esprit*, No. 255 (November, 1957): "Relais," 465–467; Jean-Marie Domenach, "Esprit, nouvelle série," 468–485; and Jean Conilh, "Mounier et notre génération," 486–499. See also "Mounier de nouveau," *Esprit*, No. 391 (April, 1970), 643–680.

[48] François, "La revue qui a formé une génération chrétienne," 13.

[49] See "Notes de lecteur et calendrier" section of *B.A.E.M.*, Nos. 1–37 (February, 1952– October, 1970) *passim*.

[50] On English and American personalism, see B. Darling, "La pensée de Mounier en Grand-Bretagne," *B.A.E.M.*, No. 22 (June, 1964), 1–7; Paul de Gaudemar, "Tendances personnalistes anglaises," *Esprit*, No. 143 (March, 1948), 373–388; G. R. Taylor, "Rapport du groupe personnaliste anglais," *Esprit*, No. 143 (March, 1948), 365–372; J. B. Coates, *The Crisis of*

Western civilization which called into question the institutions, the ideas, and the values of that civilization possesses special relevance and urgency in those nations of Europe in which such a total crisis became clearly discernible as a result of war or domestic upheaval and repression. His search for a "third way," his condemnation of capitalist disorder, and his persistent support of Christian-Marxist dialogue have understandably found a receptive audience in the countries of Eastern Europe; and similarly, the opponents of Franco and Salazar have found in Mounier's example and message the spiritual and intellectual resources for their battle against "the established disorder" which is so visible to them.

The foregoing admittedly provides only a very rough gauge of the intensity of Mounier's influence and suggests that the extent of that influence has been unusually broad. Beyond this, an examination of the heritage of Mounier, even in his native land, encounters serious difficulties. Certainly, the number of lectures, conferences, study circles, and scholarly works devoted to Mounier and *Esprit* in France leaves no doubt as to the extent of his remarkable posthumous fame. In October, 1964, for example, the Municipal Council of Grenoble met to vote on the name to be given a new lycée and Mounier defeated his fellow native of Grenoble, Condillac, by a vote of nineteen to nine. And several years later, Mounier became an official ornament of French culture when there was a special display of documents, photographs, and even a recording of the voice of Emmanuel Mounier in the French pavillon of the World's Fair in Montreal. So explosive has been the posthumous fame of Mounier that it is tempting to agree with a French writer who has said that

There is an endemic French illness in which the works of serious thinkers mysteriously spread beyond the small circle of initiates for whom they are intended and become the object of a cult. The thinker is afflicted with disciples he never wanted, preaching a gospel he never taught. He is hailed by worshippers who never have read a line of his work.[51]

the Human Person: some personalist interpretations (New York: Longmans, Green and Co., 1949), 15–28; J. W. Lapierre, "Le personnalisme à l'Américaine," *Esprit*, No. 195 (October, 1952), 535–548; and "Le personnalisme aux Etats-Unis," *Esprit*, No. 143 (March, 1948), 385–389. In the United States only the weekly *The Commonweal* and the quarterly *Cross Currents* have shown an interest in Mounier. On the influence of Mounier in Poland, Portugal, and Spain, see Andrezej Bukowski, "L'Actualité de la pensée de Mounier en Pologne," *B.A.E.M.*, No. 21 (December, 1963), 3–18; Jorge Dias, "Emmanuel Mounier et la Portugal," *B.A.E.M.*, No. 21 (December, 1963), 19–25; José-F. Fontecha Inyesto, "Attrait et avenir du personnalisme de Mounier en Espagne," *B.A.E.M.*, No. 22 (June, 1964), 8–14; and Alfonso Comin, "Deux inspirateurs: Mounier et Machado," *Esprit*, No. 342 (October, 1965), 451–467.

[51] Sanche de Gramont, "There Are No Superior Societies," *The New York Times Magazine* (January 28, 1968), 28.

That this is an accurate description of Mounier's fate cannot be ascertained without careful examination by some future student of Mounier's life, work, and influence. As Adrien Dansette has pointed out, not for half a century will "an aspirant to a *doctorat-ès-lettres* be able to investigate minutely how the influence ... of a Mounier has proceeded." [52]

Just how formidable a task this will be has been recognized by both friends and critics of Mounier. One of the former emphasizes both the danger of unduly limiting the influence of Mounier and *Esprit* and the difficulty of determining its extent with any measure of accuracy when he asks:

> How many others who have never read *Esprit*, who have never met the serious gaze and good humor of its founder, have benefitted from an impulse whose source they could not have been aware of? Did Mounier himself imagine the innumerable stages by which his *témoignage* nourished in a substantial way all of the generous movements of his time? [53]

And a harsh critic of Mounier writes that

> If there is today, in Christian circles, an accepted vocabulary, a vehicle of a moral orientation and dynamism towards action, it is in great measure in the gifts of Emmanuel Mounier that its source must be sought. If certain words recur frequently like an echo, ...it is because the work of Mounier has radiated very widely even among those who have never read him and are sometimes ignorant of his existence. [54]

Jean-Marie Domenach has expressed the fear that Mounier's thought has been perverted by the tendency to separate it from the concrete applications that provide its strength. A hundred students are writing theses on Mounier and his personalism has found its way into manuals of philosophy like any other philosophy. Domenach grants that some of Mounier's ideas have been deprived of their shock value for "today it seems quite natural to have been against Munich, against the alliance of the spiritual and the reactionary, for the reconciliation of the Church with the authentic values of the modern world." But there is, Domenach stresses, no *mouniériste* catechism. "True fidelity to Mounier, for me," Domenach affirms, "does not consist in following him theoretically, but practically, by continuing what he had undertaken. ..." This is a difficult task, for in the world today there is greater tolerance for ideas but less tolerance for certain kinds of behavior. "One has the

[52] Dansette, *Destin du catholicisme français*, 123.
[53] Baboulène, "Emmanuel Mounier et le mouvement catholique," 523.
[54] Clément, "Emmanuel Mounier (II)," 61.

right to think and to say anything, provided that one behaves like everyone else. This is what we must refuse: the odious politeness of the world which constrains you to live ... according to its laws, as a result of which you have permission to turn off the television in the evening and to read Marx or Mounier if that appeals to you." The example and heritage of Mounier consist living in another way: of speaking openly to others, of disobeying any command which conflicts with justice and truth; in short, in living a life of risk. "Personalism," Domenach says, "is first of all a pedagogy, a philosophy of service and not of domination. Its success is not measured in terms of power or numbers, but in terms of a change in the spirit of men and in their rapport with one another, in the development of a sense of disquiet, in the awareness of a responsibility." [55]

In this sense, as Mounier himself wrote in 1946, "the best future one could wish for Personalism is that it should so awaken in every man the sense of the whole meaning of man, that it could disappear without trace, having become the general climate of our days." [56] That such is the case with certain of the major themes of personalism has been suggested by Domenach. This judgment, however, conflicts with the views of several veterans of the *Esprit* group. Nicolas Berdiaev believed that "the only drawback [to the *Esprit* movement] was that it, like so many similar movements, was confined to a comparatively small group, unable to do anything which could effectively influence its environment. It could only 'endure' and try to understand the modern world, in which everything seemed to move in a direction contrary to the aims of *Esprit*." [57] Similarly, Hélène Iswolsky has said that

it is to be regretted that the *Esprit* movement never went beyond a small elite. I believe that one of its shortcomings was that it remained somewhat too "academic." It was mostly supported by university men, schooled in fixed frames of thought. Their ideas though dynamic and revolutionary were often couched in scholarly language, inaccessible to the public at large. They did not appeal to the average person or to the lower middle-class.[58]

Marcel Moré recounts that "shortly after I joined *Esprit* [in 1934], I began to doubt the efficacy of the 'proletarian revolution' for the present and the future. ... While Mounier still believed in the efficacy,

---

[55] Domenach, "Présence de Mounier," 217–228. See also Gaston Maire, "Présence d'Emmanuel Mounier en France," *B.A.E.M.*, No. 22 (June, 1964), 17.
[56] Mounier, *Qu'est-ce que le personnalisme?*, trans. in *Be Not Afraid*, 111–112.
[57] Berdyaev, *Dream and Reality*, 275.
[58] Iswolsky, *Light Before Dusk*, 115.

for the liberty of the world, of a proletarian revolution, provided that it be truly colored by Christianity, I have lost all hope for this. ..." [59] Consequently, Moré, like François Goguel, believes that *Esprit* had no effect upon events in France.[60]

The positions of Mounier and *Esprit* never found significant expression in French political life. As a consequence, Mounier has been severely criticized for attributing greater efficacy to his *engagement* and *témoignage* than they actually possessed. His critics have charged that the source of Mounier's difficulty was that he took insufficient account of the evil possibilities of modern life, that he had excessive faith in the actual progress of history, and that he welcomed change almost for its own sake.[61] One critic argues that Mounier was "almost a Pelagian" and another that "there is no doubt that Mounier meant to be a man of action more than a prophet. There is no doubt that he was only a prophet." [62]

To many such criticisms – though certainly not to all of them – Mounier's life and work provide certain answers. His was a "tragic optimism" which denied neither the Christian sense of human frailty nor the humanist faith in the possibilities of bettering the human condition. To the man who turns his back in despair on the almost infinite complexities of modern industrial civilization, Mounier cried out: "'You, there, you are carrying off the finest machines in the world.' And as he turns around, I point to his hands and his feet, and his tireless heart. These mechanisms do not prevent him from seeking perfection. Why should the others do so?" [63] Mounier's métier, his vocation, and the function he assigned *Esprit*, however, facilitated many criticisms for they were so easily open to serious misunderstanding. Mounier himself noted in his diary in March, 1941 that

I am a man of conversation, of mediation, of dialogue, who feels a strict responsibility for his mediation among men, who wishes only to pursue a permanent communication and service. It is in this sense that I undertake action. I care nothing, nothing for engaging in offensive action of a political nature.... I am too sensitive to everything that deforms men in action, too much a relati-

[59] Marcel Moré, *Accords et dissonances, 1932–1944* (Paris: Gallimard, 1967), 233–234.

[60] *Ibid.*, 236; and François Goguel, "Six Authors in Search of a National Character," in Hoffmann *et al.*, *In Search of France*, 387. See also Beigbeder, *Lettre à "Esprit*," 28.

[61] See, for example, Copleston, "Mounier, Marxism, and Man," 203–207; Rouquette, "Positions et oppositions d'Emmanuel Mounier," 150–151; Pierre de Boisdeffre, "Le drame d''Esprit': le personnalisme au carrefour," 14ff.; Moré, "Emmanuel Mounier," 237; and Clément, "Emmanuel Mounier," *Itinéraires*, No. 35 (July-August, 1959), 65–77, and "Emmanuel Mounier (II)," 61–76.

[62] Leslie Paul, "Foreword," in Mounier, *Be Not Afraid*, xx; and Rouquette, "Cheminements tragiques d'Emmanuel Mounier," 252.

[63] Mounier, "La machine en accusation" (1949), *O.M.*, III, 390.

vist in matters of political regimes, too little impassioned in what concerns them. I am aware that this subjective position, erected into a doctrine, will engender an error (the a-politicism that I have often denounced because I feel myself too close to it). But I must protect the clear perception of my vocation, and my methods of efficacy. I see myself working freely on all political tendencies so long as they remain open. . . . Perhaps this is not a position of political efficacy; I make no pretensions about it. But this is not simply a position of disengagement. *I concern myself with being efficacious* but in a manner other than the political.[64]

Mounier was not a political figure and *Esprit* did not publish political directives. Mounier did not found a political party nor did he ever identify personalism with any existing party. Although he himself attempted to work within the realm of the possible and to exert a practical influence, Mounier was primarily an educator, a "pedagogue of action," a man of dialogue, rather than the political tactician or strategist that some of his followers wanted him to be and that many of his opponents believed him to be. "The *raison d'être* of *Esprit*," a veteran member affirms, "was not to furnish theoreticians, militants, and ministers for a Left Center, but to bring together men capable of thinking politically on a level of inquiry and honesty in which the spiritual would not be betrayed in either ends or means. . . . There is a form of commitment . . . which consists of saying what is right in the face of all the voices of collective or individual egoism and in never waiting for the establishment of justice in the world while personally practicing justice." [65] "The virtue of Mounier," writes a friendly critic, "was to jolt our conformities, to place our opinions on trial; at least to show us that our political decisions perhaps inevitably always remain impure; he has made us see that what we take so easily for absolute good is only perhaps a lesser evil. Nothing is more uncomfortable than to be forced out of our shell of ready-made certitudes." [66]

Mounier was also "a witness." François Mauriac explained that

Emmanuel Mounier, it seems, never tried to convert anyone; he had no direct method for gathering young minds into the Church's nets or for holding them there. I do not know whether in the *Esprit* groups the believers and "practicers" were in the majority. Perhaps Mounier himself never tried to find out. He simply lived his Christian life among his fellow-men. The only thing that concerned him was to help them find, here and now, an answer to the questions of every sort that they raised. The lamp that he held high over his generation and with which he cleared up every problem was that of the Gospel. He advanced in this light, but as though it were of value only to him. To him, it would have seemed a silly idea to treat his comrades like some sort of spiritual quarry. . . .

[64] Mounier, "Entretiens XI, 30 mars 1941," *O.M.*, IV, 701.
[65] Simon, "Emmanuel Mounier et le personnalisme d'*Esprit*," 40–41.
[66] Rouquette, "Cheminements tragiques d'Emmanuel Mounier," 252.

He worked among them and for them without trying to make any impression on their consciousness save by the example of his life.[67]

Similarly, Ignace Lepp said that "I have never known a believer less bigoted than Emmanuel Mounier. However, anyone who met him knew that he was in the presence of a believer, and this awareness was never reproachful. Nevertheless, Mounier was not in the habit of interpolating pious considerations into his political, philosophical, or literary discussions. . . ." [68] Another man testifies that Mounier "knew that Christ is not a conqueror and that the term 'success,' taken in its fully temporal sense, has no place in the vocabulary of a religion in which one is called upon to imitate the Crucified. The essential thing for the Christian is to bear witness in order to arouse consciences. And Mounier bore witness." [69]

Mounier was able to pursue his task of making Catholics and non-Catholics, Christians and non-Christians, believers and nonbelievers work together because he did not present "Christianity as a haughty doctrine which has all of the solutions to worldly affairs." [70] His was a philosophy of openness and dialogue which was at once the consequence and the means of a profound ecumenism – an ecumenism witnessed in Mounier's association with the *Davidées*, Nicolas Berdiaev's meetings of Orthodox and Roman Catholics and Protestants at Clarmat, Maritain's gatherings at Meudon, and within the *Esprit* movement itself. At the *Rencontres Internationales de Genève* in 1963, Mounier's friend Père Yves Congar discussed the aim of that dialogue which is the underlying principle of ecumenism in essentially personalist terms. Men are so prone to possessiveness, Congar declared, that they tend to regard themselves as *subjects* and to treat others as *objects*. But other people are also *subjects* and "they do not wish to be mere *objects*, not even objects of solicitude." Congar continued that "the only escape from this deadlock lies in our own conversion to the acceptance of others as *subjects* with their own views of the world, their own ideas, joys, sorrows and plans, all of which are as individual and legitimate as our own." [71] To the problem posed by the Churches and dogmatic truth Congar stated: "Openness to dialogue necessarily entails an adequate

---

[67] François Mauriac, "More about Scouts and Guides," in *Letters on Art and Literature*, trans. Mario A. Pei (New York: Philosophical Library, Inc., 1953), 101–102.

[68] Lepp, *Atheism in our time*, 158.

[69] Moré, "Emmanuel Mounier," 236. See also Simon, "Emmanuel Mounier et le personnalisme d'*Esprit*," 34.

[70] Marrou, "La signification religieuse de la pensée d'Emmanuel Mounier," 30.

[71] Yves M.-J. Congar, *Dialogue Between Christians. Catholic Contributions to Ecumenism*, trans. Philip Loretz (Westminster, Md.: The New Press, 1966), 57.

realization that I cannot completely identify what I now hold, and the way in which I hold it, with the absolute truth to which I profess to be dedicated." [72] Congar then distinguished between "a sort of immediate and superficial faithfulness and a fidelity in depth." True fidelity, he contended, consists of a kind of continuous examination of conscience. It does not consist of abandoning one's own position "since one professes nothing else than the desire to grasp the whole truth, nor of minimizing or relativizing the latter but of giving it the greatest possible plentitude." [73] Finally, Congar stated that

It is thus that Emmanuel Mounier envisaged the well-being of the Christian in a divided world, actually face to face with "others" who are really different. It is our relation to the "absolute" which seemed to him to force dialogue upon us and to keep the individual in a state of dialogue. Far from being a game for dilettanti, like a drawing room conversation in which no one is committed to anything, the dialogue of which we are speaking is the confrontation of another person with someone who has convictions to which he is genuinely committed: reference to the "Absolute" is essential to it and is what gives it life. Far from enfeebling the convictions of those who engage in it, ecumenical dialogue strengthens and deepens them.[74]

Mounier's religious ecumenism and his advocacy of Catholic pluralism in temporal affairs were inextricably bound together. The essence of his work and his message as "a witness and a guide" can best be expressed in the term "dialogue." As a man of dialogue, Mounier was the exemplar of a new relationship between politics and belief, between the temporal and the spiritual, for his co-religionists. Even though his influence is admittedly difficult to trace with any measure of accuracy, there has been a striking reorientation in the historic social and political complexion of French Catholicism since 1930, and this change, in turn, has conformed in many ways to the example and message of Mounier. In a number of developments Mounier has been explicitly recognized as an exemplar or guide, and in others traces of his influence are clearly discernible. Among the clearest indications of the new orientation of Catholicism in France is the development of a genuine Catholic Left as well as of a movement towards "de-confessionalization" or "secularization" within a number of the most important Catholic organizations of Mounier's time. The diminution of the ghetto mentality of French Catholics and the growth of a new pluralism in temporal affairs manifested themselves ultimately within Christian democracy

[72] *Ibid.*, 59.
[73] *Ibid.*, 60.
[74] *Ibid.*

itself. Seventeen years after the French press had published obituaries of the founder of *Esprit*, it published the obituary of Christian democracy in France. There were some doubts as to the precise time of death, so little of the old party remained at the time of its formal demise, but the cause of death was fairly clear. Emmanuel Mounier had long before diagnosed the fatal illness. That few Catholics mourned the passing of the M.R.P. was but one indication of the extent of the changes which had taken place in French Catholicism since the birth of *Esprit*.

At the time of Mounier's death in 1950, the major components of what can best be called a "Christian Left" were generally opposed to the idea and the politics of Christian democracy. Two of the organizations which had provided both leaders and militants for Christian democracy for two generations were on the verge of major internal crises and had already produced important elements of a genuine Christian Left. Within the venerable A.C.J.F., a number of veterans of the J.O.C. had organized the *Mouvement Populaire des Familles*. Within the C.F.T.C. also, an organization called the *Groupes Reconstruction* had taken form and, after a long period of debate and serious dissension concerning both the character and the program of Christian syndicalism, the C.F.T.C. redefined its program as one of democratic socialism and rechristened itself the *Confédération Française Démocratique du Travail* (C.F.D.T.). In addition, at the time of Mounier's death, the Christian Left included not only the *Union des Chrétiens Progressistes*, but a study circle called *Economie et Humanisme*, the little *Jeune-République*, a "Mouvement d'education et d'action communautaire" called *La Vie Nouvelle*, and a small wing of the M.R.P. itself.[75]

The heritage of Mounier, the development of a Christian Left, and the debilitating effects of both upon Christian democracy in France can nowhere be more clearly traced than in the evolution of the A.C.J.F.[76] Founded in 1886 by Albert de Mun as a middle and upper class movement, its original purpose was to organize and coordinate the efforts of "Catholic youth with a view to restoring the Christian social order." Well before the Great War, however, the conservative Social Catholic propensities of the A.C.J.F. had given way to the Christian democratic sympathies of its leaders and many of its militants. During the 1920s

---

[75] For a brief survey of the Christian Left in 1950, see Jean-Marie Domenach, "Espoirs et impossibilités d'une gauche chrétienne," *France-Observateur*, June 22, 1950.

[76] On the early years of the A.C.J.F., see Charles Molette, *L'Association Catholique de la Jeunesse Française, 1886–1907. Une prise de conscience du laïcat catholique* (Paris: Armand Colin, 1968). On the later years, see A. Latreille *et al.*, *Histoire du catholicisme*, III, 604–609, 651–657; and *A.C.J.F. Signification d'une crise, passim*.

the A.C.J.F. became almost a training school for future Christian democrats and, during the presidencies of Charles Flory and François de Menthon, the period of "specialization" began. This "new springtime of the French Church" obscured beneath its enthusiasm many problems relating to both the structure and the mission of the A.C.J.F. and its specialized branches. From its early years, the A.C.J.F. was both a youth movement and a movement of the Church and the precise relationship of these two characteristics was unclear. In the strict sense, the A.C.J.F. was a "Catholic movement" or a "movement *within* the Church" and not "Catholic Action" or a "movement *of* the Church," a distinction which was to be the source of major difficulties in the future. Indicative of the complexity of this problem was the fact that the J.O.C. had been founded outside of the A.C.J.F. as an organization of Catholic Action and had later affiliated with the A.C.J.F., which was not, strictly speaking, an organization of Catholic Action.

What the enthusiasm of the 1930s had tended to submerge, the experiences of 1940–1944 brought to the surface. The War, the Occupation, and the Resistance clearly demonstrated that the lives of the members of the A.C.J.F. were profoundly affected by temporal structures and institutions and that the task of evangelization was inseparable from the temporal conditions in which this work was undertaken. The fundamental problem was the proper relationship between the temporal and the spiritual. In the immediate postwar period, two differing conceptions of the mission of the A.C.J.F. were voiced. One conception emphasized the traditional character of Catholic Action as a religious apostolate in which the laity shares in the spiritual mission of the hierarchy. The other conception emphasized the necessity of transforming temporal conditions, of rendering them more compatible with human liberty and the practice of Christianity.

Compounding these already difficult problems was the question of the structure of the A.C.J.F. Was it one movement with five branches or a confederation of five autonomous movements (the J.O.C., J.E.C., J.A.C., J.I.C., and J.M.C.)? In the late 1940s, the specialized branches were increasingly independent of the A.C.J.F. and increasingly activist in temporal affairs. Religious authorities became fearful that the concern for "humanization," for transforming temporal conditions, would lead the members of the A.C.J.F. to neglect their spiritual apostolate. The discord within the A.C.J.F. reached crisis proportions in 1955–1956 over a number of seemingly minor internal issues, but these differences were more the occasion for than the actual cause of the crisis which brought about the demise of the A.C.J.F. in 1956. The basic issue was the mission of the A.C.J.F. and its specialized branches – and, in a larger sense, the role of the laity in the Church itself. Whereas religious author-ities, supported by the J.O.C., stressed evangelization, the A.C.J.F. conceived of its task as "rather to act at once on the men and on the structures of a milieu so as to enable each person to develop his talents fully."

In the background of these developments was the experience of the *Mouvement Populaire des Familles* (M.P.F.).[77] The M.P.F. was a clear illustration of the tendency of certain movements of Catholic Action to abandon their social, religious and apostolic preoccupations in favor of specific political commitments. The M.P.F. originated among members of the *Ligue Ouvrière Chrétienne* (L.O.C.), a movement of Catholic Action which was a kind of adult J.O.C. During the Occupation, the L.O.C. expanded substantially and sought to collaborate with non-Christians. In 1942 the L.O.C. and its feminine counterpart, the *Ligue Ouvrière Chrétienne Feminine*, merged to form the M.P.F. The circum-stances in which the M.P.F. was born undoubtedly contributed to its future evolution, for the immediate problems confronting its members were of a politico-religious character: whether they should go to Berlin or to the Vercors, whether they should join the Resistance or obey the urgings of those members of the hierarchy who supported the S.T.O. Moreover, the word "Christian "was not included in the name of the new organization, and whether or not it was still a branch of Catholic Action was unclear. The M.P.F. itself was apparently uncertain for it was both a "movement of working class life" and a "movement of Christian conquest." By 1946 the immersion of the M.P.F. in political affairs had become so pronounced that its leaders asked the Assembly of Cardinals and Archbishops to recognize that it was not a movement of Catholic Action, and in October, 1949 its official mandate as a movement of Catholic Action was withdrawn by the Assembly. The following October, the M.P.F. transformed itself into the *Mouvement de Libération du Peuple* (M.L.P.), thereby not only abandoning its emphasis upon problems concerning the life, culture, and welfare of the

---

[77] On the M.P.F., see Suffert, *Les catholiques et la gauche*, 99–105; Roland Talleux, "Chré-tiens dans le combat ouvrier," *La Nef*, No. 5 (January, 1954), 157–170; Jacques Viard, "Réponse. Catholiques de droite? Catholiques de gauche?," *Chronique sociale de France*, 64ᵉ année, No. 7–8 (December, 1956), 730; Dansette, *Destin du catholcisme français*, 372–378; Micaud, *Communism and the French Left*, 153–176; Duquesne, 424–425; Pierre Bigo, *La Doctrine sociale de l'Eglise. Recherche et dialogue* (Paris: Presses universitaires de France, 1966), 165–167; and *Pour un renouveau du socialisme. Mouvement de Libération du Peuple* (Paris: Imprimerie commerciale, 1956).

family but also making more explicit its "revolutionary conscience."
Finally, in May, 1951 a minority of the M.L.P. split from the parent
organization to form the more moderate *Mouvement de Libération
Ouvrière* (M.L.O.).

The M.L.P. did not join the Communist Party as the dissidents of the
M.L.O. feared; nor did the M.L.O. affiliate itself with the M.R.P. as the
majority in the M.L.P. feared. Rather, although many of the members
of the M.P.F. had earlier supported the M.R.P., the M.L.O. devoted itself to educational and cultural endeavors, while the M.L.P. actively
sought a middle way between the bourgeois and capitalist M.R.P. and
the Marxist Communist Party. In this quest for a third way, the M.L.P.
adopted many positions familiar to any reader of *Esprit*. Its members
refused to separate themselves from the working classes, many of them
joined the *Confédération Générale du Travail*, and several of them did,
in fact, join the Communist Party. They believed that capitalism was
fundamentally evil and had to be replaced by socialism as "the only
method for the emancipation of the working class and the mass of
laborers." In a lengthy manifesto published in 1956, the M.L.P. called
for both the nationalization of the means of production and the decentralization of economic and political power without, however, clearly
indicating the means for achieving these seemingly contradictory aims.
One of its members contended that the aim of his organization was to
construct "a socialism of Christian, that is, of personalist inspiration."[78]

In December, 1957 the M.L.P. joined with a group of dissident Socialists and a majority of the members of the *Jeune-République* in organizing the *Union de la Gauche Socialiste* (U.G.S.) whose purpose was to
form a "New Left" between the S.F.I.O. and the Communist Party and
to further the dream of a "popular socialism." At Issy-les-Moulineaux
in April, 1960, the U.G.S. joined the *Parti Socialiste Autonome*, which
was made up of a group of dissidents from the S.F.I.O., a number of
Mendèsistes, a group of Communist Party dissidents who called themselves the *Tribune du Communisme*, and representatives of various political clubs and groups, to form the *Parti Socialiste Unifié* (P.S.U.). The
stated purpose of the P.S.U. was "to construct the VIe Republic or the
First Socialist Republic." Included in its ranks were a large number of
the members of the new Christian Left. It has been suggested that with
the exception of the M.R.P. the P.S.U. probably "included proportion-

---

[78] Jacques Viard, "Réponse, Catholiques de droite? Catholiques de gauche?," *Chronique
sociale de France*, 64e année, No. 7–8 (December, 1956), 730.

ally the greatest number of Christians concerned with prolonging their faith by means of a political commitment." [79]

Among the members of the P.S.U. were a number of Christian syndicalists. Within the C.F.T.C., a dissident minority had developed rapidly immediately after the War. The core of this minority was the *Syndicat Général de l'Education Nationale* (S.G.E.N.) which was founded by François Henry, Bernard Vacheret, and Paul Vignaux in 1937. Vignaux and his group believed in "the necessity of dialogue with all those who worked for a better world," opposed subsidies to the Catholic schools, and consistently made a careful distinction between their religious convictions and their temporal options. In the *Cahiers Reconstruction,* the members of the S.G.E.N. increasingly differed with the older generation of Christian syndicalists and supported significant changes in both the statutes and the program of the C.F.T.C. [80]

The War and the Resistance provided additional impetus to the changes supported by the *Groupes Reconstruction.* Referring to the ideological evolution of the C.F.T.C., Vignaux said that

in certain regions in the North and the East, references to encyclicals continued in the Christian syndicalist milieu, but this kind of discussion based upon documents of the Church diminished progressively throughout the confederation. Do not forget that the C.F.T.C. which emerged from the Resistance was very different from the one which had entered it. The Social Catholic tradition was diluted in the socialist ideology of the Resistance. The common ground became the search for a syndicalism in the French tradition.[81]

The first step in the "secularization" or "de-confessionalization" of the C.F.T.C. for which the *Groupes Reconstruction* worked occurred in 1947 when the first article of its statutes was altered. A specific reference to the social doctrine of the Church as defined in *Rerum novarum* was deleted and in its place reference was made only to "the principles of Christian social morality." In spite of this victory by the C.F.T.C. minority, differences between Vignaux's group and the majority of the C.F.T.C. persisted. The minority declared its intention of working for

[79] René Rémond, "Forces religieuses et partis politiques," in Rémond (ed.), *Forces religieuses et attitudes politiques,* 81.
[80] On the evolution of the C.F.T.C., see Adam, *La C.F.T.C.*; Gérard Adam, "De la C.F.T.C. à la C.F.D.T.," *Revue française de science politique,* XV, No. 1 (February, 1965), 87–103; Suffert, *Les catholiques et la gauche,* 86–99; Micaud, *Communism and the French Left,* 177–193; Paul Vignaux, "Evolution et problèmes de la C.F.T.C.," *La Nef,* 11e année, No. 5 (January, 1954), 125–134; Marcel David, "Catholicisme et action syndicale ouvrière," in Rémond (ed.) *Forces religieuses et attitudes politiques,* 177–201; Paul Vignaux, "Communication," in Rémond (ed.), *Forces religieuses et attitudes politiques,* 207; and "L'évolution du syndicalisme ouvrier et la C.F.T.C.," *Chronique sociale de France,* 72e année, No. 7 (November, 1964), 379–487.
[81] Vignaux, "Communication," 207.

"a socialist and democratic alternative to the present regime." Its brand of democratic socialism included the nationalization of banks and possibly the steel, chemical, cement, oil, and naval construction industries as well. Moreover, the *Groupes Reconstruction* were vehement in their opposition to the M.R.P. Max Lyon, a leader of the minority, criticized Christian democracy in almost precisely the language used by Mounier. He called it a "sanctimonious party" whose members expected Catholic doctrine to provide precise directives in civic affairs.[82]

As a result of pressure from the increasingly powerful *Groupes Reconstruction*, a special study group was established in 1960. After four years of discussion, consultation, and debate, an extraordinary congress of the C.F.T.C. was held in Paris on November 6 and 7, 1964. The "centrists" opposed a proposal to delete the second "C" in the title of the organization and to revise the statutes. Supported by seventy per cent of the membership, however, the *Groupes Reconstruction* triumphed. The C.F.T.C. was officially rechristened the *Confédération Française Démocratique du Travail* (C.F.D.T.) and the reference to "the principles of Christian social morality' was replaced by a preamble which stressed "the contributions of different forms of humanism, including Christian humanism, to the definition of the fundamental exigencies of the human person." Although the C.F.D.T. retained its ties to the *Confédération Internationale des Syndicats Chrétiens* and five to six per cent of the membership refused to accept the decision to change the title and statutes of the organization, the process of "deconfessionalization" was complete.

The War and the Resistance also contributed to the development of another important element of the new Christian Left, the Study Center called *Economie et Humanisme*. The founder of *Economie et Humanisme* was Père Louis-Joseph Lebret, a Dominican priest whose response to the crisis of the early 1930s was not dissimilar to that of Mounier and the founders of *Esprit*.[83] A former merchant marine officer, Père Lebret worked among the fishermen of Saint-Malo during the 1930s, first as a chaplain for the *Jeunesse Maritime Chrétienne* and then as the founder of the *Secrétariat social maritime*. The economic crisis of the early 1930s had a profound impact upon the inhabitants of the coastal areas of Brittany and convinced Lebret of the insufficiency of a narrowly religi-

---

[82] Max Lyon, "Laïcité et cléricalisme," *Cahiers des Groupes Reconstruction*, April, 1955, cited in Micaud, *Communism and the French Left*, 181.

[83] On *Economie et Humanisme*, see "Le dossier de la quinzaine. Un Centre d'Etudes: Economie et Humanisme," *Informations catholiques internationales*, No. 67 (March 1, 1958), 15–21; Duquesne, 393–394; Poulat, *Naissance des prêtres ouvriers*, 415ff. and 525ff.

ous apostolate. "The misery of the people, the inhumanity of an economy based upon profit, the anarchy of the liberal economy – the possibility for men who were competent technically, who were personally disinterested and aware of the common good, to change structures – the union of the spiritual and the temporal – the necessity of constructing, beyond capitalism and Marxism, a human economy" – these were the concrete realities and needs Lebret discovered in Saint-Malo.[84] In 1938 Lebret organized a study group whose purpose was to discover "a fourth way" based upon a rejection of the ideologies and regimes of Marxism, capitalism, and National Socialism.

It was not, however, until after the fall of France that Lebret organized *Economie et Humanisme*. "The designation *Economie et Humanisme* that I proposed was adopted," Lebret recalled; "the word *Economie* signified a desire not to be tied to the social palliative but to call structures into question; the word *Humanisme* expressed a reaction against the false humanisms then dominant and an emphasis on the whole man and on all men. ...." The new movement proposed to seek a way between "capitalist chaos" and "socialist statism," between "the capitalist myth of profit" and "the socialist myth of equality," and to return "to the direct observation of human facts." [85] Fundamental to the work of *Economie et Humanisme* was the communitarian idea which pervaded the thought of so many Frenchmen during the war years. The merit of *Economie et Humanisme* was that it proposed that Catholics should seriously study economic realities and no longer content themselves merely with being "social." *Economie et Humanisme* held numerous conferences, organized study circles, and, over the years, published many studies in economics, sociology, and religious sociology, and on such subjects as Marxism, lay spirituality, and the problems of action and *engagement*. *Economie et Humanisme* responded to Emmanuel Mounier's old complaint concerning the technical inadequacies of Christians in temporal affairs.

The purpose of *Economie et Humanisme* was not to work at tasks that properly belonged to syndicalism, Catholic Action, or political movements. Rather, it was to place the results of its labors at the disposal of others. Among the movements which drew upon the resources of *Economie et Humanisme* was a "Mouvement d'éducation et d'action communautaire pour adultes" called *La Vie Nouvelle*. Outside of the *Esprit* movement itself, no organization was so explicit in admitting its

---

[84] "Le dossier de la quinzaine. Un Centre d'Etudes: Economie et Humanisme," 16.
[85] *Ibid.*, 17–18.

debt to Mounier and the inspiration it drew from his communitarian personalism. And few movements so vividly illustrated the gradual shift from the political Right to the Left as well as from confessional to non-sectarian organizations by a number of French Catholics in the past generation: the seedbed of *La Vie Nouvelle* was the conservative Catholic Scout movement but the ultimate political affinities of many of its leaders and members were with such elements of the Left as the *Jeune-République* and the P.S.U.

The prehistory of *La Vie Nouvelle* dates from the year of the founding of *Esprit*.[86] In 1932 the *Route des Scouts de France* was organized by Pierre Goutet and André Cruiziat. Goutet and Cruiziat remained the national directors of the *Route* during the 1930s and after the fall of France they both joined the *Compagnons de France*. Convinced of the need for communitarian organizations in the new France, Goutet and Cruiziat succumbed temporarily to the National Revolution. Soon they turned to Mounier's communitarian personalism. Both men, like Mounier and many other members of the *Compagnons*, then entered the Resistance. In late 1942 Cruiziat began to meet with a number of former Scouts and veterans of the *Compagnons* in what was to be a kind of adult *Route* called the *Amitiés scoutes*.

Under the somewhat paternalistic guidance of Cruiziat, the *Amitiés scoutes* emerged from the War and the Resistance with a clear orientation towards "education and action conceived of as complementary and equally indispensable to one another." In 1945 and 1946 a major split in the membership occurred. One group viewed the *Amitiés* as little more than a prolongation of its work as Scouts and looked to the organization for support and friendship in the Scout tradition. Another group wished to make the *Amitiés* an instrument not only of education but of revolutionary changes in the social, economic, and political structures of France. Cruiziat and the other leaders of the *Amitiés* supported this view. As a result, a schism took place within the *Amitiés*. Cruiziat and his supporters went forward to obtain the formal independence of the *Amitiés scoutes* from the parent *Scouts de France*, a confessional organization which had provided financial support for the *Amitiés*. On July 31, 1947 the *Amitiés scoutes* was renamed *La Vie*

---

[86] On *La Vie Nouvelle*, see "Le dossier de la quinzaine. Une mouvement de laïcs: 'La Vie Nouvelle,'" *Informations catholiques internationales*, No. 220 (July 15, 1966), 17–25; Jean Lestavel, "Le Mouvement 'La Vie nouvelle,'" in Rémond (ed.), *Forces religieuses et attitudes politiques*, 167–172; Jean Lestavel, *Introduction aux personnalismes* (Paris: La Vie Nouvelle, 1962); "Déclaration d'associations," *Journal Officiel de la République Française. Lois et décrets*, No. 303 (December 24, 1949), 12323; Suffert, *Les catholiques et la gauche*, 107–113; Duquesne, 392–393; and Bosworth, 163–165.

Nouvelle, an action which, in the view of its leaders, had the advantage of expanding the recruitment possibilities of the organization beyond veterans of the *Scouts de France.*

The years from 1946 to 1949–1950 were a time of "generous enthusiasm more than of efficacy" in the history of the *Amitiés* and *La Vie Nouvelle,* and most of the new recruits to the movement were veterans of the Scouts. Beginning in 1949–1950, new members from other milieux joined *La Vie Nouvelle.* Some were militants of the *Groupes Reconstruction,* others were members of the *Jeune-République* or the *Nouvelle Gauche,* and still others were dissidents from the M.R.P. With the influx of these new members, *La Vie Nouvelle* began to forge a general political orientation. Increasingly after 1950, *La Vie Nouvelle* organized local groups, national teams, and national congresses devoted to the study of current problems.

Paralleling the new emphasis upon careful study of specific problems by various specialists, particularly in the domain of the human sciences, was a search for a coherent philosophical framework upon which *La Vie Nouvelle* could build. More than one member of the organization discovered that "there was a convergence between the course *La Vie Nouvelle* followed and the communitarian personalism of Emmanuel Mounier." Due in large measure to the work of Jean Lestavel, the thought of Mounier henceforth became the official frame of reference for the men of *La Vie Nouvelle.* Although much of the membership of *La Vie Nouvelle* was middle class, an effort was made to recruit members of the working class and concern for the poor led members of *La Vie Nouvelle* to turn their attention to the problems of overseas peoples and to support de-colonization. These two departures manifested the increasing importance that many members of *La Vie Nouvelle* attached to politics in its broadest sense. The crisis of parliamentary democracy signalled by the return to power of Charles de Gaulle further accentuated the political concerns of *La Vie Nouvelle* and led it to embark on the task of defining the conditions of a "communitarian socialism." The increasing political activism of many of the leaders and members of *La Vie Nouvelle* again brought to the surface the basic cleavage within the movement which had first appeared in 1945–1946. Between 1956 and 1958 two fairly specific points of view concerning the nature and purpose of *La Vie Nouvelle* crystallized. One view was that "the communitarian spirit signified fidelity to a labor of personal development and of general mutual aid" and was void of any genuine political content. The other view was voiced by André Cruiziat and was more faithful to Mounier's conception of personalism: by its very nature personalism was a guide to political action and demanded commitment. Cruiziat's view prevailed and 1958–1959 ushered in a new phase in the history of *La Vie Nouvelle*.

Ideologically, the movement attempted to develop the ramifications of personalism and it organized a study session devoted to communitarian personalism at Jouy-en-Josas, where a number of *Esprit* congresses had been held during the 1930s. Of particular concern was the study of pluralism. Here also the message and example of Mounier were clearly in evidence, for *La Vie Nouvelle* worked against the historic ghetto mentality of French Catholics. *La Vie Nouvelle* also concerned itself with the relationship between the Christian and the modern world, ecumenism, dialogue with non-Christians, the role of the laity in the Church, and the exigencies of evangelical poverty in contemporary society. Politically, in the words of Jean Lestavel, *La Vie Nouvelle* "is anxious [to maintain] the autonomy of politics and the necessary collaboration with nonbelievers: the lesson of Mounier has been fully understood." [87] Although composed almost entirely of Catholics, *La Vie Nouvelle* emphatically distinguished between the religious commitment of its members and the political positions they adopted. Fearful of a tendency towards "de-politicism," *La Vie Nouvelle* founded a journal called *Citoyens 60* in 1958 and around this journal the political clubs *Citoyens 60* developed.

Among the other political clubs of the last years of the Fourth Republic and the Fifth Republic was the *Jeune-République*. Although the *Jeune-République* was technically a political party, it had become in fact "a Club of modest dimensions." [88] The evolution of the *Jeune-République* from its origins among the veterans of Sangnier's *Sillon* to its affiliation with the P.S.U. is, in itself, a remarkable chapter in the history of Catholicism in contemporary France. The men of the *Jeune-République* were not the "poor, pale, generous débris" to whom Mounier had referred thirty years before. Not only had their political options during the final crisis years of the Third Republic been strikingly similar to those of Mounier and *Esprit*, but increasingly after the War their political path had converged with that of *Esprit*. Moreover, the personalism which had long been implicit in the doctrine of the *Jeune-République* became more and more explicit as the little party examined

[87] Lestavel, "Le Mouvement 'La Vie Nouvelle,'" 172.
[88] Jean-André Faucher, *Les Clubs politiques en France* (Paris: Editions John Didier, 1965), 106.

and re-examined its *raison d'être* and determined its political course of action. Finally, Mounier's communitarian personalism was adopted as a guide to the action of the *Jeune-République* and Mounier himself was recognized as one of the party's intellectual mentors.

The *Jeunes Républicains* emerged completely unsullied by their activities during the War and the Occupation. The party's deputies had voted against Pétain in July, 1940, and after the suppression of their Resistance journal, *Valmy*, and the arrest or dispersal of its collaborators, the *Jeunes Républicains* entered into a number of Resistance movements.[89] None of them, however, played a significant role in either the *Combat* movement or the series of clandestine meetings which led to the organization of the M.R.P. With the formation of the M.R.P., the *Jeune-République* lost a number of its militants, including Maurice Schumann. Under the leadership of Maurice Lacroix, the party adamantly refused to disband and join the new Christian democratic party. The *Jeunes Républicains* were particularly incensed by an appeal issued by a group of former party members urging the *Jeune-République* to join the M.R.P.[90]

In its decision to remain independent of the M.R.P., the *Jeune-République* was motivated by various considerations but three of them appear to have been particularly compelling. First, the party feared that the M.R.P. would be a purely confessional party whose program would inevitably be regarded as the political position of the Church. For this reason alone, a majority of the members of the *Jeune-République* believed that the continued existence of another party of "spiritualist inspiration" was necessary. Second, the *Jeune-République* feared that the electoral clientele of the M.R.P. would prevent it from fulfilling the requirements of the revolutionary changes spelled out in the Resistance Charter. And finally and perhaps most important of all, the *Jeune-République* retained its historic faith in the advent of a great republican party. Immediately after the war, the *Jeune-République* supported the formation of a "great Labor Party." [91] It remained an "open" party and demonstrated its willingness to work with other parties as a "building stone" of a French Labor Party. In 1945 and early 1946 the little party attempted to form an electoral entente with the M.R.P., the S.F.I.O., and the *Union Démocratique et Socialiste de la Résistance* (U.D.S.R.). When the M.R.P. refused to enter into such a

[89] *La Jeune-République*, May 31, 1945.

[90] *La Jeune-République*, August 24 – September 12, 1946; and "Origines et mission du M.R.P.," 29.

[91] *La Jeune-République*, February, 1945.

pact and the Socialists failed to renew their short-lived pact of unity of action in early 1946, the *Jeune-République* was forced to content itself with an alliance with the small U.D.S.R.[92]

As a result of this failure, the *Jeune-République* re-examined its *raison d'être*. In mid-1946 it reverted to its old practice of subordinating purely electoral concerns to a program of popular civic education.[93] Quoting Mounier, one of the party's publicists argued that a new socialism constructed by new men was something that went well beyond the cadres of the presently constituted political parties.[94] Like Mounier also, the *Jeune-République* accused the M.R.P. of being a "prisoner of its conservative clientele, narrow ideas, and confessionalism" and opposed the Gaullist R.P.F. as a manifestation of a nascent Fascism.[95] By late 1948 the similarities between the positions of the *Jeune-République* and those of *Esprit* were becoming more and more obvious. At its National Congress of November, 1948, the party accused the Third Force of practicing a negative, "stupid and dangerous" anti-Communism.[96] Echoing Mounier's arguments, the party declared that "anti-Communism is always the beginning of Fascism" and was creating a fatal division in the body politic of France. Consequently, it suggested that conversations with the leaders of the *Rassemblement Démocratique et Révolutionnaire*, the *Union des Chrétiens Progressistes*, and the Communist Party be initiated with a view to forming a political entente. Time and again during the Congress, members of the *Jeune-République* took the rostrum to repeat Mounier's dictum that "anti-Communism is not a program."[97]

In February, 1949 the little party explicitly recognized its kinship with Mounier and *Esprit*. The editor of *La Jeune-République* declared that the men of *Esprit* "are at the center of that meeting ground between humanist socialists and revolutionary spiritualists ... [who are working] for the defense of the dignity and liberty of the human person, for the establishment, in short, of a 'personalist and communitarian' State."[98] The leaders of the party also affirmed their acceptance of part of the Marxist critique of capitalism and liberal democracy and admitted to an "instinctive tendency" to regard the Communists with

[92] *Ibid.*; and *La Jeune-République*, April 5–11, 1946.
[93] *La Jeune-République*, July 6–12, 1946.
[94] *La Jeune-République*, January, 1948.
[95] *Ibid.*
[96] *La Jeune-République*, December, 1948.
[97] *Ibid.*
[98] *La Jeune-République*, February, 1949.

sympathy.[99] The motto on the masthead of the party's journal was then changed from "A Free Journal in the Service of Free Men" to "For a Socialist, Personalist and Communitarian Revolution," and its pages were filled with discussions of personalism and communitarianism.[100] In succeeding years, the party supported the European federalist movement, opposed the Atlantic Alliance and the Indochinese War, and supported Algerian independence. In December, 1957 a majority of the militants of the little party joined the *Union de la Gauche Socialiste*, leaving only a tiny nucleus of men in the party. Finally, in April, 1960 the *Jeune-République* ceased, for all intents and purposes, to exist as the *Jeunes Républicains* joined the P.S.U. and the party's journal suspended publication.[101]

In 1956 a critic of the *Jeunes Républicains* charged them with holding "an intellectual vision of the facts." In the formation of public opinion, the *Jeunes Républicains* performed a necessary task but "on the terrain of political action, they expend a great deal of energy in vain." [102] A *Jeune Républicain* deputy also complained that "the disproportion between the political influence of the Christian Left and its importance in the intellectual life of the country is astonishing." [103] The practical political influence of the *Jeune-République* – the most overtly political of all the groups which carried the stamp of Mounier – was negligible. When Pierre Bourdan died in 1948, he was the only parliamentary representative of the *Jeune-République*, and, at the National Congress of November, 1948, only 730 members were in attendance.[104] Beginning just prior to the M.R.P. Congress of Nantes in 1950, the *Jeune-République* received intermittent political transfusions from the M.R.P. as some of the dissident Christian democrats entered the ranks of the little party. Among them were Charles d'Aragon, André Denis, and Henri Bouret, all of whom were deputies, and Léo Hamon, who was a Senator. There is, however, no reason to challenge Jean-Marie Domenach's assessment of June, 1950. Although the *Jeune-*

---

[99] *La Jeune-République*, July, 1949; and *La Jeune-République*, December 3, 1949.

[100] See, for example, *La Jeune-République*, March, 1949; *La Jeune-République*, May, 1949; and *La Jeune-République*, April 18, 1950.

[101] Faucher, 107; and Estier, 254.

[102] André Laurendeau, "Réponse. Catholiques de droite? Catholiques de gauche?," *Chronique sociale de France*, 64ᵉ année, No. 7–8 (December, 1956), 641.

[103] Charles d'Aragon, "Réponse. Catholiques de droite? Catholiques de gauche?," *Chronique sociale de France*, 64ᵉ année, No. 7–8 (December, 1956), 705.

[104] *La Jeune-République*, January-September, 1948; and *La Jeune-République*, December, 1948.

République still had supporters in many regions of France, it was already a "society of thought" instead of a political party.[105]

Numerically, the most important component of the Christian Left is probably *La Vie Nouvelle* and its *Citoyens 60*. In 1966 *La Vie Nouvelle* had 144 groups throughout France and 7000 people were actively engaged in the work of these groups. Since its organization, the leaders of *La Vie Nouvelle* believe that about three times this number of people have been directly influenced by its activities.[106] The membership of *Citoyens 60* was estimated to have been between 6000 and 7000 in 1964–1965 and the circulation of its journal, *Les Cahiers Citoyens 60*, was 3500.[107] The Christian Left as a whole, therefore, is not of particular numerical importance. "In order to avoid overestimating the importance of this current of the Left," René Rémond stated in 1963, "it is necessary to remember that if it includes a stratum of intellectuals and a fringe of militants generally drawn from the popular milieux, it has never represented more than a very small fraction of the members of French Catholicism." [108] The *Union de la Gauche Socialiste*, which so many members of the Christian Left supported in late 1957, was able to obtain only two or three per cent of the popular vote, and the P.S.U. received only three or four per cent of the vote cast in the presidential election of June, 1969.[109]

There was no direct numerical correlation between the development of a Christian Left and the decline and demise of the M.R.P. The main criticisms and losses suffered by the M.R.P. in the years between the founding of the party and 1951–1952 came from the Right as the party lost both militants and electoral support to conservative parties, most notably the Gaullist R.P.F. For a number of years after 1951 criticism and defections came primarily from the Left as many members of the M.R.P. found the party to be too timid, irresolute or confessional for their tastes, and moved in the direction of the *Jeune-République*, the renovated Radical Party of Mendès-France, the M.L.P., and, later, the *Union de la Gauche Socialiste* and the P.S.U.[110] Beginning in 1958, the M.R.P. declined as its electorate turned to the Gaullist *Union de la*

105 Domenach, "Espoirs et impossibilités d'une gauche chrétienne," 13.
106 "Le dossier de la quinzaine. Une mouvement de laïcs 'La Vie Nouvelle.'"
107 Georges Lavau, "Les clubs politiques," *Revue française de science politique*, XV, No. 1 (February, 1965), 103–113.
108 Rémond, "Forces religieuses et partis politiques," 81.
109 Micaud, *Communism and the French Left*, 156; and *The New York Times*, June 2. 1969.
110 Rémond, "Forces religieuses et partis politiques," 81.

Nouvelle République.[111] While a reader of the Catholic press might well have received the impression that French Catholics were becoming far more favorable to the Left, in actual fact Catholic voters continued to support the M.R.P., the Moderates, and the Gaullists.[112]

The development of a genuine Left within French Catholicism by its very existence as well as because of the caliber of its members, however, possesses an importance which clearly transcends its numerical size. The Christian Left forced the largest Christian democratic party in French history into the same relative position within the increasingly broad spectrum of Catholic opinion that the M.R.P. held in French opinion as a whole. Between the Christian Left and the M.R.P. there were differences over a broad range of specific political issues – colonialism, Mendès-France, the interminable question of the Catholic schools, Gaullism, socialism, and Communism – but the fundamental differences between the two went well beyond purely political questions. The fundamental problem was the role of the Christian in temporal affairs, and this role, as it was defined and acted upon by members of the Christian Left, called into question not merely the politics but the very *raison d'être* of Christian democracy. In an important sense, the Christian democracy of the M.R.P. was the adventure of one generation of French Catholics and the new generation regarded it as an anachronism.

Etienne Borne was particularly forthright and consistent in dealing with the basic criticism raised by Mounier and the Christian Left. But even his efforts to revitalize the M.R.P., to return the M.R.P. to the sources of its original *mystique,* were unsuccessful. Less than a year after Mounier's death, the first issue of a new journal appeared. An English reporter observed that

On the cover, the title *Terre Humaine* stands out in white letters against a black background and underneath runs the sub-title, *Revue de Doctrine et d'Action.* This new paper is obviously meant to have both feet firmly on the ground and to influence events; but a white star, set in perspective beyond the words of the title, warns us that events are seen in relation to something above the earth. *Terre Humaine* is, in fact, a new Catholic paper, directed by Etienne Borne, and it seems to stem, although on a more practical level, from the same Left-Wing Péguy-ist current as *Esprit.*[113]

---

[111] *Ibid.*, 83–85; Aline Coutrot, "Les mouvements confessionnels et la société politique," in Rémond (ed.), *Forces religieuses et attitudes politiques dans la France contemporaine,* 148–150; and Coutrot and Dreyfus, 199–200.

[112] Coutrot and Dreyfus, 201–202.

[113] J. G. Weightman, "The French Reviews," *The Twentieth Century,* CXLIX (April, 1951), 294.

The purpose of *Terre Humaine* was to re-examine the *raison d'être* of Christian democracy and, most important, to revive its *mystique* which Borne believed had degenerated, in the *péguyste* sense, into a *politique*.[114] In terms which were familiar to readers of *Esprit*, Borne condemned the "moralist deformation" of his party and criticized the "tragic personalism" with which it tended to excuse its political deficiencies.[115]

In the second issue of *Terre Humaine*, Borne responded to Mounier's fundamental criticisms of Christian democracy.[116] He prefaced his response by admitting that much of Mounier's criticism was not without merit and that the most effective response was to continue the work of Mounier. Then, after summarizing Mounier's idea of the peculiar "Christian democratic temperament" – albeit with much of the sarcasm with which he accused Mounier of treating the Christian democrats – Borne addressed himself to "the heart of the debate" between Mounier and the Christian democrats. On the basis of a careful distinction between Christendom and Christianity, Mounier believed that for Christians to organize themselves in social, civic, and temporal organizations is "to go to the wrong side of history and to perpetuate those confusions of the sacred and the profane which are fatal to the development of the Church and the progress of the Kingdom of God." According to Borne, Mounier wanted "to make a world worthy of man, side by side with all men of good will, believers and nonbelievers. All attempts to restore Christendom will imprison Christians in an impossible ghetto." The Christian union, the confessional school, the Christian party were all anachronisms. Christian democracy, in Mounier's lexicon, was no more than "a moribund sequel to 'the late Christendom.'" Borne expressed his agreement with much of the foregoing, but he protested Mounier's identification of the essence of Christian democracy with its closest and most probable temptation. Borne contended that some Christian democrats were capable of elaborating and applying a political doctrine; some of them repelled moralizing evasions of temporal problems; some of them recognized that politics is a lay and not a religious matter; some of them did not seclude themselves within their spiritual family. Borne argued that the very idea of "the late Christendom" was ambiguous. If it meant the Christendom of the Holy

---

[114] Etienne Borne, "Contributions à l'espérance," *Terre Humaine*, No. 1 (January, 1951), 12–14.

[115] *Ibid.*,; and "Positions," *Terre Humaine*, No. 1 (January, 1951), 1–2. See also François Goguel, "Destin du M.R.P.," *Terre Humaine*, No. 6 (June, 1951), 100.

[116] Borne, "Emmanuel Mounier, juge de la démocratie chrétienne," 65–71.

Empire or of Paul Claudel's epic *Satin Slipper*, Borne too condemned it. But if it meant that one must refuse "to deduce from the spiritual not only the specifics of a temporal activity but even an attitude when confronting the temporal," then Mounier propounded a double standard of truth – one for the temporal and one for the spiritual. Borne did not believe the latter to be the case but he contended that many had gone beyond Mounier in this direction, perhaps making reference to the *Chrétiens Progressistes*. In a bit of sarcasm, Borne explained that

the purpose of Emmanuel Mounier was to distinguish between the spiritual and the temporal by destroying a certain number of received ideas and honored prejudgments, but he did this in order to unite them in a new, more secret, more pure, more efficacious manner. . . . This led to restoring meaning to the idea of Christendom: for the *Esprit* community, whether one likes it or not, has been and remains a cell of the new Christendom that many of us are building.

Borne's effort to revive the declining M.R.P. by returning it to its *mystique* continued despite the fact that *Terre Humaine* was forced to cease publication after only two years. Time and again, ne restated his conviction that while Mounier's criticism of Christian democracy was only partially justified the Christian democrats could profit from the *mouniériste* critique. Borne reasserted his belief that *Esprit* owed a debt to its Christian democratic predecessors. Making reference, for example, to Francisque Gay and the Dominicans who published *Sept* and *la Vie intellectuelle*, Borne contended that these men had created a "climate for a new departure and a new beginning, a kind of little Pentecost [which] makes the creation of *Esprit* so readily understandable. . . ." [117] In an address to the tenth National Congress of the M.R.P. in Lille in May, 1954, Borne claimed that the primary criticism of Christian democracy made by *Esprit* was that by its very nature Christian democracy resulted in social conservatism and clericalism. If this was true, Borne said, why exaggerate the defects of "the unfortunate victims of an inevitable fate?" Borne then argued that the charge that Christian democracy was congenitally prone to social conservatism and clericalism would be valid only "if either Christianity or milieux of Christian tradition posed spiritual or sociological barriers to human and social progress." The Christian democrats wagered optimistically on precisely the opposite – that there is a human efficacy in Christianity and its adherents. But then Borne confessed that Christian democrats suffered from an excess of moralism; in reaction against

[117] Etienne Borne, "Souvenirs de l'autre temps," *la Vie intellectuelle* (August-September, 1956), 103.

the immoralism of "political realism," they too often assumed that a clear conscience and honesty were sufficient for the practice of a good and effective politics. "Many of us trained in the movements of Christian youth and Social Catholicism," Borne admitted, "have believed too readily that they were depositories of a ready-made social doctrine, ... [and have failed to understand] that work and inventiveness were necessary to transform into a [political] program a spiritual inspiration which was as necessary as it was, by itself, insufficient." The criticisms of *Esprit*, Borne concluded in this part of his speech, "can be helpful if they remind us that our duty is not to give political expression to the sociological and psychological position of the Christian milieux which support us, but to furnish them with that social and civic education which can correct prejudices and weaknesses, ... [and which] may cause us some embarrassment in the present but will assure the future of our message, our thought, our action." [118]

Two years later, on the occasion of the publication of *Mounier et sa génération*, Borne once again turned his attention to the complex relationship between Mounier and Christian democracy and its adherents. He suggested that this book might well have been entitled "Emmanuel Mounier ou la Justice faite homme." [119] Borne called Mounier "the prince of our youth" and "a kind of archangel of justice," but he also recounted once again "the incomprehensible" misunderstanding which had separated Mounier from the Christian democrats. Not without some of his customary irony, Borne called Mounier a "patrician" of justice, intelligence, and moral purity who, because of his prophetic vocation, was unable to appreciate "us other plebians" whose labors were "more humble, more modestly political." In the pages of the M.R.P. journal *Forces Nouvelles*, Borne made much the same point: "*Esprit* was a society of thought which had the immense merit of posing in all of their dimensions – spiritual and technical, human and economic – the great problems of a difficult and tumultuous time." [120] Borne continued that when a member of *Esprit* wanted to undertake genuine political action he felt himself compelled to leave *Esprit*. In Borne's judgment, Mounier's revolutionary vocabulary reflected a "certain mythology of the absolute" which was incompatible with the

---

[118] Etienne Borne, "1944–1954. Le sens de notre engagement politique. Texte du rapport présenté par Etienne Borne au 10ᵉ Congrès National du MRP. Lille, 27, 28, 29, 30 mai 1954," *Forces Nouvelles*, June, 1954.

[119] Borne, "Pour un tombeau d'Emmanuel Mounier," 100–113.

[120] Etienne Borne, "Emmanuel Mounier. Témoin de son temps," *Forces Nouvelles*, April 1, 1956.

requirements of political activity. The Christian democrats were correct in the position of "integral resistance" they had adopted in 1940. The "third way" against liberal capitalism and Marxist totalitarianism that Mounier pursued throughout his life was a worthy and honorable endeavor; but history had demonstrated that the most fruitful "third way" was to be found in neither "a crypto-Marxist progressivism" nor a bankrupt variant of something called "radicalism" but rather in Christian democracy in its largest sense.

Borne's somewhat forced optimism concerning the future of Christian democracy proved to be unfounded. His responses to Mounier's criticisms revealed that the continued existence of Christian democracy was increasingly open to question. One of the most vehement attacks on Christian democracy came from Joseph Hours, one of the founders of the M.R.P. and Gilbert Dru's history professor in Lyons. The gist of Hours' charge was that the historical antecedents and history of Christian democracy in France revealed that, by its very nature, Christian democracy was an anti-national and clerical movement. Hours argued that the European policy of the M.R.P. was a clerical, anti-national, and Germanic effort to construct a new Holy Roman Empire in cooperation with the German and Italian Christian democratic parties and under the auspices of the Vatican. Hours was so angry that he called the M.R.P. the first political expression of the Ultramontane tradition in France; he accused the party of loving the Church, hating the State, and running the risk of losing its "sense of the Country"; he went so far as to point out that Robert Schuman, "the father of Europe," had once studied in Bonn and there Schuman had breathed a *"grossdeutsch* atmosphere," and that di Gasperi, the Italian Christian democratic leader, had once been a student in Vienna; and, finally, Hours stated that the Archduke Otto, the Habsburg pretender, was a contributor to a European federalist publication.[121]

More damaging to the M.R.P., as well as to most other non-Gaullist parties, were the events of May, 1958, and their aftermath. Joined together by little more than their classic Christian democratic bonds of "friendship" and their consistent support of the Catholic schools, the members of the M.R.P. witnessed first the slow fragmentation of their party and finally voted its dissolution. Charles de Gaulle's return to power created an immediate schism within the M.R.P. Georges Bidault,

---

[121] Joseph Hours, "L'Idée européenne et l'idéal du Saint-Empire," *L'Année politique et économique*, 26e année, No. 111–112 (January-March, 1953), 1–16; and Joseph Hours, "Les Catholiques français et la patrie," *L'Année politique et économique*, 28e année, No. 123–124 (January-March, 1955), 1–24.

its president, organized the *Mouvement pour la Démocratie Chrétienne* in June, 1958, largely on the basis of his support of "L'Algérie Française." The M.R.P. supported de Gaulle in the referendum of September, 1958, but it suffered serious setbacks in the elections of the following month. Not even the influx of militants from various rural Catholic Action groups was sufficient to compensate the M.R.P. for the defections it suffered to the Gaullist electorate in the following year. In the elections of 1962, the party which had at one time been the largest party in France was reduced to a size comparable to the combined strength of the old *Parti Démocrate Populaire* and the prewar *Jeune-République*.[122]

In the winter of 1962–1963 the M.R.P. re-examined its *raison a'être*. In a special issue of *Forces Nouvelles* appropriately entitled, "La démocratie chrétienne en question," Etienne Borne explained that the Christian democratic parties of Western Europe were undergoing the same crisis that the democratic idea itself was confronting. Borne argued that the Christian democratic parties had already accomplished important historical tasks:

Against politico-theological integralisms, they have dissociated the spiritual and the reactionary; *against totalitarianisms* of the Right and the Left, they have defended pluralism, dialogue between doctrines, public liberties; *against nationalisms,* they have been the champions and the pioneers of the communitarian spirit in Europe; and [they have] supported the open society against the closed society. . . .

But like other democrats the Christian democrats had not lived up to their democratic ideal and as a result "the unity and even the existence of Christian democracy are in jeopardy. . . . Certainly, no party, not even a Christian democratic party, is absolutely necessary to democracy," Borne confessed.[123]

In May, 1963 at the National Congress of La Baule, Jean Lecanuet, the new president of the M.R.P., said in his closing address that the party was ready to disband and to join with other French democrats in building "a great political force." [124] The parliamentary group of the party had already renounced its autonomy and entered the *Centre Démocratique*. At the Congress of La Baule, a motion to join with all other men who supported "social, economic and political democracy,

---

[122] For surveys and brief analyses of the foregoing, see Pezet, *Chrétiens au service de la cité*, 145ff.; Coutrot and Dreyfus, 196ff.; and Rémond, "Forces religieuses et partis politiques," 57–87 *passim*.
[123] Quoted in Pezet, *Chrétiens au service de la cité*, 152–153.
[124] *Ibid.*, 154.

and the United States of Europe" carried unanimously. "This large union cannot be realized by a simple regrouping of existing parties. It requires the creation of an entirely new organization. ...." [125] While Borne continued his efforts to revitalize the dying party, primarily under the auspices of the political club *France-Forum* and its journal of the same name,[126] the leadership of the party reached the painful conclusion that the M.R.P. should join the *Centre Démocratique*, an amalgam of various centrist men and groups which was officially organized in February, 1966. The following year, the remnants of the M.R.P. voted the official dissolution of their party.[127] Albeit under extraordinary circumstances, Emmanuel Mounier's prophetic judgment was fulfilled.

Like that other prophet of an earlier generation, Mounier condemned the "Catholic party" of his day. He believed that France had need of a *mystique* and in his life and work he gave substance to that belief. What has been said of Charles Péguy applies, in its essentials, equally to Mounier:

His passionate belief in personal integrity, obedience to conscience against all authority at whatever the cost, the quality of his revulsion against the forces which tried to crush Dreyfus, made him the hero of modern Republican individualism....

. . . .

He presented, in vivid personal shape, the eternal protest of the prophet against the lawgiver, the spiritual against the material. He did much to ennoble the ideas and sentiments of the young men of his generation. The incorrigible nonconformist, in a perpetual minority of one; the rebel ... cherishing integrity above power, exerted a strong fascination over many Frenchmen.[128]

Mounier's Dreyfus affair was less climactic but no less important than that of Péguy: the alliance of Christianity and "the established disorder." In his lifelong battle against this alliance, he, like Péguy, found no party he could support. Just before founding *Esprit*, he indicated his distrust of "castes and their prejudices, parties and their decrees, and that regimentation which impairs the best of causes. ...." [129] Between the Christian democrats and Mounier, as François Mauriac

[125] Jacques Moreau, "Le XXᵉ Congrès du M.R.P.," *Revue française de science politique*, XIII, No. 3 (September, 1963), 715.

[126] See, for example, *La démocratie à refaire. Colloque "France-Forum."* (Paris: Les Editions Ouvrières, 1963); and Faucher, 104.

[127] See, for example, Charles d'Aragon, "Elogé funébre du M.R.P.," *Esprit*, No. 4 (April, 1968), 629–641; and Peter Steinfels, "Christian Democracy – R.I.P.," *The Commonweal*, LXXXVII, No. 9 (December 1, 1967), 294–296.

[128] Thomson, 124–125.

[129] Mounier, "L'Action intellectuelle ou de l'Influence," 11.

pointed out, there was "the eternal dispute between Mary and Martha. Did not Mounier, who had chosen the better part, abuse those who, in order to serve the State, consented to necessary compromises and to soiling their hands a bit?" [130] But by delineating the characteristics of "the Christian democratic temperament," and by constantly criticizing the politics it produced, Mounier performed a necessary, though inevitably thankless, task. To a generation of Christian democrats, his last words are perhaps to be found among his earliest writings. The most truly human vocation, he wrote, is "discerner, choisir, transfigurer." [131]

---

[130] François Mauriac, "Emmanuel Mounier," *Le Figaro*, March 27, 1950.
[131] Mounier, "L'Action intellectuelle ou de l'Influence," 16.

BIBLIOGRAPHICAL ESSAY

For a complete bibliography the reader should consult the footnotes.

A. Emmanuel Mounier. Primary Sources

The most complete bibliography of Mounier's works is in *Oeuvres de Mounier*. Vol. IV: *Recueils posthumes. Correspondance* (Paris: Editions du Seuil, 1963), 833–876. The *Oeuvres de Mounier*, 4 vols. (Paris: Editions du Seuil, 1961–1963) also contain reprints of Mounier's major books as well as the most extensive published collection of his letters and journals. The latter includes the letters and journals originally published in *Emmanuel Mounier, 1905–1950* (Paris: Editions du Seuil, 1951) but this book remains of value because of Albert Béguin's editorial notes, the recollections of many of Mounier's friends and associates, and the articles on Mounier by a number of veterans of *Esprit. Mounier et sa génération. Lettres, carnets et inédits* (Paris: Editions du Seuil, 1956) is included in Vol. IV of the *Oeuvres*. Additional journals and letters have been published in the *Bulletin des Amis d'E. Mounier*, Nos. 1–36 (February, 1952–October, 1970) as well as in *L'Amitié Charles Péguy*, No. 84 (May, 1961) and No. 85 (June, 1961) and the *Revue Montalembert*, No. 4–5 (1963). The various issues of the *Bulletin des Amis d'E. Mounier* contain reprints of many of Mounier's articles in journals and periodicals that are less accessible than *Esprit* as well as transcripts of a number of Mounier's radio addresses and interviews. *Communisme, anarchie et personnalisme* (Paris: Editions du Seuil, 1966), *L'engagement de la foi. Textes choisis et presentés par Paulette E. Mounier* (Paris: Editions du Seuil, 1968), and *Malraux, Camus, Sartre, Bernanos. L'espoir des désespérés* (Paris: Editions du Seuil, 1970) all consist of reprints of previously published materials.

B. Emmanuel Mounier. Secondary Sources

There is no complete bibliography of books and articles on Mounier. The best bibliography is in the *Bulletin des Amis d'E. Mounier*. To date, the most valuable studies of Mounier are Candide Moix, *La penseé d'Emmanuel Mounier* (Paris: Editions du Seuil, 1960) and *Mounier ou le combat du juste* (Bordeaux: Guy Dueres, 1968), a collection of essays published by the editors of the journal *Frères du monde*. Also of value are Jean Conilh, *Emmanuel Mounier. Sa vie, son oeuvre avec un exposé de sa philosophie* (Paris: Presses universitaires de France, 1966), Lucien Guissard, *Emmanuel Mounier* (Paris: Editions Universitaires, 1962), and Roy Pierce, *Contemporary French Political Thought* (London: Oxford University Press, 1966). On the *Jeunes équipes* of the 1930s, J.-L. Loubet del Bayle, *Les non-conformistes des année 30. Une tentative de renouvellement de la pensée politique française* (Paris: Editions du Seuil, 1969) is indispensable. Among recollections and memoirs of value are Pierre-Henri Simon's contribution to Robert Aron (ed.), *Histoire de notre temps* (Paris: Plon, 1968), Denis de Rougemont, *Journal d'une époque, 1926–1946* (Paris: Gallimard, 1968), Helen Iswolsky, *Light Before Dusk. A Russian Catholic in France, 1923–1941* (New York: Longmans, Green & Co., 1942), Marcel Moré, *Accords et dissonances, 1932–1944* (Paris: Gallimard, 1967), Nicolas Berdiaeff, *Dream and Reality. An Essay in Autobiography*, tr. by Katherine Lampert (New York: Macmillan Company, 1951), and the special issue of *Arts* (March 28–April 3, 1956) devoted to *Esprit*.

Much of the literature on Mounier is of a polemical nature. See, for example, Marc Beigbeder, *Lettre à "Esprit" sur l'esprit de corps et la contrainte par corps* (Paris: Gallimard, 1951) and *Les vendeurs du temple* (Paris: Editions de minuit, 1951); Roger Garaudy, *Lettre à Emmanuel Mounier, homme d'Esprit* (Paris: Editions de "La Nouvelle Critique," 1950); Jean Madiran, *Ils ne savent pas ce qu'ils disent* (Paris: Nouvelles Editions Latines, 1955) and *Ils ne savent pas ce qu'ils font* (Paris: Nouvelles Editions Latines, 1955); and Jean Calbrette, *Mounier le mauvais esprit* (Paris: Nouvelles Editions Latines, 1957).

A bibliography of articles on Mounier would run to many pages. In addition to those published in *Emmanuel Mounier, 1905–1950* and either published or reprinted in the *Bulletin des Amis d'E. Mounier*, the following were of particular value in this study: Pierre Andreu, " 'Esprit' (1932–1940)," *Itinéraires* (May, 1959); Pierre de Boisdeffre, "Le drame d'Esprit,' " in Boisdeffre's *Des vivants et des morts. Témoignages 1948–1953* (Paris: Editions Universitaires, 1954); Marcel Clément, "Emmanuel Mounier," *Itinéraires* (July–August, 1959 and September, 1959); Frederick C. Copleston, "Mounier, Marxism and Man," *The Month* (October, 1951); Joseph Folliet, "Emmanuel Mounier," *Chronique sociale de France* (July, 1955); Michel François, "La revue qui a formé une génération chrétienne," *France-Observateur* (April 2, 1959); Henri Marrou, "L'action politique d'Emmanuel Mounier," *Cahiers de la République* (1956); Robert Rouquette, "Positions et oppositions d'Emmanuel Mounier," *Etudes* (February, 1951) and "Cheminements tragiques d'Emmanuel Mounier," *Etudes* (February, 1952); and Donald Wolf, "Emmanuel Mounier: A Catholic of the Left," *The Review of Politics* (July, 1960).

With the exception of a section of Paul Archambault, *Pierres d'attente pour une Cité meilleure* (No. 29, "Cahiers de la Nouvelle Journée"; Paris: Bloud & Gay, 1935), the most important works on Mounier written by Christian democrats are to be found in journals and periodicals. In the early years of *Esprit* Archambault paid careful attention to Mounier: "Esprit," *Politique* (November, 1932), "Problèmes et doctrines du personnalisme," *Politique* (April, 1939), and "Du personnalisme au marxisme: une aventure spirituelle," *Politique* (May, 1950). The debate between Archambault and Mounier on "La démocratie et la révolution" in *l'aube* (January 21–22, February 28, and March, 9, 1934) is invaluable. After the war Etienne Borne wrote numerous articles on Mounier: "Le parti intellectuel contre la Troisième force," *l'aube* (January 11–12, 1948), "Pour un dialogue créateur," *l'aube* (January 18–19, 1948), "Emmanuel Mounier n'est plus," *l'aube* (March 23, 1950), and "Une philosophie ouverte: le personnalisme," *l'aube* (March 25–26, 1950). Borne addressed himself to Mounier's criticisms of Christian democracy in "Emmanuel Mounier, témoin de son temps," *Forces Nouvelles* (April 1, 1956), "Notre jeunesse," *Forces Nouvelles* (August 2, 1960), and "1944–1954. Le sens de notre engagement politique," *Forces Nouvelles* (June, 1954), but Borne's most penetrating critiques of Mounier are "Pour un tombeau d'Emmanuel Mounier," *la Vie intellectuelle* (June, 1956) and "Emmanuel Mounier, juge de la démocratie chrétienne," *Terre Humaine* (February, 1951).

C. Christian Democracy. Primary Sources

On Christian democracy in twentieth century France, the newspapers *le Petit Démocrate*, *La Jeune-République*, and *l'aube* as well as the journals *Politique, Terre Humaine*, and *Forces Nouvelles* should be consulted. So also should many of the volumes of Paul Archambault's *Cahiers de la Nouvelle Journée* and *La Nouvelle Journée*. Francisque Gay, *Pour un rassemblement des forces démocratiques d'inspiration chrétienne. Mémoire confidentiel* (Paris: Bloud & Gay, 1935), *Pour en finir le légende: "Rouges-Chrétiens"* (Paris: Editions de "l'aube," 1937), and *Les démocratiques d'inspiration chrétienne à l'épreuve du pouvoir* (Paris: Bloud & Gay, 1951) reveal much about the internal tensions and disputes of the Christian democrats. Paul Delourme [Abbé Trochu], *Trente-cinq années de politique religieuse ou l'histoire de "l'Ouest-Eclair"* (Paris: Editions Fustier, 1936) serves the same purpose with reference to conflicts between Christian democrats and more conservative Catholics, both lay and clerical.

On the *Parti Démocrate Populaire*, the *Cahiers du Parti Démocrate Populaire*, Raymond-Laurent and Marcel Prélot, *Manuel politique. Le programme du Parti Démocrate Populaire* (Paris: Spes, 1928), and the many works of Robert Cornilleau and Raymond-Laurent should be consulted. Of particular value also are *Robert Cornilleau. Souvenirs et témoignages* (Rennes: Imprimerie bretonne, 1959), Ernest Pezet, *Chrétiens au service de la cité, de Léon XIII au "Sillon" et au M.R.P.* (Paris: Nouvelles Editions Latines, 1965), Abbé Desgranges, *Journal d'un prêtre député, 1936–1940* (Paris–Geneva: La Palatine, 1961), and Marcel Prélot's articles: "Les démocrates d'inspiration chrétienne entre les deux guerres," *la Vie intellectuelle* (December, 1950); "Les démocrates populaires français (Chronique de vingt ans: 1919–1939)," in *Scritti di sociologia e di politica in onore di Luigi Sturzo*. Vol. III (Bologna: Zanichelli Editore, 1953); and "Histoire et doctrine du Parti démocrate populaire," *Politique* (July–December, 1962). On the *Jeune-République*, Marc Sangnier, *Une politique nouvelle. A propos du "Parti Nouveau," les catholiques et le "Parti Nouveau," la "Ligue de la Jeune-République."* (Paris: "La Démocratie," 1912), the *Cahiers de la Démocratie, Ligue de la Jeune-République. Programme et statuts* (Paris: "La Démocratie," 1912), and Georges Hoog, *Histoire, doctrine, action de la "Jeune-République"* (Paris: Société coopérative d'édition et de propagande, 1925) should be consulted. On the M.R.P., the stenographic accounts of the national congresses published by the Fondation Nationale des Sciences Politiques, the *Cahiers de formation politique*, and Albert Gortais, *Démocratie et libération* (Paris: Société d'éditions Républicaines Populaires, 1947) are invaluable. On the founding of the M.R.P., see "La naissance d'un grand Mouvement," *Forces Nouvelles* (June 16, 1945), the articles by Gilbert Dru in the *Cahiers de notre jeunesse* (September, 1941–August, 1942), Jean-Marie Domenach, *Gilbert Dru, celui qui croyait au ciel* (Paris: Editions du Livre Française, 1947), and Raymond-Laurent, *Figures de militants. Les origines du Mouvement Républicain Populaire. Quelques souvenirs* (Paris: Editions du Mail, n.d.).

D. Christian Democracy. Secondary Sources

Although there are, as yet, no full scale studies of the *Parti Démocrate Populaire*, the *Jeune-République*, or the M.R.P., there are several good general surveys of Christian democracy and many valuable specialized works. On the early years of Christian democracy see Hans Maier, *Revolution and Church. The Early History of Christian Democracy, 1789–1901*, tr. by Emily M. Schossberger (Notre Dame: University of Notre Dame Press, 1969); Peter Stearns, *Priest and Revolutionary: Lamennais and the Dilemma of French Catholicism* (New York: Harper & Row, 1967) and Stearns' article on *Avenir* in *The American Historical*

Review (July, 1960); René Rémond, *Lamennais et le démocratie* (Paris: Presses universitaires de France, 1948); and Alec Vidler, *Prophecy and Papacy. A Study of Lamennais, the Church and the Revolution* (London: S.C.M. Press Ltd., 1954). No student of Christian democracy in France can neglect the standard studies of Social Catholicism by Jean-Baptiste Duroselle and Henri Rollet. The best general surveys of Christian democracy are Maurice Vaussard, *Histoire de la démocratie chrétienne.* Vol. I: *France. Belgique. Italie* (Paris: Editions du Seuil, 1956), Louis Biton, *La démocratie chrétienne dans la politique française. Sa grandeur, ses servitudes* (Angers: H. Siraudeau, 1955), Michael P. Fogarty, *Christian Democracy in Western Europe: 1820–1953* (Notre Dame: University of Notre Dame Press, 1952), and Mario Einaudi and François Goguel, *Christian Democracy in Italy and France* (Notre Dame: University of Notre Dame Press, 1952).

In recent years a number of more specialized studies have been published. André Darricau, *Marc Sangnier* (Paris: Les Editions Ouvrières, 1953) and Maurice Carité, *Francisque Gay, le militant* (Paris: Les Editions Ouvrières, 1966) are useful, brief introductions to the lives and work of two of the patriarchs of contemporary Christian democracy. The most comprehensive study of the *Sillon* is Jeanne Caron, *Le Sillon et la démocratie chrétienne, 1894–1910* (Paris: Plon, 1967) but Jean de Fabrègues, *Le Sillon de Marc Sangnier. Un tournant majeur du mouvement social catholique* (Paris: Librairie académique Perrin, 1964) is also very useful. Jean-Marie Mayeur, *Un prêtre démocrate. L'Abbé Lemire, 1853–1928* (Paris: Casterman, 1968) is a superb study of one of the leading *abbés démocrates.* Mayeur's study of the Christian democratic congresses of the 1890s in the *Revue d'Histoire moderne et contemporaine* (July–September, 1962) is an important addition to the literature as is Maurice Montuclard's *Conscience religieuse et démocratie. La deuxième démocratie chrétienne en France, 1891–1902* (Paris: Editions du Seuil, 1965). On the early years of the Christian democratic journal *l'aube,* François Mayeur, *l'aube. Etude d'un journal d'opinion, 1932–1940* (Paris: Armand Colin, 1966) is indispensable. Another standard work is Aline Coutrot, *Un courant de la pensée catholique. L'hebdomadaire "Sept" (mars 1934–août 1937)* (Paris: Les Editions du Cerf, 1961). The histories of the major ancillary movements of Christian democracy have yet to be written but Charles Molette, *L'Association Catholique de la Jeunesse Française, 1886–1907. Une prise de conscience du laïcat catholique* (Paris: Armand Colin, 1968) is the definitive study of the seminal years of the A.C.J.F. and *A.C.J.F. Signification d'une crise. Analyse et Documents* (Paris: Editions de l'Epi, 1961) is useful on the crisis leading to the demise of the A.C.J.F. Gérard Adam, *La C.F.T.C., 1940–1958. Histoire politique et idéologique* (Paris: Armand Colin, 1964) supplemented by Adam's "De C.F.T.C. à la C.F.D.T.," *Revue française de science politique* (February, 1965) examines the later period in the history of Christian trade unionism.

E. General Secondary Sources

Every student of contemporary French Catholicism owes a debt to René Rémond. Although Adrien Dansette, *Histoire religieuse de la France contemporaine.* 2 vols. (Paris: Flammarion, 1948–1951) and *Destin du catholicisme français, 1926–1956* (Paris: Flammarion, 1957) are still useful surveys, Rémond's brilliant synthesis in André Latreille *et al., Histoire du catholicisme en France.* Vol. II: *La période contemporaine* (Paris: Spes, 1962) is unlikely to be surpassed for many years. Rémond's *The Right Wing in France. From 1815 to de Gaulle,* tr. by James M. Laux (Philadelphia: University of Pennsylvania Press, 1966) is already something of a classic. In addition, a number of Rémond's other works are indispensable: *Forces religieuses et attitudes politiques dans la France contempo-raine* (Paris: Armand Colin, 1965), *Les catholiques, le communisme et les crises, 1929–1939* (Paris: Armand Colin, 1960), *Les deux congrès ecclésiastiques de Reims et de Bourges, 1896–1900. Un témoignage sur l'Eglise de France* (Paris: Sirey, 1964), "Les partis catholiques" in M. Carrouges *et al.*, *Le monde se fait tous les jours* (Paris: Les Editions du Cerf, 1953), "L'évolution du journal 'La Croix' et son role auprès de l'opinion catholique (1919–1939)," *Bulletin de la Société d'Histoire Moderne* (1958), and "Droite et gauche dans le catholicisme français," *Revue française de science politique* (September, 1958–December, 1958). The work of Emile Poulat is also valuable: *Histoire, dogme et critique dans la crise moderniste* (Paris: Casterman, 1962), *Le "Journal d'un prêtre d'après-demain" (1902–1903) de l'abbé Calippe* (Paris: Casterman, 1962), *Intégrisme et catholi-cisme intégral. Un réseau secret antimoderniste: La "Sapinière" (1909–1921)* (Paris: Casterman, 1969), and *Naissance des prêtres ouvriers* (Paris: Casterman, 1965). On the priest-workers, Gregor Siefer, *The Church and Industrial Society. A survey of the Worker-Priest Movement and its implications for the Christian Mission*, tr. by Isabel and Florence McHugh (London: Darton, Longman and Todd, 1964) should also be consulted.

Among other works on French Catholicism, Aline Coutrot and François Dreyfus, *Les forces religieuses dans la société française* (Paris: Armand Colin, 1965) is a good introduction; Henri Guillemin *et al.*, *Les chrétiens et la politique* (Paris: Editions du Temple présent, 1948) and Ignace Lepp, *Espoirs et déboires du progressisme* (Paris: La Table Ronde, 1956) are important for an under-standing of the *Chrétien progressiste* movement; Alexander Sedgwick, *The Ralliement in French Politics, 1890–1898* (Cambridge: Harvard University Press, 1965) and Harry W. Paul, *The Second Ralliement: The Rapprochement Between Church and State in France in the Twentieth Century* (Washington, D.C.: The Catholic University of America Press, 1967) deal with aspects of the two ralliements; William Bosworth, *Catholicism and Crisis in Modern France. French Catholic Groups at the Threshold of the Fifth Republic* (Princeton: Princeton University Press, 1962) surveys Catholic organizations; and Jean-Marie Domenach and Robert de Montvalon (eds.), *The Catholic Avant-Garde. French Catholicism Since World War II*, tr. by Brigid Elson *et al.* (New York: Holt, Rinehart and Winston, Inc., 1967) is an excellent anthology of the writings of many of the leaders of French Catholicism. No student of French Catholicism should fail to consult periodical literature, particularly the special issues of the *Chronique sociale de France* and "Le dossier de la quinzaine" section of *Informations catholiques internationales*.

Literature on the years 1940–1944 is massive. The best history of Vichy is Robert Aron, *Histoire de Vichy, 1940–1944* (Paris: Librairie Arthème Fayard, 1954) but it should be supplemented by Stanley Hoffmann, "Aspects du régime de Vichy," *Revue française de science politique* (January–March, 1956), a pre-liminary reinterpretation of Vichy. A semi-official history of the Church during this period is Msgr. [Emile] Guerry, *L'Eglise catholique en France sous l'occupa-tion* (Paris: Flammarion, 1947). On the Resistance, the volumes in the "Esprit de la Résistance" collection published by the Presses universitaires de France are indispensable. Jacques Duquesne, *Les catholiques français sous l'occupation* (Paris: Bernard Grasset, 1966) is an important and controversial interpretative account. On youth movements, Jean Délage, *Grandeur et servitudes des Chantiers de la jeunesse* (Paris: Editions André Bonne, 1950); and Robert Hervet, *Les Chantiers de la Jeunesse* (Paris: Editions France-Empire, 1962) and *Les Compag-nons de France* (Paris: Editions France-Empire, 1965) are biased but useful. On *Uriage*, the following are essential: Janine Bourdin, "Des intellectuels à la recherche d'un style de vie: l'Ecole nationale des cadres d'Uriage," *Revue française de science politique* (December, 1959); Raymond Josse, "L'Ecole des cadres d'Uriage (1940–1942)," *Revue d'Histoire de la deuxième guerre mondiale* (January, 1966); Gilles Ferry, *Une expérience de formation de chefs. La stage de six mois à Uriage* (Paris: Editions du Seuil, 1945); and Gilbert Gadoffre, *Vers le style du XXe siècle* (Paris: Editions du Seuil, 1945). On the most important Catholic journal founded during the Resistance, see François and Renée Bedarida, "Une résistance spirituelle, aux origines de 'Témoignage chrétien,' " *Revue d'Histoire de la deuxième guerre mondiale* (January, 1966) and Jean-Pierre Gault, *Histoire d'une fidélité. Témoignage chrétien, 1944–1956* (Paris: Editions Témoignage chrétien, n.d.). On the press, Claude Bellanger, *Presse clandestine, 1940–1944* (Paris: Armand Colin, 1961) should be consulted.

Among other works on contemporary France, the following were particularly useful: H. Stuart Hughes, *The Obstructed Path. French Social Thought in the Years of Desperation, 1930–1960* (New York: Harper and Row, 1968); David Caute, *Communism and the French Intellectuals, 1914–1960* (London: André Deutsch, 1964); Jean-André Faucher, *Les Clubs politiques en France* (Paris: Editions John Didier, 1965); Stanley Hoffmann *et al.*, *In Search of France* (Cambridge: Harvard University Press, 1963); François Goguel, *La Politique des partis sous la Troisième République* (Paris: Editions du Seuil, 1946); Charles Micaud, *The French Right and Nazi Germany, 1933–1939* (Durham, N.C.: Duke University Press, 1943) and *Communism and the French Left* (New York: Frederick A. Praeger, 1963); Jean-Pierre Maxence, *Histoire de dix ans, 1927–1937* (Paris: Gallimard, 1939); Yves Simon, *La grande crise de la République française. Observations sur la vie politique des Français de 1918 à 1939* (Montreal: Editions de l'arbre, 1941) and *La campagne d'Ethiopie et la pensée politique française* (Lille: S.I.L.I.C., n.d.); Eugen Weber, *Action Française. Royalism and Reaction in Twentieth-Century France* (Stanford: Stanford University Press, 1962); Philip Williams, *Politics in Post-War France. Parties and the Constitution in the Fourth Republic* (London: Longmans, Green & Co., 1954); David Thomson, *Democracy in France. The Third and Fourth Republics* (London: Oxford University Press, 1958); and the studies of Charles Péguy by Alexander Dru, Majorie Villiers and Hans A. Schmitt.

INDEX